ARTHUR
AND THE
KINGS OF BRITAIN

About the Author

Dr Miles Russell is a senior lecturer in archaeology in the Faculty of Science and Technology at Bournemouth University and a Fellow of the Society of Antiquaries of London. His research and publications focus on the prehistoric and Roman periods and he is currently involved in fieldwork across southern Britain. Miles is a regular contributor to television and radio.

ARTHUR AND THE KINGS OF BRITAIN

MILES RUSSELL

AMBERLEY

To Mum and Dad, who first inspired my love of the past, Glynis, who patiently proofread everything, and Bronwen, Megan and Macsen, who have, over the last eight years, seen their home turned into a research centre and suffered countless detours down obscure country lanes, along overgrown and extremely muddy footpaths and into all manner of local museums, in search of the Matter of Britain.

This edition published 2018

Amberley Publishing
The Hill, Stroud
Gloucestershire, GL5 4EP

www.amberley-books.com

Copyright © Miles Russell, 2017, 2018

The right of Miles Russell to be identified as the Author of this work has been asserted in accordance with the Copyrights, Designs and Patents Act 1988.

ISBN 978 1 4456 8282 2 (paperback)
ISBN 978 1 4456 6275 6 (ebook)

British Library Cataloguing in Publication Data. A catalogue record for this book is available from the British Library.

Typesetting and Origination by Amberley Publishing.
Printed in the UK.

Listening to such tales it often seemed to me that among the ordinary people the legend had become more important than the history. The continued retelling of the story in the folk tradition had produced its own narrative, accumulating fabulous detail over many centuries; ending up far more wonderful than mere historical fact, but still in some mysterious way reflecting a kind of crystallised essence of the original story.

Michael Wood, *In Search of Myths and Heroes*

CONTENTS

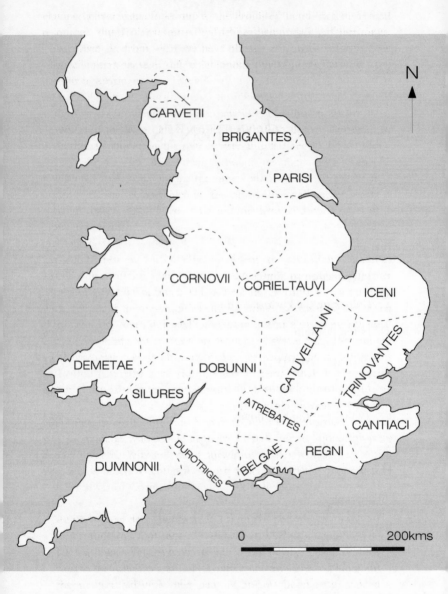

The Late Iron Age tribes of Britain.

PREFACE

For most people the 'Dark Ages' are just that: a period hidden by a fog of myth, legend, and extreme chronological uncertainty. While academics endlessly theorise about the survival of the Roman Empire and the arrival of barbarian groups, popular culture revels in a fantastic world of warriors, wizards and sorcery. Period perception is fuelled by epic matter – dragons, giant-killers, Avalon, the sword in the stone, and the round table – while British folklore, tales and legends coalesce around key mythical figures such as Lear, Coel Hen, Arthur, Merlin, Mordred, Ambrosius Aurelianus, Guinevere and Morgana. Most of the characters that appear in legendary accounts, loosely termed 'the Matter of Britain', have been so extensively distorted by the passage of time that it is often difficult to see when or how particular tales began, and to whom they originally related. Macsen Wledig, who appears in the Welsh epic the Mabinogion, for instance, seems to bear little resemblance to the Magnus Maximus of fourth-century Roman history, while Ambrosius Aurelianus, though cited in sixth-century historical sources, appears in legend gathering monoliths from Ireland and re-erecting them on Salisbury Plain in order to create Stonehenge.

Perhaps the biggest problem for anyone attempting to make sense of the years following the collapse of Roman administration in Britain is the apparent paucity of contemporary historical material. Within the textual desert there are, of course, the writings of Dark Age stalwarts Gildas and Bede. There are other sources, such as the ninth-century Historia Brittonum (History of the Britons), allegedly compiled by Nennius, comprising a variety of disparate texts, dynastic lists and topographical information, all lumped together to form a single narrative. Building on this is the Historia Regum Britanniae (History of the Kings of Britain), an epic work compiled by Geoffrey of Monmouth in around AD 1136 which purports to chronicle the rulers of Britain from earliest times until the seventh century AD. Both Historiae contain much that is clearly fictional and, as a result, have often been ignored or derided. As pieces of literature, however, both are among the most important works produced in Europe, laying the ground for the story of King Arthur and the Knights of the Round Table.

The verdict of history upon Geoffrey of Monmouth has been harsh: he is at times treated as a fantasist, a spinner of tall stories, a serial hoaxer or a misguided patriot. The Historia Brittonum has fared little better, not contributing much to the 'Matter of Britain' other than with regard to Arthurian mythology. Aside from introducing the world to the life and reign of King Arthur, both the Historia Brittonum and the Historia Regum Britanniae also chronicle the history of the Britons from the first settlers, migrants from the Trojan Wars, to the arrival of Rome. None of this material is ever seriously considered as being even remotely factual and is usually dismissed out of hand. There is, it is thought, no truth in these accounts; there is no 'lost voice' helping us understand the political, economic and social life before Rome.

In this book I hope to begin the process of changing that perception. By ignoring or dismissing sources like the Historia Brittonum and the Historia Regum Britanniae we are discarding a large data set, turning our back on information that could help us interpret the past. The accounts compiled by Geoffrey of Monmouth and Nennius need to be considered objectively if their context and significance is to be understood. It is time to put our cultural prejudices aside for one moment and, with open minds, begin the process of re-evaluating the Matter of Britain.

A note on italicisation: we decided not to italicise the names of texts cited as it was thought to be distracting.

I

INTRODUCTION TO SOURCE MATERIAL

The popular view of life in post-Roman Britain has been shaped by only a few primary and not-so-primary indigenous sources. Together these portray a society of anarchy, violence, moral decline and collapse into barbarism.

Gildas and Bede

The earliest and most influential text describing the chaos that followed in the wake of Roman Britain is De Excidio et Conquestu Britanniae (On the Ruin and Conquest of Britain) by Gildas:

> The townships and high wall are abandoned; once again the citizens are put to flight; once again are scattered with less hope of recovery than usual; once again they are pursued by the enemy; once again massacres yet more cruel hasten upon them. The pitiful citizens are torn to pieces by their foes like lambs by butchers.[1]

Gildas has been described as 'the basic building block for the traditional political historical narrative' of post-Roman Britain[2] and also a 'largely untrustworthy' author of a 'tedious and exasperating work'.[3] As we shall see, he is both these things and more. Little is really known about Gildas the man, although two partially contradictory hagiographies were compiled and he was later worshipped as a saint, his mortal remains (or at least part of them) resting at the church of Saint-Gildas-de-Rhuys in Brittany. Writing at some point in the first three decades of the sixth century, though most historians prefer a date around 540, Gildas was an eyewitness to the political turmoil of 'Dark Age' Britain. Unfortunately, from a modern perspective, De Excidio Britanniae is not an objective text, instead being a robust polemic, a fearsome moral sermon outlining the anarchy and violence of his own time, urging the British population to turn from sin and seek forgiveness in God. It is a work in three discrete sections: the first providing a narrative for Britain up to Gildas' own time; the second, a scathing attack upon British Kings Aurelius Conanus, Constantine, Cuneglas, Maelgwn and Vortiporius; the third, a condemnation of the clergy. In this landscape of horror, debauchery and death, the wretched Britons struggle desperately to survive while the barbarian invaders, be they Saxon, Angle, Jute, Frank, Scot or Pict, are seen as a form of divine punishment, a cleansing force sent by God to purge his immoral and degenerate flock. However one views this particular form of history, there can be no denying that it's dramatic stuff.

After Gildas, the next indigenous source that we have to describe the early history of the British Isles is the Historia Ecclesiastica Gentis Anglorum (An Ecclesiastical History of the English People), compiled in the monastery of Monkwearmouth-Jarrow, now in Tyne and Wear, during the early eighth century. The author of this great work was Bede, and, although less of an obvious sermon than Gildas' work, the Historia Ecclesiastica is still, of course, written from an overtly Christian perspective. Unlike his predecessor, Bede is more favourable to the Saxon English, viewing them as God's chosen people and less an Old Testament plague. There is much in the Historia Ecclesiastica that is taken directly from the De Excidio et Conquestu Britanniae, sometimes almost word for word, although there are other obvious borrowings from continental texts such as the fifth-century Chronicon (Chronicle) by Prosper of Aquitaine and Historiarum Adversum Paganos (History Against the Pagans) by Orosius.

Nennius: The History of the Britons
The first source that claims to examine and chronicle aspects of British history that occurred before the arrival of Rome and the Saxons, where Gildas and Bede begin their accounts, is the Historia Brittonum (History of the Britons). The Historia is a structurally irregular mix of

chronicle, genealogical table, legend, biography, bardic praise-poem, itinerary (which includes the 'Wonders of Britain') and folklore. Some would also argue it is full of 'fakelore' whereby stories, characters and events were back-projected into Antiquity in order to explain a place, people or nation. It was probably first written down in the late 820s, although the precise nature of authorship remains disputed. Throughout much of the nineteenth and twentieth centuries the work was credited to 'Nennius', a name that appears in certain later copies of the manuscript in a section often referred to as 'the Nennian Prologue':

> I, Nennius, disciple of St Elved, have with great care written down some passages which the dullness of the British nation had caused to be thrown aside, for there was no mention in books, and the teachers were without knowledge, of the island of Britain. Moreover I have also gathered together all that I have found from the annals of the Romans and the chronicles of the Holy Fathers, that is Hieronymous, Eusebius, Isidore, Prosper, and from the annals of the Scots and Saxons, and from the traditions of our ancestors, which many teachers and scribes have attempted to write.[4]

More recently, doubt has been cast as to whether Nennius (or Nemnius/Ninnius) was indeed the author, some suggesting that the prologue, where it exists, was 'a false and late addition', possibly created in the mid-eleventh century.[5] I will continue to refer to Nennius here, not only because the name appears in so many works published in the twentieth century – hence most readers are familiar with him – but also to help distinguish it from, and to avoid potential confusion with, other Historiae, such as Bede's Historia Ecclesiastica Gentis Anglorum and Geoffrey of Monmouth's Historia Regum Britanniae. 'Nennius' is a useful nom de plume under which to park authorship.

The Historia Brittonum is an eclectic and, at times, hugely entertaining piece. Its importance rests not only on the fact of it being the first attempt to record the origin stories of the Britons, but also on it providing the earliest acknowledgement of the existence of Arthur, crediting him with an impressive battle list. This list cites twelve points of combat in which Arthur, the leader of battles, was ultimately triumphant. The Historia Brittonum, although less obviously infected with the overtly religious tone of Gildas and Bede, can be infuriatingly vague and, at times, contradictory in detail. This latter point may derive from the fact that, as Nennius himself notes, the work was a heap of disparate and diverse sources woven together to create a coherent whole. Despite modern attempts to suggest that the Historia Brittonum was no simple compilation but a work with a single, unified structure and outlook, its irregular tone, combined with its repeated change in emphasis, style and focus, strongly suggest that multiple and diverse sources were indeed stitched together in order to create the piece, albeit with the guiding hand of an author with vision. That's not to say there isn't material contained within the Historia Brittonum that is derived from an earlier period, possibly considerably earlier than the ninth century, but that it has been selected and, quite possibly, been 'massaged' in some way in order to fit the overarching narrative. Finding where these individual sections begin and end within the text is relatively easy; understanding their precise nature, origin and significance, far more difficult.

A vital document that covers the Saxon perspective during this period is the Chronologia Anglo-Saxonica (Anglo Saxon Chronicle), a compilation of stories and events which attempts to explain the origin of certain English kingdoms. The Chronologia was a piece of historical revisionism designed to present a single and coherent official version of the history and origins of Wessex and, by default, of the first Saxon kings in Kent, Sussex and South West Britain. It appears to have been compiled in or around AD 892 from a variety of diverse sources to legitimise the dynasty of Wessex while defining Saxon ethnicity at a time of sustained Danish attack. The story is presented in clear-cut terms as a war of Briton against Saxon; the finer blurring of ethnic, social and political backgrounds is neither discussed nor examined. As a chronicle, the events discussed are all supplied with a date, although doubt surrounds the reliability of the sequence supplied, much of the detail for which appears to have been culled from Bede's Historia Ecclesiastica Gentis Anglorum. Because the main purpose of the Chronologia was to legitimize the Saxon monarchies through the judicious rewriting of dynastic lists and the fabrication of origin stories, we cannot take the work as an objective and factual account, although comparison with Gildas, Bede and Nennius does, as we shall see, provide some interesting and alternative perspectives on post-Roman Britain.

Geoffrey of Monmouth

There are other sources such as the Trioedd Ynys Prydein (The Triads of the Island of Britain), the Annales Cambriae (Annals of Wales) and the Mabinogion, the significance of which we will examine on the way. The main aspect of the 'Matter for Britain' that we will be considering in this book, however, is the Historia Regum Britanniae (History of the Kings of Britain). Compiled in around 1136, Geoffrey of Monmouth's work is a sprawling narrative epic, purporting to chronicle the rulers of Britain from earliest times until the seventh century AD. Containing the first reference to well-known literary characters such as Cole (the merry old soul), Lear and Cymbeline (both later immortalised by Shakespeare), as well as King Arthur, Merlin the magician and Mordred the traitor, the Historia was a medieval bestseller, and its influence upon European culture cannot be overstated.

We know next to nothing about Geoffrey, whose association with Monmouth, in the borderlands between Wales and England, is unclear. He was certainly familiar with the geography of Cornwall, Brittany and South Wales, the Roman fortress town of Caerleon, near Monmouth, appearing many times in his text, and he may have been part Welsh or part Breton, working and researching in an England that was very much under the Norman yoke. Geoffrey spent most of his working life in Oxford, his name appearing on a number of charters there, as Galfridus Monemutensis (Geoffrey of Monmouth) between 1129 and 1151, where he is referred to as magister, or teacher.[6] He apparently conceived the Historia Regum Britanniae at the request of Walter, archdeacon of Oxford, who presented him with 'an ancient book written in the British language' for him to translate into Latin.[7] The book provided the British with their own heroic mythology – a national epic to rival any produced by the Saxons or Normans.

Geoffrey's subsequent 'translation' contains a number of stories which, if not fictional, are clearly fantastical, and it's hardly surprising that, within a few years of the Historia being produced, serious doubts were being cast on its authenticity. William of Newburgh, in his Historia Rerum Anglicarum (History of England) produced in 1190, declared that 'it is quite clear that everything this man wrote about Arthur and his successors, or indeed about his predecessors from Vortigern onwards, was made up, partly by himself and partly by others, either from an inordinate love of lying, or for the sake of pleasing the Britons'.[8] Eight centuries later, Geoffrey Ashe insisted that 'Monmouth is an entertaining and memorable companion, so long as one never believes anything he says'.[9] John Burrow has described him as 'a parodist of near-genius'.[10] The fact that Geoffrey's ancient, unnamed book, written in the British tongue, remains utterly elusive has added weight to the conviction that it was nothing more than a bluff.

The Trojans Are Coming

Perhaps the most incredible claim contained within Geoffrey of Monmouth's Historia Regum Britanniae, and the greatest impediment for believing that it contains a 'lost truth', is the assertion that the British monarchy was descended from Trojan nobility. On the face of it, this appears ludicrous; a piece of fervent pro-British or Welsh propaganda perhaps, intended to prove that the social foundations of Britain surpassed those of the English, preserved in the Anglo Saxon Chronicle and celebrated by the likes of Bede, William of Malmesbury and Henry of Huntingdon. The problem with such a view, however, is that it is derived from those who look at the story from an early twelfth-century mindset. What if this apparently rather bizarre tale, linking the blood-heritage of the Britons to that of the eastern Mediterranean, was not, after all, a medieval delusion but part of a much earlier attempt to establish that the people of Britain and Rome were one and the same?

There are, of course, earlier versions of the Trojan tale preserved in the Historia Brittonum. These accounts are all rather contradictory, something which may be due to the fact that Nennius was trying to integrate multiple sources, each of which provided a slightly different version of the story. This suggests that the concept of the Trojan diaspora was no mere piece of twelfth-century fabrication. Geoffrey of Monmouth may have expanded the tale but he clearly did not invent it for it was already in existence by the early ninth century. Can the story be taken any further back? Certainly Virgil's Aeneid was a popular work in late first-century BC Rome, the story of the Trojan adventurer Aeneas being reworked into an epic national foundation myth, but what about European prehistory: can a place for the story be found in prehistoric Britain? Certainly, the story of Aeneas and the escape from Troy was a major and constantly recurring theme within the aristocratic circles of Augustan Rome, with whom Iron Age Britons were in contact. A creation myth placing Trojan refugees in the British Isles would have put prehistoric dynasts on an equal footing with the Roman elite.[11]

The possible existence of an early foundation myth surrounding the Trojans seems more plausible when we realize that evidence for claiming common ancestry with the Senate and People of Rome was not something that was restricted to Britain. When discussing the origins of the Gauls, Ammianus Marcellinus, a Roman historian from the fourth century AD, observed that 'some maintain that after the destruction of Troy, a few Trojans fleeing from the Greeks, who were then scattered over the whole world, occupied these districts, which at that time had no inhabitants at all'.[12] The source for this exotic origin myth is unknown, although it has been suggested that Ammianus drew heavily upon Timagenes, a Greek writer from Alexandria, who had been taken captive and brought to Rome in 55 BC.[13] Ammianus may also have consulted the works of the poet Lucan, who, in the mid-first century AD, reported that the Arverni tribe of the Auvergne district in France 'dared to invent that they were brothers to Latium from the blood of the Trojan people'.[14]

The tradition of a shared Gallic/Trojan blood-heritage therefore seems to have been in circulation by the later first century BC, being recognized by commentators in Rome. This could explain Julius Caesar's statement that the allied pro-Roman Aedui tribe of the upper Loire in central France were 'often hailed by the Senate as brethren and kinsmen'.[15] The Aedui and Arverni were both keen to associate with Rome, their coinage proudly utilizing a range of images taken directly from Mediterranean examples. Such collective myths of descent, creatively appropriating stories of the Trojan diaspora, could therefore be seen in the light of groups who were seeking to declare both their loyalty to Rome and to negotiate their place in the Roman world.[16] Such an association became more important following the rise to power of Augustus, first emperor of Rome, a man whose family traced their line directly back to Aeneas himself.

If what appears at first glance to be the most fantastical, and certainly the most openly ridiculed, idea in the Historia Regum Britanniae – that the Britons thought they were of the same Trojan stock as the people of Rome – is, in the context of Late Iron Age Britain, actually plausible, where does that leave our overall understanding of both the book and its context? Could it be that Geoffrey of Monmouth did, after all, employ a lost source whose origin extended back at least as far as the mid-first century BC?

Where Did Medieval Writers Get Their Information?

Some early scholars made a point of citing their sources, often as a matter of pride. In 1125, William of Malmesbury, in the preface to Gesta Regum Anglorum (Deeds of the English Kings), acknowledged his debt to Bede, 'a man of singular learning and modesty' from whom 'I shall cull somewhat'. He also referred, almost in passing, to the 'notices of antiquity, written in the vernacular tongue', presumably the Anglo Saxon Chronicle. Henry of Huntingdon, in the preface to the Historia Anglorum (History of England) produced in 1129 also praised the Venerable Bede whose work, he notes, 'I have followed, as far as possible' before adding, in rather vague terms, that he has also made 'compilations from the chronicles preserved in ancient libraries'. Geoffrey of Monmouth, of course, claimed to have gathered all the material he needed for the Historia Regum Britanniae from 'a very ancient book in the British tongue' given to him by Walter, archdeacon of Oxford. Frustratingly, neither the name nor the origin of this book is mentioned, leading many to suggest that this was all part of a ruse designed to deceive readers into thinking that the narrative was genuine.

It is clear that despite what Geoffrey of Monmouth says at the outset, his material was not all gleaned from a single primary source. At several points within his text, for example, he expressly refers to the works of earlier writers such as Gildas and Bede as well as quoting from Roman sources such as Juvenal. He further inserts his own point of view, indicating that whatever he wants us to think, this was not verbatim translation of a much older text. He also hints that he had access to a variety of oral sources. Early on, for example, he observes that 'I found nothing said of those kings who lived here before the Incarnation of Christ, nor of Arthur and many others who succeeded after the Incarnation, though their actions both deserved immortal fame, and were also celebrated by many people in a pleasant manner and by heart, as if they had been written.'[17] Actions celebrated in a pleasant manner and by heart seems to suggest the survival and transmission of an oral tradition, but it is not clear who was preserving material in this way nor quite what the mechanism for passing it on was. The nature of transmission down the generations is one which we shall return to later but it is worth noting that William Malmesbury also hinted at the spoken word when he says, rather off-handedly, that 'it is of this Arthur that the Britons fondly tell so many fables, even to the present day'.[18]

Scholars today present their arguments and conclusions within densely written articles where every last fact, example and scrap of information is referenced. Without a detailed presentation of the nature and location of source material, the conclusions of any academic paper can be considered void, being based on hearsay rather than objective and demonstrable fact. Referencing, whether as in-text citation or as endnotes, is an essential component of presentation demonstrating how widely a subject has been researched, the variety of sources used, the nature and basis of the central argument and, most critically of all, in order to avoid charges of plagiarism. Plagiarism is something that is today rarely off the academic agenda, with constant and easy access to downloadable internet information. In the modern world of publishing, the lifting of someone else's thoughts, ideas or inventions and passing them off as your own is quite rightly considered a major transgression, the exposure of which often results in grovelling public apologies, the recall and pulping of books and, in the most extreme cases, the termination of an academic career. In the medieval world, however, the theft of another's work was a far less serious offence. Gildas,

Bede, Nennius, William of Malmesbury, Henry of Huntingdon and Geoffrey of Monmouth were, in the modern sense, all inveterate plagiarisers, cutting large sections of writing from those who had gone before and liberally pasting them into their own work, sometimes with only a minimal amount of editing or textual adjustment.

Medieval chroniclers and historians were less concerned about literary or academic theft than we are today, there being no real concept, before the renaissance at least, of intellectual property and the integrity of primary research. Plagiarism was a practice that was not only acceptable for Ancient Greek, Roman or medieval writers, who were forever borrowing ideas and text from earlier sources, sometimes without significant acknowledgement, but it was in some instances also positively encouraged. The blatant appropriation of another's words was, after all, a good way of demonstrating the reliability of material under discussion.[19] Far more important than originality in medieval writing was the concept of a perceived 'truth'. Many believed that the works of ancient Greek, Roman and Christian authors possessed a truth that simply couldn't be improved upon. To change another's writing was to somehow reduce its significance and muffle the voice of authenticity.

Identifying Source Material: William of Malmesbury

The practice of cut-and-paste in early medieval texts can be considered in a positive light, for there is much from the ancient world that would simply not have survived to this day had it not been paraphrased, quoted or appropriated, sometimes word for word, from an original work. A good example of where primary source material can be identified from within a later text is the so-called 'lost life' of the Saxon King Athelstan, preserved within the body of William of Malmesbury's Gesta Regum Anglorum.

Athelstan was arguably the most powerful of all post-Roman rulers in Britain, the first to establish the kingdom of England as a political, military, judicial and economic reality. Our understanding of the precise nature of his life and reign, however, is limited by the fact that no full contemporary biography survives, other than the detail that may be reconstructed from various charters and law codes. Even the Anglo Saxon Chronicle, which supplies so much information on the early Saxon monarchies, fails when it comes to the deeds of this, the most successful son of Wessex. Only one medieval scholar, writing some two centuries after Athelstan, laid any claim to understanding the character of the Saxon king and that was William of Malmesbury.

William lived and worked within the monastery of Malmesbury in Wiltshire, probably as the librarian. At some point in the 1120s he embarked upon the work that would establish him as 'the best English historian since Bede'.[20] The Gesta Regum Anglorum was intended to chronicle, for the benefit of a Norman audience, the rich and diverse story of England and the English monarchy as well as helping, undoubtedly, to restore a sense of pride to the English themselves following the horrors inflicted in the aftermath of 1066. Key to the establishment of England as a strong and viable kingdom, as William would no doubt have been well aware, was the reign of King Athelstan. But where to find information on this the most elusive of Saxon monarchs? Malmesbury itself was a good place to start, the abbey housing both his tomb and mortal remains. The importance of the town to the king probably meant that there were many sources, both written and remembered, to draw on in order to reconstruct his life. No surprise, then, when it comes to recounting the deeds of Athelstan, William directly addresses his audience, noting that he was 'versed in literature I discovered a few days since, in a certain old volume'.[21]

Discovery of an 'old volume' in which significant amounts of lost information could be resurrected reminds us of the statement made, a decade after the first appearance of William's magnum opus, by Geoffrey of Monmouth concerning the nature of source material recovered for the Historia Regum Britanniae. William's lost work clearly did not generate as much primary information of the sort deployed by Geoffrey, being less of a 'book' perhaps than a short manuscript or heroic poem. The fact that the source claimed by William is unnamed and remains lost has unfortunately not helped his cause, many since doubting the veracity of the account supplied as a 'flight of fancy' or, less charitably, as a rather crude fake or forgery.

Unusually for the time, William does not quote the lost text verbatim, but chose to summarise the account, explaining that, in the original,

> ... the writer struggles with the difficulty of the task, unable to express his meaning as he wished. Indeed I would subjoin his words for brevity's sake, were they not extravagant beyond belief in the praises of the king, and just in that style of writing which Cicero, the prince of Roman eloquence, in his book on rhetoric, denominates 'bombast'. The custom of that time excuses the diction, and the affection for Athelstan, who was yet living, gave countenance to the expression of praise. I shall subjoin, therefore, in familiar language, some few circumstances which may tend to augment his reputation.[22]

In other words, the account of Athelstan that William claims to have found was written in a style that his own readers would find difficult to follow. Possibly the information was originally contained within a panegyric or bardic praise-poem, an undiscriminating form of verse written in high praise of Athelstan's great achievements.[23] Such a eulogy would certainly explain William's description of the primary source as bombastic and extravagant beyond belief. It would also potentially resolve the occasional repetition of certain key events in Athelstan's life and reign as set out in the Gesta Regum Anglorum for, as Rodney Thompson has pointed out, the original source probably comprised 'sections of prose, more or less narrative, alternating with verse panegyric'.[24] Perhaps, in order to rectify this awkward format, while at the same time removing those segments of the story that he felt were either irrelevant or hopelessly sycophantic, William rewrote the original in a more acceptable style, working the direct quotes into 'the Latin of his own day'.[25]

By the late twentieth century academic opinion surrounding this 'lost life' of King Athelstan was almost universally negative. Criticism focused not only upon the vague nature of William's account surrounding the discovery of the 'old volume', which he never specifically names, but also his failure to quote it verbatim, preferring instead to modify and paraphrase in a different style. The critique supplied by Michael Lapidge was particularly damning, going so far as to suggest that the entire account had been fabricated, probably in the 1120s. William of Malmesbury, it would appear then, was nothing more than a faker and his account of King Athelstan could be safely ignored.[26] This is not, of course, the end of the story for, as is so often the way in academia, not everyone agreed.

If we are to believe the story of Athelstan, as supplied in the Gesta Regum Anglorum, and treat it as the only useful source recounting the achievements of his reign, then we need to show that the account is not wholly make-believe and that aspects clearly derived from a genuine tenth- or eleventh-century source. A detailed analysis of the relevant section, conducted by Michael Wood, suggests that, despite having been edited and partially summarised by William of Malmesbury, sufficient remains to demonstrate that there was indeed a primary, possibly even near-contemporary, source recounting Athelstan the king.

> Rather as a modern translator would, William has tried to give an impression of the lost book, and in many places his account shows traces of the older text underneath it. Vocabulary, syntax, favourite words, even line ends and internal rhymes – all show traces of the tricks used by poets of the tenth century.[27]

William seems, therefore, rather than rewriting the primary source in the 'familiar language' of his day, as he claims to have done, to have in fact edited with a very light touch, substantially retaining elements of the compositional framework and word structure of the original. The detail supplied by William of Malmesbury, especially with regard to Athelstan's character, the battles fought and his investiture in the presence of his grandfather, King Alfred, are all further suggestive of a genuine tenth-century account, rather than a twelfth-century flight of fancy.[28]

Disassembling the Narrative: Geoffrey of Monmouth

In specifically describing his 'lost book', William of Malmesbury was unusual, for most medieval writers copied without acknowledging the source. Whether such scholars were actively trying to steal another's text, passing it off as their own, or were more simply collating a scattered set of material into a single volume for the benefit of humankind, is unknown. Nennius, for example, the scribe who may have been responsible for the Historia Brittonum, noted, in a preface that appears in some (but not all) versions, 'I have made a heap of all that I could find as well from the annals of the Romans as from the chronicles of the sacred fathers ... and from the annals of the Scots and Saxons, and from our own ancient traditions.' A 'heap' is an appropriate way of describing the contents of the Historia for there is little here that can be attributed to a single voice or unified vision. Instead we find a mass of information, sometimes contradictory, suggesting that documents and manuscripts have simply been transcribed and stuck together with no attempt at internal consistency. Hence we encounter origin myths, genealogies and king lists mixed with more obviously mythological stories, Christian hagiographies and fantastical topographies as well as oral tales transcribed for the first time (the 'ancient traditions' mentioned by Nennius). It is an irregular assortment of material; an act of compilation in which wealth of diverse primary data, secondary information and assorted miscellanea, most of which would have been inaccessible to the ordinary reader, has been amassed into a single, albeit still strangely indigestible, format.

Identifying text that has been appropriated from another source is relatively easy, especially when examining the work of medieval manuscript writers. Here the editing of borrowed sections in order to fit the style of the secondary piece was either poor or non-existent. Today, the tricks of the plagiarist are detectable in many ways, from the vague allusion to, or poor acknowledgement of, minor detail when whole sections of text have been lifted, to the disassembly and rewording of complete passages. In the worst and most blatant cases of textual appropriation, the expressions, thoughts and phrases of the first writer are sometimes so inelegantly stitched together that the tone, content and style of the new work switches abruptly from paragraph to paragraph often with minimal attempt to disguise the join. The trick to understanding this is to note where individual components in works such as the Historia Brittonum and the Historia Regum Britanniae rub up against one another. Once these fault lines have been identified, discrete stories and independent sources of material can be separated from the overarching narrative.

Geoffrey of Monmouth's Historia Regum Britanniae, as has been noted, is filled with material culled from a variety of other sources. It is not proposed here to attempt a resolution to the mystery of the so-called 'missing book' that Geoffrey of Monmouth claims to have used. So many other writers have attempted to do just that, often with intriguing and thought-provoking, if ultimately rather fruitless, results. Rather I hope to show here that there are significant sections of text which supply archaeological and historical detail in sufficient quantity to show that they can only have come from sources earlier than Geoffrey of Monmouth. The question of precise attribution will, in most cases, have to wait.

The most obvious signs of appropriated text are unexpected changes in the format, where style changes, diction alters or the overall register shifts suddenly from sentence to sentence or within a matter of paragraphs. Repeated duplication of specific phrases or ideas hints that the author may have copied chunks of another text without fully digesting its meaning or understanding its significance. Shift in tense or confusion between a first- or second-person narrative can also warn of liberal 'plagiarism', as can the inclusion of anachronistic detail or inconsistencies in diction, tone, audience, vocabulary and spelling combined with a change in direction or focus, between perhaps religious, political, social or military concerns. Sometimes literary theft can be strongly suspected if there is something in the text that simply doesn't seem right: something that jars or seems 'out of place'. Such feelings cannot always be proved, although a nagging doubt remains.

A Note on Names and Naming

At its heart the Historia Regum Britanniae is a big book of names, many of which are strange and unusual. Trying to resolve issues surrounding the identification of a specific personal or place name is not helped by the many different spellings within the many variant examples of the Historia Regum Britanniae that exist today. In some cases an inconsistency in spelling within the same manuscript may reflect the preference of a particular medieval copyist, hence the spelling of Brit(t)annia and Brit(t)ones, which probably depends on which scribe was at work.[29] While the misspelling of common Latin words by a scribe or copyist would be almost unthinkable, unfamiliarity with nomenclature, especially if already irrevocably garbled or corrupted in earlier versions, is understandable. The original form and spelling of ancient names and titles would have seemed completely alien to writers of the ninth, tenth, eleventh and twelfth centuries and sometimes they simply made a best guess or 'corrected' a name-form to better suit their own time period.

Whether it was Nennius or Geoffrey of Monmouth who was at fault, perhaps confused by the precise nature of the sources, where sometimes the same person may have been referred to in different ways (or with different titles) in texts compiled from multiple authors, each with varying perspectives, is unclear. It is more likely that inaccuracies in nomenclature came later during reproduction of the text, corruption and cumulative error increasing to the point that name-forms became incomprehensible. Neil Wright, in his introduction to the most recent translation of the Historia, in which fourteen discrete manuscripts were examined, makes this point well: 'The worst problem concerns names, of which there are over 900, many recurrent. In collating each manuscript I heaved a sigh of relief when Gualguainus finally perished.'[30]

Unfortunately, but perhaps understandably for the sake of the sanity of both translator and reader, modern editions of the Historia Regum Britanniae often make the decision to either clarify variant spellings contained within the same manuscript or to use a name that is better suited and more familiar and therefore more comprehensible, to the audience of today. As Wright notes: 'With few exceptions, therefore, I have plumped for one attested spelling and stuck to it ... Would anyone have been grateful for fidelity to the manuscripts?' While we can certainly agree with the sentiment, the replacement of the unfamiliar variants with a fixed and standardised version carries with it many dangers. In the 1966 translation of the Historia by Lewis Thorpe, the introduction observes that 'where Geoffrey's Latinized names represent persons well-known to English readers, I have printed the standard English form, e.g. Guenhuueram,[31] Ganhumaram,[32] Ganhumare[33] and Ganhumere,[34] in its various spellings and cases, becomes Guinevere'.[35] Unfortunately, the name 'Guinevere' carries with it a significant amount of cultural and literary baggage.

As a character in the medieval romantic cycles of Chrétien de Troyes, Thomas Malory and subsequent writers, Guinevere is far removed from the Ganhumara / Guenhuueram / Ganhumaram / Ganhumare / Ganhumere of the twelfth-century writings of Geoffrey of Monmouth. By backdating this particular 'correct' name-form into the Historia, Thorpe was unwittingly creating an anachronism, adding legitimacy to the later romantic characterization of Arthur's queen. Neil Wright's most recent translation of the Historia has commendably retained the Latin form of most personal names, such as Kaius and Gualguainus, usually equated with Kay and Gawain, although relents when it comes to 'very familiar characters such as Vortigern, Merlin and Arthur'.[36]

Similar problems arise with regard to place names. There is a temptation to equate strange name-forms appearing in the Historia Regum Britanniae with more established locations, hence 'London' instead of Trinovantum as Geoffrey of Monmouth frequently describes it, or 'Scotland' instead of Albany or Albania. Such a practice, of course, is not dissimilar to what Geoffrey himself was doing in rendering unfamiliar prehistoric name-forms such as 'Catuvellauni', 'Trinovantes' or 'Cantiaci' into place names that would have meant more to an eleventh-century audience, even if by doing this the geographical context of the original story became hideously distorted. Wright admits that, in his translation of 2007, in order to aid the reader 'most places appear under their modern names, in so far as these can be identified'.[37] While this is perfectly understandable, we can never be sure whether our interpretation of a place was really the same as that intended by Geoffrey, nor whether his identification matched that of the earlier source material.

2

UNLOCKING THE HISTORIAE

Key to the understanding and unlocking of Geoffrey of Monmouth's Historia Regum Britanniae, and indeed the Historia Brittonum of Nennius, is the story of Julius Caesar's two expeditions to Britain, the first events in either work that can be independently verified from other historical sources and cross-compared.

Caesar documented his military adventures of 55 and 54 BC in a collected series of despatches from the front line, which today are referred to as de Bello Gallico (the Gallic Wars). The commentaries are an invaluable source of information: first-hand observations made by someone who was there. Written entirely in the third person, as if Caesar were describing the exploits of another, de Bello Gallico provides a unique and totally Roman perspective on the populations of Gaul, Germany and, most crucially, Britain. Unfortunately, Caesar rarely provides any useful geographical information, seldom placing battles fought or tribes encountered in their respective landscapes, something that can make tracing his exploits on the ground difficult. A Roman audience, eagerly lapping up the account of alien races in distant lands, would probably not have cared too much for precise detail about the geography of Britain. Such information, although vital to modern researchers, would undoubtedly have slowed the pace of Caesar's account. In fact, the only time the Roman general pauses from the action is to provide incidental detail surrounding the customs, appearance, culture, fighting techniques and unpleasant proclivities of the tribes that he encountered.

Caesar in Britain

By 55 BC, Caesar had subjugated much of Gaul (France) and had led troops on a punitive campaign across the Rhine into Germania Magna (Greater Germany), to much acclaim back in Rome. His aim in all this was threefold: to increase Roman dominion, neutralizing any barbarian threat; to raise his own popular profile as saviour of Rome; and to build up his own private resources through the acquisition of loot, the sale of slaves and the establishment of an army that was loyal only to him. In such a context, the expeditions that Caesar directed against the tribes of Britain do not seem to have been intended to form the basis of permanent conquest, but, like earlier exploits in Gaul and Germania, they were a fantastic public relations success, capturing the imagination of the Roman public like nothing before.

Truth be told, the first expedition to Britain was not a great military success. Trapped on the beachhead, hemmed in on all sides by the enemy, Caesar could only watch helplessly as his cavalry reinforcements were scattered at sea in a storm, and his own transport vessels, anchored off the coast of Kent, were dashed to pieces on the shore. A stalemate followed, the British tribes being unable to dislodge Caesar from his coastal base, the Romans being unable to break out in order to attack British targets and gather provisions. Eventually both sides sued for peace and Caesar departed with what was left of his army in a fleet of hastily repaired ships. Characteristically, writing in de Bello Gallico, Caesar makes even this sound like a victory.

In a year he was back, this time hoping to obtain a more impressive outcome, ideally defeating the British tribes in battle, acquiring slaves and 'tribute' and capturing at least one major native town. Landing unopposed late in 54 BC, Caesar immediately gathered prisoners in order to learn where the Britons were massing. A swift night march 'of about twelve miles' brought his army in sight of the enemy who, so Caesar tells us, had 'advanced to a river with their cavalry and chariots'.[1] Routed by Caesar's cavalry, the British forces fled into the woods 'where they occupied a well-fortified post, of great natural strength'. No details are provided for this defensive position, which was presumably a hill fort, although Caesar notes that 'all the entrances were blocked by felled trees laid close together'. Harried by natives, the 7th legion locked their shields together, piled earth up against the fortifications and stormed the place 'at the cost of only a few men wounded'.

Unfortunately for Caesar, although his blitzkrieg was proving remarkably successful, another severe coastal storm meant that he had to return to base in order to oversee repairs to the fleet. When he finally returned to the fray some ten days later, he found that 'larger British forces had now been assembled from all sides by Cassibellaunus, to whom the chief command and direction of the campaign had been entrusted by common consent'.[2] Caesar refers to the unifying British king as Cassibellaunus, although today Cassivellaunus and Cassivellaunos are more commonly used (the spelling will vary in this book depending on the text being referenced). Unification, with an enemy acting together under a single authority, was precisely what Caesar did not want. Sadly, we learn nothing about this first named Briton from Caesar, save that his territory lay 75 Roman miles from the sea, being 'separated from the maritime tribes by a river called the Thames'.[3]

Ambushing the Roman column as it advanced, Cassibellaunus' charioteers were beaten back, Caesar's cavalry 'killing a good many, but also incurring some casualties themselves'.[4] A second attack, this time upon troops engaged in fort construction, resulted in 'a violent battle' in which Caesar notes that one of his military tribunes, Quintus Laberius Durus, was killed. The following day, troops sent by Caesar on a foraging expedition were ambushed by the Britons who successfully pressed their attack 'right up to the standards of the legions'.[5] Only after very fierce fighting, in which 'a great many were killed', were the legions able to disperse the natives, the rout being so decisive that Caesar notes 'the Britons never again joined battle with their whole strength'. Now determined to bring the campaign to a swift conclusion, he sent his troops across the Thames noting that sharp stakes had been fixed along the bank and within the riverbed. The Britons, surprised by the speed of the attack on two fronts, were overpowered and fled.

Cassivellaunus, who, according to Caesar, had now 'given up all hope of fighting a pitched battle', disbanded the main part of his army, retaining 4,000 chariots with which he proceeded to disrupt the Roman advance.[6]

He would retire a short way from the route and hide in dense thickets, driving the inhabitants and cattle from the open country into the woods wherever he knew we intended to pass. If ever our cavalry incautiously ventured too far away plundering and devastating the country, he would send all his charioteers out of the woods by well-known lanes and pathways and deliver very formidable attacks, hoping by this means to make them afraid to go far afield.[7]

Luckily for Caesar, at the very point in the campaign where his strategy was appearing to unravel, dispatches arrived from the Trinobantes tribe (or 'Trinovantes' as they are usually referred to today). Mandubratius (or Mandubracius), 'a young prince of the tribe' who had fled to Caesar just prior to the invasion, was needed, the envoys promising 'to surrender and obey Caesar's commands and asked him to protect Mandubratius from Cassibellaunus and send him to his people to rule as king'.[8]

The Trinobantes/Trinovantes were therefore the first British tribe to embrace 'the protection of Caesar', a wonderful Roman euphemism. Having earlier fought against and been defeated by the tribe of Cassibellaunus, they probably viewed Caesar as the lesser of two evils. That any tribal blood feud would at some point destabilize the British resistance to Caesar must have always been a risk for the British king, for it was likely that certain groups would view the arrival of Caesar as the perfect opportunity to level old scores and destroy a more ancient foe. Cassivellaunus' ultimate failure in keeping the tribal alliance together, therefore, says much about the politics, squabbles and inter-ethnic tensions of groups in southern Britain at the end of the Iron Age.

Following the surrender of Mandubracius to Caesar, Cassivellaunus' anti-Roman coalition collapsed. When the other tribes saw that 'the Trinobantes had been protected against Cassibellaunus and spared any injury,' so Caesar tells us, 'the Cenimagni, Segontiaci, Ancalites, Bibroci and Cassi sent embassies and surrendered.'[9] Of the groups noted by Caesar as capitulating to Rome, only the Cenimagni are known to us, being, quite plausibly, the Iceni or 'Iceni Magni' (Great Iceni), a tribe later identified as occupying Norfolk and northern Suffolk. None of the remaining groups – the Cassi, Ancalites, Bibroci and Segontiaci – are ever mentioned again (either by Caesar or by any later source) and frustratingly Caesar provides no geographical location for them. As his campaigns were restricted solely to south-east England (Kent, Essex and Hertfordshire), we might expect all tribes to have existed in this general area. The Cassi are perhaps the most intriguing, given that not only was the British war leader's name 'Cassi-Vellaunus', but also because Caesar neglected (or forgot) to provide him with any form of tribal affiliation. Given that Bellaunos/Vellaunos is a perfectly acceptable British name (roughly meaning 'excellent'), that the leader of the resistance against Rome was actually called 'Bellaunos/Velaunos of the Cassi' then seems reasonable, and that somehow this identity was mis-transcribed (or misunderstood) by Caesar, becoming Cassibellaunus/Cassivellaunus. The remaining three tribes, the Ancalites, Bibroci and Segontiaci, may have been discrete clans within 'Cantium', a geographical name possibly meaning 'corner land' (relating to the promontory of Kent). Caesar mentions 'four kings of that region, Cingetorix, Carvilius, Taximagulus and Segovax'[9] who were later to make an attack on his naval base, but does not ascribe tribal affiliation. It is possible that the four may have ruled over any of the three remaining groups mentioned by Caesar.

The surrender of multiple British tribes brought Caesar vital tactical information concerning the leader of the resistance movement, namely the location of his capital, which, he noted, was 'protected by forests and marshes' being 'filled with a large number of men and cattle'.[11] Assaulting from two sides, the legions successfully got in, a large quantity of cattle being rounded up and many of the defenders being captured or killed. In a last attempt to draw Caesar away, Cassivellaunus ordered the four kings of Cantium 'to collect all the troops and make a surprise attack' on the Roman beachhead. This was successfully repelled.[12] With the capture of his capital, combined with the failure of the Kentish tribes to destroy the Roman base, Cassivellaunus realized the game was up. Both sides now agreed to a cessation of hostilities, Caesar, keen to return to Gaul, setting out terms that in future Cassivellaunus would 'not wage war against Mandubratius nor the Trinobantes'.[13] Mandubracius was now an ally of the Roman state, his tribe a fully fledged protectorate. Having resolved the war, the Roman troops set sail in their repaired transport ships. Caesar was never to return.

Gildas and Bede on Caesar

Gildas, the earliest British writer to describe first contact with Rome (albeit 600 years after the event), is vague on detail, apparently conflating Caesar's expeditions with the later invasion under the emperor Claudius in AD 43. Having subjugated 'all the neighbouring regions and islands', Gildas tells us, Rome 'could not be restrained or extinguished by the blue torrent of the ocean'.[14]

> Crossing the strait, and, meeting no resistance, it brought the laws of obedience to the island. The people, unwarlike but untrustworthy, were not subdued, like other races, by the sword, fire and engines of war, so much as by mere threats and legal penalties. Their obedience to the edicts of Rome was superficial: their resentment they kept repressed, deep in their hearts.[15]

Unsurprisingly perhaps, from what we shall see later in Gildas' De Excidio et Conquestu Britanniae, the Britons are depicted as un-militaristic and deceitful. After successfully reducing them through 'mere threats and legal penalties', Gildas tells us that 'the conquerors soon went back to Rome, allegedly for want of land, and had no suspicion of rebellion'.[16] The statement that, having established a foothold the Romans went home is curious for, on the face of it, this can only relate to Caesar's expeditions, following which he returned to the Continent. It could be that Gildas was simply misunderstanding his primary source material for, following the later Claudian invasion of AD 43, Roman troops did indeed move out of central south-eastern Britain to garrison the north. Perhaps this gave the impression, at least to Gildas, that they had left the island completely. Alternatively, it could be that he just didn't care, the key facts of the Roman invasions not being central to his idiosyncratic moral thesis.

Bede, writing in the early eighth century, provides a neatly abridged summary of Caesar's two campaigns, largely following detail supplied in de Bello Gallico. Presumably Bede either had direct access to a manuscript copy of the commentaries or, at least, a decent summary account, such as that provided by the fifth-century writer Orosius (in his Historiarum Adversum Paganos). He certainly did not appear to employ the sources that Nennius and Geoffrey of Monmouth later used in their very different accounts of the war and, as a consequence, does not suffer from the same degree of textual confusion.

> During a campaign against the Germans and Gauls, whose common boundary was the Rhine, he entered the province of the Morini, from which is the nearest and quickest crossing into Britain. Here he assembled about eighty transports and galleys, and crossed into Britain, where his forces suffered a fierce battle. Next encountering a violent gale, he lost most of his fleet and many troops, including almost all of his cavalry. So he returned to Gaul, dispersed his legions to winter quarters, and gave orders for the construction of 600 vessels of both types.[17]

Bede, as noted, seems to have based his version of the Roman invasion on material appearing in Caesar's de Bello Gallico via the later treatise by Orosius, the fifth-century writer having neatly abridged Caesar's account of the first campaign in a very similar way:

> Thence he came to the territories of the Morini where is to be found the nearest and shortest passage to Britain, to which, after preparing about eighty transports and swift ships, he set sail. In Britain he was first harassed by a bitter conflict and then overtaken by a disastrous storm; in the end he lost the greater part of the fleet, a considerable number of soldiers, and almost all of his cavalry. Returning to Gaul, he sent the legions into winter quarters and ordered six hundred ships to be built of every kind needed.[18]

Having prepared for war, so Bede continues, Caesar made a second attempt to conquer Britain in the spring:

> But while he was advancing against the enemy with large forces, the fleet lying at anchor was struck by a storm, and the ships were either dashed against each other, or driven on the sands

and destroyed. Forty ships were wrecked, and the remainder were only repaired with great difficulty. At the first encounter, Caesar's cavalry suffered a defeat at the hands of the Britons, and the tribune Labienus was killed. In a second battle, which involved considerable risk, he put the Britons to flight. His next objective was the Thames, where a vast host of the enemy under Cassobellaunis was holding the far bank, and had constructed a defence system of sharpened stakes which ran along the bank, and under the water across the ford. Traces of these stakes can still be seen; cased in lead and thick as a man's thigh, they were fixed immovably in the river-bed. But they were noticed and avoided by the Romans, and the barbarians, unable to resist the charge of the legions, hid themselves in the forests and harassed the Romans by frequent fierce sorties.

The curious defensive strategy of deploying wooden stakes along the Thames is mentioned by Caesar and also by Orosius, although Bede adds the touch of adding that the stakes can still be seen in his time, although it is unclear whether he actually saw them himself. Descriptions of them being cased in lead suggests perhaps that, rather than being a defence against military attack, the timbers were actually part of a later structure such as piers for a bridge. The death of tribune Labienus picks up on a detail mentioned by Orosius when describing the second expedition (although this is not explicitly clear in the later description): 'Caesar's cavalry was defeated by the Britons in the first battle, in which the tribune Labienus lost his life.'[19] Titus Atius Labienus, who appears with some regularity in Caesar's de Bello Gallico, was one of Caesar's most competent and trusted officers. It is not clear, however, whether he was in any way involved with the first campaign in Britain, although he certainly played a major part in crushing the Morini in Gaul who rose in revolt on Caesar's return.[20] In 54 BC it was Labienus who Caesar left behind on the Continent 'with three legions and two thousand cavalry with orders to guard the ports, provide for a supply of corn, watch events in Gaul and act as circumstances from time to time might require'.[21]

Orosius, then, seems to have misread, or at least misunderstood, a key aspect of Caesar's narrative when summarising de Bello Gallico for his own Historiae Adversus Paganos. Titus Atius Labienus did not die in Britain, but another officer, Quintus Laberius Durus, certainly did. During a particularly fierce encounter with the Britons, who swooped down upon Legionaries busy building a fort, Caesar notes that his men were unnerved by the unfamiliar tactics of their enemy, not having encountered war chariots before. It was during that battle that Laberius Durus was killed,[22] suggesting that the enemy were able to inflict serious injury on Caesar's troops. Orosius's error, confusing Laberius Durus with Atius Labienus, is repeated by Bede and later also by Geoffrey of Monmouth, further suggesting that neither writer had direct access to the primary source: de Bello Gallico.

Bede continues with his account of the war:

> Meanwhile the strongest city of the Trinobantes and its commander Androgius surrendered to Caesar and gave him forty hostages. Following its example, several other cities came to terms with the Romans and, acting on their information, Caesar, after a severe struggle, captured the stronghold of Cassobellaunis, which was sited between two swamps, flanked by forests and well provisioned. After this, Caesar left Britain for Gaul.[23]

Cassobellaunis and Androgius are garbling of the name-forms Cassivellaunus (Cassibellaunus) and Mandubracius (Mandubratius), the two key protagonists mentioned by Caesar in his account of the second campaign. Once again Bede seems to have copied directly from Orosius' summary account of Caesar's campaigns, repeating the fifth-century author's error in transcribing the Roman general's description of 'States' or tribes, the Trinovantes (or Trinobantes) being one, believing instead that they were cities. A similar confusion seems to have occurred later with Nennius, who described 'Trinovantum', believing it to be a town or centre of population rather than a tribe, such things no longer having any meaning when he was writing. Bede also appears to contribute further to the garbling of the name Mandubracius, as he appears in Caesar's de Bello Gallico, and Mandubragius in Orosius, providing the name-form Androgius.

Caesar in the Historia Brittonum

Nennius, compiling information on the campaigns of 55 and 54 BC for the Historia Brittonum, provides a brief account of the British conflict that, although essentially similar to that recorded by Caesar, Orosius and Bede, diverges considerably at a number of critical stages.

> The Romans, when they had achieved dominance over the whole world, sent legates to the Britons to demand hostages and tribute from them, as they received from all other countries and islands. The Britons however, tyrannical and swollen with pride, treated the Roman legates with contempt. Then Julius Caesar, the first who had achieved absolute power at Rome, was greatly enraged, and sailed to Britain with sixty ships, and came into the mouth of the Thames, where his ships were wrecked while he fought with Dolobellus, the proconsul of the British king, who was called Belinus and who was the son of Minocannus who held all the islands of the Tyrrhenian Sea; and Julius returned home without victory, his soldiers slain and his ships wrecked.[24]

It is interesting that, in this account, Caesar's ships 'came into the mouth of the Thames'. On the face of it this represents a major geographical error on Nennius' part, for the Roman fleet, as we can tell from Caesar's own account, landed somewhere on the south coast, probably the shingle beaches of Kent. It is also clear that, during this campaign, the range of the Roman expeditionary force did not extend far from the initial beachhead, the Thames not being reached until the following year. This raises the possibility that either Nennius confused the campaigns of 55 and 54 BC, substituting 'the Thames' for the Kent coast, for Caesar seldom supplied specific geographical detail, the Thames being the only named feature that he mentions in either account, or that the sources that he gathered for the Historia had simply got the details wrong. A third possibility is that, in describing the 'first invasion', Nennius is actually describing the events of the second, outlining a Roman advance deep into British territory and a successful crossing of the Thames. In such a scenario, the fact Nennius' narrative begins with the Thames crossing itself, which he describes as the point of disembarkation for the Roman legions, rather than the main landing in Kent could be explained. If the source material that Nennius claims to have accessed had been written from the perspective of tribes settled to the north of the Thames, then everything that occurred prior to the crossing of that river would either be deemed irrelevant or would have been unknown or otherwise unrecorded.

The fact that Nennius mentions 'Dolobellus', whom he describes as 'the proconsul of the British king', further suggests that the account of Caesar's initial campaign to Britain is not all that it seems. This is not a personal name at all but a garbled version of a specific place. In modern Welsh, 'dol', 'dolau' and the plural 'dolydd' are common place-name elements meaning a water or riverside meadow, hence 'Dolaucothi', 'the meadows of the River Cothi', in Carmarthenshire or Dolwyddelan, 'the meadow of (Saint) Gwyddelan' in Conwy. The second element, 'Bellus', could derive from the Latin Bellum for war, hence, perhaps, the 'meadow of war'/'battle of the river meadows', possibly representing a mis-transcription of a specific event or location. Dol/dolau/dolydd do not, however, appear much within the established place-name evidence for Roman Britain, the only known example 'Dolocindo' occurring in the Roman geography known as the Ravenna Cosmography. This particular name-form, however, is thought to be a garbling of either Durocintum or Dunocitum,[25] the Duro-/Duno- element, meaning 'fort' 'fortress' or 'walled town', being far more common in Romano-British contexts (hence Branodunum, Camulodunum, Durobrivae, Durotriges etc.). In Kent, the later tribal capital established for the Cantiaci by the Roman State was named Durovernum, which can be translated as the 'walled town by the alder swamp'.[26]

If we assume that 'Dorobellus' was a place (a fort, fortress or walled town) rather than a person, we have to turn to the second campaign, undertaken in 54 BC, in Caesar's narrative for an explanation. Three particular battles with the Britons are described, in some detail, by Caesar during the primary expedition: the point of disembarkation; the rescue of the 7th Legion, ambushed a short distance from the camp while foraging for corn; and the defence of the beachhead itself. It is only during the second campaign, in 54 BC, that Caesar is able to directly target two British settlements: the first, a 'well-fortified post of great natural strength' in the woods some 12 miles from the coast,[27] the second a place 'of great natural strength and excellently fortified' to the north of the Thames.[28] We shall return to this site and its potential name when we examine the account preserved by Geoffrey of Monmouth later.

Further interpretative complications arise with regard to the name that Nennius supplies for 'the British King' opposing Caesar, whom he calls Belinus, as well as that of his immediate predecessor Minocannus, neither of who are known from other sources. This is not necessarily a problem, for Caesar names no specific individual from the British side during his first campaign, so there may have been a Belinus, possibly ruling in Kent, that he was unaware of. Alternatively, given that a later king of the south-east was named Cunobelinus, it could be that Nennius supplied an anachronistic detail, or that somewhere the names of two very different rulers were substituted or irrevocably garbled.

A second expedition by Caesar against the Britons is described by Nennius:

> And again, after three years, he came with a great army and three hundred ships to the mouth of the river which is called Thames. And there they commenced battle, and many of his horses and soldiers were killed, for the above named proconsul had placed iron stakes and seeds of war, that is Cetilou, in the shallows of the river, and this invisible ruse caused great damage to the Roman soldiers; and they departed again without peace or victory.[29]

This sounds very much like a duplication of the first expedition. Once again, Caesar lands his troops directly at the River Thames, thus avoiding the tribes of Kent completely, this time with 300 rather than sixty transport ships. Mention of the 'proconsul' Dorobellus adds further credence to the theory that this is, in fact, a retelling of the same event, possibly taken from a different source. Description of the 'iron stakes and seeds of war' in this variant may well have convinced Nennius that it was, in effect, a different conflict and therefore led him to place it 'three years later' in his narrative.

Confusion over the precise number, and timing, of Caesar's expeditions to Britain is amplified by Nennius who goes on to cite yet another Roman invasion:

> For a third time war was waged between the Romans and the Britons, near the place called Trinovantum; and Julius gained imperium over the Britons, forty-seven years before the birth of Christ, two thousand two hundred and fifteen years from the creation of the world.[30]

There was, of course, no third invasion by Caesar of southern Britain. What we appear to have here, therefore, is another account of the campaign of 54 BC, specifically detailing the action undertaken to the north of the Thames. Trinovantum is presumably a place associated with the Trinovantes tribe, possibly Camulodunum or perhaps another site in Essex, for neither of the two strongholds mentioned by Caesar as having been taken by his troops were in Trinovantian territory. Alternatively, 'Trinovantum', as noted above, could be a simple misunderstanding on the part of Orosius, Bede and then Nennius, deriving from the fact that Caesar received the surrender of the Trinovantes 'state', as opposed to 'Trinovantum' the city, under their King Mandubracius. The comment that Caesar 'had imperium over the Britons' makes sense in this context, the Trinovantes being left as a Roman protectorate once Caesar had left for Gaul.

It is possible that the differences between the accounts of Caesar's campaigns as recorded by Bede and Nennius, which both appear to have derived, at least in part, from Orosius' Historiae Adversus Paganos, was that while Bede's narrative was a history of the English people, focusing on the Roman Republic as bearers of civilization and culture, Nennius was perhaps more resolutely 'patriotic' when it came to the Britons. There may well, therefore, have been a degree of subjectivity in the description of both sides and outcome, especially if Nennius had been relying upon indigenous sources, Bede utilizing a more extensive classical and religious library in the eighth-century monastery at Monkwearmouth-Jarrow, including copies of the primary Latin texts for the purposes of his research.

Geoffrey of Monmouth and Caesar: the First Invasion

By the time Geoffrey of Monmouth came to compile the Historia Regum Britanniae, it is clear that there were multiple accounts of Caesar's campaigns in circulation. Elements of the three campaigns cited by Nennius and the detail outlined by Bede enter into his narrative, although he too does not appear to have had direct access to a copy of de Bello Gallico. Geoffrey's description of the expeditions is a greatly expanded version of those appearing in all of the earlier sources, the extra detail concerning the nature of the conflict, the places involved and the relationship of key protagonists all deriving from sources untapped by either Bede or Nennius. This has led some critics to suggest that Geoffrey simply made it all up, generating a patriotic fantasy of British resistance to the superior military might of Rome. As we shall see, this is not the case and the version of the Caesarean War as described by Geoffrey of Monmouth, which is clearly neither patriotic nor particularly flattering to the British, does indeed appear to derive from older sources, much as he claimed.

In Caesar's own account of his second invasion, there are three main protagonists: the hero (himself, naturally); the villain, a British king called Cassibellaunus whom Caesar defeats after much fighting; and the ally, a young British aristocrat called Mandubratius. In the Historia Regum Britanniae, however, Geoffrey duplicates the events of 54 BC, like Nennius, setting them down as if they were two discrete military operations. In the first campaign, Caesar, enraged by an arrogant letter from the British King Cassibellaunus saying that he will not submit to Rome, immediately sets sail for Britain, landing 'with his army in the estuary of the River Thames'.[31] The Nennian perspective that the Roman invasion began only when Roman troops reached the Thames is repeated here, either because Geoffrey of Monmouth is directly using the Historia Brittonum or because the sources he had access to were similarly focused upon the geography of what is now Hertfordshire and Essex, rather than Kent.

> As soon as the Romans had come ashore in their boats, Cassibellaunus marched to meet them with the whole of his force. He reached the town of Dorobellum and there took counsel with the princes of the kingdom as to how he could best

drive the enemy back. With him was Belinus, the commander in chief of his army, with the help of whose planning and advice the whole kingdom was governed. Androgeus, duke of Trinovantum, and Tenuantius, duke of Cornubia, the two nephews of Cassibellaunus, were also there; and so too were the three kings holding sway under Cassibellaunus: Cridious of Albania, Gueithaet of Venedocia and Britahel of Demetia.[32]

Once again having reference to a commander in chief called Belinus, possibly replicating Nennius' confusion surrounding the later character of 'Cunobelinus' (of whom we will hear more later), Geoffrey resolves the problem of 'Dolobellus', correctly interpreting the name-form as a place rather than Nennius' confused description of the 'proconsul of the British king'. Dorobellum, as a town or 'fort of war', makes far more sense, especially if it is chosen by the British leaders as a place to do battle.

Mention of Androgeus, duke of Trinovantum, and Tenuantius, duke of 'Cornubia' or Cornwall, whom Geoffrey also says were the nephews of Cassibellaunus,[33] are characters absent in Nennius' account. Caesar, of course, describes Mandubratius, the name-form becoming Mandubragius in Orosius' summary and Androgius in Bede,[35] as a prince and heir apparent to the throne of the Trinobantes (Trinovantes) tribe. None of these sources, however, mention Tenuantius (or Tenvantius as he also sometimes appears), although as we shall see later, coin evidence attests a genuine figure from history, albeit one whose name-form was Tasciovanus. Tasciovanus' coin distribution covers an area to the north of the River Thames, from Hertfordshire to Essex, the mint marks VER and VERLAMIO (for Verulamium or St Albans) suggesting that he started his career as king of the Catuvellauni. If the Androgeus of the *Historia Regum Britanniae* was the Mandubratius/Mandubracius of Caesar, Trinovantum the town actually being Trinovantes the tribe, how then do we reconcile Tenuantius/Tenvantius' territory as being the dukedom of Cornwall (Cornubia)?

Whether name confusion is derived from the primary accounts or from subsequent manuscript copying is difficult to determine. But if the character or place can be identified from archaeology or from an alternative written source, the problem can usually be resolved.

Such is the case with Tenuantius/Tenvantius, a person who is not referenced within any surviving ancient account of the Caesarean war. He is known solely from archaeological evidence and his kingdom and sphere of influence can thus be determined. 'Catuvellauni' was a name-form that was either incomprehensible to Geoffrey of Monmouth, it being difficult to resolve or one which possessed no obvious geographical location; unlike Trinovantum, which he interpreted as derived from 'Troia Nova' or 'New Troy' (and hence, in his view, being the antiquated name for London). If the story that Geoffrey was writing was indeed one of the 'Kings of Britain' then an obvious resolution presented itself: Catuvellauni, or in whatever corrupted form the name appeared, could only really be 'Cornubia', the kingdom of Kernow/Curnow, or Cornwall.

This has dramatic consequences for our understanding of the Historia Regum Britanniae. It would appear that the geographical scope of the narrative was not as vast as Geoffrey of Monmouth intended. Rather than being the dukes of London (Trinovantum) and Cornwall (Cornubia/Kernow), a curious combination of places in any case, Androgeus (Mandubracius) and Tenuantius (Tasciovanus) were respectively heirs to the tribes of the Trinovantes and Catuvellauni. This point is further emphasized when we consider Geoffrey of Monmouth's earlier statement that, when Cassibellaunus came to the throne, he granted significant power to his two nephews:

> He did not wish the young men to be cut off from the kingship, and he allowed a large share of his realm to the two of them. He granted the town of Trinovantum and the duchy of Cantia to Androgeus; and to Tenuantius he gave the duchy of Cornubia. Cassibellaunus himself remained in authority over both of them and over the princes of the entire island, for he was the overlord by virtue of his crown.[36]

Androgeus, therefore, was not just provided with Trinovantum, the tribal lands of the Trinovantes in Essex, which Geoffrey of Monmouth identified with London, but also the 'duchy of Cantia', the name-form equating with Kent – home, so Julius Caesar tells us, of the 'kings of Cantium'. The sources that Geoffrey employed for his narrative were, it would therefore appear, recounting not a pan-British conflict, but a regionalized dispute involving two neighbouring clan groups, the Catuvellauni and the Trinovantes/Cantiaci, joined, or at least led by, their overking, Cassivellaunus.

A shift in the geographical placement of Geoffrey's account to the Iron Age tribal groups of central south-eastern England may further help with the identification of the three 'sub-kings' mentioned, almost in passing, as being with Cassibellaunus at the gathering in Dorobellum: 'Cridious of Albania, Gueithaet of Venedocia and Britahel of Demetia'.[37] Most modern translations equate Albania with Albany or Scotland and Demetia with the Demetae tribe of south-west Wales, with Venedocia or Venedotia being unlocated. The problem, again, is that such an identification conforms to the view that this was a pan-British war and that Cassibellaunus had power over all areas. The reality is probably far more prosaic: Geoffrey of Monmouth, or the sources he had access to, had garbled the name-forms of tribes local to the Catuvellauni/Trinovantes. Any one of the leaders or tribal subgroups mentioned by Caesar could have formed the inspiration for Albania, Venedocia and Demetia as they appear in the Historia Regum Britanniae, their name-forms and place of origin being hopelessly corrupted and subsequently 'reconstructed' by a medieval copyist, even perhaps by Geoffrey of Monmouth himself.

Advising Cassibellaunus to attack Caesar immediately, Geoffrey tells us the counsel agreed that should the Roman 'occupy any city or fortress', then the 'task of expelling him would be all the more difficult'. The army then marched forward to the shore in order to do battle.[38] The conflict that develops in the Historia then shifts register, becoming more poetic in its description of the subsequent carnage, hinting at either a lost source, such as a battle-saga, or the direct copying from a bardic praise-poem.

> The two armies were drawn up in battle-array and the Britons engaged the enemy in hand to hand combat, matching javelin with javelin and sword-thrust with sword-thrust. On both sides the wounded fell in heaps, with the weapons of war sticking in their entrails. The earth was drenched with the blood of the dying, as when a sudden south west wind drives back the ebbing tide.[39]

Particular attention is given to the actions of Nennius, brother of Cassibellaunus, and Androgeus, Cassibellaunus' nephew, together with 'the men of Cantia and the citizens of Trinovantum who were under their command', who 'fell upon the battalion which was guarding the emperor's person'.[40] Such a combat citation, reflecting significant gallantry on the battlefield, would appear to indicate that the account was written by, or at least on behalf of, the Trinovantes/ Cantiaci coalition, demonstrating that it was they, and they alone, who successfully fought to the heart of the Roman line, almost to Caesar himself. The sense that this section of the Historia has been directly appropriated by Geoffrey from a warrior panegyric without significant editing or modification in order to fit his own distinctive house style increases as the detail of battle focuses in upon an aspect of the combat and the bravery of one Briton in particular.

As the two sides made contact the emperor's company came very near to being scattered by the close ranks of the invading Britons. They all fought together in a confused melee and Nennius had the extraordinary luck of meeting Julius in person. As he rushed at Caesar, Nennius rejoiced in his heart at the fact that he would be able to deal at least one blow at so great a man. Caesar saw Nennius charging at him. He warded his opponent off with his shield and struck him on his helmet with his naked sword. Caesar lifted his sword a second time with the intention of following up his first blow and dealing a fatal wound. Nennius saw what he was at and held out his own shield. Caesars's sword glanced off Nennius' helmet and cut into his shield so deeply that, when they had to abandon their hand to hand fight because of the troops who crowded in on them, the emperor could not wrench his sword out. Having acquired Caesar's sword in this way, Nennius threw away his own, dragged the other weapon out and hurried off to attack the enemy with it.[41]

The battle, as described, now takes on a mythic feel, containing fantastic elements that echo the berserker frenzy or warrior trope so commonly encountered in later Celtic praise-poems, Nennius almost single-handedly winning the war for the Britons.

Everyone whom Nennius struck with this sword either had his head cut off or else was so seriously wounded as Nennius passed that he had no hope of recovery. As Nennius raged up and down in this way the tribune Labienus came to meet him, but Nennius killed him on the spot. So passed the greater part of the day.[42]

Mention by Geoffrey of Monmouth of the tribune Labienus replicates the error made by Orosius, and repeated by Bede, that Titus Atius Labienus, one of Caesar's most trusted officers, died in Britain whereas the casualty, according to Caesar in de Bello Gallico, was Quintus Laberius Durus. Geoffrey, of course, adds further detail that it was Nennius, the brother of Cassibellaunus the overking, who slew the Roman, either because he was taking the detail, provided by Bede and Orosius, and creating a British opponent or because there was an earlier tradition linking the two combatants. Mention of Laberius, of course, together with the nature of a battle fought inland, suggests that it is not the first campaign of 55 BC that Geoffrey is describing here but the second, in 54 BC, when Caesar's legions engaged in fighting across Kent and into Hertfordshire.

We have already noted the confusion surrounding the precise number and timing of Caesar's expeditions to Britain in the Historia Brittonum, Nennius describing three discrete invasions, all of which repeat aspects of the second campaign. This suggests that, rather than recording three discrete invasions, Nennius, and later Geoffrey, set down three different accounts of the same invasion, the change in emphasis and detail reflecting the perspective and concerns of the three original authors.

According to Geoffrey, the tide of the battle now began to turn against Julius Caesar.

The Britons pressed forward with their ranks undivided. As they charged boldly on, God favoured them and victory was theirs. Caesar withdrew to a line between his camp and the ships, for his Romans were being cut to pieces. That night he re-formed his ranks and went on board his ships, glad enough to make the sea his refuge. His comrades dissuaded him from continuing the fight and he was happy to accept their advice and return to Gaul.[43]

Cassibellaunus' joy at trouncing Rome was tempered with grief, Nennius having been mortally wounded. Dying fifteen days later, the aristocrat was buried 'in the town of Trinovantum'.[44]

Geoffrey of Monmouth: the Second Invasion

Two years later, so the Historia Regum Britanniae tells us, Caesar was back. His primary aim seems to have been 'to avenge himself upon Cassibellaunus', who, when he heard this, 'garrisoned his cities everywhere', repairing walls, stationing soldiers in the ports and planting stakes 'as thick as a man's thigh and shod with iron and lead' in the river Thames in case Caesar planned to approach Trinovantum by sea.[45] Caesar, embarking with 'so many troops that no one could count them', sailed into the Thames Estuary 'in the direction of Trinovantum' where his ships struck the metal-clad stakes. 'Thousands of soldiers were drowned as the river flowed into the holed ships and sucked them down,' Geoffrey tells us, before the survivors could get ashore.[47]

Witnessing the chaos and carnage, Cassibellaunus ordered his army to attack.

Despite the danger which they had endured in the river, once they reached dry land the Romans withstood the onslaught of the Britons bravely enough. Bolstered up by their own courage, they inflicted no small slaughter; but the carnage they themselves suffered was greater than the damage they did. They had been sorely tested in the river and now they moved forward with their ranks thinned. The Britons on the other hand were reinforced as each hour passed, by the moving up of additional troops, until they outnumbered the Romans by three to one; and thus they were victorious over their weakened enemy.[47]

Although being presented as the 'second invasion', and mentioning both the River Thames and the iron-shod stakes, as well as describing the active involvement of Cassibellaunus/Cassivellaunus, it is clear that the action, as set out in the Historia Regum Britanniae, is in part taken from Caesar's first campaign, in 55 BC, for the hard-fought landing strongly echoes the initial struggle for the beachhead in Caesar's de Bello Gallico.

The size of the ships made it impossible to run them aground except in fairly deep water and soldiers, unfamiliar with the ground, with their hands full, and weighed down by the heavy burden of their arms, had at the same time to jump down from the ships, get a footing in the waves, and fight the enemy, who, standing on dry land or advancing only a short way into the water, fought with all their limbs unencumbered and on perfectly familiar ground.[48]

As the legions began the difficult process of troop-ship disembarkation, they were harried all the time by the Britons. 'The enemy knew all the shallows,' moaned Caesar, and when they saw groups of Roman soldiers entering the sea 'they galloped up and attacked them at a disadvantage, surrounding them with superior numbers'.[49] Eventually, and after much fighting, Caesar's troops prevailed in 55 BC and the enemy were beaten back. Although this is a different outcome to the account appearing in the Historia, given the context of Caesar's and Geoffrey's versions we would perhaps expect nothing less.

The interesting point about the second Caesarean war as described by Geoffrey of Monmouth is that the battle for the beachhead was not described by Orosius, who says simply that in Britain Caesar 'was first harassed by a bitter conflict and then overtaken by a disastrous storm' and thus it is not mentioned by Bede. Nennius, it is true, describes an abortive landing in the Thames Estuary, but says only that, after great damage to their ships, caused by the iron stakes, the Romans 'departed again without peace or victory'.[50] The desperate nature of fighting in the water, the Romans trying to gain advantage over the constantly reinforced British front line, as reported in the Historia Regum Britanniae, does not, therefore, appear to have been influenced by the usual suspects. This would further suggest that Geoffrey had an alternative source on Caesar's campaigns, perhaps a shortened version of de Bello Gallico or another story or tradition in which the fighting on the beaches was recounted in detail.

The second campaign of Caesar, as it appears in the Historia Regum Britanniae, is brought to a sudden conclusion by the inability of his soldiers to gain a significant foothold. Accepting defeat, Caesar 'fled to his ships with the few men left to him and gained the safety of the open sea'.[51] Getting back to 'the shore of the Moriani' (the Morini) in Gaul, the Romans immediately took shelter while Caesar planned his next move.

Geoffrey of Monmouth: the Third Invasion

The events of the third Caesarean war in Britain, as told by Geoffrey of Monmouth, are essentially a repeat of the first invasion: a successful, and apparently unopposed, Roman landing, followed by a swift military response by Cassibellaunus, a fierce battle near to a British fortress and an eventual armistice. Key elements in the story, however, are different, something which, together with the final outcome, with Caesar triumphant, may have convinced Geoffrey that he was dealing with two different military operations, hence their treatment as discrete events.

In the Historia Regum Britanniae, following a dispute with Androgeus, which involved Cuelinus, his nephew, accidentally killing the nephew of King Cassibellaunus, a man called Hirelgdas, Cassibellaunus moves to ravage the duchy of Trinovantum 'with fire and sword'[52] as revenge. Androgeus immediately writes to Caesar, apologizing for participating in the resistance during the previous war and explaining his earlier actions.

> If I had refused to take part in that campaign, then you would
> have beaten Cassibellaunus. Since his success in that battle he
> has become so arrogant that he has now made up his mind to
> drive me into exile from my own land – me, with whose help
> he won his victory. That is how he thinks my efforts should be
> rewarded! I saved his inheritance for him, and now his is trying
> to disinherit me.[53]

Explaining that the overking has invaded his dukedom, Androgeus asked for Roman help in order that he may be restored to his position of honour, adding that 'through me you may become master of Britain'. Caesar demanded that hostages be sent to him in order to ensure the security of any landing. Geoffrey tells us that, so needful was Androgeus of Roman support, he 'immediately sent his own son Scaeva to Caesar' to secure the alliance.[54] This element of the story, unparalleled in the writings of Orosius, Bede and Nennius, echoes the account of Mandubratius/Mandubracius whom Caesar records 'fled for his life' and placed himself under the protection of Rome just prior to the invasion of 54 BC. Caesar in return 'demanded forty hostages and grain for his troops, and then allowed Mandubratius to go'.[55] That this side of the bargain was fulfilled is confirmed by Caesar, although whether the son of Mandubracius/Androgeus was among them (and whether or not he was called Scaeva) is not recorded.

Reassured, Caesar set sail a third time for Britain, landing at 'Rutupi Portus' or Richborough (Rutupiae) in Kent. Cassibellaunus was on the verge of laying siege to Trinovantum, the capital of Androgeus, having already started 'sacking the villas on the outskirts of the city', when he heard the Romans had returned. Immediately lifting the siege, the overking began the journey south to meet the invaders. 'As he marched into a valley near Durobernia,' Geoffrey tells us, Cassibellaunus 'saw there the Roman army busy pitching its camp and putting up its tents'. In the first Caesarean war, the British Army came together at Dorobellum, prior to attacking the Romans; in the third, they mass at Durobernia. Both place name-forms are sufficiently similar to suggest that, with minimal corruption and transformation, they were originally one and the same.

We have already seen that 'Dorobellum' could plausibly derive either from a Celtic-form, originally meaning something like 'meadow of war' or 'battle of the river meadows', or alternatively from a corruption of a Duro-/Duno- name-element, deriving from 'fortress' or 'walled-town'. A good example of this was the name given by Rome to the tribal capital of the Cantiaci at Canterbury, 'Durovernum', which can be translated as the 'walled town by the alder-swamp'.[56] Durobernia could therefore easily be equated with variant forms 'Dolobernia' or even 'Durobellum', given that 'b' can sometimes being used instead of 'v' in British and Gallic place and personal name-forms appearing in ancient Greek or Latin texts – hence, for example, Trinobantes/Trinovantes. It is also conceivable that the Durobernia appearing in the Historia Regum Britanniae is in fact Durovernum/Durovernia (Canterbury), relating in particular to an important Iron Age settlement or centre that predates the Roman city.[57] Later in the Historia Regum Britanniae Geoffrey notes that the post-Roman

King Vortigern was at Dorobernia, which he helpfully adds is 'now called Cantuaria' (Canterbury) when the Saxons first land in Kent.[58] It could also, possibly, derive from the name Durobrivae (Rochester), a Roman town on the River Medway in Kent, which can be translated as 'the fort by the bridge' or 'bridge-fort',[59] although the etymology here is less convincing.

The Romans had, Geoffrey tells us, been brought to Durobernia by Androgeus 'for he wanted them to occupy the town of Trinovantum in secret'.[60] When the legions realized Cassibellaunus was approaching, they drew up in companies and prepared for battle; Cassibellaunus did the same. Androgeus, however, 'lay hid with five thousand armed men in a certain forest glade' nearby 'ready to run to Caesar's help and to make a sudden unexpected charge against Cassibellaunus and his companies'.[61] Although on the face of it this would appear to be the ultimate betrayal of his people, helping Caesar fight Cassibellaunus, Androgeus, as we shall see, comes out of this extremely well, especially when we consider that it is the overking himself who has just been characterized as a brutal and unforgiving despot, sacking the settlements of Trinovantia.

As the forces of Cassibellaunus and Caesar came together, the textual style of the Historia shifts again, moving away from the rigidly descriptive and falling effortlessly into a lyrical description of battle carnage. The style also hints at another epic struggle, similar to that memorialised in the Historia Regum Britanniae as the 'battle of Dorobellum', the conflict that brought Caesar's first campaign in Britain to a close.

> When the two sides came together in this way they immediately started hurling death dealing weapons at each other and exchanging equally mortal blows with their swords. The companies of men charged at each other and much blood was shed. On both sides the wounded fell to the ground just as autumn leaves drop from the trees.[62]

Androgeus' actions ultimately proved decisive, giving victory to Caesar. Emerging from the grove, his cavalry attacked the rear of Cassibellaunus' battle line 'on which', Geoffrey tells us, 'the whole contest depended'. As a consequence, 'the forces of Cassibellaunus were scattered; he turned in flight and ran from the battlefield'.[63] Caesar had won the day, but only with the help of the warlord Androgeus of Trinovantum. Cassibellaunus fled the battlefield to the safety of 'a rocky hill'. Once there he seems to have recovered his courage sufficiently and 'defended himself manfully', slaying 'such of the enemy as pursued him'. Neither the Romans nor the soldiers of Androgeus could get to Cassibellaunus, so Caesar decided to starve him into submission.

At this point in the narrative Geoffrey digresses into a rather uncharacteristic moment of praise, saluting the heroic nature of Britons past, something which possibly hints at the inclusion of another primary source such as a bardic praise-poem.

> How remarkable the British race was at that time! Twice it had put to flight the man who had subjugated to his will the entire world. Even now, when driven off the battlefield, the Britons went on resisting the man whom the whole world could not withstand. They were ready to die for their fatherland and for liberty.[64]

Whether this sentiment came from another, possibly ancient, source, or whether it was Geoffrey taking a swipe at the later Britons who, in his day lived at the margins of the Anglo-Norman world, it represents a rare example of the editor/author expressing his own feelings. It also jars somewhat with the developing nature of the story, for at this point in the narrative we are being asked to sympathise with Androgeus, the wronged Duke of Trinovantum and Cantia, who has brought Julius Caesar to Britain in order to help end the tyranny of Cassibellaunus. This is therefore less an example of how bravely the Britons defended themselves against the might of the Roman legions and more how the legions were able to support a prince of the Trinovantes against an oppressive native regime.

As the story arc reaches its climax, it is clear where the sympathies of the reader are supposed to lie, for it is Androgeus who emerges the hero. After Cassibellaunus sends a message to the duke, asking him to negotiate a truce with Rome, Androgeus notes, with regard to his erstwhile overking, that 'the leader who is as fierce as a lion in peace time but as gentle as a lamb in time of war is not really worth much' adding, 'The man who piles insults and injuries upon the comrades in arms by whose very help he has triumphed is nothing but a fool. Victory is not won by any particular commander, but rather by those who shed their blood for him in the fighting'.[65]

Turning to the Roman general, Androgeus then says:

> All that I promised you, Caesar, was this, that I would help you humble Cassibellaunus and to conquer Britain. Well, Cassibellaunus is beaten, and, with my help, Britain is in your hands. What more do I owe you? The Creator of all things does not intend that I should permit my leader to be bound in fetters, now that he has asked mercy of me and assured me of retribution for the injury he has done me. I cannot allow you to kill Cassibellaunus while I myself remain alive. If you do not accept my advice, I shall not scruple to give him all the help I can.[66]

In fear of Androgeus, so the Historia tells us, Caesar made his peace with the British king and the terms of the tribute were resolved: an annual tax of three thousand pounds of silver. Cassibellaunus and Caesar now made friends, exchanged presents and, the following spring, the Roman returned to Gaul.

Conclusions

Most people, when reading the Historia Regum Britanniae, observe that it records three invasions by Julius Caesar into Britain, the first two being thrown back into the sea by the defiant indigenous tribes. This, of course, did not happen, at least according to the account written by Caesar himself, there being only two expeditions, both of which were, in his view, successful. What, then, are we to make of the alternative claims made by Geoffrey of Monmouth concerning the events of 55 and 54 BC? A close reading of the text has demonstrated that Geoffrey was describing not three invasions but two, the second one being recorded twice. This has important ramifications not only with regard to how we view the reliability of information contained within the Historia Regum Britanniae, but also how we understand the nature of Geoffrey's primary sources. Once it is realized that the Caesarean wars described in the Historia are not only duplicated but are also presented incorrectly, then we can deconstruct the data set and reassemble it in the right order.

The first expedition by Caesar, in 55 BC, is actually described second. The battle for the beachhead, which so dominated the operation, is concisely summarized by Geoffrey, although he transplants the fighting to the Thames Estuary, probably because this is how it is described in the Historia Brittonum. Nennius, apparently compiling information on the campaigns directly from Orosius and Bede, adds information on the conflict from an alternative source. Critically, he describes three invasions by Rome, the first two landing in 'the mouth of the Thames' rather than on the shingle beaches of Kent. Analysis of his text shows that, in outlining what he purports to be the first invasion, a Roman advance deep into British territory and a crossing of the Thames combined with the mention of 'Dolobellus', Nennius is also describing the events of the second. The next expedition undertaken by Caesar, as it is then described, is a duplication of the first: Roman troops landing at the Thames, struggling against the ship-damaging 'iron stakes' and dealing with 'Dorobellus'. The third campaign is yet another retelling, albeit this time concentrating on the action undertaken by Rome to the north of the Thames, confusing the Trinovantes tribe with 'Trinovantum'. This time Caesar is credited with establishing 'imperium over the Britons'.

Geoffrey of Monmouth uses the basic sequence established in the Historia Brittonum, presumably because he too was not working directly from Caesar's primary account, otherwise he would have noticed that the wars, as they are described in de Bello Gallico, are different in both detail and, more crucially, number. Importantly, Geoffrey adds material relating to Caesar's beach war of 55 BC, unmentioned by Gildas, Orosius, Bede and Nennius, and places it in the narrative of the second campaign, transplanting the fighting from Kent to the Thames, apparently so as not to contradict the Nennian framework. More interesting, however, is that the events of the third campaign, as described in the Historia Regum Britanniae, replicate those of the first, albeit with key differences in outcome.

In the first invasion, Julius Caesar, the aggressor, is defeated by Cassibellaunus (Cassivellaunus) at the 'battle of Dorobellum', thanks to the bravery of the British king's brother, Nennius, and his nephew, Androgeus, together with the men of Trinovantum (the Trinovantes) and Cantia (the Cantiaci) who distinguish themselves with honour. The Romans are driven back into the sea. In the third invasion, a few pages later, Cassibellaunus is now the bad guy, waging a largely unprovoked war of terror upon his nephew Androgeus (Mandubracius). Androgeus strikes a deal with Caesar, in an attempt to neutralize his tyrant uncle. When Cassibellaunus hears that Caesar has landed on the coast, he marches south to repel him. At the 'battle of Durobernia', Caesar prevails, thanks to the timely intervention of Androgeus who appears at the last minute, fighting on the Roman side. Fearing the power of Androgeus, Caesar makes peace with Cassibellaunus and departs, all previous animosity forgotten.

It is clear that in recounting the invasion, Geoffrey of Monmouth did not realise he was using multiple versions of the same event as they had been written from different perspectives. The first, with Cassibellaunus, as the hero, ultimately triumphing thanks to the bravery of Androgeus and the self-sacrifice of Nennius, appears to have been generated by supporters of the British overking. The second account seems to have been written from the perspective of Cassivellaunus' rival, Mandubracius, as it justifies his actions, portraying Cassivellaunus as a despot and the armies of Caesar as a good thing, freeing the citizens of Trinovantum from tyranny. If we compare these two accounts with that set down by Caesar himself, then the differences and similarities in the narratives can be explained.

In de Bello Gallico, Caesar marches 12 miles inland from his beach camp and engages the Britons at an unnamed 'well-fortified post of great natural strength'.[67] Following his return from the naval base, where he repairs ships damaged in a storm, Caesar arrives at the place 'from which he had come' only to discover the Britons are massing against him under the command of Cassibellaunus.[68] After a 'fierce encounter' in which many on both sides were killed, the Britons were driven 'into the woods and hills'.[69] A second encounter, the Britons attacking while the legions establish a fort, is beaten off, but Cassibellaunus' chariots escape leaving many Romans dead, among them the tribune Quintus Laberius Durus. The following day, 'three legions and all the cavalry' were attacked, the Britons 'pressing their attack right up to the standards of the legions'.[70] A strong counter-attack again disperses the British forces, Caesar noting that 'a great many were killed and the rest were given no chance of rallying'.[71]

The two accounts provided in the Historia Regum Britanniae agree that the first battle between the armies of Cassibellaunus and Caesar was of an epic nature, the conflict probably being commemorated in bardic praise-poems which note that 'the earth was drenched with the blood of the dying, as when a sudden south west wind drives back the ebbing tide'[72] and 'on both sides the wounded fell to the ground just as autumn leaves drop from the trees'.[73] In the first, it is the Trinovantes and Cantiaci, led by Androgeus (Manudubracius) and Nennius, who press the attack deep into the ranks of the Roman legions, where they 'contact the emperor's company', Nennius himself engaging in single combat with Caesar, stealing his sword and then killing 'the tribune Labienus'.[74] The bravery of the Britons eventually drive Caesar from the battlefield. In the second account, both sides are equally matched, 'hurling death dealing weapons at each other and exchanging equally mortal blows with their swords'[75] until Androgeus intervenes and wins the battle for Caesar, driving Cassibellaunus from the battlefield.

It may therefore be wrong to search for a single primary source for the account presented in the Historia Regum Britanniae; after all, as Geoffrey says in his foreword, the lives of the early kings were in his day 'celebrated by many people by heart, as if they had been written'. As one might expect for a pre-Roman society, their heroes and heroines were commemorated not because they had been transcribed to parchment, but because they had been transmitted from generation to generation by word of mouth. The battle of Dorobellum/ Durobernia, as described in the Historia Regum Britanniae, evidently took on a mythic feel, fantastic elements expanding as the conflict evolved in folklore, but it is clear this is the same conflict described by Caesar. The difference is, where Caesar portrays himself as the hero by writing his own, no doubt overblown and inflated, account, the testimonies of both Cassibellaunus/Cassivellaunus and Androgeus/ Manudubracius also play fast and loose with the facts. History, as they say, is written by the victors. Here, with a judicious re-editing of the events, there can be said to have been multiple victors. Thanks to the accounts preserved unknowingly by Geoffrey of Monmouth, we now have the testimony of all three protagonists participating in the campaign of 54 BC, each of whom were keen to place themselves in the forefront of the action.

The account of the Caesarean wars preserved in the Historia Regum Britanniae demonstrates that Geoffrey of Monmouth was indeed drawing on traditions that stretched back to the mid-first century BC. It also shows, rather critically, that he did not appear to realise this, duplicating the same event in his magnum opus simply because it had been recorded from different perspectives, further distortion of detail and corruption of name-forms persuading him that he was indeed looking at two, albeit rather similar, events. Geoffrey tried to impose a degree of editorial control over his primary evidence, attempting to weave it all into a single coherent narrative, but the bones of the source material remain visible for all to see.

3

IN THE BEGINNING

With the key to unlocking individual sections of the Historia Regum Britanniae revealed, it is time to go back to the most sensational claim made by Geoffrey of Monmouth: that the Britons were descended from Trojan refugees. We have already seen that just such a creation myth was prevalent among the tribes of central Gaul (France) in the first century BC, but how do we interpret the tale as presented by Geoffrey?

The story of how the British monarchy carried the bloodline of Aeneas is outlined in both Geoffrey of Monmouth's Historia and the Historia Brittonum of Nennius, although, perhaps surprisingly, given he was writing three centuries after Nennius, it is Geoffrey who supplies the greater detail. The celebrated ancestry of the Britons is something that Geoffrey keeps coming back to throughout his book, the most notable example being in the prelude to the clash of empires between Cassibellaunus and Caesar, where Caesar observes that 'those Britons come from the same race as we do, for we Romans too are descended from Trojan stock' adding that 'all the same, unless I am mistaken, they have become very degenerate when compared with us'.[1] Cassibellaunus too makes the link when writing to Caesar, noting that 'a common inheritance of noble blood' is shared by Briton and Roman alike, adding that 'our two races should be joined in close amity by this link of glorious kinship'.[2]

Brutus

The story of the Trojan progenitor Brutus, his birth, exile from Italy, travels through the Mediterranean and exploits in Gaul, fills the whole of Book 1 in Geoffrey's Historia, the journey being similar to that of the Israelite exodus from Egypt: Brutus, like Moses before, leading his people towards the Promised Land. Old Testament allusions to a divinely chosen race are, in fact, made explicit by Geoffrey in one scene where, upon encountering an abandoned city in 'an island called Leogetia', Brutus enters a temple and makes a sacrifice to the goddess Diana. Asking Diana to 'say in which lands you wish us to dwell', the goddess responds:

> To the west, beyond the kingdoms of Gaul, lies an island of the ocean, surrounded by the sea; an island of the ocean, where giants once lived, but now is deserted and waiting for your people. Sail to it; it will be your home for ever. It will furnish your children with a new Troy. From your descendants will arise kings, who will be masters of the whole world.[3]

It is Brutus' destiny, therefore, to establish a glorious homeland for his people at the edges of the known world, and to start a noble line of monarchs.

Every society has its own origin myth, a story of creation which helps explain the world and justify the order of things. Origin myths serve to legitimize monarchies, demonstrating through complex genealogical tables and lines of dynastic descent why a particular family has been 'chosen' to rule. They help to establish, explain and fossilize a specific religious doctrine, sometimes helping a belief system to gain prominence over others. In some cases they are also used to support intolerance, extremism and an overwhelming sense of political, cultural and ethnic supremacy, especially when employed to justify invasion and conquest.

The first Anglo Saxon kings established their credentials by demonstrating ancestry stretching back to Woden, a Germanic deity who appears as Odin in Norse mythology. Such a dynastic link, to a divine progenitor, appears in no less a text than Bede's Historia Ecclesiastica Gentis Anglorum, where it is recorded that the Saxon war leaders Hengist and Horsa 'were the sons of Wictgils, whose father was Witta, whose father was Wecta, son of Woden, from whose stock sprang the royal house of many provinces'.[4] Having a powerful deity as a founding father was of course extremely useful, demonstrating not only a 'god-given' right to rule, but also that those who wielded power were set above the mere mortals who served them. Once Christianity took hold as the faith of choice within Saxon society, the dynastic tables, rather than being completely rewritten, were merely edited so that Woden became a real person, a genuine king from deep time. The Norman King William I had his very own pedigree, tracing his ancestry back, via Old Testament stalwarts Noah and Abraham, to Adam and Eve. Earlier in the first century BC, Octavian, who as 'Augustus' became the first Roman emperor, could underscore his position by tracing the origins of his family back through Romulus, founder and first king of Rome, and Aeneas. The benefit here, of course, was that Octavian could not only claim descent from the most important people in Roman history, but also from the gods, for in Greek mythology Aeneas was the son of the goddess Aphrodite (Venus). Such a pedigree made Octavian special and helped justify his title 'First Citizen' and use of the name Augustus, meaning 'revered one'.

Roman society was unusual in the ancient world for having two very different origin myths, both of which, at face value, appeared mutually exclusive. In one, Rome was founded by Romulus, twin brother of Remus, son of Rhea Silvia and grandson of Numitor, king of Alba Longa, while the other suggested a much older Hellenic foundation thanks to Aeneas who had successfully escaped the horrors of the Trojan War. By the first century BC, as Rome established itself as the pre-eminent force in the Mediterranean, serious thought was given as to how these two very different traditions could be joined. This was achieved by having Aeneas arrive in Italy, marry Lavinia, the daughter of King Latinus, king of the Latins, and then establish the city of Lavinium. Aeneas' son, Ascanius, later established Alba Longa, the thirteenth king of which, Numitor, was the father of Rhea Silvia. With Numitor deposed by his brother Amulius, Rhea Silvia was made a virgin priestess of Vesta, but was impregnated by the god Mars, subsequently giving birth to Romulus and Remus.

No two versions of this revised foundation myth were exactly alike, the greatest disparity being between those who claimed that Ascanius was actually Iulus/Julus, the son of Aeneas and Creusa, daughter of King Priam, and had been born before the sack of Troy, and those who suggested that he was the product of Aeneas' later union with King

Latinus' daughter Lavinia. Another tradition stated that Ascanius was originally called Euryleon prior to the flight from Troy, and that Iulus was in fact Euryleon's son (therefore making Iulus the grandson of Aeneas and Creusa). As with the multiple versions of the same story presented by Nennius in the Historia Brittonum, it would seem likely that divergent aspects in the tale of Aeneas and his bloodline ultimately derived from the 'rich oral tradition' that surrounded the myth prior to it being written down.[5]

No doubt the first tribal rulers of Britain were also in possession of self-aggrandizing foundation myths that upheld their distinctiveness and right to rule. We have already noted that the story of Trojan inheritance, the claim by Nennius and Geoffrey of Monmouth that the earliest kings of Britain were, like the Senate and people of Rome, descended from Aeneas, may actually have its origins in the first century BC. British hostages taken from key aristocratic families were brought up in Rome from the time of Julius Caesar and Augustus, the first emperor recording royal refugees from the island that had sought sanctuary with him. As Augustus formalized his power base in Rome, he affirmed familial links back to Romulus, Aeneas and ultimately to Venus. A key weapon in this fight for identity and legitimacy was the retelling of Roman origins and the flight from Troy, best represented in Virgil's epic the Aeneid.

Living in Rome at this time of seismic political, literary, artistic and architectural change, those Britons in the imperial court would have first absorbed, and later enthusiastically transmitted, aspects of Romanitas: the Roman way of being. Indeed, it would seem surprising if, as 'guests' of Rome who grew up in the city, they were not in some way affected by it. As John Creighton has observed, 'the ideological and perceptual framework within which such a myth would be created is clear: in Augustan Rome in the late first century BC, Troy was a recurrent theme'.[6] Could it be that we owe the story of Trojan heritage to the political aspirations of a first-century indigenous aristocratic elite rather than to a ninth-century copier of dynastic fiction or a twelfth-century spinner of political fantasy? Nowhere does this appear more likely than in the coins minted by British rulers following first contact with the Mediterranean world.

Coinage first appears in southern Britain around the mid-second century BC. The earliest issues are stamped with images influenced by those produced by the Macedonian royal family in the eastern Mediterranean. This may be because tribesmen, recruited largely from the Balkans and northern Italy, had, during the fourth and third centuries BC, been employed as mercenaries by a variety of Mediterranean city states. Any warriors returning home at the end of their employment may therefore have been carrying coins as payment for services rendered. Such coins, stamped with a variety of strange and exotic images, may have influenced regional native aristocracies, inspiring them to produce something similar. The earliest Celtic coins appear to copy Macedonian designs, such as the laurel-wreathed head of Apollo appearing on the obverse (front) and a two-horse chariot on the reverse (back). Referred to as being of 'Gallo-Belgic' type, such images may have crossed the English Channel into Britain on coins either as payment for goods received, or with those returning from military service. Some may also have appeared in the purses of migrants, Caesar noting that the south-eastern coastal strip of Britain was, by 54 BC, under the control of 'those who had passed over from the country of the Belgae for the purpose of plunder and making war'.[7]

The exact function of Celtic coins is not easy to resolve as Late Iron Age society was not, in the modern sense, a monetary economy. Coin produced was, in any case, seldom low-denomination units of base metal, but gold and silver which could not easily be used in day-to-day transactions. Instead of representing disposable cash, therefore, coins may more logically have been used by tribal leaders as a way of storing wealth, perhaps to later give a proportion as a gift to the gods. Alternatively they could be used to pay the Roman State for bulk commodities such as wine or olive oil, or for use in purchasing important necessities such as horses, grain or mercenaries, from their neighbours. They could also have been used as a form of political gift, buying loyalty from another tribe, paying people off or helping to cement alliances and inter-tribal cooperation.

As the concept of coinage spread through Britain, a distinct series of regional variations began to develop. From 70 to 50 BC a wide range of heavily distorted heads and horses appeared on some while others sported lively geometric patterns and overtly stylised images. Towards the end of the first century BC there was a change in imagery combined with a greater desire among some groups to use Latin words, names and phrases. Sometimes the words used relate to forms of tribal affiliation; sometimes they may have been the name of a particular deitiy, leader, town of manufacture, royal title or line of descent. Coins now appear to have been used as weapons in a propaganda war; overt statements of wealth and power with the names of successful individuals firmly impressed upon them. Although incomplete, and often frustratingly vague, as the first examples of a history written by the British about themselves, coins present an invaluable resource.

The pictures deployed on the reverse of the new series of coins were also a departure from what had been previously used, designs having close ties with those used in the Roman world but which were almost certainly incomprehensible to a British audience. Such images, which included cornucopiae, wreaths, vine leaves, oared galleys, classical temples, mythical animals (such as griffins, capricorns, sphinxes and hippocamps) and Roman deities (like Neptune, Mars and Apollo), reflect 'a British aristocracy perfectly in touch with the visual language of the developing Principate and its network of friendly kingdoms'.[8] The tribal leaders of central and south-eastern Britain were, in the decades before the Claudian invasion, not just in the orbit of Rome, but very clearly part of the Roman world.

The Arrival of Brutus According to Nennius

For the earliest known version of the Trojan heritage and the story of Brutus in Britain we have to turn to Nennius, writing in the early ninth century AD. Nennius claims that he merely transcribed the tale into the Historia Brittonum exactly as 'it is written in the annals of the Romans', an unfortunately vague allusion to the nature of the primary source material.

> They trace their origin from the Romans and the Greeks, that is, on the mother's side, from Lavinia, daughter of Latinus, king of Italy, of the race of Silvanus, son of Inachus, son of Dardanus. This Dardanus was son of Saturn, king of the Greeks, who took

a part of Asia, and there built the city of Troy. Dardanus was the father of Troius, who was the father of Priam and Anchises; Anchises was the father of Aeneas, who was the father of Ascanius and Silvius; and this Silvius was the son of Aeneas and Lavinia, daughter of the king of Italy. From the sons of Aeneas and Lavinia there descended Romulus and Remus, who were the sons of the holy queen Rhea, and the founders of Rome. Brutus was consul in Rome when the Roman Empire conquered Spain and made them slaves of Rome, and afterwards he took the island of Britain, where lived the Britons, descended from the Romans, from the line of Silvius Posthumus. He was called Posthumus because he was born after the death of his father Aeneas; and his mother Lavinia stayed in hiding while she was pregnant. He was called Silvius because he was born in a wood; for this reason the kings of Rome were called Silvian, as were the Britons, who descended from him, but they were called Britons from Brutus, and were of the line of Brutus.[9]

Nennius thus established, in rather complex fashion, that both the Britons and the Romans were descended from the Trojan Aeneas, the British kings, as with those of Rome, having the moniker 'Silvian' thanks to their common ancestor, Aeneas' son (with Lavinia), Silvius Posthumus. His explanation of how the Britons got their name, however, differs significantly from subsequent writers, such as Geoffrey of Monmouth, claiming that this was due to a Roman consul rather than a Trojan refugee.

Brutus was a popular choice for the third name (or cognomen) used in the Roman tripartite system of nomenclature, the 'tria nomina', used to amplify the second family element (the nomen) of a specific clan. Within the prominent Junii clan, 'Brutus' became a popular choice of male cognomen, arguably the most famous recipients being Lucius Junius Brutus, first consul of the Roman Republic (in 509 BC) and Marcus Junius Brutus, one of the leading conspirators in the assassination of Julius Caesar (in 44 BC). Given the number of 'Bruti' appearing in Roman history, it is perhaps unsurprising that some degree of textual confusion could arise regarding which particular Brutus took the island of Britain, an event which, it must be pointed out, is certainly not supported in archaeology or Roman literature. Presumably Nennius had some reason to link his narrative with the consul Decimus Junius Brutus, who pacified north-western Spain between 138 and 137 BC (and therefore has a good case to be the 'consul in Rome when the Roman Empire conquered Spain'), although why this should be so is not clear. Possibly the name association and subsequent confusion can be traced back to the fourth-century writer Eusebius of Caesarea, who mentions the Spanish activities of this particular Brutus in the Chronicon (or Chronicle), a work that seems to have influenced Geoffrey of Monmouth.[10]

Having established the origins of the Britons, Nennius then recounts the story again, this time in more detail. Presumably this was because at this point in the narrative he was attempting to integrate a second source concerning the creation myth which contained a slightly different version of the tale.

After the Trojan war, Aeneas arrived in Italy with his son Ascanius, and having defeated Turnus, married Lavinia, daughter of Latinus, son of Faunus, son of Picus, son of Saturn; and after the death of Latinus, he gained the kingdom of the Romans, or rather of the Latins. Ascanius built Alba, and afterwards took a wife, who bore him a son called Silvius. Ascanius took a wife, and she became pregnant, and Aeneas was told that his daughter in law was pregnant; and he sent his son Ascanius to command his magician to examine his wife, to discover whether the child in her womb were male or female, and the magician examined the wife and returned. On account of the prediction the magician was put to death by Ascanius for he said to Ascanius that the woman held a male in her womb, and that he was a son of death, who would slay his father and his mother, and would be hated by all men. So it happened; the woman died at his birth, and the boy was raised and given the name Brutus. After a period of time, as the magician had predicted, while he was playing with other boys, he shot his father with an arrow, not intentionally but by accident. And expelled from Italy, he left the country, and came to the Tyrrhenian Sea, and he was driven off by the Greeks on account of the death of Turnus, who had been slain by Aeneas,

and he travelled on to Gaul, and there he built the city of the
Turoni, called Tours. And later he came to this island, which is
called after his name, that is Britannia, and he populated it with
his people, and he lived there. And Britain has been inhabited
from that day to this.[11]

Nennius thus presents two versions of the identity of the Brutus but,
critically, makes no attempt to explain the contradictory nature of his
evidence. Undoubtedly the two accounts derive from very different
traditions, both of which accepted that the Britons were named after
Brutus, but with neither agreeing on which particular Brutus that was.
The second, more detailed, version establishes the lineage of Brutus
as the descendant of Aeneas, legendary founder of the Roman race,
while the second links more directly with a prominent member of the
republican Roman aristocracy.

Nennius then goes on to record the story of Brutus again when,
following a brief summary of the world according to the Old
Testament, he notes the island 'derives its name from Brutus, a Roman
consul'.[12] This may all be a slip on behalf of Nennius, or one of the
many of those to subsequently transcribe his words, misidentifying
a more ancient 'Brutus' with the man from Rome. Why the link was
not made with Lucius Junius Brutus, traditionally the founding father,
and one of the first consuls, of the Roman Republic is unclear. Lucius
Junius Brutus would, perhaps, have been a more obvious choice for
the 'Brutus' of the Britons, joining them more directly to the creation
of the Roman State. As we have already noted, Nennius 'made a heap'
of all the material he could find in order to compile the Historia
Brittonum, a text which, unlike Geoffrey of Monmouth's, was not
intended as a single, grand, sweeping narrative. Nennius certainly
did not attempt to conceal contradictory points of view encountered
during the course of his research in an attempt to provide internal
consistency; in fact he seems to positively revel in disparity.

At the beginning of section 10, for example, when outlining
the origins of the Britons, he notes that 'if anyone wishes to know
when after the flood this island became inhabited, I have found two
accounts'. Later, when recounting the final moments of King Vortigern,
Nennius describes three different versions of the monarch's death. The

first, from 'the book of the blessed Germanus', has Vortigern and his household destroyed by heavenly fire, Nennius concluding soberly that 'others said otherwise'.[13] A second version of Vortigern's demise has him wandering 'from place to place' until 'his heart was broken and he died, with no honour', while a third has him devoured by the earth, which 'opened up and engulfed him'.[14] The presentation of divergent, contradictory accounts helps us to understand the variety of different sources available to Nennius. It also highlights which tales were considered particularly important to a British audience and also which, potentially, possessed considerable antiquity.

Following on from the two different versions of the Brutus/Britain myth, Nennius again goes back to Aeneas, presumably because he was attempting to integrate another genealogy or king list.

> Aeneas reigned over the Latins for three years; Ascanius reigned for thirty-seven years, after whom Silvius, son of Aeneas, reigned for twelve years; Posthumus, from whom the kings of Alba are called Silvia, reigned for thirty-nine years; he was the brother of Brutus. When Brutus ruled in Britain, Eli the priest was the judge in Israel, and at that time the Ark of the Covenant was taken by foreigners. Posthumus his brother was then reigning among the Latins.[15]

Then, after a lengthy digression into the origins of the Picts and Scots, mixed with detail taken, among other things, from the Old Testament, Nennius suddenly states, 'I have learned another account of this Brutus from the ancient books of our ancestors.'[16] Once again the nature of the source is left vague, although this time we are presented with a more Bible-influenced genealogy explaining the origin of both the Britons and the other major races of the ancient and early medieval world:

> The Britons are called after Brutus. Brutus, son of Hisicion, Hisicion of Alan, Alan son of Rea Silvia, daughter of Numa Pompilius, son of Ascanius; Ascanius son of Aeneas, son of Anchises, son of Troius, son of Dardanus, son of Flisa, son of Iovan, son of Japheth. And Japheth had seven sons; from the first,

Gomer, came the Gauls; from the second, Magog, the Scythians and the Goths; from the third, Madian, the Medes; from the fourth, Iovan, the Greeks; from the fifth, Tubal, the Hebraei and the Spanish and the Italians; from the sixth, Mosoch, the Cappadocians; from the seventh, Tiras, the Thracians. These are the sons of Japheth, son of Noah, son of Lamech.[17]

Thus not only can the origins of Britons be traced back to Lamech, father of Noah and descendant of Cain, but so too can the Trojans, Gauls, Alans, Scythians, Goths, Medes, Greeks, Hebrews, Spaniards, Cappadocians, Thracians and Italians. Such a complex genealogical table presumably derives from an early medieval text or 'Table of Nations'[18] which was not seen, or which was ignored, by Geoffrey of Monmouth when compiling the Historia Regum Britanniae.

The Arrival of Brutus According to Geoffrey

Geoffrey's tale of the great Trojan journey to, and ultimate acquisition of, Britain is different again. After outlining Aeneas' flight from Troy, the landing in Italy and subsequent founding of Alba, Geoffrey treats the reader to a detailed account of the birth of Brutus, in which his mother dies, he is exiled from Italy following the death of his father Ascanius, and his journey through Greece, which is essentially an expanded version of the story as it appears in the Historia Brittonum. Freeing the many 'descendants of Helenus, Priam's son' (fellow Trojans who had been kept in captivity by the Greeks),[19] Brutus' expanded retinue stumbled upon the temple of Diana in the island of Leogetia. Here the goddess prophesied that Brutus would find his home in 'an island of the ocean, where giants once lived' and found a great dynasty of kings.[20]

After a brief sojourn in Mauretania, Brutus and his followers encounter 'four generations born to exiles from Troy' led by a man named Corineus.

As soon as they had realized that his stock was of such high antiquity, they took him into alliance with them straight away, together with the people over whom he ruled. Later Cornwall was called after the name of this leader. In every battle he was of more help to Brutus than anyone else.[21]

Aside from reiterating the origin of the name Britain (from Brutus), Geoffrey of Monmouth digresses in order to explain the etymology of Cornwall – this time deriving from another Trojan, Corineus. This is, of course, not just simple wordplay nor idle patriotism for those who remained free of Saxon influence in the south-west of Britain for, as we have already seen, Cornubia plays an important role in Geoffrey's story. In fact, an understanding of who the 'Cornish' were, in this early part of the Historia, and what precisely the position 'duke of Cornwall' meant, is vital to our understanding of where the primary source material for Geoffrey's account came from, and which tribal group it was intended to celebrate and promote. The fact that Corineus was described as the greatest of all Brutus' warriors adds further credence to the suggestion made in the previous chapter, that it was the Catuvellauni who considered themselves pre-eminent of all tribes in southern Britain and that this particular story was undoubtedly part of their own creation mythology, a point we shall examine further below.

The now significantly enlarged group of Trojans 'came to Aquitaine', casting anchor in the Loire estuary. Exploring the land they immediately annoyed Goffarius the Pict, who ruled the area. In the skirmish that followed, Corineus proved his worth, dodging an arrow aimed at him and breaking the head of the would-be assassin with his own bow. The skirmish predictably led to a more significant battle and, once again, it was Corineus who showed the way:

> He took fresh heart, called his own men over to the right of the battle, arranged them in fighting formation and charged headlong at the enemy. With his troops in close order he broke through their ranks in front and went on killing the enemy until he had worked right through their force and compelled them all to flee. He lost his sword, but by good luck he had a battle axe: and anything he struck with this he cut in two from top to bottom. Brutus was greatly impressed by his boldness and courage. So were his comrades, and so indeed were the enemy.[22]

As his foe started to flee, one of the 'Poitevin leaders called Suhardus' turned to face Corineus, charging him with 'three hundred fighting men'. The combat, as it is described, follows the standard recurring theme of the frenzied warrior, largely immune to injury, which can be found in so much 'Celtic heroic' literature. The importance of Corineus as battle-berserker at this point, however, cannot be overstated, not only because of what he means to those who later claimed him as an ancestor, but also because the description of battle represents a clear divergence in Geoffrey of Monmouth's narrative style, suggesting the appropriation of an epic source.

> Corineus received on his outstretched shield the blow which Suhardus dealt him. Then he remembered the battle axe which he was holding. He swung it up in the air, struck Suhardus on the crest of his helmet and at the spot where he made contact split him in two halves from top to bottom. Then he rushed at the others, twirling his battle axe, and went on causing the same destruction. Up and down he ran, avoiding none of the blows which were dealt him and never pausing in his destruction of the enemy. From one he severed an arm and a hand, from another he carved the very shoulders from his body. At a single blow he struck off one man's head, while from another he cut away the legs. He was the one whom they all attacked, and he in his turn took them all on.[23]

We encounter the warrior trope repeatedly in the Historia Regum Britanniae. It is important to reiterate, however, that where it occurs, not only can we detect the underlying presence of a separate, older epic celebrating the achievements of an individual on the battlefield through exaggerated combat manoeuvres and an excessive body count, but also that we can identify and isolate those characters deemed of vital import to those writing the primary chronicle – in this case the Catuvellauni.

With the Trojans victorious, Brutus revealed his less appealing side, sacking the country and burning all the cities 'far and wide, heaping fire upon fire', slaughtering everyone he found 'for his plan was to exterminate this unhappy race down to the last man'.[24] Emboldened,

Brutus then set about establishing a camp in 'the place which is now called Tours'. Following attack by Goffarius and the Gauls, the 'Picts' now vanished from the narrative, successfully repelled, and Brutus' army inflicted great slaughter upon his enemy in an ambush organised by Corineus. Dismayed that the Gauls were receiving continual reinforcement from neighbouring tribes, Brutus finally decided to 'seek out the island which divine prophecy had promised would be his'. Setting sail, ships loaded with riches, he 'sought the promised land', eventually arriving in Britain by coming ashore at Totnes in Devon.[25]

Totnes was a popular choice of destination for many making first contact with Britain. Brutus comes ashore here in the Historia, an event that is today commemorated by the 'Brutus Stone', a block of granite set into the pavement of the town and which, according to local legend, was the first piece of the British Isles that his feet touched. Totnes also features in the Historia as the port where the Roman general Vespasian lands when planning an attack against the British King Arvirargus[26] as well as being the place Constantine II, Aurelius Ambrosius, Utherpendragon and a Saxon army, escaping from the victorious King Arthur, all make for. Why this particular market town, set at the head of River Dart in Devon, should prove so popular, is unclear, given its relative geographical isolation from events which focus upon central south-eastern Britain. Presumably Geoffrey of Monmouth was interpreting a place name-form that had become irrevocably garbled.

At the time of Brutus' first footfall, so Geoffrey tells us, 'the island of Britain was called Albion', being 'uninhabited except for a few giants'.[27] Having driven the indigenous species into mountain caves, Brutus and his people 'began to cultivate the fields' and to build permanent forms of habitation.

> Brutus then called the island Britain from his own name, and his companions he called Britons. His intention was that his memory should be perpetuated by the derivation of the name. a little later the language of the people, which had up to then been known as Trojan or Crooked Greek, was called British, for the same reason.[28]

Having delivered his followers to the Promised Land, rich in natural resources, the Trojans started to define their individual territories. Unsurprisingly, from what we have already read with regard to the Catuvellaunian sense of self, chief among the splinter groups was the one led by Corineus.

> Corineus, following in this the example of his leader, called the region of the kingdom which had fallen to his share Cornwall, after the manner of his own name, and the people who lived there he called Cornishmen. Although he might have chosen his own estates before all the others who had come there, he preferred the region which is now called Cornwall, either for its being the cornu or horn of Britain, or through a corruption of his own name.[29]

Evidently wrestling with two very different sources of information as to the origin of the name 'Cornwall', Geoffrey provides two rather contradictory explanations. This is probably because he was dealing with the belief that, etymologically speaking, Cornwall was derived from the word 'cornu', based on its horn-like projection into the sea, and the very different creation myths of the Catuvellauni, the primary sources that he accessed having been concerned more with the origins of an Iron Age tribe in central southern Britain, rather than a specific geographic locale in the south-west.

Corineus began to clear his land of the giants that infested it. Geoffrey tells us that the most 'repulsive' of these indigenous creatures was Gogmagog who 'could tear up an oak-tree as though it were a hazel wand'. With all the giants slain and only Gogmagog left, Brutus saw much potential for sport, ordering that the poor creature be kept alive for Corineus alone to kill.

> Corineus was delighted by this. He girded himself up, threw off his armour and challenged Gogmagog to a wrestling match. The contest began. Corineus moved in, so did the giant; each of them caught the other in a hold by twining his arms around him, and the air vibrated with their panting breath. Gogmagog gripped Corineus with all his might and broke three of his ribs, two on

the right side and one on the left. Corineus then summoned all his strength, for he was infuriated by what had happened. He heaved Gogmagog up onto his shoulders, and running as fast as he could under the weight, he hurried off to the nearby coast. He clambered up to the top of a mighty cliff, shook himself free and hurled this deadly monster, whom he was carrying on his shoulders, far out into the sea. The giant fell on to a sharp reef of rocks, where he was dashed into a thousand fragments and stained the waters with his blood.[30]

Now Britain was settled and the wild aspects of nature, represented by Gogmagog and his fellow giants, had been neutralised, Geoffrey of Monmouth tells us that Brutus settled down to the more practical aspects of establishing the kingdom. First, a capital was required.

In pursuit of this plan, he visited every part of the land in search of a suitable spot. He came at length to the River Thames, walked up and down its banks and so chose a site suited to his purpose. There then he built his city and called it Troia Nova. It was known by this name for long ages after, but finally by a corruption of the word it came to be called Trinovantum.[31]

In Geoffrey of Monmouth's hands, the foundation of a capital became an important part in the creation mythology of Britain for Troia Nova was equated with London, thus establishing noble Trojan origins for the city. Despite the evident popularity of Brutus, Corineus and Gogmagog in the mythology and folklore of London, effigies of 'Gog and Magog' still being carried at the head of the annual Lord Mayor's Show procession, the cold, hard stare of the scientific world has been completely unforgiving.

Some legends may incorporate a germ of truth, a folk-memory of actual events. Trinovantum is not such a legend. In origin it was artificial, a strange melange of unscholarly errors and scholarly inventions. It is irrelevant to any discussion of the existence or non-existence of a pre-Roman London. It reflects not the origins of London but London's need for a pedigree, and perhaps the lack, in the twelfth century, of any earlier tradition on the subject strong enough to compete with Geoffrey's speculation.[32]

Of course the association of Trinovantum with London was not the intention of the original source material. It was Geoffrey who, apparently unfamiliar with the name Trinovantes given to the Late Iron Age tribe of what is now Essex, made sense of the term within his own theories concerning the origins of Britain. Trinovantum was therefore Troia Nova or 'New Troy'. This further confirms that Geoffrey was not making use of Julius Caesar's primary account of the conflict, for Caesar directly references the Trinovantes (or Trinobantes) as a tribe or state. Confusion may have arisen from secondary or tertiary sources, such as the early fifth-century Historiarum Adversum Paganos by Orosius, which uses the term 'civitas Trinobantum' for the 'nation of the Trinobantes'. Civitas is also the term for the market towns built by the Roman provincial government in Britain. In such a context it is easy to see how the 'tribe' mutated into becoming the 'town'. As it stands, in the Historia, it is clear that it is Trinovantum the place that is being founded by Brutus, rather than Trinovantes the tribe. With a better understanding of Late Iron Age politics than was evident in the twelfth century, perhaps we can now see this relates to the founding not of London, but a Trinovantian royal centre, presumably Camulodunum (Colchester). This seems to further confirm the suspicion that, in compiling this part of his magnum opus, Geoffrey was accessing information taken from the creation myths of two different Iron Age groups: the Catuvellauni with Corineus and the Trinovantes with Brutus.

This is an important point to make for Geoffrey of Monmouth was struggling to integrate two different, but evidently deep-seated, traditions. Those who claim that the tale of Brutus and his Trojan followers as it appears in the writings of Nennius and Geoffrey was a bizarre slice of early medieval fantasy are missing a crucial point. The tale of Brutus and Corineus was no simple explanation of how Britain and Cornwall were named; there is something far more fundamental at work. As well as leading his people to the Promised Land, Brutus created 'Trinovantum', both the capital and the tribe, while Corineus is cited as the founder of their immediate neighbour, the Catuvellauni. Here, then, are two discrete creation stories with both tribes claiming descent from Trojan migrants. It is Brutus who ultimately claims precedence in Geoffrey's narrative, for he is both the descendant of Aeneas and first king of the Britons, giving his name to both settlers and homeland. The ancestry of Corineus is left unresolved by Geoffrey, other than noting 'his stock was of such high antiquity',[33] and may well have been downplayed, making Corineus and his people, the Catuvellauni, ultimately subservient to Brutus and the Trinovantes. Whether it was Geoffrey of Monmouth who created this relationship in the Historia or whether it possessed far earlier origins is unclear, for Nennius did not mention the second Trojan.

The strength, bravery and heroic stature of Corineus as depicted in the Historia Regum Britanniae, where 'he was of more help to Brutus than anyone else',[34] is of particular interest for Corineus gets far more attention on the battlefield than his erstwhile leader Brutus. As we have noted, the detail in the description of combat, most notably in the fight against the army of Goffarius the Pict, the single combat with Suhardus and the wrestling match with the giant Gogmagog, suggests the underlying presence of a different epic source, one which excessively praises the achievements of 'the Other Trojan'. This alternative saga, no doubt compiled by the Catuvellauni, may not actually have mentioned Brutus at all, for it seems curious why anyone would feel the need to insert a second batch of Trojan refugees into the narrative. More likely the addition of Corineus to the Brutus story occurred when someone combined the differing origin myths of two Iron Age tribes. The Catuvellauni and the Trinovantes were, it seems, both claiming Trojan blood-heritage, something that set them on a par with the Romans. Both groups were, however, evidently in competition and the story, as it appears, has the potential to explain critical aspects of their relationship. Nennius seems to have only had access to the Trinovantian source material, which established Brutus as king, whereas the Catuvellaunian point of view emerged only later in Geoffrey of Monmouth's work. It seems reasonable to suggest, perhaps, given what we know about both tribes in the Late Iron Age and Early Roman period, that the subservient nature of Corineus, and by implication of the Catuvellauni, may have had its origins in deep time.

The prestige with which 'Trinovantum', the political centre, was held can be seen in the proud boast, repeated throughout Historia Regum Britanniae, that it was surrounded 'with lofty walls and with towers built with extraordinary skill'.[35] Intriguingly, the eventual rebuilding of Trinovantum was, so Geoffrey of Monmouth tells us, conducted by 'Lud, the brother of Cassibellaunus, who fought with Julius Caesar'. Lud, having 'seized command of the government of the kingdom', not only remodelled the Trinovantum's defences, but also decided on a not-too-subtle piece of rebranding.

> He ordered it to be called Kaerlud, or Lud's city, from his own name. As a result a great quarrel arose later on between him and his brother Nennius, who was annoyed that he should want to do away with the name of Troy in his own country.[36]

This significance of this curious dispute is, at first, not apparent, other than providing Geoffrey of Monmouth with the etymology for 'London'. As Kaerlud became corrupted through time, he tells us, it became 'Kaerlundein', then 'as languages evolved, it took the name London'.[37] If, as seems likely, Trinovantum was not London at all but the Trinovantian tribal centre, an intriguing possibility develops for the capital (or oppidum) of the Trinovantes was, at the time of the AD 43 invasion, known as Camulodunum (the 'fortress of Camulos'). Is it too far a stretch of the imagination to suggest that the rebranding of Trinovantum to Kaerlud as recorded was not the result of an actual character named Lud but the distorted remembrance or recording of the name Camu-LOD-unum? If so, then the character of Lud himself may have been created from the name 'fortress of Camulos', presumed to be a prehistoric war god rather than a British king, and back-projected as an explanation for Kaerlud/Kaerlundein/London. If we develop this theory further, another possibility presents itself: the rebuilding of Trinovantum, with its 'lofty walls', skilfully constructed towers and rebranding as 'Kaerlud' may echo a seismic shift in the geopolitics of Late Iron Age Britain, namely the appropriation of the Trinovantian capital by another tribe or faction.

Celtic coins recovered primarily from areas to the north of the River Thames (Hertfordshire/Essex) containing the name element

TAS/TASC for Tasciovanus were, unusually for coins manufactured in British prehistory, stamped with two mint marks: VER / VIR / VERL / VERO / VERLAMIO and CAM/CAMVL. The first was Verulamium/Verulamio (St Albans), an Iron Age oppidum remade in the Roman period as the civitas of the Catuvellauni, while CAM was Camulodunum (Colchester). To be in possession of two centres of coin manufacture may seem unusual for an Iron Age dynast, but it is possible that Tasciovanus, either through war or marriage, did indeed control them both. Generally, the oppida are thought to have been created by two different tribes, Verulamium by the Catuvellauni and Camulodunum by the Trinovantes. If Tasciovanus had first been a king of the Catuvellauni, it is possible that his power later extended over Camulodunum, an oppidum that started life within Trinovantian territory, thus providing the landlocked Catuvellauni with direct access to the sea. If this was so, then it was Tasciovanus and not the manufactured 'Lud' who may finally have completed the process of expansive war and absorption of the Trinovantes that began with Cassivellaunus.

Whatever the case, and whichever scenario is the more likely, it does appear that by the first century AD Camulodunum and Verulamium were under the control of a single monarch. Could the appropriation of the Trinovantian capital by a ruler of the Catuvellauni therefore have provided the basis of the story echoed in the Historia Regum Britanniae? If so, then it was no mere change in nomenclature of a settlement that generated the 'great quarrel', which Geoffrey records as being between Nennius and Lud, but the capture of the Trinovantian capital and its subsequent identity change to Camulodunum, a city taken by the Catuvellauni and dedicated to Camulos, a Celtic god of war.

A Noble House

With Kingdom and capital established, Brutus, according to Geoffrey of Monmouth, went on to fulfil the next part of Diana's great prophesy by establishing a noble house of kings.

> Brutus had consummated his marriage with his wife Innogin. By her he had three sons called Locrinus, Kamber and Albanactus,

all of whom were to become famous. When their father finally died, in the twenty-third year after his landing, these three sons buried him inside the walls of the town which he had founded.[38]

The 'town' inside which Brutus is laid to rest is undoubtedly Trinovantum, which, as discussed in the previous chapter, can best be equated with Camulodunum/Colchester rather than Troia Nova (New Troy), which Geoffrey and all subsequent writers have linked with London. Camulodunum/Colchester, of course, was, by the first century AD, the premier oppidum of southern Britain, centre of trade, politics and religion, being claimed on the coins of a number of Iron Age kings. It was also Rome's main target in the invasion of AD 43, and scene of the Emperor Claudius' great triumph where, we are told, he took the surrender of eleven British kings. It is hardly surprising then, that Brutus, father of Britain, should have been placed within the town of those who claimed priority over all tribes in southern Britain. Archaeological investigation has produced significant evidence for wealthy burial in the Late Iron Age and Early Roman period in and around Camulodunum[39] and, although none of these can lay claim to be Brutus, they demonstrate the association of the site with the aristocratic elite of the tribe.

The blood-heritage of Brutus, and the exploits of his many descendants and subsequent rulers up until the arrival of Julius Caesar, fills the entirety of Book 2 in the Historia Regum Britanniae. Sometimes the tale reads like a simple king-list, with names, line of descent and years ruled, while at other times more significant, and sometimes bizarre, detail is supplied. It is not intended to provide a full interpretation of the data set here, for there is much that is unknown and, in the context of pre-Roman Britain, ultimately unknowable. If, however, we accept that the Historia Regum Britanniae contains information that was not originally part of a single epic, but instead a mass of stories, myths, chronologies and lists, all of which was put together by Geoffrey of Monmouth in order to form a coherent narrative, then individual elements can be teased out. Comparative, and perhaps slightly more objective, information, especially that from Greece and Rome, which would help us to place the characters, events and geographies of the Historia in context, is hard to come by. Given that the majority of stories that we have examined so far appear to have derived from central southern Britain, predominantly from the area of the Trinovantes and Catuvellauni tribes of the later first century BC and early first century AD, however, then it is here we should perhaps focus our attention. Both tribes were in contact with the Mediterranean, were defining the nature of statehood and were attempting to establish themselves as equals to Rome. Within this comparatively limited geography and time frame, some intriguing comparisons with the established archaeo-historical data set can be made.

Some of the information employed by Geoffrey of Monmouth has clearly been derived from dynastic tables, given that the detail surrounding particular monarchs is sparse, relating to simple facts concerning line of descent and length of reign. Hence, in Book 2, following on immediately from a descriptive section outlining the violent reign of King Mempricius, we receive an abrupt listing for the family of King Ebraucus:

> ... by the twenty wives which he had, he was the father of twenty sons and of thirty daughters. For forty years he ruled over the kingdom of Britain with great firmness. The names of his sons were as follows: Brutus Greenshield, Margodud, Sisillius, Regin, Morvid, Bladud, Lagon, Bodloan, Kincar, Spaden, Gaul, Dardan, Eldad, Ivor, Cangu, Hector, Kerin, Rud, Assarcus and Buel. The names of his daughters were: Gloigan, Ignogin, Oudas, Guenlian, Guardid, Angarad, Guenlodoe, Tangustel, Gorgon, Medlan, Ourar, Mailure, Kmbreda, Ragan, Gael, Ecub, Nest, Chein, Stadudud, Cladus, Ebrein, Blangan, Aballac, Angoes, Galaes (the most beautiful of the young women who lived at that time in Britain or in Gaul), Edra, Anor, Stadiald and Ergon.

This divergence from flowing narrative into basic citation of names suggests that, at this point in writing, Geoffrey had become reliant upon a dynastic list, or perhaps even detail taken from a post-Roman memorial, where the ancestry of a particular monarch was recorded. How corrupted were the names when Geoffrey encountered them in the twelfth century is unknown. We may suspect, given what we have already seen, that unusual or divergent names were simplified or 'interpreted' in order that they complied with established or familiar name-forms, either personal (such as Ivor, Hector, Angarad, Gorgon or Ragan) or geographical, relating to specific groups of people (such as Gaul, Gael and Galaes). Furthermore, the repetition of names in the list, such as Brutus (with 'Greenshield' attached), and the appearance of others, such as Sisillius and Bladud, who occur more prominently later as the offspring of different rulers, may indicate a garbling of sources – perhaps an alternative list of Trojan descent which Geoffrey found and then tried to fit, filling in any chronological gaps. We have already seen, for example, that when compiling the Historia Brittonum, Nennius cited multiple versions of the same story, without imposing any degree of editorial control by the deletion of those tales he felt contradicted the main account. Geoffrey seldom does this, his skill being the way in which he creates order from potential narrative chaos, placing characters and events within a single grand chronology. Sometimes the desire to make everything fit creates a paradox, specific names and events appearing more than once, albeit with key strategic details altered.

Another example of a basic king-list, or citation of royal blood-heritage, appears to be in Book 2 of the Historia Regum Britanniae, where we hear that,

> After the death of Cunedagius, his son Rivallo succeeded him, a peaceful, prosperous young man who ruled the kingdom frugally. In his time it rained blood for three days and men died from the flies that swarmed. Rivallo's son Gurgustius succeeded him. Sisillius came after Gurgustius, then Jago the nephew of Gurgustius, then Kimarcus the son of Sisillius and after him Gorboduc.[40]

The name Cunedagius is an intriguing one for it is the Latinised form of the Welsh Cunedda, the name of a mythologized fourth- or fifth-century leader who is frequently cited as the founding father of the royal house of Gwynedd. Names could, of course, easily be duplicated over time, especially if an ancestor was subsequently held in very high regard. If Cunedagius is, however, the Cunedda cited as progenitor in a number of early Welsh dynasties, then perhaps his appearance in Book 2 of the Historia Regum Britanniae is due to Geoffrey of Monmouth misunderstanding the nature and chronological context of a particular post-Roman king-list. The anachronistic placement of Cunedda/Cunedagius back into the depths of 'Trojan prehistory' could explain why this particular king does not feature in the Historia Regum Britanniae, at least not in that name-form or in the correct time period. Cunedda certainly makes an appearance in prominent welsh genealogies, as does Maelgwn (or Maglocunus), his great-grandson, whom Gildas decries as being 'mightier than many both in power and malice, more profuse in giving, more extravagant in sin, strong in arms but stronger still in what destroys a soul'.[41]

Listed by Gildas as one of the 'five tyrants', Maelgwn/Maglocunus may well be the 'Maglo' whom Geoffrey of Monmouth says 'was a man brave in battle' and 'more generous than his predecessors' as well as being overly given 'to the vice of sodomy'.[42] Maglo's ancestry is not cited in the Historia Regum Britanniae, possibly because Geoffrey was not interested in, or did not have access to, family details of those dynasties that followed the collapse of Roman power in the west. More likely, perhaps, he had already cited Cunedda/Cunedagius, the great-grandfather of Maelgwn/Maglocunus/Maglo, as an early king from the immediate bloodline of the first Trojans (as son of Henuinus and Regau) and could not, therefore, find room for him in the dynasties of post-Roman Britain.

Such an explanation, the brief details produced by Geoffrey having been lifted from a king-list or dynastic chronology, may further resolve the summary nature of individual rule as it is appears in the Historia, the descendants of Cunedagius (namely Rivallo, Gurgustius, Sisillius, Gurgustius, Jago, Kimarcus and Gorboduc) receiving no more than the briefest of citations. The only additional detail provided, the three-day rain of blood that occurred during Rivallo's reign in which 'men died from the flies that swarmed' could, in this respect, be a reflection of one of the great mortalities or plagues that swept through the Mediterranean and western Europe throughout the fifth and sixth centuries. One such catastrophic death event is described in the Annales Cambriae for the year 547: 'Here a great death in which Maelgwn, king of Gwynedd died. Thus they say "the long sleep of Maelgwn in the court of Rhos". Then there was the yellow plague.'

The name Gorboduc raises some interest for Iron Age coins minted in the area of Cirencester just prior to the Roman invasion contain the name BODVO/BODVOC, which, if assumed to be a personal name, may conceivably have been Boduoc[43] or Boduocus. While not attempting to claim that the Goboduc of the Historia can in any way be equated with the Boduoc appearing on the coinage, it is interesting to note the comparatively large numbers of names, both personal and tribal, recorded from Britain that possess the 'boud' or 'bod' prefix. Boud itself may be translated as meaning something akin to 'victorious', the name of the British queen Boudicca, who led an independence war against the Roman government in in AD 60, perhaps being the most famous. The tribe of the 'Bodunni' whom the Roman historian Dio Cassius says had been 'subject to the Catuvellauni' just prior to the invasion of AD 43,[44] represent another potential example of the name-form.

The coinage of Boduoc was the first in the Cotswolds to be branded with the name of a ruler. Given that the name-form, as it survives, is gender-neutral, and there being no further helpful titles such as 'Rex' on the coin, it is unfortunately not known whether Boduoc was male or female. What we can say, however, is that the style, form and iconography that Boduoc deployed, together with the flagrant use of Latin, marked a radical change in the coin design of the region. This could indicate that, as some have suggested, the ruler 'was of Catuvellaunian origin'.[45] Either way, it is a shame that Geoffrey of Monmouth does not expand upon the nature of Gorbuduc, for it would be interesting to see if his survival as a king in the Historia Regum Britanniae came from either the remembrance of a genuine Iron Age dynast, who may have been cited as progenitor or founder in later genealogical tables, or was simply the reuse of a popular name-form.

As the narrative of the Historia Regum Britanniae marches to the arrival of Rome under the generalship of Julius Caesar, Geoffrey of Monmouth seems keen to get all remaining rulers dispensed with. The lack of detail surrounding specific reigns (dates, events, etc.) and obvious repetition of name-forms again suggests that Geoffrey was employing information derived from genealogical tables, none of which provided any significant incidental data other than perhaps the occasional, and sometimes bizarre, detail being focused instead upon the critical line of descent. Towards the end of Book 3, for example, we hear,

> Enniaunus was replaced by his cousin Iduallo, the son of Ingenius, and he, warned by the fate of his predecessor, was just and righteous in all that he did. Runo, the son of Peredurus, succeeded Idvallo. Then came Gerontius, the son of Elidurus; and after Gerontius his own son Catellus. After Catellus came Coillus, then Porrex, then Cherin. Three sons were born to Cherin: Fulgenius, Eldadus and Andragius, who all reigned one after the other. Next came Urianus, the son of Andragius, and then in turn Eliud, Cledaucus, Clotenus, Gugintius, Merianus, Bledudo, Cap, Oenus, Sisillius and Beldgabred. This last surpassed all the musicians of ancient times, both in harmony and in playing every kind of musical instrument, so that he was called the god of minstrels. After him reigned his brother Arthmail. Eldol came after Archmail, then Redion, then Rederchius, then Samuil, then Penissel, then Pir, then Capoir. Cligueillus, the son of Capoir, came next, a man modest and prudent in all his actions and one who cared above all for the fair administration of justice among his people.[46]

A Kingdom Divided

Almost from the moment that Britain is established as the kingdom of Brutus and his people, we are told that there are regional subdivisions. Corineus, leader of a second group of Trojans picked up by Brutus en route to Gaul, formed the first group to splinter from the whole. It is Corineus who deals with the giants that infest his territory, especially the fearsome Gogmagog, an allusion to the wild forces of nature that required taming before the land could rightfully be his. The followers of Corineus formed 'Cornwall', an apparently semi-autonomous political unit, Corineus himself being a companion (albeit a subservient one) to Brutus and not his son or heir. The precise status of Cornwall and the Cornish, especially as far as the Historia Regum Britanniae is concerned, is vague.

Geoffrey of Monmouth's Cornwall is a key territory essential to the establishment of Britain as a vibrant, independent kingdom. It is referred to by the Historia on a number of occasions as a 'duchy', although quite what this means to Geoffrey, and what degree of authority a duke actually possessed, remains unclear. Cornwall is depicted as standing apart from other areas of Britain, something that was evidently true at the time Geoffrey was writing. The dukes of Cornwall were powerful, frequently acting as advisors to the monarchy, defending Britain from attack, supplying military resources, making critical decisions on the battlefield and, when need arose, providing marriage partners for the king.[47] Arthur, the hero of the Historia, was of Cornish descent, his mother being Ygerna, duchess of Cornwall, Arthur himself being conceived at Tintagel on the north Cornish coast, although Geoffrey does not say whether he was actually born within the duchy.

Perhaps it was that Corineus, the founder of Cornwall, was simply not of the same bloodline as King Brutus, although still Trojan, that made all the difference. Perhaps it was this crucial distinction that meant Cornwall was not, nor was ever, designated by Geoffrey as one of the constituent parts of Britain, the three elements being Albany/ Albania (Scotland), Kambria (Wales) and Loegria (England). The threefold division of Britain is established early on in the narrative. When Brutus, first king of Britain, dies, the territory is divided between his three sons by queen Innogin: Locrinus, Kamber and Albanactus.

> They divided the kingdom of Britain between them in such a way that each succeeded to Brutus in one particular district. Locrinus, who was first born, inherited the part of the island which was afterwards called Loegria after him. Kamber received the region which is on the further bank of the River Severn, the part which is now called Wales but which was for a long time called Kambria from his name. As a result the people of that country still call themselves Kambri today in the Welsh tongue. Albanactus, the youngest, took the region

which is nowadays called Scotland in our language. He called it Albany, after his own name.[48]

Thus, conveniently for Geoffrey, not only is Britain subdivided, but an order of primacy was established, the eldest son receiving Loegria, the second Kambria and the third Albany. This degree of authority was further enforced by what happened next. Within a short time Albanactus was killed by Humber, king of the Huns, meaning that, apart from imprinting the land with his name, the first king of Albany achieved little. Locrinus persuaded Kamber to join forces and together the two destroyed Humber's army, the Hun drowning in the river which thereafter took his name. Dubious etymology aside, the key point here is that Locrinus of Loegria (England) now had control of Albany (Scotland), something that would certainly have appealed to Geoffrey's Norman masters.

Locrinus immediately encountered a problem for, Geoffrey tells us, in dividing the spoils of war, the king found a female captive on board one of Humber's ships. This was Estrildis, daughter of the king of Germany, and she was 'of such beauty that it would be difficult to find a woman to be compared with her'.[49] Locrinus was love-struck and immediately wanted Estrildis for his wife, something that angered Corineus of Cornwall as his daughter Guendoloena was promised to the king in marriage. In a clear demonstration of his relative autonomy and independent status, Corineus went to the court of Locrinus and addressed him as follows, brandishing his battle-axe as he did so:

'These then, Locrinus, are the rewards you offer me in exchange for all the wounds which I have received through my allegiance to your father, at the time he was waging war with unknown peoples? My daughter is to be passed over and you are to demean yourself to the point where you will be prepared to marry some barbarian woman or other! You will not do this unpunished – as long, that is, as strength is left to this right hand of mine which has torn the joy of living from many a giant up and down the Tyrrhenian shores!' He bellowed out these words again and again, brandishing his battle-axe as if he was going to strike Locrinus.[50]

Corineus is presented as a strong character, who can force his will upon the king without fear of punishment or retribution. Locrinus eventually submitted and married Guendoloena, Corineus' daughter, the two of them going on to have a son together by the name of Maddan. The houses of Brutus and Corineus are thus joined, Loegria and Cornwall being linked at last through a single bloodline. Maddan, as he grew, was 'handed over to his grandfather Corineus to be taught his early lessons'.[51] Unbeknownst to either Corineus or Guendoloena, however, Locrinus had dug a cave beneath the streets of Trinovantum, where he kept Estrildis in secret. She too bore Locrinus a child, a daughter called Habren.

When Corineus died, Locrinus felt he no longer needed to hide Estrildis. Divorcing Guendoloena, the king married his German lover, making her queen. Guendoloena was, as Geoffrey says, 'most indignant at this'[52] – probably an understatement.

> She went off to Cornwall and there she assembled all the young men of that region and began to harass Locrinus with border forays. At last, when both sides had gathered an army together, they joined battle near the River Stour. There Locrinus was struck by an arrow and so departed from the joys of this life.[53]

Guendoloena now 'took over the government of the kingdom, behaving in the same extravagant fashion as her father had done'. Evidently the Cornish aristocracy were, at least in Geoffrey's mind, exceeding their authority. Guendoloena had Estrildis and Habren drowned and then 'ruled for fifteen years'.[54] As soon as her son Madden was of age, she 'passed the sceptre of the realm to him, being content herself with the province of Cornwall for the remainder of her life'.

Now, if we take this story entirely at face value, we therefore possess a set of origin myths for the kingdoms of England, Scotland and Wales, all three created by the logical subdivision of Britain between the three sons of Brutus, with Cornwall as an ill-defined but apparently semi-autonomous territory. Formed from a 'subset' of Trojans, Cornwall nevertheless appears to wield a significant degree of power over the throne of Loegria, to which it is further bound by marriage and eventually by blood, via Guendoloena and her son Maddan. Alternatively, if we reflect upon what has already been established with regard to Trinovantum as representing not the chief city of Brutus (London) but the 'Trinovantes' tribe, with the duchy of Cornwall representing the Catuvellauni, then the geographical and geopolitical uncertainties of Geoffrey's narrative melt away. This is not a dispute between the king, based in London and a duke from the other end of the country, but two tribal neighbours competing for supremacy.

Geoffrey of Monmouth was evidently attempting to make coherent sense of a mangled series of tribal names preserved within the sources he encountered, none of which were clear in twelfth-century Britain. The description of kingdoms at war, disputed succession, marriage alliances and political intrigue that he encountered in his primary sources resonated with a medieval audience, even if the ethnic identities of the people under discussion did not. To Geoffrey, the 'reality' of England, controlled by a Norman monarchy still desperate to prove its legitimacy, was self-evident. Cornwall was part of this still-developing kingdom, although, like many areas governed from London, it still felt independent and 'different', while the Norman elite were casting their greedy eyes further afield to Wales and Scotland. Reference to unfamiliar tribal units in the oral tradition or early written sources could also be clarified or liberally interpreted within the mindset of someone inhabiting the 1130s. Hence, to Geoffrey, the Catuvellauni were evidently the Cornish while Trinovantum was the capital, London. Whoever was in charge of Trinovantum evidently controlled the kingdom.

Locrinus, Kamber and Albanactus, the three sons of Brutus, appear to be a literary or etymological device, an attempt by Geoffrey of Monmouth to clarify the confused nature of tribal identities provided within multiple and somewhat confused traditions, some of which clearly established competing and contradictory perspectives. If, as seems likely, the bulk of the material deployed within the Historia Regum Britanniae derived from, and related to, central southern Britain, then reference to the kingdoms of Kambria and Albany/Albania also require reconsideration. Kambria/Cambria seems to be a Latinisation of the word Cymry (or 'Welsh' in the Welsh language) and, although appearing before Geoffrey's time, was not particularly popular, failing to catch on 'as a term for Wales among other Anglo-Norman, Cambro-Norman and even Welsh writers'.[55] To the Anglo-Saxon and later Norman aristocracy, the indigenous population of Britain were predominantly described as 'Welsh', from wylisc, walas or wealh in Old English. This was an all-encompassing term that may loosely be translated as meaning 'foreigner'. Over time this developed to have a more specific meaning within Anglo-Saxon society, being used to mean 'serf' or 'slave', probably reflecting the English, and later Norman, view of the average Briton. The Britons, perhaps understandably, did not view themselves as 'foreigners' or 'slaves', preferring instead a variety of alternative terms such as Combrogi,[56] something which may be defined as meaning 'us', 'fellow countrymen' or simply 'the people'. It is a term that continues to fuel debate but which may survive in the modern names Cymru/Cymry and Cumbria.

Kambria/Cambria therefore is a term which, although not particularly widespread, was recognized by both Geoffrey of Monmouth and his audience. If, however, the original identity of Geoffrey's 'Kambria' was not that of Wales/Cymru, there is a variant within central south-eastern Britain, and within the political influence or geographical scope of the Catuvellauni/Trinovantes, which fits the name-form. Given that Kambria, in the Historia Regum Britanniae, seems to be subservient to Trinovantum/Loegria or treated in a secondary capacity, either being taken over by a militaristic king such as Dunvallo Molmutius[57] or spoken of in the same breath as Loegria/Trinovantum and Cornwall, the probability is that the original name-form was Cantium. Cantium, from which the modern term 'Kent' is derived, appears to have a confused identity in Julius Caesar's narrative, being neither a tribal name (Cantium perhaps meaning 'corner land') or specific political entity, Caesar telling us that Cantium was ruled by four kings (Cingetorix, Carvilius, Taximagulus and Segovax),[58] all of whom appear to have been dominated in some way by Cassivellaunus, the British war leader and overking. By the time Britain was taken over by Rome and ruled as a province, Cantium seems to have been used as a tribal signifier, the 'Cantiaci' having their civitas or town at Canterbury (Durovernum Cantiacorum).

Where does that leave Loegria? Here we are on more dubious ground, something compounded by the fact that we do not possess the source material or primary tradition that Geoffrey accessed, the original name-form, or indeed context of use, being unknown. Although still in use, the origins of the name Lloegr, standing for 'England' in modern Welsh, are unclear. Eric Hamp has suggested that Lloegr/Lloegyr could have derived from a compound meaning 'having a nearby border, being from near the border'.[59] This doesn't help, geographically speaking, for it could as easily apply to the Welsh/English border as anywhere else. It may suggest that from the perspective of the sources used, it referred to a state nearby or sharing a border, without the tedious need of having to name them. Whatever the case and origin of the term, it is reasonably clear that when Geoffrey of Monmouth uses Loegria in his magnum opus he is refereeing to the Trinovantes. Perhaps the repeated use of Trinovantum to mean Troia Nova (New Troy) meant that other terms were necessary in order to avoid confusion. If a pro-Catuvellauni source called the kingdom of the Trinovantes 'those over the border', then perhaps the root of the name, at least in the Historia, can be found.

Albany/Albania causes more etymological headaches. There have been many attempts to resolve the meaning of Albany or Albion, traditionally thought to be an early, perhaps even insular/indigenous, name for the British Isles, although the most popular explanations derive from the Welsh elbid/elfydd, roughly meaning 'the habitable surface of the world' or the earlier name-form found in the Gaulish or Galatian Albio/Albiorix ('King of the World).[60] Quite how this relates to the tribal framework of southern Britain is unclear. It could be that the term is substituted for the Iceni, the Cenimagni in Julius Caesar's de Bello Gallico, the fourth tribe occupying the eastern margins of Britain and northern neighbours of the Trinovantes. While this would make sense geographically speaking, especially as Albania/Albany is regularly grouped together in the Historia Regum Britanniae with Trinovantum/Loegria (the Trinovantes) and Cornwall (the Catuvellauni), where it is usually referred to as being the most northerly of all the kingdoms, it is not clear how the name-form could easily mutate from Iceni to Albany, unless it is a complete twelfth-century fabrication. It is just possible, of course, that Albany/Albania derived from a medieval 'clarification' of Atrebates, a tribal group that occupied north Hampshire and Berkshire, to the south-west of the Catuvellauni. Although it is clear that the Atrebates were one of the more Romanised of tribes in southern Britain, their story does not seem to impinge much upon the Historia's narrative and so the association is unlikely.

4

A TROJAN DYNASTY

Expanded sections within Book 2 of the Historia Regum Britanniae, which supply additional information beyond the simple 'A followed B and ruled for xx years' expected in a king-list, strongly suggest Geoffrey of Monmouth chanced upon a major epic or other independent source, which he then 'crowbarred' into the narrative. We cannot be sure of being able to assign identity to every name, some tales having been duplicated or the name-form having been irrevocably garbled over time. Worse, given our incomplete understanding of the tribal leaders that came before Rome, the historical source material and archaeological evidence being fragmentary, not every name can be interpreted or assigned to its rightful time period. A few key characters appearing in Book 2 are, however, worthy of extraction and discussion.

Dunvallo Molmutius

Perhaps the most obvious place to start is with Dunvallo Molmutius, the twenty-first monarch of Trojan origins, so Geoffrey of Monmouth tells us, to rule over the descendants of Brutus. If we are looking for associations, whereby one original name-form from the past has been corrupted or mutated into another, as we have already seen with the likes of Mandubracius/Androgeus, then there is only one clear parallel for Dunvallo Molmutius, and we shall look at him first: Dubnovellaunus.

In Britain, following the departure of Julius Caesar in 54 BC, we hear no more of the two prominent leaders Cassivellaunus and

Mandubracius, either in Roman sources or on indigenous coinage. When named coin issues appear, in the area to the north of the River Thames, the first to be identified is Tasciovanus, followed by Cunobelinus and Epaticcus, who claimed to be his sons. So far so good for, despite chronological issues surrounding the specific nature of a bloodline and whether someone on a coin identified as the son of another is really their grandson (or even great-grandson), at least the inscriptions provide us with a concept of dynastic succession. Where individuals did not cite their ancestry, our understanding of where, how and, rather more critically, when they originally fit becomes rather less clear. A good example of such dynastic and geographical uncertainty comes with Dubnovellaunus.

Coins with the inscriptions DV / DVB / DVBNO / DVBNOV / DVBNOVELL / DVBNOVALLA / DVBNOVALLAVNOS occur in Kent,[1] while in Essex DVBN / DVBNOVIILL / DVBOVALAVNOS / DVBNOVIILLAVN / DVBNOVALLAVNOS commonly occur.[2] It seems sensible to consider these as representing the same person, even though, geographically speaking, their distribution covers two broad tribal areas, that occupied by the Cantiaci (in Kent) and the Trinovantes (of Essex). Not everyone agrees, and it has been suggested that the two main distribution patterns reflect two different people ruling at very different times,[3] hence we sometimes hear of 'Dubnovellaunus of Kent' before a similarly named 'Dubnovellaunus of Essex'. While it is understandable that caution be exercised when attributing specific individuals to territories, the creation of a complex framework of dynasties, relationships and chronologies based upon the limited evidence appearing on the coins is a dangerous thing to do for, as John Creighton has politely observed, 'the evidence offers a wide degree of latitude'.[4]

The huge variety of name-forms for what, on the face of it, appears to be the same individual should also not cause too many concerns, nor spur us to create multiple rulers in order to fit the coin evidence. All the variety really shows is that the Latinization of British/Celtic names did not follow a set path or that the coin-die inscription cutter was used to the spoken, rather than the written, version of the name-form and that ultimately no one really cared all that much. If the intended audience for the coins was not literate, there being no prehistory of the written word in the British Isles, then the names would either appear as incomprehensible 'squiggles' or, perhaps, suggest a guide to pronunciation. Today, the names that we give to people and places tend to be fixed, but such things were more fluid in the distant past. One has, for example, only to think of the many variant forms of surname provided for that the great Elizabethan poet and playwright Shakespeare as Shakespeare / Shakspeare / Shakespere / Shakespear / Shackspeare / Shakspere / Shakspear / Shakspeare / Shakespheare / Shaxspere, and so on, to realise that certainty in spelling is a curiously modern phenomenon.

Given the similarity of name-forms for DVB/DVBNO etc. as they appear on coins, it would seem perverse to create two discrete individuals, especially if, as we have already observed, the tribal boundaries identified for Late Iron Age Britain appear to have been relatively fluid. There seems to have been little to distinguish the ruling aristocracies of the Catuvellauni, Trinovantes and Cantiaci in either the testimony of Roman writers or on coin, which, to our eyes at least, display a significant degree of intertribal confusion. Julius Caesar, in de Bello Gallico, seems to suggest that Cassivellaunus had authority over 'the kings of Cantium' (Kent) while also claiming suzerainty over the Trinovantes (even if they only recognized Mandubracius as their leader). In a later account, the Roman historian Suetonius noted that Adminius (or Amminus) of Kent was the son of Cunobelinus, a king minting coins in both Camulodunum (Colchester) in Trinovantian territory and Verulamium (St Albans) at the heart of Catuvellaunia, while Epaticcus, the brother of Cunobelinus, and Caratacus, Cunobelinus' son, seem, from the evidence of their coinage, to have claimed both Verulamium and the Catuvellauni. Perhaps, as we have noted, the concept of fixed tribes with fixed borders and a clear 'sense of self' was, at least for this part of Britain in the Late Iron Age, an alien concept.

With such evident concerns regarding the nature of the written record, we must exercise considerable caution when interpreting the coin data set. Yes, there are coins proclaiming a DVB / DVBN / DVBNO / DVBNOV / DVBNOVELL / DVBNOVALLAVNOS in both Kent and Essex, but there is no reason to suggest that these were different people, merely that they appear to have been in control of discrete areas, areas that, to the Roman State at least, comprised different tribes. Perhaps the divergence in coin imagery reflects the nature of separate audiences in Kent and Essex, the Cantiaci and the Trinovantes possessing differences in cultural heritage which could only be managed through the use of alternative messages. The Iron Age coin sequence itself is also unhelpful for it is by no means chronologically secure, few of the recorded coins having been obtained from datable contexts while, unlike those produced by Rome, no British coin possesses titles or images which tie them to a specific time period.

Sometime between 30 BC and AD 14, however, a character whom the Roman State called Dumnobellaunus was in Rome. Dumnobellaunus was mentioned in the Res Gestae – a monumental 'look what I've done for you' statement commemorating the achievements of Augustus, grand-nephew, adopted son and principal heir of Julius Caesar – as a British king 'seeking refuge' with the emperor. What (or whom) precisely Dumnobellaunus was seeking refuge from is not recorded. Whatever the reason for his flight from Britain, it seems likely that he was trying to persuade Augustus to honour the promises and assurances of 'protection' made by Caesar to the friends of the Roman people, the Cantiaci and Trinovantes in particular. If he had been ousted from power then perhaps he was seeking some form of military assistance. Certainly, as we shall see later, Augustus made plans to invade Britain on three occasions – in 34, 27 and 26 BC – ostensibly because the Britons 'would not come to terms'.[5] It is possible that plans for invasion were aided by characters such as 'Dumnobellaunus' whispering in the emperor's ear while discreetly supplying tactical information with regard to harbours and natural inland obstacles.

That 'Dumnobellaunus' was Dubnovellaunus seems clear enough, a point upon which most academics today agree, further underlining the dangers of taking British name-forms too literally. This raises the problem of whether this particular king ever managed to return to Britain, either with or without the backing and support of Rome. It is possible that the coin series discovered in Kent and Essex reflects two discrete phases of power in Britain: 'before' and 'after' his flight to Rome. That would perhaps represent an exercise in modern myth-making and, although certainly tempting, cannot yet be supported by the archaeological and historical evidence.[6]

So, with little more to go on than a coin series and a fleeting reference by the emperor Augustus, what can we actually say about Dubnovellaunus (as we shall continue to call him)? The coins reveal little other than, perhaps, an idiosyncratic relationship with spelling and an increasing predilection for the classical imagery of Rome. Those coins produced to the north of the Thames, in the area traditionally ascribed to the Trinovantes, and which may represent the earliest produced, display crescents, 'disjointed' horses and stylized heads, possibly inspired by portraits of Apollo. Those found predominantly in Kent carry more overtly Mediterranean images, including the eagle and the lion as well as more 'Celtic-style' representations of wild boar. Also apparent are images of a seated figure holding what could be a hammer, suggesting this is a representation of a metalworker[7] or a curved staff (lituus) used with augury and sacrifice.[8] Either way the image does not appear to imitate nor derive from Roman coin issues. If it was meant to 'suggest the paraphernalia of Roman rites of sacrifice' it could indicate that British rulers were adopting more overtly Roman forms of divination,[9] another sign perhaps that the native aristocracy were actively emulating the ways of Rome's elite.

The name-form Dubnovellaunus / Dumnobellaunus / Dubnovalla / Dubnovallaunos / Dubovalaunos / Dubnovbouiillaun gets yet another mangling in the Historia Regum Britanniae, emerging as Dunvallo Molmutius – hardly surprising given the diversity of spelling that occurs on his official coins and the variant form that appears in the only Roman source, the Res Gestae. Geoffrey of Monmouth tells us that Dunvallo came to power during the traumatic and disruptive period of civil war that followed the violent death of his predecessor Porrex, who was brutally assassinated by his own mother.

As a result of this the people of Britain were for a long time embroiled in civil war; and the island came into the hands of five kings who kept attacking and massacring each other's men in turn.[10]

It is Dunvallo who is presented as a saviour during this time of anarchy, the description provided for him being both positive and glowing.

> Some time later a certain young man called Dunvallo Molmutius came into prominence because of his personal courage. The son of Cloten king of Cornwall, he excelled all the other kings of Britain by his good looks and his bravery.[11]

Dunvallo was evidently an important character in Catuvellaunian, or as Geoffrey of Monmouth calls it, 'Cornish' history; a major dynastic figure upon whom later rulers claimed descent. Although, as king of Catuvellaunia/Cornwall, Dunvallo is, in Geoffrey's mind, of noble Trojan stock, it must be presumed that, as his ancestry is not specifically cited within the Historia, that he was considered to have descended from Corineus, rather than directly from the bloodline of Brutus. Unless he was from the marriage of Locrinus and Guendoloena or from another unspecified or uncredited union between the clans, Dunvallo was, from Geoffrey of Monmouth's perspective, evidently not descended from the great Trojan Aeneas.

The civil war that brought Dunvallo to power may reflect a period of tribal expansion, such as that noted by Julius Caesar when discussing the background of his rival Cassibellaunus/Cassivellaunus, whom he says 'had been continually at war with the other tribes',[12] or dynastic squabbling in the wake of a disputed royal succession. Alternatively the account may have had its origins in, or be a remembrance of, the internal discord that drove Dubnovellaunus and others to seek sanctuary in the court of Augustus. Whatever the cause and nature of the strife, which we shall examine again later, it appears that the ultimate effect was to propel a son of the Catuvellaunian house to power.

> Almost as soon as he had succeeded to the kingship of Cornwall after his father's death, he attacked Pinner, king of Loegria, and killed him in pitched battle. As a result Rudaucus, king of Kambria, and Staterius, king of Albany, met to make an alliance with each other. They then led their armies into Dunvallo's territory, destroyed his buildings and killed his peasantry.

If we are right in our identification of Cornwall, Loegria, Kambria and Albany as they appear in the Historia Regum Britanniae, as Catuvellauni, Trinovantes, Cantiaci and Iceni, then the civil discord that swept Dunvallo/Dubnovellaunus to action was actually concentrated within the tribes of central south-eastern Britain, rather than within the broader geography of Cornwall, England, Wales and Scotland as suggested by Geoffrey of Monmouth, who was making sense of the prehistoric political situation in the context of his own twelfth-century understanding of Britain. The nature of conflict as he describes it suggests a catastrophic period of instability in which the aristocratic elite of four discrete kingdoms felt that they could only resolve their differences on the battlefield.

At the first battle, Pinner of Loegria was killed. Following the logic of name-form corruption and medieval interpretation, what we are seeing here is a direct attack by the Catuvellauni upon their eastern neighbours, the Trinovantes. Quite who in such a scenario 'Pinner' was is unclear, for his twelfth-century name-form as it appears in the Historia does not seem to equate with any recorded on the eastern British coin series. It is possible, therefore, that his name has become irrevocably garbled or that he did not live long enough, or receive sufficient support from, either his own people or those of Rome, to issue coins.

The death of Pinner, defeat of Loegria and subsequent attack by Rudaucus of Kambria and Staterius of Albany upon the people of Dunvallo's kingdom further exacerbated an already dangerous situation. Determined to resolve the peace militarily, Dunvallo raised an army.

Dunvallo himself marched to meet them at the head of thirty thousand men and joined battle with them. When a great part of the day had been passed in fighting, Dunvallo found himself still as far as ever from victory. He summoned six hundred of his boldest young men and ordered them to strip the arms from those of their enemies who lay dead around them and then to put those same arms on. He himself cast to one side the protective clothing which he was wearing and did the same as his men. He then led the way through the enemy lines, moving his men forward as if they had actually been enemy troops. He reached the spot where Rudaucus and Staterius were and signalled to his comrades to attack them. As Dunvallo's men charged forward, the two kings were killed and many others with them. Dunvallo Molmutius then came back with his companions and disarmed, for he was afraid of being attacked by his own men, He once more put on his own arms which he had earlier cast aside. He then exhorted soldiers to charge at the enemy and attacked them himself with great ferocity. Almost immediately he won the battle, for his enemy was put to flight and scattered. Now at last Dunvallo was free to march through the lands of those whom we have listed as killed. He destroyed their cities and fortresses and forced their people to accept his rule. When he had completely subjugated the entire island, he fashioned for himself a crown of gold and restored the realm to its earlier status.

The tale of conflict between the army of Dunvallo and the combined forces of Rudaucus and Staterius is a familiar one of ferocity and ultimate triumph (for the hero). A curious feature though is the occurrence, once again, of battlefield duplicity: the hero gaining victory through an act of deception. Dunvallo switches armour, clothing and identity in order to get close to his foe and cause significant damage, killing Rudaucus and Staterius 'and many others with them'. Such deceit may be considered 'unsporting' within the rules of combat, such as they are, and yet they occur time and again in the Historia. Androgeus betrays his people to Caesar, joining the Roman general to attack the warrior Cassibellaunus, yet Androgeus is the hero. In a similar vein, Lelius Hamo, as we shall see later, changes clothing mid-combat in order to attack and kill the British King Guiderius. All these events, it could be argued, simplify or telescope more complex situations where alliances are made then torn up, where old friendships and previous treaties are rewritten. Such was, undoubtedly, the nature of intertribal relationships between the Catuvellauni, Cantiaci, Trinovantes and Iceni; client states fighting for supremacy at the margins of the Roman world.

Having established peace through the merciless, but, from the perspective of the original source writer entirely justified, subjugation of the defeated foe, their cities being 'destroyed' and the people 'forced to accept his rule', Dunvallo set out on the second part of his reign: the creation of order. The apparently incidental comment that the king 'fashioned for himself a crown of gold' is of interest far beyond the apparently trivial detail of regal fashion. The crown represents the physical embodiment of the power of an individual and their legitimacy to govern. It demarcates their authority and celebrates their victory in politics and on the battlefield. It is a signal of majesty to be worn on state occasions and a signal of dynasty, to be passed down through the generations at the point of coronation. The introduction of such an iconic piece of headgear in the narrative marks a discrete break in what has gone before, suggesting that Dunvallo's reign would mark the beginning of a new age.

Intriguingly, one specific coin issue established within the sequence of Dubnovellaunus (in Kent) portrays a 'laurate head'; that is to say the portrait of a man wearing an extremely ornate piece of head attire.[13] The item, which comprises a series of highly decorative prongs or coiled points, each ending in a looped terminal, is similar in effect to the radiate diadem, or solar crown, in which the rays of the sun appear to emanate from the head of the wearer, as worn by Alexander the Great and later by a multitude of Roman emperors on third-century coin portraits. Could it be that this was intended to represent an image of Dubnovellaunus himself wearing a diadem that signified not only his own prestige and power, but also the official backing of Augustus as Rome's nominated king in southern Britain? It is certainly possible and, if so, it has undeniable resonance with the 'crown of gold' fashioned by Dunvallo in the Historia Regum Britanniae.

Every society needs its primary lawmaker; a legislative founder upon whom the basic structure of society rests. Athens had Draco and Solon, Rome had Numa Pompilius and Brutus while Anglo-Saxon England had Alfred the Great and Athelstan. Individuals such as these are credited with the basis of a legal constitution. Rome's legislature was traditionally based upon the Code of the Twelve Tables, a strict set of laws allegedly written in the early days of the Republic. The Code, which established the key rights and obligations of the plebeian underclass as well as the powers available to the patricians, was formalized by the aristocracy and so tended to favour their particular (and sometimes rather peculiar) interests. Although neglected, overwritten and revised, the Twelve Tables were frequently cited as the bedrock of civil freedoms within the Republic. In a similar way today, the Magna Carta (the 'Great Charter') of Liberties, agreed between the English King John and his barons in 1215, is cited as the cornerstone of both British and American legislature. Although the original charter was more to do with the protection of the church and the baronial classes from the divine right of a monarch to rule as they saw fit, rather than the rights of the common man or woman, the Magna Carta has obtained a near mythical status and today remains a potent symbol of liberty.

What then of the Ancient Britons; shouldn't the descendants of Aeneas have a legal constitution equivalent to that of their (distant) relations in Rome? Geoffrey of Monmouth evidently thought so and the Historia Regum Britanniae provides the solution:

It was Dunvallo Molmutius who established among the Britons the so-called Molmutine Laws which are still famous today among the English. Included in the other things which Gildas of blessed memory wrote about him many years later was this: that it was he who decreed that the temples of the gods and the cities should be so privileged that anyone who escaped to them as a fugitive or when accused of some crime must be pardoned by his accuser when he came out. Dunvallo it was, too, who decreed that the roads which led to these temples and cities should be included in the same law and that the ploughs of the peasantry should be inalienable. During Dunvallo's lifetime no bandits were allowed to draw their swords and the outrages of robbers came to an abrupt end, for no one dared to do violence to his fellow.[14]

Setting aside the specifics of the 'Molmutine Laws', which possess a curious medieval mindset with regard to the concept of 'sanctuary', not to say the declaration that Gildas apparently described these (which he did not), what can be made of the reference to a prehistoric legislature?

We have no evidence that Dubnovellaunus returned to Britain from his enforced stay with Augustus in Rome, although, as a client king, allied prince or hostage (obsides) it would be expected that he should ultimately fulfil his obligations by going back to claim his throne, possibly with military help, and introduce the full benefits of Roman civilization to his people. A safe, and no doubt triumphal, return would bring with it patronage, enhanced trade deals and more overtly Roman ways of doing things. As we have already noted, the two phases of coin production for DV / DVB / DVBNO / DVBNOV / DVBNOVELL / DVBNOVALLA / DVBNOVALLAVNOS (in Kent) and DVBN / DVBNOVIILL / DVBOVALAVNOS / DVBNOVIILLAVN / DVBNOVALLAVNOS (in Essex) may hint at two discrete phases of rule, perhaps before Rome and after. Certainly the enhanced classical image-forms that appear in the Kent series, especially those depicting a seated figure suggesting familiarity with Roman augury and sacrifice,[15] hint that the king had by then a more openly Roman mindset. Another way of emulating Rome's elite would be to introduce more classical laws, especially if these were explicitly modelled upon the 'Code of the Twelve Tables'.

Perhaps the key to understanding the significance of Dunvallo Molmutius is that his story, as it appears in the Historia, represents only one aspect of his life: the Return of the King. Dubnovellaunus, we know, was in Rome seeking protection from Augustus at some time after 30 BC. Neither Augustus nor his successors tell us what ultimately happened to the king, but, if he did make his way back to Britain, possibly with the full backing of the emperor as Rome's preferred choice, would this have brought an end to the instability? Are the large numbers of men recorded in the Historia merely an echo of imperial reinforcements; a Roman peacekeeping army dispatched in order to stabilize the succession and restore order to Rome's northern frontier. Fighting and retribution against those who had stood against Dunvallo would certainly make sense within the context of Dubnovellaunus' return, as indeed would the subsequent introduction of Roman law.

Whether the 'Molmutine Laws' were as wide-ranging as Geoffrey of Monmouth indicates, and whether they really included the provision of sanctuary in temples, the banning of highway robbery as well as the inalienable right of peasants to their ploughs, we cannot say, although it does seem unlikely. The point is that the introduction of a new law code under Dunvallo was remembered as a significant event, just as significant, say, as Dubnovellaunus returning from Rome with a mandate supported by the emperor and a desire to get the kingdom working more efficiently as a client state. It helped that a pride in the new (Roman) order brought in by Dunvallo/Dubnovellaunus, and reflected in the sources mined for the Historia Regum Britanniae, also suited Geoffrey of Monmouth, who could demonstrate that the Britons had a working legislature long before Alfred, Athelstan or the Normans.

Rud Hud Hudibras

On the face of it there is little to the story of King Rud Hud Hudibras as he appears in the Historia Regum Britanniae, Geoffrey of Monmouth telling us simply,

> Leil lived on for twenty-five years after mounting the throne, but towards the end he ruled the kingdom feebly. As result of Leil's prolonged inactivity a civil war suddenly broke out in the realm. Leil's son Rud Hud Hudibras reigned for thirty-nine years after him. Once the civil war was over, Hudibras restored peace once more to the people. It was he who built Kaerreint: that is Canterbury. He also founded Kaerguenit, or Winchester, and the fortress of Paladur, which is now called Shaftesbury. There the Eagle spoke, while the wall was being built. If I believed its Sayings to be true, I would not hesitate to hand them down to history with my material.[16]

Mention of the Eagle who spoke, presumably to Rud Hud Hudibras himself (although that point is not particularly clear), strongly suggests the presence of a separate source or literary tradition that either Geoffrey or his audience was familiar with, as it appears as 'the Eagle' rather than simply 'an eagle'. Quite why it was felt that a talking eagle was inappropriate, in the wider context of the Historia where magical and curious phenomena abound, is unclear. Strange that Geoffrey mentions the bird, before immediately dismissing its sayings. Why he should do this is not explained, 'unreliability' being a rather bizarre choice, and the Eagle is never mentioned again. Of course it could be that Geoffrey had a rather garbled account of a specific event which, although potentially well-remembered, made no real sense in the primary source material and so was redacted, allowing the narrative to move swiftly to Hudibras' son, Bladud, and grandson, Leir.

It is possible, of course, that the Eagle story was a misremembered account of interaction with Rome, the 'eagles' sometimes standing as a metaphor for the Roman army, each legion having as its ensign an eagle (Aquila) to be protected and revered. By the Late Republic, the eagle had become a sort of 'brand' logo or symbol for Rome itself, having originated as the animal most associated with Jupiter, chief deity of the Roman pantheon. The will of Jupiter was often interpreted through birds – the terms augur/auspices/auspicious are all from the Latin auspex, which can be translated as meaning 'an observer of birds' – and the eagle had precedence over all other animals in the sky. Critically, perhaps, the practice of augury, or the interpretation of omens, was vital in making State decisions or prior to the execution of a major public act, such as the declaration of war or the commencement of a building project. The foundation of Rome itself by the twins Romulus and Remus had, so the legend goes, been dependent upon the will of the gods as determined through augury. Remus, who wanted to build upon the Aventine Hill, saw six vultures in the sky, whereas Romulus, who favoured the Palatine, spotted twelve.

It is perhaps in the context of Rud Hud Hudibras establishing the towns of Kaerreint and Kaerguenit together with the fortress of Paladur that the story of 'the eagle that spoke' makes sense, for this may relate to the taking of the auspices, the most significant aspect in Roman town-building. Having first set out the limits of a new city, by driving a plough around the proposed boundary, it was the job of the augury to assess the will of the gods.

> The auspices were taken by delineating a field of vision in the sky. This was conceptually marked out in the air not by the hand but by using the augur's curved staff or lituus. Within this square in the sky, omens were sought. These took the form of the flight

of birds, or even, on rare occurrences lightning bolts. On the
basis of these signs, judgements were made.[17]

Determining divine favour was therefore fundamental to the successful
formation of a new city, the layout of which was connected to
a range of preordained and strictly ordered ritual activities. Anyone
working within the Roman mindset of town planning would be
aware of the 'structured practices' tied up with the founding of
a new urban centre and it is likely that a client king or queen, even in
a territory as far away from Rome as Britain, would know precisely
what to do and the correct order in which to do it. The reading of
the auspices required both secret knowledge, in order to accurately
interpret and read the signs, and a good relationship with the gods.
Only royalty could interpret divine will and, within the societies of
Ancient Greece, the founding of towns was integral to the role of
Hellenistic kingship.[18]

That the kings of Britain were familiar with basic Greek and
Roman ritual practices is clear enough from the coins produced where
the lituus, or staff deployed by the Mediterranean augur, can at times
be identified. John Creighton, for example, has observed the presence
of a lituus on a quarter stater produced by Tincomarus, a king
whom the emperor Augustus records (in the Res Gestae) as being in
Rome sometime before AD 14, 'almost as if the coin was used for
a one-off event'.[19] A lituus also appears on a single issue of a stater
manufactured for Tasciovanus and the design of a single gold coin of
Dubnovellaunus, making Creighton wonder whether such a restricted
application could possibly relate 'to the specific foundation rites'
associated with the creation of important native centres such as
Silchester, Verulamium and Canterbury.[20]

Could it be that the story of the Eagle, as it came down to Geoffrey
of Monmouth, actually related to the reading of aupices in the primary
stages of the foundation of a new settlement by a British dynast
emulating the ways of Rome? It seems very probable, especially as it
is the eagle, the animal most associated with the will of Jupiter, that
is mentioned as speaking to Rud Hud Hudibras. Perhaps Geoffrey,
or the compiler of the primary source that he accessed, was aware of
the overtly pagan associations of augury and, although many other

explicitly non-Christian activities made it into Geoffrey's narrative, for example the sacrifice made by Brutus to Diana and her resultant prophesy,[21] this particular one was excised.

As to the towns of Kaerreint and Kaerguenit 'and the fortress of Paladur', which the Historia claims Rud Hud Hudibras constructed, little can really be said. Geoffrey of Monmouth interpreted Kaerreint as Canterbury and Kaerguenit as Winchester, although on what evidence this was based is not clear. There is no clear etymological reason for equating the two ancient places with towns in Kent and Hampshire, but it is possible that Geoffrey was drawing on more discrete geographical information contained within his primary sources, such as those which presumably told him what the Eagle had said to the king. If it were Canterbury and Winchester to which the activities of Rud Hud Hudibras were in some way connected, it is interesting that it is Cantium, irrevocably linked in both archaeological and literary sources to the Catuvellauni and Trinovantes, and the northern fringes of Hampshire, bordering the lands of the Atrebates, that are identified. Could this be a remembrance of a form of territorial acquisition, perhaps of the sort that Caesar claimed his rival Cassivellaunus was conducting across southern Britain prior to 54 BC? It is possible, although ultimately unprovable.

In this context, perhaps, the 'fortress of Paladur, which is now called Shaftesbury' would not appear out of place, even though it suggests significant involvement to the west of the traditional Catuvellauni/Trinovantes homeland into what is now northern Dorset and south Wiltshire. At the time of the Claudian invasion of AD 43, the Roman historian Dio Cassius tells us that, having prevailed over Caratacus and Togodumnus, the 'sons of Cunobelinus', the general Aulus Plautius 'accepted terms of surrender from that part of the Bodunni having been subject to the Catuvellauni.[22] The Bodunni, in this account, are assumed to have been the 'Dobunni', a native tribe occupying lands roughly centred upon Gloucestershire and northern Somerset. Could the positioning of 'Paladur' in the Historia indicate some form of western expansion by the Catuvellauni? It is a tempting theory but again, given the dangers inherent in taking Geoffrey of Monmouth's place-name evidence too literally, one which we should perhaps not take any further.

What then of Rud Hud Hudibras himself; can we equate him with any of the documented kings of pre-Roman Britain? The name-form is certainly distinctive and, given his importance, as father to Bladud, the founder of Kaerbadun, and grandfather to Leir, whose life fills a large part of Book 2 of the Historia Regum Britanniae, we should not be surprised to find him featured somewhere in the, admittedly rather fragmentary, historical record. In fact, in the list of British rulers preserved on native coin, the closest comparison to the sound-form can be found in Addedomarus.

The name Addedomarus appears predominantly on coins found within territory assigned to the Catuvellauni in Hertfordshire, although a small amount have also been recorded from Trinovantian lands in Essex. The significance of Addedomarus is that he appears to have been the first ruler north of the Thames to add his moniker to coinage,[23] neither Cassivellaunos nor Mandubracius identifying themselves in such a distinctive way. Perhaps it is due to the primary nature of coin inscription that means the name-form, as it appears, does not always adhere to Latin, with more Hellenistic letter conventions AΘΘ/AΘΘIIDOM/AΘΘEDOMAROS occurring. As Addedomarus, whose name probably meant 'charioteer' or 'great in chariots',[24] does not feature in any Roman history, the nature and precise chronology of his reign cannot be gauged. A best guess would perhaps place him somewhere between 45 and 25 BC.[25] His reign certainly postdates that of Cassivellaunus and he would appear to precede that of Tasciovanus and probably Dubnovellaunus. More than that cannot really be said, at least from archaeological sources.

Whoever Addedomarus was, he appears to have been important because he was remembered not just in the pages of the Historia Regum Britanniae, but in other early source material. In the manuscripts that collectively form what has become known as Trioedd Ynys Prydein (The Triads of the Island of Britain), Aedd Mawr (Aedd 'the Great') appears as the founding father of the Britons.

The first Name that this Island bore, before it was seized or occupied: Myrddin's Precinct. And after it was seized and occupied, the Island of Honey. And after it was conquered by Prydein son of Aedd the Great it was called the Island of Prydein.[26]

Rachel Bromwich, who has extensively studied the various textual elements preserved within the Trioedd Ynys Prydein, contends that the Enweu Ynys Prydein (The Names of the Island of Britain) contains detail which 'is long anterior to the time of Geoffrey of Monmouth'. As to why this particular contribution to the origins of the British kings does not feature in the Historia Regum Britanniae, she speculates that the reference in the Triads to the seizure and occupation of Britain by Prydein son of Aedd Mawr and the subsequent naming of 'Britain' (Prydein) was intentionally suppressed by Geoffrey 'since he would not tolerate any rival to his account of the settlement of Britain by Brutus and his Trojan companions'.[27] This is certainly plausible, for Geoffrey, as we have seen, had difficulty synthesizing different origin myths – namely that of Brutus (for the Trinovantes) and Corineus (of the Catuvellauni). To insert a third individual at the critical point would perhaps have risked undermining the entire narrative, which was already crowded with multiple secondary characters. It is possible, of course, that Geoffrey simply did not see or have access to Trioedd Ynys Prydein during his research, although it has to be said that the explanation of how Britain was named after the hero Prydein as it appears in the Triads directly contradicts that of Brutus and, unlike Nennius, Geoffrey of Monmouth did not appear to enjoy ambiguity in storytelling.

The fact that Addedomarus/Aedd Mawr was remembered as primogenitor is significant. Perhaps he was originally not the father of 'the Britons' but the father of a specific dynasty, one which later came to consider themselves pre-eminent of all people (and of all tribes) in Britain. It should not surprise us that the coinage of the historically attested Addedomarus comes predominantly from Hertfordshire, for this was territory belonging to the Catuvellauni and we have seen, time and time again, that it was their mythology that shaped the Matter of Britain as it appears in both the Historia Brittonum and the Historia Regum Britanniae.

Bladud

The curious tale of Bladud, son of Rud Hud Hudibras, occupies only a few lines within the Historia Regum Britanniae, and yet it is one which has been significantly expanded since the time of Geoffrey of Monmouth, Bladud being one of the few characters described by Geoffrey who has a life beyond the Historia. Geoffrey is, as far as we can tell, the first person to describe the reign of Bladud, noting that, after Hudibras, his son 'ruled the kingdom for twenty years'.[28] Apart from being the father of Leir, the title character (as 'Lear') in arguably Shakespeare's most celebrated play, Bladud's fame was due primarily to his establishment of a new city.

> It was he who built the town of Kaerbadum, which is now called Bath, and who constructed the hot baths there which are so suited to the needs of mortal men. He chose the goddess Minerva as the tutelary deity of the baths. In her temple he lit fires which never went out and which never fell away into ash, for the moment that they began to die down they were turned into balls of stone. At that time Elijah prayed that it should not rain upon the earth so that for three years and six months no rain fell.[29]

Mention of 'Kaerbadum' provides us with a firm geographical placement for the exploits of Bladud for Bath was Aquae Sulis, an important Roman spa town and pilgrimage centre in Somerset. The significance of Bath is its thermal spring. Here, on a daily basis, over 1,100,000 litres (or 250,000 gallons) of water, heated to 46 °C, emerges through limestone aquifers from deep underground. The supposed healing properties of the water, which contains calcium, sulphate, sodium and chloride, have been much celebrated, especially from the mid-first century AD when the Roman State embarked upon a major building project, attempting to tame and control the spring. The construction of a great temple, bathhouse and urban centre unfortunately swept away all earlier signs of prehistoric settlement, although evidence of Iron Age religious activity is preserved in the name of the later town Aquae Sulis: 'the waters of Sulis'.

The Roman State was remarkably tolerant of native religions, often absorbing pre-Roman deities into its own belief system. The rejection of indigenous gods and goddesses in conquered territories would, Rome knew, lead unfailingly to resistance – the acceptance of local religions being a successful way of winning hearts and minds and helping to maintain control. The Romans were also deeply spiritual and superstitious. Beating disorganized native armies on the battlefield was one thing, but winning over their gods quite another. If the spiritual world of the conquered could be brought gently into line with Rome, native deities being worshipped, honoured with new temples and, ideally, merged with acceptable Mediterranean counterparts, so much the better.

Conflation with classical gods and goddesses, a process referred to as religious syncretisation, is often the only way that the names of pre-Roman gods and goddesses have survived to the present day. Iron Age society did not record the names of their gods either on altars or upon the countless pieces of metalwork they deposited in springs, bogs and other watery places. They did not write down the nature of religious practice and neither did they build monumental temple structures in which specific deities could reside. It is only through Roman altars and religious dedications do we encounter the familiar names of Roman deities fused with unfamiliar-sounding names of indigenous gods, goddesses and spirits of the place; hence at Lydney, in Gloucestershire, we hear of Mars Nodens,[30] a Romano-British god of healing, and in Colchester we find Mars Medocius[31] and at Carlisle Mars Belatucadrus.[32] The classical-style temple established at Bath was dedicated to Sulis Minerva, Minerva being the Roman deity associated with wisdom, craft, war and healing, while Sulis, it would appear, was her local Iron Age equivalent: the native goddess of the hot spring.

Classical temples were built to a standard design throughout the Roman world, with an enclosed room or cella that contained the cult statue of a specific deity. The cella, usually set out according to the principle that its length should not exceed one and a quarter times its width, was approached through a set of doors surrounded by an ornate set of columns, which in turn supported a highly decorated pediment. The temple was a place where the public could make a dedication or pray to their god or goddess but, as worship was not a congregational activity, they would not enter the cella, the focus of religious fervour being contained at the front of the building, which explains why so many classical temples possess ornate façades. Temples were usually set within their own temenos, or sacred precinct, something which helped further distance the holy structure from the noises, smells and harsh reality of the outside world. Upon approaching a temple, the request, gift or prayer was either left on the main altar in front of the building, or passed directly to a priest or priestess who would then safely convey it inside. The cella therefore acted as a sort of celestial hotline connecting the priestly class to the heavenly realm; a transmitter for talking to the gods.

Few classical temples have been recorded in the British Isles. In Colchester, the Roman town of Colonia Claudia Victricensis built over the native Camulodunum, a temple was dedicated to the deified emperor Claudius. Sadly, nothing remains above ground of this once imposing structure, although the vaulted foundations of the great podium are preserved beneath the later Norman castle.[33] At Bath, the foundations to the temple of Sulis Minerva have been more securely identified while a significant amount of the temple building itself, especially the ornately decorated pediment, has been unearthed, sawn up for use in later building projects.[34] The main temple was set within its own walled precinct together with other religious buildings, a sacrificial altar and a vaulted chamber that covered the sacred spring. The baths, which were architecturally conjoined to the temple complex along the south-eastern edge where the spring emerged, focused upon the lead-lined Great Bath, effectively an enormous swimming pool fed by the naturally warmed waters of Sulis. An additional, furnace-heated suite of baths were built on the westernmost edge of the Great Bath and all excess water piped through drains out to the River Avon.

The central pediment of the temple at Bath contained one of the most visually arresting images from Roman Britain: a stern male face with penetrating gaze and hair a writhing mass of snakes and serpents. Some have attempted to identify the face in the Bath temple with the Roman sea deities Neptune or Oceanus, but the presence of wings, evident at either side of the head, just behind the ears, clearly indicate that the figure was intended to be Medusa – albeit a male, moustachioed Medusa – the Gorgon whose stare could turn people to stone. In Greek mythology, Medusa was the daughter of the marine god Phorcys and the sea monster Keto. Together with her two sisters Stheno and Euryale, the three women were known as 'the Gorgons'.

In her youth Medusa was famed for her beauty and for her luxurious golden hair. Seduced by Neptune in the temple of Minerva, Medusa was later cursed by the outraged goddess, who transformed the young woman into a hideous, snake-haired creature. Later, after helping arrange the assassination of Medusa, Minerva took the severed head of the Gorgon and wore it on her armour.

Perhaps the sculptor commissioned to generate the face in the Bath temple pediment was unfamiliar with the iconography of the Gorgons and wrongly provided Medusa, who appears in classical art with snakes and wings spouting from her head, with male attributes, namely the moustache. Given the prominence given to the piece, however, this seems unlikely. More probably we are seeing an attempt to portray a perfect syncretisation or fusion between Neptune and Minerva, the two deities whose actions conspired to create the monster of legend. Anyone seeing the face should automatically have made the connection, the head of Medusa appearing on the temple pediment as a form of ident or branding. To those who did not make the association, additional attributes more obviously signifying the goddess Minerva/Athene, such as an owl, were added, as was the wreath, a symbol of victory.

The temple soon became a major pilgrimage centre, far exceeding all others in Britain and no doubt generating large amounts of money for those in control of the establishment. By the early third century the fame of Aquae Sulis was such that the Roman writer Gaius Julius Solinus could state,

> The circumference of Britain is 4,875 miles, within which there are many great rivers and hot springs richly adorned for the use of men. Over these springs the divinity of Minerva presides and in her temple the perpetual fires never whiten into ash, but when the flame declines it turns into rocky lumps.[35]

The collector of curiosities may well have visited Bath in person and seen the never-whitening fires for himself, for a dedication has been recovered from the city asking Sulis Minerva, on behalf of one 'Solinus', to curse those who took his 'bathing costume and cloak', ensuring they are to be deprived of 'sleep or health' until returned to the temple.[36] Whether Solinus' anger at the theft of his clothing was ever assuaged, or his bathing costume returned, we sadly don't know.

Our main interest in Solinus' brief description of the fires in the temple of Minerva, of course, is that it clearly inspired Geoffrey of Monmouth, who notes that it was King Bladud who first lit the 'fires which never went out and which never fell away into ash' in Kaerbadum, the holy flames, when starting to die down, turning immediately 'into balls of stone'.[37] Geoffrey had seen, or had access to, the Collectanea Rerum Memorabilium, or at least had a source in which Solinus' description of the hot springs of Britain was quoted. This would perhaps explain how he was able to identify the temple at Bath as having been dedicated to Minerva, although, to be fair, Solinus does not specifically name Bath/Aquae Sulis as the centre of the cult to the goddess,[38] so it is possible that Geoffrey possessed an additional source that confirmed this, had access to an oral remembrance that this was so or just 'got lucky' with the identification. Certainly it was not until the first significant antiquarian exploration of Bath in the eighteenth century that the association of the Roman building with Minerva became apparent.[39] Whether Solinus had Aquae Sulis in mind when he was writing his guide in the third century or not, archaeologists have been quick to interpret the story of 'fire-into-stone' as demonstrating the use of Somerset coal in the temple.[40]

There is no archaeological indication, of course, that monumental construction work began at Bath under the direction of King Bladud, let alone that this commenced in deep antiquity, as Geoffrey implies when he associates the building of Kaerbadun with the prophet Elijah. The building of the temple to Sulis Minerva, the composite British/Roman super deity, which erased any earlier native site, seems to have commenced somewhere between AD 75 and 90. Although by no means proven, it seems likely that complex was conceived, or at least part sponsored, by a native aristocrat keen to Romanize his people and demonstrate fidelity to the State. The temple to Sulis Minerva at Bath was first established at broadly the same time as another classical religious establishment was being built at Chichester in West Sussex.

The Chichester temple has not been identified archaeologically, although a dedicatory inscription found close to the site names the deities worshipped as Neptune and Minerva.[41] The combination of Minerva, daughter of Jupiter and Juno, and the god Neptune was not common within the Roman world,[42] although their Greek counterparts, namely Athene and Poseidon, representing the combination of land and sea, were widely known as the co-guardians of ancient Athens.[43] The temple to Neptune and Minerva in Chichester was sponsored, so the inscription tells us, by Tiberius Claudius Togidubnus, the full text stating that he was 'Great King in Britain'. Addition of the Roman names Tiberius and Claudius to the more Celtic name-form Togidubnus tells us that not only was this individual a Roman citizen, but, far more importantly, his sponsor was the emperor Claudius himself, whose full name was Tiberius Claudius Caesar Augustus Germanicus. Fortunately, a second textual source provides more information on this Great King, for the Roman historian Tacitus, writing at the end of the first century AD, noted that in Britain 'certain states were handed over to King Cogidumnus – he in fact remained totally loyal down to our times'.[44] Cogidumnus in Tacitus' text is assumed to have been the Togidubnus of the Chichester inscription, the differences in spelling being either due to Roman misunderstanding of the ethnic name-form or, perhaps more likely, later scribal mis-transcription. It is worth noting that as a client king in possession of 'many states', Togidubnus is also the logical choice for sponsor of the temple at Bath.[45] Could Togi-dubnus therefore be Bladud? The name-form derivation from To-GIDUB-nus is difficult but certainly not impossible.

Geoffrey of Monmouth provides us with a rather startling, if not downright bizarre, end to the story of Bladud, founder of Kaerbadum:

> Bladud was a most ingenious man who encouraged necromancy throughout the kingdom of Britain. He pressed on with his experiments and finally constructed a pair of wings for himself and tried to fly through the upper air. He came down on top of the temple of Apollo in the town of Trinovantum and was dashed to countless fragments.[46]

What to make of this curious twist? Bladud was evidently an inventor, magician and polymath, all things which, in the cold light of the early twelfth century, could also be considered akin to necromancy, as Geoffrey states, or simple pagan blasphemy. But can we seriously consider that Bladud was a pioneer of flight, or was this simply an allusion to the classical tale of Daedalus and Icarus, a tale of tragedy born of arrogant pride?

There is a curious parallel to the story of early flight and it comes from the pages of William of Malmesbury's Gesta Regum Anglorum. Geoffrey's Historia Regum Britanniae appears to have been conceived, at least in part, as a riposte to the overtly English perspective of historians such as William of Malmesbury and Henry of Huntingdon. We should not, therefore, be surprised if anything William tells us concerning the great deeds of the English clergy could be eclipsed by Geoffrey's proof of the inventiveness of the earlier Britons. Inspiration for the tale of Bladud 'the flying king' can perhaps therefore be found in a short digression in the life of King Edward 'the Confessor' into which William inserts the story of Elmer (or Elimer), 'a certain monk of our monastery' at Malmesbury.

> He was a man of good learning for those times, of mature age, and in his early youth had hazarded an attempt of singular temerity. He had by some contrivance fastened wings to his hands and feet, in order that, looking on the fable as true, he might fly like Daedalus, and collecting the air on the summit of a tower, had flown for more than the distance of a furlong; but, agitated by the violence of the wind and the current of air, as well as by the consciousness of his rash attempt, he fell and broke his legs, and was lame ever after. He used to relate as the cause of his failure, his forgetting to provide himself a tail.[47]

This particular story, quite understandably, has had a significant afterlife, Elmer being sometimes referred to, or considered as, a pioneer of human flight. It is, of course, not known how much of the story, as presented, is true; for example whether Elmer really managed to fly for a distance of more than a furlong (over 200m), or whether this is simply an allusion to biblical or classical texts.

As the tale relates to a monk of Malmesbury Abbey, we can at least expect William to be employing a degree of local knowledge, possibly even pride in his own institution. Perhaps the story of the flying monk inspired Geoffrey of Monmouth to enhance or elaborate upon the tale of Bladud in order to show that a Briton 'got there first'. Such an attempt at demonstrating primacy can also be gleaned in the writings of the seventeenth-century historian Ahmed Mohammed Al-Makkari, who made great claims for the ninth-century polymath Abu'l-Qasim Abbas ibn Firnas of Cordova in southern Spain, noting that when attempting to fly, using methods similar to Elmer, he injured his back 'not knowing that birds when they alight come down upon their tails, he forgot to provide himself with one'.[48]

There is another potential solution. As long ago as the late 1880s it was suggested that Bladud as he appears in the Historia Regum Britanniae may be an echo of a pre-Roman deity, one whose image may have provided the inspiration to the 'Gorgoneion', the central face on the temple pediment at Bath, Archibald Sayce describing it as being 'the face of a deity of orb-like shape, and surrounded by flames of fire in place of hair'.[49] Although there is no reason to suggest that the pediment head was that of a Celtic deity, rather than the Gorgon Medusa, Sayce's 'flames of fire' clearly being serpents, it remains possible that, as A. T. Fear has observed, 'it was the sculpture of the gorgon that gave rise to the legend, not vice versa'.[50] The startling image of the wide-eyed, moustachioed Gorgon would certainly have had an impact on all those who saw it in situ, especially in the context of a predominantly Christian, post-Roman society, and could easily have given rise to stories of an old god, spirit of the spring or founder of the bathing/temple complex.[51] Had the pediment itself collapsed, together with a larger part of the temple building, bringing the Gorgon down in a single catastrophic event, could this have been remembered long after, giving rise to myths of a king who fell to earth?

Perhaps. This is certainly an attractive hypothesis but one which appears to be critically flawed. First, we have no way of knowing when, if ever, the temple pediment fell, for it may have been deliberately taken down rather than collapsing in a dramatic and memorable way.

Secondly, even if the Gorgon did stand for some significant time, into the late or even post-Roman period, we have no way of establishing the impact that it had upon any observers, or indeed whether they would have made the link between sculptured head and the legendary founder of Bath. Thirdly, and perhaps rather more importantly, Geoffrey of Monmouth states that Bladud was dashed to pieces upon the 'temple of Apollo in the town of Trinovantum' and not the temple of Minerva in Kaerbadun.

If we deal with the location first, this is not a wholly insurmountable problem. Trinovantum, which Geoffrey and others have identified with London (Troia Nova) is, as we have already noted, in reality the capital of the Trinovantes, later called Camulodunum, Colonia Claudia Victriensis and finally Colchester. There was indeed a great temple at Colchester, dedicated to the imperial cult and, in particular, Claudius, emperor and god, rather than to Apollo, although Geoffrey and others may not have realized this. Either Bladud died at or near to Camulodunum/Colonia Claudia Victriensis, or was buried, as so many tribal aristocrats were, close to the temple of Claudius or the royal Trinovantian/Catuvellaunian burial grounds to the east. Perhaps Geoffrey had an account of a great temple and, naturally repositioning it in his narrative to be closer to the capital of Brutus, as he saw it, the event was shifted to Troia Nova (London), as many stories seem to be.

The thorny issues surrounding the longevity of remembrance and the persistence of oral myth are rather trickier to resolve. John Clark felt that the likelihood of the Gorgon (or 'Gorgoneion') being remembered for some significant time following the fall of the Roman administration, and conceivably of the temple building itself, being transmitted from generation to generation without the obvious visual prompt of the sculpture itself, to be unlikely.[52] For such a survival to occur, he considered we must

... envisage the circulation of the story in oral tradition for some 700 years until Geoffrey of Monmouth made use of it, tradition surviving the near total collapse of the culture in which it had originated, the influx of many new people of a different race and culture, and translation into a new language-and all this in the absence of the one piece of concrete evidence, the sculpture, to which the teller could refer in corroboration of his story.[53]

But, of course, the survival of stories over considerable periods of time, and over many countless generations, is precisely the thing that can be demonstrated, even if the precise circumstances of transmission are lost.[54] Having dismissed the likelihood of direct remembrance of the temple Gorgon, Clark felt that the theory was still persuasive and could be explained by the presence of a second, now lost, sculpture, perhaps of the kind apparently seen by John Leyland during a visit to Bath in 1542.[55] While possible, such an explanation does appear overly complicated and, using the maxim of Occam's Razor, one must ask why the simplest explanation is not the better one: that it was indeed the fall of the Gorgon-headed temple pediment at the heart of Aquae Sulis that provided the basis of Bladud's unusual demise.

Key to understanding whether the Bath Gorgon was 'Bladud the flying king' is the length of time that the temple pediment remained open to view. We know that the Gorgon, together with significant quantities of sculptured masonry blocks, was rediscovered in the 1790s during the rebuilding of the Pump Room, causing quite a stir at the time.[56] Unfortunately, given the rather haphazard nature of recovery, with little attention being paid to context, and certainly none regarding stratigraphy, our understanding of the final phases of the temple are limited. Literary sources suggest that the hot springs and temple/bathing complex at Bath continued to be used and experienced, in some form, well into the sixth century.[57] The oft quoted poem 'The Ruin', which appears in the tenth-century Codex Exoniensis, has usually been taken to indicate the collapse of Aquae Sulis as seen through the eyes of an eighth- or ninth-century visitor: 'Wonderous is this masonry, shattered by the Fates. The fortifications have given way, the buildings raised by giants are crumbling. The roofs have collapsed; the towers are in ruins.'[58]

Quite when the fortifications gave way and the roof fell in has been a matter of some significant debate. In the final report of the 1976–84 excavations conducted within the inner precinct of the temple, Barry Cunliffe and Peter Davenport suggested that the final collapse of buildings occurred during a period of deliberate demolition in the late fifth or even early sixth century.[59] Reanalysis of the artefactual material, combined with a new suite of radiocarbon dates, however, has suggested to James Gerrard that the destruction of the temple and bathing complex (referred to as Period 6) should be placed shortly after AD 450 and probably no later than AD 500.[60] Prior to this, sporadic activity seems to have taken place within the area of the temple precinct and baths, possibly suggesting continued veneration of the hot springs associated with low-level maintenance of the main buildings,[61] all of which was brought to a sudden end by the collapse of the temple.

> The 400-year-old buildings were excised from the townscape, an act which stands as a powerful testimony to the ability of a late fifth century society to change and reshape the world around it.[62]

Is it too much to suggest that this attempt to forcibly expunge the Roman buildings at the heart of Aquae Sulis, in which 'the superstructure of the portico and possibly part of the reservoir collapsed, or was pushed over, creating a scree of massive stone blocks mixed up with slabs of concrete and shattered tiles from the vaults',[63] was remembered? Certainly the scale of the demolition, the ground 'heavily disturbed by the impact of the large stone blocks which collapsed on to it'[64] and the tumbled mass of stone still lying, as it had fallen, to be recovered in the late twentieth century[65] demonstrates this was not some minor event easily forgotten. The great temple portico, which had proudly stood as monumental testament to Roman power for almost four centuries, had fallen. Surely that was something that was worthy of a story? Ultimately, the connection between Bladud of the Historia Regum Britanniae and the collapse of the temple portico at Bath in the late fifth century must remain unproven, but the description of the king being 'dashed to countless fragments' sounds wonderfully architectural.

Leir

The brief account of Kings Rud Hud Hudibras and Bladud in Book 2 of the Historia Regum Britanniae serve as little more than the prelude to the greater story of King Leir, the first tale since the story of Brutus and Corineus, which Geoffrey of Monmouth felt worthy of a more detailed account. Our understanding of Leir, of course, is significantly clouded by later reworkings of the narrative, not least of which is *The Tragedie of King Lear*, widely regarded as one of William Shakespeare's finest plays. Written in 1605, Shakespeare's King Lear is a study in pride, deceit and wilful ignorance combined with the slow descent into madness and death. It is not a happy play. The inspiration for Lear came from Raphael Holinshed's Chronicles of England, Scotlande, and Irelande published in the 1580s, which mined the Historia Regum Britanniae as source material. Given that Shakespeare's narrative, although using the accounts of Raphael Holinshed and Geoffrey of Monmouth as the foundation, diverges significantly from these, introducing many additional characters along the way, it is best to go back to the source and summarise the story as it was first set down in the 1130s.

In the Historia Regum Britanniae, Leir, son of Bladud, is propelled to the throne in the aftermath of his father's flying accident. His reign, as it is recorded, appears uneventful, Geoffrey telling us only that 'he built the city on the River Soar which is called Kaerleir'.[66] Having no male heir, Leir decided, as old age approached, to divide his kingdom into three between his beloved daughters Gonorilla, Regau and Cordellia, whom he decided should be married to husbands 'suited to them and capable of ruling the kingdom along with them'. In order to ascertain which of the three was best suited to inheriting the larger part of his realm, Leir asked his daughters the fateful question 'which of them loved him most'. Gonorilla stated that her father was 'dearer to her than the very soul which dwelt within her body'. Pleased, the king immediately granted Gonorilla a third of the kingdom, allowing her to take the husband of her choice. She chose Maglaunus, Duke of Albany. Regau, the next to be questioned, swore that she loved the king her father 'more than any other living person'. Leir duly gave her a third of the kingdom and she chose Henuinus, Duke of Cornwall, as her husband. Cordellia, the most favoured daughter, answered the same question with:

> I have always loved you as my father, and at this moment I feel no lessening of my affection for you. If you are determined to

wring more than this out of me, then I will tell you how much I love you and so put an end to your inquiry. You are worth just as much as you possess, and that is the measure of my love for you.[67]

Dissatisfied with this final answer, Leir immediately disinherited Cordellia, telling her she would never be married with honour. After taking advice from his nobles he divided his territory between Gonorilla and Regau and their respective husbands, the dukes of Albany and Cornwall, agreeing that 'after his own death they should inherit the entire kingdom of Britain'.

King Aganippus of the Franks, upon hearing of Cordellia's great beauty, petitioned Leir for the hand of his daughter. Apparently glad to be rid of her, Leir agreed telling Aganippus that 'there would be no land or dowry'. Aganippus, who at this time 'ruled over a third of Gaul', was not discouraged and Cordellia was duly dispatched. As time went on, Leir became ever more infirm and the husbands of Gonorilla and Regau, Maglaunus and Henuinus, took the throne from him. The deposed Leir was placed in the protective care of Maglaunus, together with 140 knights so that the ex-king would 'not end his days alone and in obscurity'. Gonorilla, however, aggrieved by the disturbance that her father's retinue was causing her household, informed Leir that he should 'content himself with the service of thirty soldiers' and dispense with the rest. Infuriated, Leir stormed off to his second daughter, Regau, where he was 'received honourably'. Within a year, relations with Regau had broken down, his daughter telling the former king that he should 'dismiss all his retainers except five'. Leir, even more annoyed, went back to his elder daughter, Gonorilla.

She upbraided her father for wanting to go about with such a huge retinue now that he was an old man with no possessions at all. She refused steadfastly to give way on his wish. For his part he had to obey her, and so the other attendants were dismissed and he was left with a single soldier.[68]

Depressed by the severe decline in his standard of living, Leir decided that he could no longer stay in Britain and crossed to Gaul to be with his youngest daughter Cordellia. Fearful of the reception he might receive at the court of King Aganippus, given how 'he had given her away so shamefully', Leir boarded a boat and left his former kingdom behind. During the crossing to Gaul, Leir was left to further reflect upon his reduced status, discovering that 'he was held third in honour among the princes on the boat'. Frustration and depression led eventually to anger, Geoffrey of Monmouth digressing in order to provide the deposed king with a lengthy speech in which Leir railed at the Fates.

> It is even more miserable to sit thinking of some past success than to bear the burden of subsequent failure. Indeed the memory of the time when, attended by so many hundred thousand fighting men, I used to batter down the walls of cities and to lay waste the provinces of my enemies saddens me more than the calamity of my own present distress, although it has encouraged those who once grovelled beneath my feet to abandon me in my weakness. Oh spiteful Fortune! Will the moment never come when I can take vengeance upon those who have deserted me in my final poverty?[69]

Landing in Gaul, and apparently still 'muttering these things to himself', Leir travelled to Karitia where, starving and dishevelled, he sent word to his youngest daughter. Cordellia, shocked to hear of her father's situation, sent gold and silver and attendants to take Leir to another city 'to bathe him, dress him and nurse him there'. At last he returned to address King Aganippus.

> Dressed in royal robes, equipped with royal insignia and accompanied by a household, he announced to Aganippus and his own daughter that he had been expelled from the realm of Britain by his own sons-in-law and that he had come to them so that he might recover his kingdom. Accompanied by their councillors and noblemen, Aganippus and Cordellia came out to meet him. They received him honourably and they granted him the rank which he held in his own country until such time as they should have restored him to his former dignity.[70]

Plans to take back control of the kingdom for Leir were swiftly made.

> Aganippus sent messengers throughout the whole of Gaul to summon all the men there who could bear arms, so that with their help he might endeavour to restore the kingship of Britain to his father-in-law Leir. When this was done, Leir marched at the head of the assembled army, taking his daughter with him. He fought with his sons-in-law and beat them, thus bringing them all under his dominion again.[71]

Now back in charge of state affairs and with all parts of the kingdom reunited, Geoffrey tells us that Leir remained in power for a further three years before his death. Following his death, and that of Aganippus, control of the state passed to Cordellia. William Shakespeare, in his reworking of the story, famously has a less upbeat ending than that provided in the Historia Regum Britanniae, with Regan (Regau) poisoned, Goneril (Gonorilla) committing suicide, Cordelia (Cordellia) hanged and, finally, Lear (Leir) dying of grief.

The story of King Leir, with its themes of self-sacrificing love, betrayal and, in Geoffrey of Monmouth's account, redemption and reconciliation, at least between the king and his daughter Cordellia, is undeniably emotive. The history and development of the tale post-Geoffrey, and its evolution into full-blown tragedy, is well known, but its origins are far less clear. It may ultimately have derived from a real sequence of events, not necessarily pre-Roman in date, or it may have been adapted from a religious myth or folk tale. A version of the Leir/Lear story appears in the Gesta Romanorum (Deeds of the Romans), a curious collection of myths, anecdotes and allegories that may originally have been intended as an aide to sermon-writing. The presence of a somewhat shortened variant in the Gesta, albeit one where King Leir is replaced by the emperor Theodosius and the narrative transplanted to the eastern half of the Roman Empire, could indicate that the basic plot was 'a popular medieval international tale';[72] one that preceded any potential British claim to it. Unfortunately, whatever the date and origin of the stories contained within the Gesta Romanorum, the version as it appears today does not seem to have been compiled much before the late thirteenth century. The account of 'the Wise Emperor' that is set down as chapter XXI would, therefore, appear to have derived from the Historia Regum Britanniae and not the other way round.

It is possible that the account of a king and the troubled succession of power to his three daughters came from religious tradition, possibly a creation myth or fable. Llyr, Lir or Ler may, for example, have been variant name-forms given to an ocean deity, such as 'implied in that of the sea-god Manannan mac Lir', 'Llyr' being certainly used at times in early Welsh literature 'as a common noun denoting the sea'.[73] The story of a sea god and his three daughters would certainly fit within what little we know of Celtic folklore. Strong female characters feature prominently within the native belief systems of Britain, Gaul and Germany, often being associated with healing and fertility. Deae Matres, or 'Mother Goddesses', usually appear in sculptured form in triplicate, often 'nursing infants or holding baskets of fruit, loaves or other fertility symbols such as fish'.[74] Dedications to three-fold mother goddesses occur throughout Roman Britain, and are to be especially found within the chief cities and frontiers of the province.

Could the curious tale of Leir, Gonorilla, Regau and Cordellia have originated from a pre- or post-Roman religious fable? It is certainly possible. Unlike the gods and goddesses of the Roman Empire, whose origin myths and background stories were preserved in the contemporary writings and artistic creations of its people, the stories that swirled around their Celtic counterparts were not formally recorded until centuries later. In the years between worship and the written word, religions changed significantly and the differences between fact and fiction, between real monarchs and those of the more ethereal world, became blurred. For a chronicle writer versed in the Christian tradition, such as Gildas, Bede, Nennius or Geoffrey of Monmouth, the distinction between a mythological character taken from the lost world of Iron Age religion and a genuine pre-Roman king who had been mythologized may not have been obvious. Iron Age religious practice was far more regionalized than that of their Roman counterparts, gods and goddesses being related to particular tribes, clans or family groups and often associated with specific natural features, such as a spring, river, mountain, hill or forest. The

Leir that appears in the Historia Regum Britanniae may, therefore, represent the earliest account of a wholly legendary and possibly even local religious figure, one for whom no place in history can reasonably be found.

So does the character of King Leir fit within our understanding of early Britain? There is one clear name-form signpost contained within the body of the Historia that can help us place both the identity and the reign of Leir in context. It comes with the character whom Geoffrey says was king of the Franks: Aganippus. Needless to say, no such 'King of the Franks' by the name of Aganippus is known to us and, in any case, the term 'Frank' is anachronistic for the pre-Roman period that Geoffrey is supposedly describing, the Franks not taking control of Gaul until the early sixth century AD. Helpfully, there is another name-form from the Later Iron Age that does equate well with 'Aganippus', but it is of someone with a solidly Roman pedigree: Agrippa.

Marcus Vipsanius Agrippa was a close friend of the emperor Augustus and, despite the significant age differences, eventually went on to marry Augustus' daughter, Julia the Elder. Away from the intrigues of Rome, however, Agrippa was also involved in the project to Romanize Gaul, creating the necessary State infrastructure, and stabilize the situation in Germanic territory to the north. In 39 BC, Agrippa was serving as governor in Gaul where, as one of his first actions, he crossed the Rhine in an effort to militarily neutralize the Germanic Suebi and Chatti, resettling the more pro-Roman Ubii on the left (Roman) side at Ara Ubiorum, later renamed Colonia Claudia Ara Agrippinensium (Cologne). The following year, Agrippa was engaged in suppressing a revolt by the Aquitani, a tribe in south-western Gaul (Aquitane) and overseeing the completion of a major new road network across the province. In 37 BC he was called back to Rome to stand as one of the two consuls of the city.

During his time in Gaul it is more than likely that, as the loyal and trusted Augustus deputy of the emperor, Marcus Vipsanius Agrippa was involved in overseeing relations with the tribes of southern Britain in order that the island remained stable and Rome's northern frontier secure. As the 'go-to' man in Gaul establishing the foundations of Romanitas, Agrippa would probably have been well known to the British tribal elite, especially when it came to renegotiating allegiances and the subsequent arrangement of hostages. In fact it is in the area of clientage, whereby allied rulers in Britain sent their offspring to Rome with a view to their eventual return as fully integrated members of the Roman elite, that the dispatch of Cordellia may alternatively be viewed. In Geoffrey of Monmouth's narrative she is sent to marry Aganippus, who 'ruled over a third of Gaul', but perhaps this is a medieval, romanticized rereading of what was originally a story of a young member of a British tribal elite being sent to the governor of Transalpine Gaul for 'processing and assimilation'. Such an interpretation could be behind Geoffrey's statement that messengers were sent 'to Leir to ask if the king would let Cordelia go back with them' not because Aganippus wanted to marry her but because Agrippa required a new round of hostages in order to secure the loyalty of British tribes.

If the name-form Aganippus may find etymological resolution in the historical sources, what then of Leir himself? Archaeologically and historically speaking, there is no specific reference, either in Roman sources or on indigenous coin issues, of anyone with that name, and yet the quantity of detail supplied by Geoffrey for the unfortunate monarch suggests that he was perceived to be an extremely important individual. We must also assume, unless Geoffrey was making the whole story of Leir up (and there seems little reason for him to have done so given that, unlike his predecessors, Leir is not credited with any aspect of constitutional change, legislative reform or infrastructural improvement other than the establishment of Kaerleir on the River Soar)[75] or unless Leir was actually a deity, that the account in the Historia Regum Britanniae was appropriated from a lengthy discourse, poem or 'saga' about the aged monarch and his complex familial relationships. This is certainly strongly suggested by the sudden expansion of detail provided for the king, with not only individual speeches provided but also the minutiae of court life, whereas earlier rulers (such as Ebraucus, Brutus Greenshield, Leil, Rud Hud Hudibras and Bladud) are supplied with little more than a concise summary of blood-heritage, reign and major achievements. The original story or poem of Leir, Gonorilla, Regau and Cordellia, with its focus upon responsibility, old age, infirmity, deceit, insanity, reconciliation and redemption, sounds very moralistic, as if written in order to make a point about human nature and the frailty of existence, things which evidently alerted Shakespeare to the possibility of composing a 'tragedie'.

The focus upon the interpersonal conflict generated within the final years of Leir's life means that most of his reign, which Geoffrey of Monmouth assures us lasted sixty years, is swiftly glossed over. Indeed, the first five lines provided in the Historia Regum Britanniae to introduce Leir to the reader, before the narrative of his decline and fall from power, fit very well with the accounts summarizing the reigns of Leir's predecessors.

> After Bladud met his fate in this way, his son Leir was raised to
> the kingship. Leir ruled the country for sixty years. It was he who
> built the city on the River Soar which is called Kaerlier after him
> in the British tongue, its Saxon name being Leicester. He had no
> male issue, but three daughters were born to him. Their names
> were Gonorilla, Regau and Cordellia.[76]

At this point, given what the readers of the Historia had come to expect, there would have been no surprise had the narrative then moved on to examine the aftermath of Leir's rule (civil war) followed by the reign of his immediate successor, in this case his youngest daughter Cordellia. No doubt the opening sentences introducing us to Leir and describing his reign were taken directly from a primary source, such as a genealogy or king-list which similarly condensed the reigns of other monarchs, and it was this which Geoffrey of Monmouth used before tacking on the more detailed account of Leir's relationship with his daughters and their husbands.

That Leir possessed such a detailed storyline should alert us to the fact that somebody perceived him to be a vital character, one who clearly stood out from the other kings, queens and rulers in Britain. It could be that the regnal instability that followed the removal of Leir, the kingdom subsequently being divided, and the civil war that ended with Leir's triumphal return at the head of a large army was remembered as a time of uncertainty and chaos. Of course, civil war was not unusual within the pages of the Historia and there is nothing in the account that seems particularly exceptional. The feeling that there is 'something missing' from the story is magnified when we encounter Leir on the boat to Gaul for here, Geoffrey of Monmouth tells us, he bemoaned the loss of his youth, remembering when 'attended by so many hundred thousand fighting men' the deposed monarch 'used to batter down the walls of cities and to lay waste the provinces of my enemies'. No further account of this fighting appears in the Historia Regum Britanniae.

The brief mention of siege warfare and the laying waste to enemy lands could, of course, all be artistic licence, Geoffrey providing the reader with the sort of activities that he felt a monarch of the period would be engaged in. Strange, though, that the warlike aspects of the king's earlier career are mentioned at all, given that they contradict the rather anodyne nature of Leir's sixty-year reign, with nothing worthy of note save for the founding of Leicester. If there had been a period of protracted and significant conflict, why did Geoffrey not mention it, at least in passing? Perhaps it was simply not covered in the brief summary of Leir's reign mined to supply the introduction of the king, but did form part of the secondary narrative appropriated by Geoffrey of Monmouth for the story of Leir, Gonorilla, Regau and Cordellia.

Intriguingly, if we assume that there were, as is suggested by the sudden switch of tone and detail within the Historia, two separate sources providing information on the reign of Leir, the former being derived from a genealogical table, it immediately becomes apparent that the basic account of his reign is duplicated. Earlier on in the Historia we hear of a king named Leil, who, in the complex bloodline of Trojan descent provided by Geoffrey of Monmouth, appears as Leir's grandfather and the son of Brutus 'Greenshield'.

> Leil, the son of Greenshield, a great lover of peace and justice, succeeded him. Leil took advantage of the prosperity of his reign to build a town in the northern part of Britain which he called Kaerleil after himself. This was the time when Solomon began to build the Temple of the Lord in Jerusalem and when the Queen of Sheba came to listen to his wisdom. About the same time Silvius Epitus succeeded his father Alba in the kingship of Rome.

Leil lived on for twenty-five years after mounting the throne, but towards the end of his life he ruled the kingdom feebly. As a result of Leil's prolonged inactivity a civil war suddenly broke out in the realm.[77]

Aside from the length of time on the throne, Leil ruling for twenty-five years and Leir for sixty, the basic details of their respective reigns are similar: both ruled successfully in times of prosperity; both built a town in the north of the kingdom, which they named after themselves; and both ruled for so long that they became infirm and incapable of good government, their inactivity sparking civil war.

That the same person, or at least the same 'reign', appears to have been cited twice is not something that seems to have bothered Geoffrey of Monmouth. In fact, assuming that the reason for duplication may have been due to the use, by Geoffrey, of two discrete sources providing slightly different levels of information about the same king, information which may have become corrupted over time – hence Kaerleil and Kaerleir – then it may be he simply didn't notice. Given that there was a clear need to fill the narrative between the arrival of Brutus two generations after the fall of Troy and the arrival of Julius Caesar in the mid-first century BC, no doubt Geoffrey was glad to obtain data on as many monarchs as possible. If their reigns could be expanded to fit the chronology, so much the better. Hence we hear that Leil's reign was contemporary with events from the Old Testament (Solomon and Sheba) and legends of Rome (Silvius Epitus, or Capetus Silvius as he is better known, one of the kings of Alba Longa descended from Aeneas), something that establishes him at a 'fixed' point in antiquity, at least from the perspective of Geoffrey's audience and setting him apart from Leir.

The duplication of people, places and events should not surprise us. We have already seen that the same episode can appear on more than one occasion within Geoffrey's narrative, subtle differences in place names, or slight change in descriptive focus, effectively masking similarity, or at least suggesting that two very different events had in fact taken place. The invasion of Julius Caesar in 54 BC, as noted, appears on three occasions in the Historia Regum Britanniae, the battle between Rome and the Britons, being placed at 'Dorobellum' and later at 'Durobernia' while in the earlier Nennian narrative of the Historia Brittonum, Dorobellum/ Durobernia is cited as a person: 'Dolobellus'. By the time Geoffrey of Monmouth came to compile the Historia Regum Britanniae, it would appear that there were multiple versions of key reigns and events in circulation, each focusing on diifferent aspects of the basic story and mutating in a slightly different way. This not only confirms to us that Geoffrey was, as claimed, using much older sources, which he modified and adapted, but it also helps us in the identification of Leir and the understanding of his reign in the context of pre-Roman Britain.

We have already observed that there is no obvious parallel for the name Leir/Leil in either the archaeological or the surviving historical sources. If, however, we reflect upon the fact that a number of name-forms presented, not only in the Historia Regum Britanniae but also other key documents of the period such as the Historia Brittonum and the Anglo Saxon Chronicle, appear in significantly edited, abbreviated or condensed form, then a whole new possibility presents itself. What if 'Leir/Leil' is merely an abridged form of a name that had, by the twelfth century, become significantly garbled or corrupted? What if it had only been a part of a much longer name-form, perhaps the aspect of the original upon which a key aspect of pronunciation or stress had been placed?

Given what has already been said with regard to Aganippus/ Agrippa and the placing of the story of King Leir/Leil in the latter decades of the first century BC, an obvious choice for the name-form interpretation of 'Leir' presents itself: Dubno-vellau-nos. Dubnovellaunus, of course, we have already encountered coins with his variant name-form DVBN / DVBNOVIILL / DVBOVALAVNOS / DVBNOVIILLAVN / DVBNOVALLAVNOS occurring in Essex while DV / DVB / DVBNO / DVBNOV / DVBNOVELL / DVBNOVALLA / DVBNOVALLAVNOS are found in Kent.[78] We have already met Dubnovellaunus of course, and equated him with the British King Dunvallo Molmutius in Book 2 of the Historia Regum Britanniae.

The obvious (and sometimes not so obvious) duplication of characters in the Historia has not, thus far, caused too much concern, however the suggestion that Leir/Leil was also Dunvallo Molmutius does perhaps require more specific justification. The lengthy tale of

King Leir in the Historia Regum Britanniae is missing significant detail surrounding the early years of the king's reign, especially the battering down of 'the walls of cities' and the laying waste to 'the provinces of my enemies', activities which Leir, on the boat to Gaul, remembers from his youth. This is something that the story of Dunvallo Molmutius supplies, for in Geoffrey's account Dunvallo comes to power in the heat of battle, defeating the armies of Loegria, Kambria and Albany before marching through the lands of his enemies where he 'destroyed their cities and fortresses and forced their people to accept his rule'.[79]

Leir, in the version provided by Geoffrey in the Historia Regum Britanniae, wanted to divide his kingdom between his three daughters Gonorilla, Regau and Cordellia. To Geoffrey, this would perhaps have made sense as the division of the larger kingdom of Britain into the constituent parts of England, Scotland and Wales. This certainly seems to have been the view of William Shakespeare when he was inspired to write King Lear, 'the disastrous division of his kingdom into three' perhaps intended to serve both as a warning but also as 'some kind of prompt towards support for a unifying king', in this case James I, whose coronation in 1603, brought the crowns of Scotland and England together.[80] The division of Britain into its traditional constituent parts was not, however, what the original compilers of the tale of King Leir had in mind. To them the story was to do with the more regionalised division of Iron Age tribes in central south-eastern Britain.

With Cordellia banished to Gaul, it is evident that Leir remained in power, albeit in a significantly reduced state, with Gonorilla married to Maglaunus, Duke of Cornwall, and Regau betrothed to Henuinus, Duke of Albany. If we take what has already been said with regard to the identification of these particular areas in the Historia Regum Britanniae, and of Geoffrey's attempts to syncretise the names of Iron Age tribes with his own twelfth-century vision of Britain, then 'Cornwall' represents the land of the Catuvellauni (in Hertfordshire) while 'Albany' is the Iceni of Norfolk. Interpolation of prehistoric name-forms would furthermore explain the prominence that Cornwall has in the narrative, rather than Kambria or Wales, a nation which would, in the context of Geoffrey's world, appear more apposite. This leaves Leir with a third area, presumably that of the Trinovantes, a tribe with borders to both the Catuvellauni and the Iceni and the territory in which the coins of Dubnovellaunus appear to concentrate. The tale of Cordellia/Maglaunus and Regau/Henuinus would therefore suggest, rather than the breakdown of relations between the kingdoms of Britain, instead the hazy remembrance of a failed attempt to ally three key Iron Age tribes through marriage alliance.

It is in the final stages of King Leir's reign that we obtain our closest parallel with the career of the historical Dubnovellaunus. Deposed by elements within two key regions of his kingdom, Albany and Cornwall, and deprived of a retinue, Leir flees to the protection of King Aganippus' court in Gaul. Dubnovellaunus, the Trinovantian king, as far as we can envisage, did exactly the same, for although there is no solid evidence for the characters Gonorilla, Regau and Cordellia, nor indeed for the complex intermarriages that were arranged for them, we can trace Dubnovellaunus at the court of Augustus around, or shortly after, 30 BC. The monumental Res Gestae, set up by the emperor in order to commemorate the achievements of his reign, records that the British King Dumnobellaunos 'sought refuge' with him. Although the circumstances of Dumnobellaunus/ Dubnovellaunus' flight from Britain do not survive, the suspicion must be that he was ousted in a palace coup, possibly orchestrated by elements from one or more of the neighbouring tribal elite. We can perhaps imagine him, just as Geoffrey of Monmouth later describes Leir, arriving exhausted from a long and tortuous journey, taking the opportunity to smarten himself up in the nearest bathhouse, before finally arriving appropriately 'dressed in royal robes' and 'equipped with royal insignia' in the hope of creating a good impression.

Ultimately we don't know what happened to Dubnovellaunus. It is possible that he lived out his final days in Rome, or in some other part of the Empire, telling anyone who would listen how he had once been a wealthy king with a large group of retainers. Perhaps he returned to Britain. That would certainly have been Augustus' hope, for he had no desire to see large numbers of refugee monarchs with their families, friends and multiple 'hangers-on' filling his capital. Better to restore them, if at all possible, to their kingdoms swiftly, in order that they may continue to promote the ideal of Empire among their people. We have noted that Augustus planned on three occasions to intervene in the affairs of Britain. Maybe he did. Maybe one such punitive action was to reinstate the fugitive Dubnovellaunus to Britain. If pro-Roman and allied leaders could be put back in power without significant loss of life, and certainly without loss of Roman life, so much the better.

Perhaps, in the description provided within the Historia Regum Britanniae of the preparations made to return Leir to Britain, Aganippus sending 'messengers throughout the whole of Gaul to summon all the men there who could bear arms' reflects the very real call to arms or the gathering together of troops for a cross-Channel adventure – a British expeditionary force designed to promote and enforce regime change. Geoffrey of Monmouth says it worked, Agannipus restoring the kingship of Britain to his father-in-law Leir. Perhaps the same was true of Dubnovellaunus who, like Leir, was able to march at the head of an army, fight his enemy, 'thus bringing them all under his dominion again'.[81]

5

LIFE WITH THE EMPIRE

The line of kings directly descended from Brutus is brought to a swift end within the Historia Regum Britanniae. After Cunedagius, whose reign Geoffrey of Monmouth equates with the founding of Rome by Romulus and Remus and also the time that 'Isaiah was making his prophesies',[1] the kings that follow are given short shrift. The story of Ferrex and Porrex, the final two, is short and violent, the bloody death of Porrex, dismembered by his deranged mother, being particularly gory.[2] The passing of the brothers marks a sad end to the line of Brutus; the civil war that follows ushers in Dunvallo Molmutius, whom we have already seen, and subsequent rise of the house of Cornwall/Cornubia (the Catuvellauni).

Belinus and Brennius

After Dunvallo Molmutius the kingdom was left in the hands of his two sons Belinus and Brennius, both of whom, the Historia Regum Britanniae tells us, were determined to inherit.[3] As before, Geoffrey of Monmouth skips over the details of the ensuing civil conflict, noting only that 'a great number of battles' were fought. Eventually the friends and advisors of the two heirs intervened and the kingdom was partitioned.

> These friends decided that the kingdom should be divided between the two of them in such a way that Belinus should be crowned king of the island and hold Loegria, Kambria and

Cornwall, he being the elder, for Trojan custom demanded that the highest office offered by the inheritance should go to him. They also decided that Brennius, on the other hand, who was the younger, should be subject to his brother but should rule Northumbria from the Humber as far north as Caithness.[4]

The accord lasted for five years until Brennius, egged on by his advisors, felt the need to make a clean break. He had, so his counsellors reminded him, 'the same nobility of birth'. Leaving for Scandinavia, Brennius married the (unnamed) daughter of Norwegian king Elsingius, hoping that an alliance would strengthen his position at home. In his absence, Belinus took the opportunity to invade Northumbria where he 'seized the cities of the people born in these parts and garrisoned them with his own men'.[5] Incensed, Brennius assembled a vast army of Norwegians and set sail for Britain. En route, however, his fleet was attacked by Ginchtalacus, king of the Danes, who 'was passionately in love with the girl whom Brennius had married'. The battle that followed was terminated by a storm that dispersed the ships, driving the Danish king and Brennius' new bride onto the Northumbrian coast and into the hands of Belinus.

When Brennius finally made it to Albany, he sent messengers to his brother requesting the safe return of his wife, threatening dire consequences if the demands were not met. In response, Belinus 'called together the entire military force of the island' and marched into Albany. Both sides met 'in a forest called Calaterium', the ensuing conflict being described by Geoffrey of Monmouth in terms of an epic struggle, the language used suggesting another lost battle-saga.

They spent the greater part of the day in their conflict, for on both sides the men who were fighting hand-to-hand were extremely brave. Much blood was shed on this side and that, and the weapons which they brandished so lustily inflicted deadly wounds. Those who were wounded where the battalions met in conflict fell to the ground as if they had been standing corn cut by the reapers' sickles.[6]

The Norwegians fled to their ships, 'their lines of battle slashed to pieces'. Belinus himself attacked them as they tried to escape 'cutting them down without pity' so that in total 'fifteen thousand men fell in that battle, and of those left alive not one thousand escaped unwounded'. Brennius fled to France leaving both his new wife and her erstwhile captor, Ginchtalacus, at the mercy of Belinus. The Danish king pledged to submit himself to Belinus, promising that, if he were allowed to depart in peace, he would provide hostages and pay an annual tribute. Belinus agreed and Ginchtalacus left for Denmark with the (still unnamed) Norwegian princess.

With his brother and rival removed, at least for the moment, Belinus took control of the entire kingdom 'from sea to sea', formally ratifying the laws that his father, Dunvallo Molmutius, had set down. Key to this was the decree that all roads leading to cities 'should have that right of sanctuary which Dunvallo had established'.[7] In order that there was no ambiguity surrounding the boundaries of said roads, Belinus set about their improvement.

He summoned workmen from all over the island and ordered them to construct a road of stones and mortar which should bisect the island longitudinally from the Cornish sea to the shore of Caithness and should lead in a straight line to each of the cities on the route. He then ordered a second road to be built, running west to east across the kingdom from the town of St Davids on the Demetian Sea over to Southampton and again leading directly to the cities in between. He built two more roads in a diagonal pattern across the island, to lead to the cities for which no provision had been made.[8]

On the face of it, this sounds like a major engineering achievement, crossing the whole of Britain with a road network stretching from its western extremities in Pembrokeshire and Cornwall to the port of Southampton and thence to the north-eastern tip of Scotland. People have of course pointed out, if it is really necessary, that this is all fantasy, no equivalent prehistoric road network ever having existed. Of course, if we break out from the twelfth-century mindset for a moment and reconfigure to the prehistoric reality to which the Historia related, an alternative presents itself. This was not a fictional pre-Roman road-building project linking every part of the British Isles, but a far more regionalized development intending to link and control a more specific area. If, as before, 'Cornwall' was in fact 'Catuvellaunia' and 'Caithness' standing in for the land of the Iceni, what we are seeing is perhaps the echo of a link, physical, political or economic, between two Iron Age tribes, one in Hertfordshire, the other in Norfolk. Mention of a highway to the west (Demetia) and south (Southampton) may further suggest an opening of communications or alliances or it may reflect a post-Roman tradition (as we shall see later) with regard to 'Demetia'.

Having established his roads, the Historia Regum Britanniae tells us that Belinus duly consecrated the highways 'in all honour and dignity', Geoffrey of Monmouth adding that if any of his readers wished to know the full details of the highway code established under Belinus, they should read the Molmutine Laws 'which the historian Gildas translated from Welsh into Latin, and which King Alfred later rewrote in the English language'.[9] Gildas, suffice to say, did no such thing, the 'Molmutine Code' remaining absent from his surviving work. Interestingly, of course, Geoffrey cannot resist another sly dig at the English legislature, claiming that the laws established under King Alfred, and much-revered by the Saxons, were merely translated or 'rewritten' from those first established by the British King Dunvallo Molmutius.

As the infrastructure of State was undergoing reform in Britain, Belinus' exiled brother was busy in Gaul, ingratiating himself with Segnius, Duke of the Allobroges. So successful was he that Segnius bequeathed the entire Dukedom to Brennius, together with the hand in marriage of his (yet again sadly unnamed) daughter. Following the death of Segnius, the new duke immediately took steps to ensure that all within his territory were content.

> He shared among them Duke Segnius' treasure, which had been hoarded since the time of his remote ancestors. What was even more attractive to the Allobroges, Brennius was most liberal in distributing food, and kept open house to everybody.[10]

This is an interesting aspect of Brennius' role as tribal leader for the 'caring and sharing' attitude described by Geoffrey of Monmouth was, as far as we can tell, exactly the sort of action expected of an Iron Age king who needed not just to simply curry favour with their own political elite, but redistribute wealth equally and fairly. Now in a position of strength, Brennius began to plot once more the downfall of his brother. Obligated by their debts of loyalty, the Allobroges agreed to support Brennius in his plan to invade Britain, and a large army was raised.

> He fitted out a fleet on the Normandy coast, put out to sea at a moment when the winds were favourable, and so landed on the island of Britain. The moment his brother Belinus learned of the coming of Brennius, he mustered the young men of his entire realm and marched forth to do battle with the invader.[11]

Fortunately for all concerned, there was no fight to the death. As Belinus and Brennius deployed their troops for close-quarter combat, their mother, the wife of Dunvallo Molmutius and former queen, Tonuuenna, brought the brothers together averting bloodshed. Disarming the soldiery on both sides, Belinus and Brennius entered the town of Trinovantum as friends. Up to this point in the narrative, the account of two brothers in competition for the throne sounds familiar, at least within the context of the Historia Regum Britanniae: the usual tale of a disputed succession followed by a disastrous period of civil war. There is, of course, far more to it for the basic framework of the Belinus/Brennius story as recounted by Geoffrey of Monmouth would have resonated with a twelfth-century Anglo-Norman audience, the tale of two brothers, their relationship, falling out and subsequent violent interaction on the battlefield reverse-replicating that which would later occur between Harold and Tostig Godwinson.

In January 1066, Edward 'the Confessor', King of England, died. Within twenty-four hours the throne had been seized by Harold Godwinson, Earl of Wessex. Harold was part of a powerful family, his brothers Gyrth, Leofwine and Tostig controlling the earldoms of East Anglia, Middlesex and Northumbria respectively. Unpopular in Northumbria, Tostig was thrown out in 1065 and sent into exile, something that, rightly or wrongly, he blamed on his brother Harold. Taking refuge first in Flanders, Tostig eventually sought sanctuary with the Scottish King Malcolm III. There he established contact with King Harold III of Norway (known to history as Harold Hardrada or 'stern-ruler'). Hardrada had a claim to the English throne via Canute, who had ruled the kingdom from 1016 to 1035 and was only too pleased to receive Tostig's delegation. Late in summer 1066, Hardrada's longships ravaged the Northumbrian coast before he and Tostig sailed up the Humber, advancing on York. Racing north with an army, Harold Godwinson was able to surprise the Norwegian forces at Stamford Bridge, a battle in which the invading army was comprehensively defeated. William of Malmesbury later observed that 'the army immediately passing over without opposition, destroyed the dispersed and flying Norwegians; King Harold and Tostig were slain'.[12] The rout was a slaughter, possibly the heaviest toll suffered by a Norse army during the Viking era.[13]

Not only does the enmity between Belinus and Brennius reverse-mirror that of Harold and Tostig Godwinson, Brennius and Tostig both losing control of possessions in Northumbria, but the desire to bring vengeance down upon their respective brothers sends both into the arms of the Norwegian king (Elsingius/Harold Hardrada). The military ambitions of Brennius and Tostig are then thwarted in their attempt to reclaim Northumbria, the invading Norse army in both cases being slaughtered almost to a man as they try to escape. Whereas Tostig is killed at Stamford Bridge in 1066, the Historia gives Brennius the opportunity to escape; the mercy shown by Harold Godwinson to Harold Hardrada's son Olaf, who is permitted to depart England in one of the remaining Viking longships, is echoed by the Belinus' treatment to Ginchtalacus, the Danish king, who returns home with his Norwegian princess.

Shifting the action to Gaul/France, Brennius then takes on the role of William 'the Bastard', Duke of Normandy. Building his forces within the tribe of the Allobroges, who were roughly centred on an area in the south of France/Switzerland, between the River Rhone and Lake Geneva, Brennius made preparations to attack. The description of him fitting out 'a fleet on the Normandy coast' then setting out 'to sea at a moment when the winds were favourable' and landing on the south coast of Britain could be taken straight from an account of the later Norman invasion of 1066. The key similarities would certainly not be lost upon an Anglo-Norman, nor indeed on a British, audience, but why would Geoffrey of Monmouth do this? What possible motive would he have, assuming there was no historical evidence for the Belinus/Brennius dispute, as it is set down in the Historia Regum Britanniae, to establish a connection between the argumentative British kings and their counterparts in the mid-eleventh century?

At a basic level, perhaps, the deeds of Belinus, first expelling a brother with strong, pro-Norwegian sentiments, before the swift march north in order to save Northumbria from an invading Norse army, equate with those of Harold Godwinson, Earl of Wessex and last king of the Saxons. Once again, it would appear, anything the English, especially the Saxon monarchy, could do, the Britons had done already – earlier and undeniably more successfully. Better still, Geoffrey's Norman readership could see that the momentous events of 1066 echoed the deeds of the British kings, possibly because, it could be argued, it was part of a divinely appointed plan; it was simply always meant to be. More significantly, perhaps, the opposing armies of Belinus and Brennius did not resolve their differences by wading in the blood of others, the dispute being resolved through words not the sword. Was this a plea by Geoffrey for reconciliation between the English and the Normans, or was it an attempt to reinforce the dangers of civil war (something that was very much in Geoffrey's mind during the political turmoil of early twelfth-century England), and the obvious benefits of peaceful conflict resolution? Perhaps it was a sly dig at the Norman aristocracy demonstrating that the Britons, however bitter their quarrel, could be reconciled while the Norman aristocracy could only take and keep their kingdom through violence and intimidation. Once again the ancient Britons were clearly superior in every way.

With an agreement made, Belinus and Brennius decided to turn their attention overseas. Like the later King William, Brennius possessed territory in France (Gaul), the tribal lands of the Allobroges in the central south-east being his through marriage. Now the British kings cast their eyes on a greater prize, Geoffrey of Monmouth noting that they intended to invade France and 'conquer all its provinces'.[14] No explanation is given for this sudden desire for territorial acquisition, unless the two brothers felt that Britain was too small a kingdom for them both. Perhaps rather than risk subdividing the homeland, Belinus felt he could help Brennius expand Allobrogian territory so that Britain and Gaul would effectively belong to one family. Perhaps this was just a continuation of the claim to French land first made by the progenitor of the British, the Trojan Brutus who had, in Book 1 of the Historia Regum Britanniae, landed in 'Aquitaine' and established the city of Tours.[15] Certainly it marks the first significant attack by the Britons upon French territory, something which many later kings, including Maximianus/Magnus Maximus, Constantine and even Arthur himself, would do. Claim to 'the provinces of France' was not peculiar to British royalty in the Historia however, for the Norman aristocracy also held significant territory on the Continent and were in an almost constant state of hostilities, armed or otherwise, with the French monarchy.

Within a year the brothers had taken control of Gaul, having 'forced all the provinces to submit'.[16] This achieved, they set their sights on Rome and, again without explanation, began plundering the cities and farms 'up and down Italy'. The two consuls of Rome, Gabius and Porsenna, immediately sued for peace, bringing 'many gifts of gold and silver' and promising an annual tribute.[17] Taking hostages, Belinus and Brennius departed, 'leading their own troops off to Germany'. No sooner were the Britons gone, Geoffrey tells us, than the Roman consuls reneged on their deal, sending aid to the German tribes in their war against the British-Allobrogian alliance. When he learned of this, Brennius 'marched towards Rome with his own armies, so that he might take vengeance on the Romans for having broken the treaty'.[18]

There is, as we've seen, much in the tale of Belinus and Brennius that is strange, obscure, and ultimately difficult to resolve. One thing is clear, however: the account of a great barbarian host sweeping down into Italy to attack Rome that we have in the Historia Regum Britanniae is actually our first verifiable historical event, the sack of Rome in 387 BC. It is also clear that, after so many anachronistic, corrupted, garbled, misplaced and misremembered individuals, cast adrift from their correct timeline and context, we also have our first historical character in the form of Brennius. Trouble is, he doesn't appear to have been remotely connected to Britain.

Brennius, or, more correctly, Brennus is the name attributed by the Roman historian Livy to the leader, or at least one of the leaders, of the Gallic tribes that threatened the cities of northern Italy in the 390s BC. In 391, a large barbarian army lay siege to Clusium (Chiusi, in Tuscany) and the citizens appealed to Rome for assistance. The Roman ambassadors sent to negotiate a truce unfortunately lost any semblance of neutrality by taking up arms against the Gauls. Blood was shed. Enraged by this act of war, so Livy tells us, the barbarian host moved south in order to attack Rome. A Roman army sent to engage and contain the enemy was defeated and, in the retreat, most drowned in the River Allia. The leader of the barbarian army, whom Livy later, almost grudgingly, admits had 'good generalship', was a man called Brennus.

After the River Allia, Rome lay undefended.

On the third day after the battle, Brennus came up to the city with his army. Finding its gates open and its walls without defenders, at first he feared a treacherous ambush, being unable to believe that the Romans were in such utter despair. But when he realised the truth, he marched in by the Colline gate, and took Rome.[19]

With all but the Capitoline Hill controlled by Brennus and the Gauls, those Romans left decided to surrender. What happened next became a defining moment for the Roman people, one which would forever shape their attitude to the northern 'barbarian' tribes of Europe.

The senate accordingly met, and the military tribunes were authorized to arrange the terms; Quintus Sulpicius conferred with the chieftain Brennus and together they agreed upon the price, one thousand pound's weight of gold – the price of a nation soon to rule the world. Insult was added to what was already sufficiently disgraceful, for the weights which the Gauls brought for weighing the metal were heavier than standard, and when the Roman commander objected the insolent barbarian flung his sword into the scale, saying 'Woe to the vanquished!' – words intolerable to Roman ears.[20]

In the account provided by the Historia Regum Britanniae, it is the treachery of the Roman consuls in sending military assistance to the German tribes that enrages the barbarian kings, Brennius marching to Rome so that he might take his vengeance.[21] Belinus, on hearing that a Roman army was planning to overtake and attack his brother, destroys them in what is clearly an echo of the Allia, pursuing the retreating legionaries 'mercilessly, never pausing in his slaughter until night came on and prevented him from completing the massacre'.[22] Joining Brennius, the joint British-Allobrogian army surrounds Rome and, after a particularly brutal siege in which the brothers execute their hostages in ever more inventive ways, the city is taken and the 'treasures of the citizens' divided up.

Master of Rome, Brennius decides to stay on in Italy, Geoffrey of Monmouth noting that 'he treated the local people with unheard-of savagery', the precise details of which he glosses over 'for the histories of Rome explain these matters'.[23] Once again, the sources actually do no such thing, the supposed reign of terror led by Brennus/Brennius being absent from all Roman histories of the Gallic invasion. Belinus, for his part, decides to return to Britain. Here, the Historia tells us, he 'governed his homeland in peace'. Having been absent for some considerable time, Belinus clearly had a lot to do.

He restored existing cities wherever they had fallen into decay and he founded many new ones. Among the others which he founded was a certain city on the bank of the River Usk, near to the Severn Sea: this was the capital of Demetia and for a long time it was called Kaerusc. When the Romans came the earlier name was dropped and it was re-named the City of the Legions, taking its title from the Roman legions who used to winter there.[24]

Geoffrey equates Kaerusc, or 'City on the Usk', with Caerleon, a town he may well have known intimately if he was indeed originally from Monmouth. There is no real evidence for a significant Iron Age settlement in or immediately around the area of the legionary fortress here, however, so it may just be empty pro-British posturing. Alternatively the primary sources used in the Historia may have been referring to an entirely different 'city' altogether. Camulodunum (Colchester), for example, was an important tribal centre in Trinovantian territory before the Roman invasion of AD 43, being overlain by a legionary fortress which itself was later converted into a city, Colonia Claudia Victriensis. Could this be the original 'Kaerusc'?

Why Belinus should be so keen to devote his attention to 'Demetia', literally the 'land of the Demetae', an Iron Age tribe that occupied an area roughly equating with Pembrokeshire in west Wales, is unclear, given that the king's main focus appears otherwise to have been central south-eastern England. This was not the only major building infrastructure project to be developed in Demetia however, for earlier in Belinus' reign, and prior to the great continental adventure with Brennius, the king had created a road 'running west to east across the kingdom from the town of St Davids on the Demetian Sea over to Southampton'.[25] Given the importance of the Welsh kingdoms in later king-lists, especially those created in the eighth and ninth centuries, this may have more to do with the back-projection of an honoured progenitor or semi-mythical founder to a part of the country that was far more significant in the immediate post-Roman period than it was in the pre-Roman Iron Age.

Moving his attention back to his capital city Trinovantum, implying that the focus of Belinus' concerns was really the territory of the Trinovantes in Essex rather than 'Troia Nova' (London) as Geoffrey of Monmouth believed, the king began another monumental building project.

> In the town of Trinovantum Belinus caused to be constructed a gateway of extraordinary workmanship, which in his time the citizens called Billingsgate, from his own name. On the top of it he built a tower which rose to a remarkable height; and down below at its foot he added a water-gate which was convenient for those going on board their ships.[26]

'Billingsgate', site of the original water gate through the Roman and medieval city wall of London, and later home to Billingsgate Market, centre of the post-medieval fish trade in England, lies at the south-eastern edge of the city on the north bank of the River Thames. The origin of the name is disputed, although, being of Old English derivation, it is very unlikely to have anything to do with a pre-Roman Belinus. Presumably this is the same sort of name-form back-projection, from person to place, that we've seen many times before in the Historia Regum Britanniae. Whether it originally was supposed to reflect a development within Camulodunum, the original 'Trinovantum', or something more specific in the later history of medieval London is unknown. More interesting, perhaps, is the fact that, having established a water gate 'of Billing', Belinus went on to stabilize the legislature of his kingdom, almost duplicating actions taken at the start of his reign.

> He ratified his father's laws everywhere throughout the kingdom, taking pleasure in the proper administration of his own justice. As a result, in his time there became available to the populace such an abundance of wealth as no previous age had ever witnessed and no subsequent era was ever to acquire.[27]

This section sounds uncannily familiar; probably because it is, for we are told by Geoffrey of Monmouth that at the start of his reign Belinus

> ... took over the kingship of the entire island from sea to sea and ratified the laws which his father had drawn up. He proclaimed that justice should be administered fairly throughout his kingdom.[28]

Later still, after hearing about Belinus' road-building project, we hear that Belinus was 'thus governing his kingdom in peace and tranquillity'.[29]

Why did Geoffrey feel the need for such obvious repetition? Surely the point of legislative ratification followed by a period of peace and prosperity under Belinus did not require hammering home so emphatically – unless, of course, the interregnum, during which time the two brothers ransacked Italy, brought considerable chaos to Britain and the eventual return of the king was in effect a second coming. Alternatively, and perhaps much more plausibly, the reason why Belinus' reign ends as it began is that Geoffrey was describing the same event, the successful administration of Belinus, albeit derived from two different sources. Taken from this perspective, aside from the period of civil instability at the beginning of his reign, Belinus' incumbency appears remarkably uneventful. True there was the invasion of Brennius and the Norwegians to deal with, then the invasion of Brennius and the Allobroges and then, after a short period, there was the invasion of Gaul, Italy, Germany and then Italy again to plan and resource but, if we take the arguments made above, we can presume that these never actually happened, at least not in the form Geoffrey describes.

The fictional invasions of France and Italy by Belinus and Brennius were important because they set the political template for future British kings in the Historia Regum Britanniae and also legitimized the military operations of the Norman monarchy against the French after the conquest of England in 1066. They also established the historical precedent that the monarchy of Britain had a legitimate claim over Rome, the religious, economic and military powerhouse for centuries to come. Similarly, the invasions of Britain by the Norwegians and then the Allobroges, both led by Brennius, and the immediate intervention by Belinus, can be interpreted as analogous to the battles later fought between Harold Godwinson and Tostig/ Harold Hardrada at Stamford Bridge and Harold Godwinson and William the Bastard at Hastings in 1066.

The deliberate appropriation of these particular campaigns by Geoffrey for his British kings not only filled out a sometimes rather Spartan timeline in the Historia, but they also proved critical to how the work was received by a twelfth-century audience. The inclusion of Brennius and Belinus turned what was, up to the end of Book 2 in the Historia Regum Britanniae, a strange and rather mysterious kingdom ruled over by a succession of long-dead monarchs, into a hard-hitting international superpower. The story of Belinus and Brennius in France, Germany and Italy made the

Historia a highly charged and politically relevant polemic against the other kingdoms, territories and peoples of medieval Europe. The fact that none of the events described actually happened was immaterial.

With the action-packed European adventure of Belinus and Brennius removed, we are left with a reign that, while not exactly dramatic, is depicted as a glorious golden age. Twice. Belinus was remembered as a 'Great King' precisely because he brought stability to a troubled succession, successfully implemented the rule of law, invested in major infrastructure projects and oversaw a period of prosperity and universal wealth. He did not, as far as we can see, originally declare an unprovoked war upon his immediate European neighbours and nor was he involved, with his putative brother, in the subjugation and destruction of Rome. These more violent elements appear to have been added to the story of a king who was remembered as being 'Great' to make him appear 'Greater' in the eyes of a medieval aristocracy used to the concept of absolute power wielded by a ruthless and divinely appointed monarch. Belinus needed to be both harsh and fair; to do this it was essential he had a brother willing to commit acts of 'unheard-of savagery'.

So, if it seems doubtful that Brennius existed, at least in the form that he appears in the Historia Regum Britanniae, where does that leave Belinus? A character called Belinus certainly appears, briefly, in the Historia Brittonum where Nennius notes that during the first invasion of Britain by Julius Caesar, the Roman 'fought with Dolobellus, the proconsul of the British king, who was called Belinus and who was the son of Minocannus who held all the islands of the Tyrrhenian Sea'.[30] Given that, as has already been established, 'Dolobellus' is likely to be the garbling of a place name rather than of a 'proconsul' or British leader, we cannot perhaps hold out much hope for the integrity of Belinus. Certainly Caesar records his primary foe in Britain as Cassibellaunus, but there is no guarantee that he was recording the name of his British adversary correctly. Perhaps Caesar got it wrong or perhaps Nennius, or another early chronicle writer, mis-transcribed the name Cassivellaunus or Cassibellaunus, shortening and simplifying it to 'Belinus' in the process.

Alternatively the textual confusion in the Historia Brittonum could have derived from a misunderstanding or misreading of other primary source material relating to the invasions of Caesar and Claudius. The name-form Belinus may therefore have derived from the mis-transcription of genuine royal names, such as that of King Cunobelinus, who is known from both British coins and from Roman written sources. Hence Suetonius, writing in the second century, notes that Adminius, a British prince and son of 'Cynobellinus king of the Britons' went over to the Roman side.[31] The relationship of prince to king is described by Suetonius in the original Latin as 'Adminius Cynobellini Britannorum regis filius', something which gets further mangled by Orosius as 'Minocynobellinus Britannorum regis filius'.[32] Given the evident corruption of the name-form, it is easy to see how it may have been thought that 'Belinus' was a real man as indeed was Minocynobellinus/Minocannus, their relationship and historical context being irrevocably garbled in the process.

That 'Cunobelinus' (or Cunobelin) existed is not in doubt. At some stage in the early first century AD, coins stamped with the name element CUN / CUNO / CUNOB / CUNOBEL / CUNOBELIN were being minted at Camulodunum (Colchester) and Verulamium (St Albans), suggesting Cunobelinus was a king of the Trinovantes or Catuvellauni (or both). As a name, Cuno-belinus seems to have meant either the cuno ('hound') of Belinos or the bel-cuno (literally 'powerful hound'). 'Cuno' could also be a diminutive suggesting 'descent from', so that Cunobelinos was the 'son/hound/puppy' of someone called 'Belinos', which would establish Belinos/Belinus as a real person within an established, if admittedly rather vague, timeline. The problem here is that the coin evidence indicates that Cunobelinus was, or at least wished to be identified as, the son of someone called Tasciovanus[33] rather than Belinus or Belinos.

Perhaps Belinus was a more distant relation claimed by a specific Iron Age dynasty. The variant name-form 'Beli Mawr' certainly figures, as the primary ancestor, in many early Welsh genealogies,[34] suggesting that he was remembered as a powerful leader. 'Mawr' (loosely translating as 'the Great') is an epithet reserved only for the most revered of ancestors, and traditionally 'Beli Mawr' appears as either the progenitor of kings or 'the prince from whom the Romans conquered Britain'.[35] The Historia Regum Britanniae establishes

Belinus as the eldest son of Dunvallo Molmutius, but the name occurs again later as the commander in chief of Cassibellaunus' army,[36] as 'Belin', the son of Ennianus and grandson of Maglo ('that mighty King of Britain who reigned fourth after Arthur'[37]) and also as King 'Heli', the son of Digueillus and father of Cassibellaunus, Lud and Nennius.[38] There is, to put it mildly, some degree of confusion here. The majority of Iron Age name-forms were incomprehensible to medieval chronicle writers and it is easy to see how an ancient name could evolve, mutate and proliferate, becoming 'Beli Mawr', the great, if contextually intangible, ancestor, in the process.

There is one further solution; just has already been suggested for Brennius (see above), the character of Belinus could originally have been a god.[39] We have already noted that the establishment of a divine origin was essential for the majority of ancient royal pedigrees. Augustus, the first emperor of Rome, could trace his family line back through Aeneas, a refugee from Troy, to the goddess Venus (Aphrodite in Greek mythology), whose father was Jupiter (Zeus), king of the gods, while the genealogical strand of many early Anglo-Saxon or Viking monarchs began with Woden/Odin, the Germanic/Scandinavian equivalent. Once Christianity became the State faith across Europe, dynastic tables were either rewritten, diverting the bloodline back via Noah and Abraham to Adam and Eve, or subtly re-edited in order to make Woden into a real person. A similar process of deity-descent within a royal pedigree being modified, in the Christian era, in order to turn a god or goddess into a more acceptable king or queen of the mortal realm, may be seen in some of the oldest Welsh pedigrees. Here, therefore, Belenos or Belinus may have begun as a super-deity, only to be altered in order to make him appear to be a genuine human progenitor, an ancient ancestor from deep-time.

Belenos/Belenus/Belinus were variant names of a pre Roman deity who appears to have been worshipped 'from the Adriatic to Scotland and as late as the beginning of the third century AD in the eastern Alps'.[40] Few Celtic deities attained a pan-European degree of veneration, most gods and goddesses of the Iron Age apparently being more localized or tribal. Although we know next to nothing of the backstory to Belenos/Belenus/Belinus, the fact that he was frequently equated with Apollo,[41] the classical sun god also associated with healing, hunting, music and poetry, suggests that he originally had some or all of these attributes. The name-form 'Belenus' itself has been interpreted as meaning 'bright' or 'brilliant'[42] and so the association with the sun was presumably the strongest within pre-Roman society. The cult of Belenus may also have been linked with Beltane/Beltene, an Iron Age solar-fire festival held in the spring.[43] As the sun god, bringer of warmth and life to the world after the cold and sterile months of winter, Belenos/Belenus/Belinus would certainly have been an appropriate royal ancestor and more than suitable explanation for the progenitor 'Beli Mawr' as he appears in a number of genealogies. It may also explain why the Historia Regum Britanniae notes that his rule was considered to have been such a golden and abundant one.

Gurguit Barbtruc

When Belinus finally died, after a long, eventful and ultimately prosperous reign, Geoffrey of Monmouth tells us that 'his body was cremated and the ash enclosed in a golden urn. The urn the citizens placed with extraordinary skill on the very top of the tower in Trinovantum which I have already described.'[44] The tower in Trinovantum had, according to the account in the Historia Regum Britanniae, been built by Belinus directly atop the water gate in Trinovantum 'called Billingsgate'.[45] We have already observed that this story appears to result, in part, as a simple back-projection of 'Billingsgate' ('Belinus' gate') in order to explain a curious London name-form. London, though, was not Trinovantum and so if there is any truth in the story of Belinus, and if he can be equated in any way with a genuine pre-Roman dynast, then it is somewhere within the territory of the Trinovantes, presumably Camulodunum (Colchester), that we should look.

At Gosbecks and Lexden, to the immediate south-west of Colchester, a religious complex and major cemetery have been recorded and partially excavated. At Lexden a burial mound, archaeologically investigated in 1924, produced a wooden chamber containing a wealth of domestic objects, furniture, a chain mail shirt, seventeen amphorae and a silver medallion of the emperor Augustus. Pottery finds suggest a date of around 15–10 BC.[46] Contrary to most discussions concerning the Lexden and Gosbecks burials, however, we do not know, and probably never will, the identity of the individuals buried there, other than to note they were aristocratic and wealthy. In any case, if the character of Belinus in the Historia had derived from early medieval attempts to 'humanise' a pre-Christian ancestor-deity, then any attempt to identify a burial place is doomed to failure. Perhaps all that can be said is that, in Geoffrey's tale of Belinus and his successors, the main focus of attention was really Trinovantum and the Trinovantes with Camulodunum as seat of pre-Roman power.

Belinus was succeed by Gurguit Barbtruc. This time the transfer of power from father to son appears to have been a peaceful one, Geoffrey of Monmouth recording that,

> He was a modest man and a wise one. In all his all his activities he imitated the deeds of his father, being himself a lover of peace and justice. When his neighbours rebelled against him, he took fresh courage from the example of his father, fought dreadful wars against them and reduced them once more to the subjection which they owed him.[47]

Once more we have an intelligent leader who strove ultimately for peace but who was prepared to destroy his enemies should they rebel or fail to pay tribute, something that, in all aspects, made him the ideal medieval monarch. Sadly, Geoffrey of Monmouth does not supply any details surrounding the rebellion against Gurguit Barbtruc, other than to note that the trouble came from his immediate neighbours. Having subjugated these local elements, Gurguit then faced a more difficult challenge from overseas.

> Among many other things it happened that the king of the Danes, who had paid tribute to Belinus while he was still alive, refused to pay it to Gurguit, saying that he owed him no allegiance. Gurguit bore this ill. He took a fleet to Denmark, fought the most frightful battles against the local inhabitants, killed the king and reduced the country to its former state of subservience.[48]

The outline story of Gurguit's reign, a 'lover of peace and justice' fighting rebellious neighbours and dealing with the troublesome

Danes, echoes the major events in that of his predecessor Belinus (if we take out the curious foreign adventure with Brennius in Italy). That could indicate that Gurguit and Belinus were originally one and the same, Geoffrey of Monmouth again perhaps employing accounts written by different people, or that the same person is being described under a different name or title. Perhaps they were even contemporaries, ruling different tribes within the same broad geographical area. Unfortunately the first part of the reign contains nothing that can really be used to tie the character of Gurguit down. The taking of a fleet to Denmark is clearly an anachronistic detail, one better suited, say, to the early eleventh century when the English and Danish kingdoms were united under king Canute, but it could represent the garbled memory of a more regional war, perhaps fought between Iron Age tribes, which Geoffrey interpolated and expanded in order to provide a more dramatic, pan-European sweep to the narrative.

The most significant event in Gurguit Barbtruc's tenure, according to Geoffrey of Monmouth, occurred when he was returning to his kingdom from Denmark via the Orkney Islands. Here he encountered thirty shiploads of refugees, men and women, led by a man called Partholoim. The newcomer asked for Gurguit's pardon, explaining that his people were called Basclenses and they were looking for a home having 'been expelled from certain regions in Spain' a year and a half ago.[49] Gurguit ordered his representatives to accompany the Basclenses to Ireland 'which at that time was a completely uninhabited desert'. Granting them free reign of Ireland, Partholoim's people 'increased and multiplied', Geoffrey adding that 'they still hold the island today'.

This story probably derived from one of the many of the Irish creation myths, akin to that of Brutus and the Trojans in Britain, that were circulating at the time Nennius compiled the Historia Brittonum. In this, we are told that,

> The Scots came from parts of Spain to Ireland. Bartholomeus was the first, with a thousand followers, both men and women, and these increased to four thousand; but a plague came upon them, and in one week they all perished, and not one of them remained.[50]

Mention of Bartholomeus/Partholoim makes it clear that this is the same story, a point underlined by Nennius and Geoffrey's perhaps rather unnecessary comment that the refugees comprised 'both men and women'. Nennius concentrates upon the quantity of migrants; Geoffrey concentrates on the total number of longships. Geoffrey's version occurs in the decades before the arrival of Julius Caesar; Nennius' version is lost in time and space. Nennius' account is also, it is fair to say, rather downbeat, Bartholomeus' expedition being wiped out through disease while Partholoim's thrives, forming the basis of the Irish race.

Having disposed of Bartholomeus, Nennius then cites further origin myths for the Irish, all of which appear to have contributed in some way to the story of Partholoim cited by Geoffrey in the Historia Regum Britanniae. First up is 'Nimeth, son of Anomen', who had 'been at sea for a year and a half' before settling in Ireland. After many years, he and his group returned to Spain.[51] Then came 'three sons of a Spanish soldier, with thirty ships and with thirty wives in each ship', neatly matching the number of vessels in Geoffrey's account. Next it was the turn of Damhoctor whose people populated parts of Ireland, the Isle of Man and Wales.[52] Finally, in a bizarre twist, no doubt taken from a Christian rewriting of Ireland's foundation mythology, Nennius explains that the region of Dal Riada in Ireland was in fact settled by the descendants of a Scythian who while in the service of Egypt, had been 'there when the Egyptians were drowned' in the pursuit of Moses. Expelled from Egypt, 'lest he should seize and occupy their land', this unnamed Scythian wandered with his family for forty-two years through Africa before settling in Spain. Eventually, with their numbers multiplied, his people came to Ireland.[53]

Quite why Geoffrey of Monmouth felt the need to insert an amalgamated series of Irish creation myths into the reign of Gurguit Barbtruc is unclear. There may have been an allusion to an Irish migration or contact with a tribe later conflated with 'the Irish' in the chronicles or king-list that he was compiling for the Historia Regum Britanniae. Alternatively he may have wished to demonstrate that the origins of the Irish did not have such a long and distinguished pedigree as the Trojans who, since the time of Brutus, had made Britain their home. As for the name 'Gurguit Barbtruc' itself, it could plausibly be a corruption of Cuno-Belinus, the early first-century king of the Trinovantes/Catuvellauni or, perhaps less convincingly, a more garbled form of Togi-dubnus/Togo-dumnus who ruled after. Either way the matter is unclear and, given the concerns already aired as to the nature of Belinus as progenitor in a number of early Welsh genealogies, the possibility must remain that Gurguit himself was also originally a deity.

Morvidus

After Gurguit Barbtruc, the reigns of the British kings race by thick and fast. Guithelin, Gurguit's son, came first, ruling 'liberally and temperately'. His wife Marcia, being 'skilled in all the arts', used her talents to invent many things, among which was a law 'called the Lex Martiana' by the Britons'.[54] This, Geoffrey of Monmouth assures us, was translated by the later English King Alfred, who called it 'the Mercian Law' in the Saxon tongue, another audacious piece of name back-projection, Mercia being a seventh- to tenth-century Saxon kingdom centred upon Tamworth in the Midlands. After Guithelin came Sisillius – presumably Sisillius II if we take Geoffrey's own list of kings at face value. At first Sisillius was too young to rule on his own, so Marcia acted as regent. After Sisillius came Kinarius, then Danius, then Morvidus.

Morvidus provides some distraction at this point. The detail of his reign has been significantly expanded beyond the simple detail provided for his immediate predecessors, something that suggests the integration of a separate myth or epic poem. Indeed the bizarre nature of the story, with its strange, supernatural ending, implies the much-repeated fable or piece of tribal folklore. His story begins with a description of his character and appearance.

> Morvidus would have been famous for his prowess had he not indulged in the most outrageous cruelty. Once he had lost his temper he spared no one, committing mayhem on the spot, if only he could lay his hands on his weapons. For all this he was handsome to look at and he distributed gifts most open-handedly. In the whole land there was no one who was as brave as he, or could resist him in a fight.[55]

This establishes Morvidus as a heroic warrior in the classic sense. He is handsome and athletic; brave and skilled in fighting. More importantly he is also generous to his supporters, distributing wealth as gifts 'most open-handedly' as Geoffrey of Monmouth recites, probably direct from source. He is also, like most combatants in Celtic art and literature, prone to 'warp spasm', the battle rage that transforms a warrior into an unstoppable fighting machine. The change in physical appearance of the soldier as they progressively work themselves up into a crazed killer 'committing mayhem' and 'sparing no one', as Geoffrey puts it, is best summed up in a single word: 'berserker'.

The berserker phase is what most Celtic warriors sought to attain prior to combat, turning themselves into a maniacal psychopath whose prowess on the battlefield could not be dulled by fatigue nor slowed by injury. A murderous, frenzied rage state was also something which, if achieved, could potentially so terrify an enemy that they would flee in disarray. Such a tactic worked to great effect the first time that Roman soldiers came face-to-face with a Gallic host at the Battle of the River Allia in 387 BC, the historian Livy noting that

> ... the main body of the army collapsed as soon as they heard the Gaulish war cry on their sides and behind them, not even waiting to see these strange warriors. They made no effort to resist, but fled in panic before they had lost a single man. None were killed in fighting, but many were cut down from behind as they fled through the crowds of their own countrymen.[56]

The berserker, capable of mowing down vast numbers of the enemy single-handed, is a popular theme in Celtic literature. It is this spasm-state, combining athletic prowess and 'outrageous cruelty' that Morvidus seems to possess and it is this that Geoffrey of Monmouth's source seems to admire in him. This is not an aspect of his personality that is being criticized, in fact it is worthy of praise; something that is self-evident in the final line, 'there was no one who was as brave as he, or could resist him in a fight'.

Having set the scene and established the character of Morvidus, the king, like any self-respecting hero, has to defend his kingdom from an external threat.

In his time a certain king of the Moriani landed in Northumbria with a strong force and began to ravage the countryside. Morvidus assembled the young men of his entire kingdom, marched forth against the invader, and met him in battle. He himself was more effective in the fight than the greater part of the army which he commanded.[57]

To some extent this sounds like a standard Celtic battle-trope: the king as defender of the realm, his individual feats of bravery being more effective on the battlefield than any of his comrades'. The name of the enemy and scale of the threat, though, are not mentioned. There is, however, a clue to the identity of the assailant and it comes from the menace as identified by Geoffrey of Monmouth: the kingdom of the 'Moriani'. The Moriani or Morini were a Belgic tribe established in the coastal districts of northern Gaul, facing Britain at the closest point between the two lands. They were mentioned by Julius Caesar on a number of occasions, not least of all when planning and conducting his military operations across the Channel in 55 BC:

Meanwhile Caesar marched the whole army into the country of the Morini, from which there was the shortest crossing to Britain, and ordered ships to assemble there from all the neighbouring districts, as well as the fleet that had been built the previous summer.[58]

On their return from Britain at the end of the campaign, two transport ships were carried to the south of the main harbour where the rest of the Roman force was disembarking. Here they were immediately attacked.

The Morini, whom Caesar had compelled to make peace before setting out for Britain, thought they saw a chance of obtaining booty and surrounded them, at first with only a small force, bidding them lay down their weapons if they did not want to be killed.[59]

On hearing what was happening, Caesar dispatched his fast-moving cavalry, who attacked the tribesmen, the Morini throwing away their arms and 'suffering very heavy casualties'. Not content with this show of force, Caesar dispatched his infantry into the marshes 'against the Morini', with most subsequently falling into his hands.[60] In the bigger picture of Caesar's narrative of campaigns in Gaul, Germany and Britain, the tribe of the Morini play a relatively small but not insignificant part. Their involvement in Caesar's first invasion of southern Britain was, however, a detail picked up on by later writers. Bede, for example, when summarizing Caesar's campaign, notes that the general 'entered the province of the Morini, from which is the nearest and quickest crossing into Britain. Here he assembled about eighty transports and galleys, and crossed into Britain, where his forces suffered a fierce battle.'[61]

If we are trying to find a 'king of the Moriani' who attacked the coastal districts of Britain with 'a strong force and began to ravage the countryside', then there is really only one candidate: Julius Caesar. So, Caesar didn't land his troops 'in Northumbria' as the Historia Regum Britanniae states the king of the Moriani did, but then secure geographical placement is not the Historia's strongpoint, many known place names and established sites having been irrevocably garbled in the final narrative. If one were invading from the land of the Moriani/Morini, through the Pas-de-Calais/Strait of Dover, Northumbria would be a strange place to land in any case. The way in which the invader is described, with no name being provided, suggests a deliberate attempt at obfuscation, if not by Geoffrey of Monmouth then certainly in the accounts which he used to compile the Historia. Mention of a Caesar-like name for the attacker, or indeed a more clear association with the Roman legions, would undoubtedly have caused consternation, creating further narrative confusion (if that were possible), Rome invading yet again, the results being similar to before. Whether it was Geoffrey himself who made the edit, or whether it was made by an earlier account writer, one key element of the original story remained intact: the assailants derived from the land of the Moriani/Morini.

Equating the unnamed foe with Julius Caesar raises a number of intriguing issues with regard to the identity of the British King Morvidus. No such individual is named in either Caesar's primary account of the war in Britain nor the multiple subsequent versions that we find in accounts by Bede, Nennius or Geoffrey of Monmouth. Given the nature of the name-form 'Morvidus', together with both the evident warrior prowess of the king as he appears in the Historia Regum Britanniae, almost single-handedly taking on the invaders from the land of the Moriani/Morini, there can really be only one identifiable candidate: Mandubracius.

Mandubracius, as we have seen, was a key player in the strategy of Caesar during his second campaign in Britain in 54 BC. As a leader of the Trinovantes, or Trinobantes as Caesar calls them, it was Mandubracius' surrender to Caesar that resulted in the collapse of the anti-Roman coalition under Cassivellaunus. As Androgeus, however, Mandubracius plays a much more significant role in the Historia Regum Britanniae as the strong-willed hero who decides that, for the good of his people, he will side with Caesar against the tyrant Cassibellaunus. It is Androgeus' decisive attack upon Cassibellaunus' troops at the Battle of 'Durobernia' that wins the war for the Romans, Cassibellaunus suing for peace through the intermediary of the Trinovantian king. When Androgeus comes before Caesar he does so from a position of strength, stating bluntly, 'Cassibellaunus is beaten, and, with my help, Britain is in your hands. What more do I owe you?' The more overtly Catuvellaunian sources employed by Geoffrey of Monmouth do not, of course, paint Androgeus/Mandubracius in such a positive light. Androgeus, 'Duke of Cornwall', has only a minor role to play in the Battle of 'Dorobellum' against Caesar, apparently fighting on the side of Cassibellaunus. In this battle it is Cassibellaunus' army that triumphs, mostly due to the extraordinary bravery of the king's brother Nennius who, in a berserker-like rage, slaughters his way through the Roman front line. Caesar, fleeing to his ships, was 'glad enough to make the sea his refuge'.[62]

The character of Morvidus in the Historia Regum Britanniae seems at first to have been inspired by the pro-Trinovantian account, the king being portrayed in the classic mould of a Celtic warrior-hero whose independent action saves the kingdom. There are also evidently traces of the more negative pro-Catuvellaunian view creeping into the narrative, Morvidus being described as having 'indulged in the most outrageous cruelty', sparing no one. Evidence for this darker side of his temperament is soon provided in the Historia for, following the victory over the forces of the king of the Moriani Morvidus took his revenge.

> Once he had proved victorious not a soul was left alive whom he did not slaughter, for he ordered them all to be dragged before him in turn and he satiated his lust for blood by killing them all one by one. When he became so exhausted that he had to give up for a time, he ordered the remainder to be skinned alive and in this state he had them burnt.[63]

His sadistic tendencies now out in the open, a particularly bizarre incident occurred which suddenly and dramatically terminated the reign of Morvidus:

> A monster of unheard-of savageness appeared from the direction of the Irish Sea and began to devour one after the other all those who lived on the neighbouring sea-coast. As soon as this news reached the ears of Morvidus, he went to meet the monster and fought with her single-handed. When he had used all his weapons against her without effect, she rushed at him with her jaws wide open and swallowed him up as though he had been a tiny fish.[64]

In one way the story of the battle between Morvidus and the sea monster seems ridiculous, a clearly mythical element inserted into the narrative. There may be an explanation, however. The story of Morvidus and the sea monster may have been allegory, a metaphorical tale hiding a deeper meaning or a literary device making sense of a genuine event from deep-time, filtered through the storytellers and bards of the post-Roman era in order to make it more comprehensible to a later audience. If Morvidus was indeed a corrupted form of the name (and character) of Mandubracius, is there anything from his story that can help us identify the nature and context of the sea monster?

Julius Caesar tells us nothing of the ultimate fate of the British prince Mandubracius. The Historia Regum Britanniae, however, confidently asserts that when Cassibellaunus died, six years after the war of 54 BC, Tenvantius was crowned king because 'Androgeus himself had gone off to Rome with Caesar'.[65] Had he actually left 'with Caesar', as the general departed the shore of Britain, would the Trinovantes have seen their man 'swallowed up' by the creature from the sea, never to return? Is it possible that, in the imaginatively distorted perspective of the storytellers, Julius Caesar, a brutal Roman warlord who brought death to southern Britain, became a savage sea monster who devoured 'all those who lived on the neighbouring sea-coast'? Stranger things have certainly happened in the early literature and folklore of Ireland, Cornwall and Wales. If Caesar was indeed the prototype for the horror that befell the coastal fringes of Morvidus' kingdom, however, quite why he became a female sea monster is unclear.

With the psychopathic Morvidus lost to the sea, power in the kingdom of Britain passed, according to the Historia Regum Britanniae, to his eldest son Gorbonianus. Gorbonianus is one of a number of monarchs whose reign is dealt with swiftly by Geoffrey of Monmouth. As a consequence we hear little about the man or his achievements other than the most basic of details.

> At that time there was no man alive who was more just than he or a greater lover of equity, and none who ruled his people more frugally. Throughout the whole of his life it was his custom to pay due honour to the gods and to insist upon common justice for his people. In all the cities in the realm of Britain he restored the temples of the gods and he also built many new ones. As long as he lived a great abundance of wealth flooded into the island, such, indeed, as was enjoyed by none of the neighbouring countries.[66]

For 'neighbouring countries' think neighbouring tribes. The Trinovantes/Catuvellauni were both prospering. Adjacent tribes, perhaps with a far less profitable trade deal with the Mediterranean, were evidently not doing so well. Following his death, Gorbonianus, so the Historia tells us, was buried at Trinovantum, perhaps affirming once again that this was the tribe to whom he ultimately owed allegiance.

Gorbonianus was succeeded by his brother Archgallo, second son of Morvidus, who, after displaying some of the less pleasant tendencies of his father, was deposed by the 'leaders of the realm'.[67] Elidurus, another son of Morvidus, was elected king, later acquiring the epithet 'the dutiful' by passing the crown back to the reformed Archgallo. When Archgallo fell into a coma, Elidurus became king for a second time. His reign was short, however, two more brothers – Peredurus and the wonderfully named Ingenius – seizing power and dividing the kingdom. When Ingenius died, Peredurus inherited the entire kingdom and, upon his death, Elidurus was released from prison to reclaim the crown.

Little in the way of interpretation can be supplied here. The transfer of power among the sons of Morvidus is convoluted and somewhat difficult to follow, possibly reflecting the reality of a disputed royal succession. Perhaps in the story of Archgallo's exile we see an echo of the banishment of Adminius/Amminus to Rome in AD 40 (see below). Perhaps in the division of the kingdom into territories controlled by Ingenius and Peredurus we see the parcelling-up of land by the Catuvellauni and Trinovantes, two groups interconnected through marriage and other forms of socio-political bonding. Perhaps the whole tale of a family torn apart was derived from folklore or a myth concerning the gods, as has already been suggested for Belinus/ Belenos. Possibly it was all an allusion to the succession crisis that was starting to destabilize England in 1135. Although 'the Anarchy' that followed the death of Henry I was only just beginning when Geoffrey of Monmouth wrote the Historia, the dangers of civil war and the benefits of reconciliation would perhaps have been foremost in his mind.

Whatever the reality of the situation, the origin of the 'sons of Morvidus' story as presented in the Historia Regum Britanniae will not detain us here. Neither will the reigns of successive monarchs Marganus, Enniaunus, Idvallo, Runo, Gerennus, Catellus, Millus, Porrex, Cherin, Fulgenius, Edadus, Andragius, Urianus, Eliud, Cledaucus, Clotenus, Gurgintius, Merianus, Bledudo, Cap, Oenus, Sisillius, Beldgabred, Archmail, Eldol, Redon, Redechius, Samuil, Penessil, Pir, Capoir or Digueillus, all of which are cited in quick succession as if culled by Geoffrey from a genealogical table or

Above: 1. Devil's Dyke, Wheathampstead, Hertfordshire. This impressive earthwork probably defined the limits to the capital of Cassivellaunus (Cassibellaunus, the eighty-first king in the *Historia Regum Britanniae*), taken by Julius Caesar in the expedition of 54 BC.

Below left: 2. Roman legionaries from a late second-century BC monument found at the Campo Marzio in Rome and now in the Louvre, Paris. This provides an idea of how the soldiers in Caesar's army would have looked as they campaigned in southern Britain.

Below right: 3. A damaged marble portrait of Julius Caesar from the sanctuary of Athena at Priene, Turkey and now in the British Museum, London.

4. Silver unit of Dubnovellaunus, probably the same king recorded as seeking shelter in Rome by the emperor Augustus. The figure, possibly a portrait of the king himself, is wearing an elaborate crown. Is this the ornate headgear that the HRB says was worn by Dunvallo Molmutius, the twenty-first king? © Chris Rudd www.celticcoins.com.

5. Gold stater of Addedomarus, meaning 'great in chariots', the first ruler north of the Thames to add his name to coinage. In the Trioedd Ynys Prydein he appears as Aedd Mawr, founding father of the Britons and in the HRB as Rud Hud Hudibras (the ninth king). © Chris Rudd www.celticcoins.com.

6. Augustus, first emperor of Rome; a plaster cast, now in the Ashmolean Museum, Oxford, of a marble portrait found at Prima Porta, near Rome. The original was made around 20 BC, when Augustus was heavily involved in the political affairs of Britain.

Above: 7. The Bath Gorgon, an image of Medusa from the pediment of the great temple to Sulis Minerva, constructed in the latter third of the first century AD. Did the fall of this building provide the inspiration for the famous flying accident of King Bladud (the tenth king)?

Right: 8. Bronze head of a goddess, almost certainly Sulis Minerva herself, from the religious complex at Bath, Somerset. Minerva was the Roman deity associated with wisdom and healing, whilst Sulis, it would appear, was her Iron Age equivalent: the native goddess of the hot spring.

9. Gold stater of Tasciovanus, a name which may mean 'Killer of Badgers', who styles himself as RICON, the British equivalent of REX. It may be the title had a specific meaning, implying over-lordship of more than one tribe. The cavalryman on the reverse is depicted wearing chainmail. © Chris Rudd www.celticcoins.com.

Above: 10. Ludgate Hill, London, looking west towards Fleet Street, from the top of St Paul's Cathedral. Despite the popularity of the story linking Lud, the eightieth king, with Ludgate, this seems to be no more than the back-projection of a personal name in order to explain a place.

Below: 11. Gold stater of Cunobelinus with an ear of corn, representing fertility and prosperity, set within 'Camv' for Camulodunum (Colchester). The name of the king appears on the reverse beneath the horse. © Chris Rudd www.celticcoins.com.

Above: 12. Bronze unit of Amminus, struck at DVNO, possibly Canterbury in Kent. Amminus is almost certainly the same character as Adminius who is recorded as seeking refuge with the emperor Caligula in AD 40 and Lelius Hamo who returned to Britain in the HRB. © Chris Rudd www.celticcoins.com.

Right: 13. Portrait of the emperor Claudius now in the Louvre, Paris. Claudius initiated the Roman invasion of Britain in AD 43 and received the surrender of eleven British kings at Camulodunum (Colchester).

Below: 14. Gold ring from Fishbourne, West Sussex with the name Tiberius Claudius Catuarus (reversed for use as a seal-stamp). We know nothing about Catuarus, although his name-form suggests a native leader made into a Roman citizen by the emperor Claudius. © Sussex Archaeological Society.

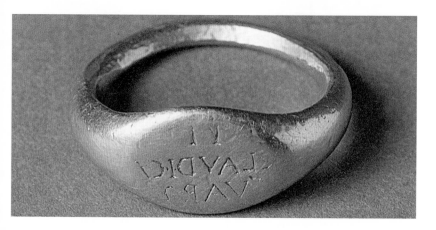

Above: 15. A monumental early twentieth-century statue of 'Boadicea' (Boudicca) by Westminster Bridge, London. Although she features briefly in the HRB with the corrupted name-form Sodric, today Boudicca is arguably the most famous of all British Iron Age monarchs.

Below: 16. The Balkerne Gate, Colchester. Although later incorporated into a city wall, the gate was originally part of a free-standing monumental arch, possibly erected around AD 50 to commemorate the creation of Colonia Claudia Victricensis, the 'city of Claudius' victory', on top of the Iron Age centre of Camulodunum. © Stuart Laycock.

Above: 17. A section of Hadrian's Wall near Housesteads, established by the emperor to mark the northern limit of Britannia in AD 122. The wall does not feature much in the Historia Regum Britanniae, Geoffrey of Monmouth following earlier writers by attributing its construction to Septimius Severus.

Below left: 18. Marble portrait of the emperor Septimius Severus, found in Alexandria, Egypt, and now in the British Museum. Cited by Nennius as the third leader of the Romans to come to Britain, Severus died in AD 211 at York after campaigning against the Caledonian tribes.

Below right: 19. Marble portrait of the emperor Antoninus (Caracalla) from Rome, now in the British Museum, made between AD 215 and 217. Remembered as 'Bassianus', the eighty-ninth king in the HRB, the eldest son of Septimius Severus did not, in reality, stay long in Britain following the death of his father.

20. Bronze coin of Allectus, emperor of Britain AD 293–6. In the HRB, Allectus is a man sent from Rome to kill Carausius 'and restore the kingdom of Britain to the domination of Rome' who becomes the ninety-first king. History suggests he was a subordinate of Carausius who staged a palace coup. © Trustees of the British Museum.

21. A gold coin of Magnus Maximus, remembered by Gildas as a tyrant, by Nennius as both the sixth and seventh emperor to rule Britain and by Geoffrey of Monmouth as Maximianus, the ninety-ninth king. He also appears as Macsen Wledig in early Welsh tradition. © Trustees of the British Museum.

22. A modern statue set up to commemorate Constantine the Great, proclaimed emperor at York in AD 306. Constantine is remembered in the HRB as the ninety-fifth king.

23. The interior of Segontium, a Roman fortress of Caernarfon, Gwynedd. Although built in the late AD 70s as a springboard to attack and control Anglesey, the site has a close association in legend with Macsen Wledig, who journeys here to find Elen of the Hosts, literally the woman of his dreams.

24. The Valle Crucis pillar (pillar of Eliseg). Set up in the early ninth century by Concenn, ruler of Powys, the inscription traces Concenn's lineage back to Sevira, wife of Guarthigirn (Vortigern) and daughter of 'Maximus the king' (Magnus Maximus). Genealogical tables linking British royalty to a Roman progenitor were an essential part of legitimising the position of the king, demonstrating his right to rule.

25. The *Hugin*, a reconstruction longship originally sailed from Denmark to Britain in 1949 to celebrate the 1,500th anniversary of the traditional landing of Hengest and Horsa in Kent (according to the Anglo-Saxon Chronicle).

Above: 26. The Iron Age hillfort of Dinas Emrys, Gwynedd, where tradition places Vortigern (the 103rd king), the young Aurelius Ambrosius (later confused with Merlin) and the story of two fighting dragons. The fortress was reused in the post-Roman period and modified in the thirteenth century, possibly by Llywelyn the Great, deliberately appropriating a site with strong mythic associations.

Below: 27. Stonehenge, Wiltshire. The first, locally sourced sarsens were set up around 2500 BC, the inner bluestone setting slightly later. The site is associated in the HRB with the coronation of Aurelius Ambrosius (the 104th king)

Above: 28. Excavations conducted at Stonehenge by Bournemouth University indicate that the bluestones were significantly modified in the sub- and post-Roman period. It is possible that the tale of the 'Giant's Ring', as it appears in the HRB, relates to this particular phase of architectural alteration.

Below: 29. The northern wall of Anderitum, a late Roman fortress at Pevensey, East Sussex, incorporating a well-preserved projecting tower. Originally built during the reign of Carausius (ninetieth king in the HRB) around AD 290, the fort remained serviceable into the post-Roman period.

Above: 30. A section of the south-west facing Roman fort wall of Anderitum at Pevensey. The Anglo-Saxon Chronicle records the storming of Andredescester by Aelle in AD 491. It is likely that the original story related to Ambrosius Aurelianus (Aurelius Ambrosius) and his war with Vortigern that was fought out here.

Below: 31. Tintagel, Cornwall. The HRB claims this was the castle of Gorlois, Duke of Cornwall, and that Arthur was conceived here when Uther (the 105th king) seduced Ygerna, Gorlois' wife. Tintagel was certainly an important sixth-century port and was probably controlled by a post-Roman business entrepreneur or warlord.

Above: 32. In an attempt to appropriate the stories of Arthur, Tristan and Yseult, Earl Richard of Cornwall built a mock-antiquated house at Tintagel in the 1230s. Richard was entranced by folklore and keen to establish himself as the obvious heir to earlier British heroes.

Below: 33. The Multangular Tower at the south-western corner of the fourth-century Roman legionary fortress of Eboracum at York. In the HRB, Arthur (the 106th king) fights his first battle against the Saxon leader Colgrin at the River Douglas, just outside York, before laying siege to the city.

Above: 34. In the HRB, Arthur attacks the Saxons, who were besieging the city of Bath, slaughtering them in the battle of Kaerbadum (Mount Badon). Earlier in the sixth century, Gildas had credited the victory to Ambrosius Aurelianus, the 'last of the Romans'.

Below: 35. The legionary amphitheatre of Isca, Caerleon in Gwent. Caerleon may have been wel known to Geoffrey, if he was originally from Monmouth. It is here, in 'the City of the Legions', that the HRB says Arthur established a plenary court where he placed 'the crown of the kingdom on his head'.

36. A fifth-century gravestone at Nevern, Pembrokeshire. This is one of a number of post-Roman inscriptions from Wales providing dynastic information as well as evidence for the survival of Latin names and phrases. This example cites Vitaliani Emerito ('Vitalianus Emeritus').

Above: 37. An early sixth-century commemorative stone or grave marker from Castell Dwyran, now in Carmarthenshire Museum. The inscription reads Memoria Voteporigis Proctictoris ('in memory Voteporigis / Voteporix the Protector'). It has been suggested that this was Vortipor 'tyrant of the Demetae' mentioned by Gildas, and Vortiporius, the 109th king in the HRB.

Below: 38. The southern wall of Portchester, Hampshire, one of the best-preserved Roman fortresses in western Europe. According to the Anglo-Saxon Chronicle, the kingdom-building activities of Cerdic and Cynric, progenitors of the House of Wessex, began here. If Cerdic is the same as Keredic (king 111 in the HRB), however, then the kingdom of Wessex requires re-evaluation.

king-list. When Heli, the son of Digueillus, ascends to the throne, Geoffrey's increasingly break-neck narrative takes a pause, the story becoming once more fleshed out with detail.

Lud

Heli, who may perhaps be equated with Beli Mawr, the shadowy progenitor appearing in many early Welsh genealogies, had three sons according to the Historia Regum Britanniae: Lud, Cassibellaunus and Nennius. Lud, the eldest, became king on his father's death.

> He was famous for his town-planning activities. He re-built the walls of the town of Trinovantum and girded it with innumerable towers. He ordered the citizens to construct their homes and buildings there in such a style that no other city in the most far-flung of kingdoms could boast of palaces more fair. Lud was a warrior king, lavish in arranging feasts. However many other cities he might possess, this one he loved above all and in it he passed the greater part of each year. As a result it was afterwards called Kaerlud and then, as the name became corrupted, Kaerlundein.[68]

Geoffrey of Monmouth tells us that Lud was the brother of Cassibellaunus and thereafter the father of two sons, Androgeus and Tenvantius. Androgeus we have already met and have shown that he can be equated with the character of Mandubracius whom Julius Caesar describes as a prince of the Trinovantes. Tenvantius can also be attested as a genuine figure from history, albeit one recorded solely from coin evidence as Tasciovanus. With characters from the pages of the Historia Regum Britanniae set at last in context, what, if anything, can we say about the ancestry of Mandubracius and Tasciovanus?

Tasciovanus does not appear to have recorded his dynastic line on those coins that bear his name, although his sons Epaticcus and Cunobelinus certainly established their lineage from him, stamping certain issues with TASC F/TASCI F and TASCIOVANI F or Tasciovanus Filius (son of Tasciovanus). Mandubracius, as far as we can tell, did not mint any coins at all although there is a passing reference to his immediate ancestry in the pages of de Bello Gallico, where in certain editions of Caesar's commentaries there exists the extended line:

> In the meantime, the Trinobantes, almost the most powerful state of those parts, from which the young man, Mandubratius embracing the protection of Caesar had come to the continent of Gaul to him, whose father, Imanuentius, had possessed the sovereignty in that state, and had been killed by Cassivellaunus; he himself had escaped death by flight, send ambassadors to Caesar, and promise that they will surrender themselves to him and perform his commands.[69]

Reference to 'Imanuentius', the father of Mandubracius, is not given in all versions of de Bello Gallico, it being just one of a number of differences, inconsistencies and variant forms within the surviving manuscripts. In the majority of modern translations, the detail surrounding Imanuentius is omitted, leaving the reasons for Mandubracius' animosity towards Cassivellaunus unclear. As early as 1967, David Ellis Evans argued that the name-form appearing in variant transcriptions was perfectly sound and that Imanuentius, together with alternative spellings Inianuuetitius, Inianuuetutus and Imannuetitius, was in all likelihood genuine.[70] Unfortunately not everyone has followed Ellis Evans' advice in this matter. If Caesar did indeed record the correct name-form of Mandubracius' father, as well as noting his fate at the hands of Cassivellaunus, can the Lud described in the Historia Regum Britanniae actually be the same character?

It is possible, considering the focus given by the Historia to Lud's remodelling of Trinovantum, that the account of his reign does indeed relate to that of a genuine Trinovantian king. Camulodunum, as opposed to Geoffrey of Monmouth's Troia Nova, was the political, religious and economic heart of the Trinovantes tribe. The term 'territorial oppida' has been applied by archaeologists to such sites in the British Later Iron Age, especially those where extensive, if discontinuous, linear earthworks define the outer edges of settlements. Territorial oppida are to be found in relatively low-lying areas of southern Britain, places where the hill forts of the early and middle Iron Age appear to have died out, often possessing complex systems of banks and ditches which define and demarcate vast blocks of the landscape.

Camulodunum represents a notable example of the territorial oppidum, the largest of its kind in Britain, the earthwork systems, or dykes, partially enclosing an area of just over 32 sq. km. There have been relatively few extensive surveys of the interior, but it seems that only a small number of areas defined were in any way intensively settled. At Sheepen, to the west of the later Roman town, an area of Iron Age settlement associated with industrial activity, coin manufacture and exotic Roman imports has been located, while at Gosbecks and Lexden to the south-west, a religious complex and major cemetery have also been recorded.[71] It is difficult to say precisely when the oppidum was founded. The banks and ditches, or 'dykes', that defined its outer limits seem to have undergone multiple phases of rebuilding and modification throughout the latter half of the first century BC and early years of the first century AD. Certainly the name Camulodunum appears as CAM/CAMVL on coins of Tasciovanus, probably from around 20 BC,[72] so the site must have not only have been in existence by then but presumably was also well-developed.

The earthwork systems of Camulodunum comprise, in total, over 12 miles of earthen bank fronted by a deep, V-shaped ditch. As noted, they did not fully enclose a specific area, instead running transversely in a north–south direction, the majority facing west, towards the Catuvellauni, presumably the direction of expected attack. Although there does not seem to be an overall masterplan to the system, their intensification over time, creating 'an impossible obstacle for chariots and a formidable one for warriors on horseback',[73] suggests they were vital for the long-term survival of both centre and tribe. Given their size and scale, it is perhaps unsurprising that their construction and modification would have been celebrated and, no doubt, commemorated in song and verse. Could one particular phase of earthwork elaboration have inspired the story, as it came down to the Historia Regum Britanniae, of Lud rebuilding 'the walls of the town of Trinovantum' and girding them 'with innumerable towers'?

To take the argument further, can this burst of construction and development at Camulodunum really be echoed in the life and reign of Lud (Imanuentius / Inianuuetitius / Inianuuetutus / Imannuetitius), father of Androgeus (Mandubracius) and Tenvantius (Tasciovanus) as celebrated in the Historia Regum Britanniae? If Geoffrey of Monmouth believed Trinovantum to be New Troy or Troia Nova, then its subsequent name change to 'London' required explanation. 'Kaerlundein', as Geoffrey calls it, was simply a back-projection of 'Lud', a name-form created specifically in order to justify the later name of the capital: 'Lud's city'. Certainly it is utilised within the Historia in order to explain a specific area of London: 'When Lud died his body was buried in the above-named city, near to the gateway which in the British tongue is still called Porthlud after him, although in Saxon it bears the name Ludgate.'[74]

Ludgate was the name given to the westernmost entrance in the circuit of London's Roman and medieval city wall. Although the gate itself was torn down in 1760, its name survives today in Ludgate Hill, Ludgate Street and Ludgate Circus in the area between St Paul's Cathedral and Fleet Street. The etymology of the name Ludgate is uncertain, but suggestions have been made for 'ludgeat', meaning postern entrance or 'back gate' or, more simply, 'flood gate'.[75] Either way 'Lud's Gate' seems unlikely. We have already observed that the oppidum of the Trinovantes at Colchester, the Trinovantum of the Historia, had, by the latter half of the first century BC, the name Camulodunum (the 'fortress of Camulos') and that Kaerlud/ Kaerlundein could actually have derived from a distorted remembrance of the original name-form Camu-LOD-unum. If so, then Lud as a specific king simply did not exist, although Imanuentius, as the rebuilder of Trinovantum/Camulodunum, certainly may have done.

Where then did the idea of 'Lud', the rebuilder of Trinovantum and father to Androgeus and Tenvantius have come from? Lludd is the central hero in the story of Cyfranc Lludd a Llefelys, which appears in the Mabinogion, the collective name given to a collection of early Welsh tales first written down in the fourteenth century. In this, Llud is one of the four sons of Beli Mawr (Beli the Great), the others being Caswallon, Nyniaw and Llefelys. Caswallon and Nyniaw can be equated with the Cassibellaunus and Nennius appearing in the Historia Regum Britanniae, but Llefelys appears to be otherwise unknown.[76]

In the tale of Cyfranc Lludd a Llefelys, Lludd inherits the kingdom following the death of Beli, ruling successfully, renewing the walls of Caer Ludd. So far, so Geoffrey of Monmouth. When Llefelys hears that the king of France has died without a male heir, he decides to marry the king's daughter and take possession of the kingdom. Lludd agrees to help and the two travel to France where the match is made. On returning to Britain, Lludd finds his kingdom to be afflicted by three plagues. The first involves the arrival of the Coraniaid, a race of people who could not be defeated because they were able to hear any conversation on the wind. The second plague was a scream that rang out every May Day, piercing people's hearts, causing women to miscarry, and leaving the animals, trees, earth and water barren. The third involved the mysterious loss of all provisions from the king's courts. With Llefely's help the plagues are resolved: the Coraniaid with 'powerful water' containing crushed insects that poisoned them; the scream emanating from two fighting dragons, both of which are caught and buried; the third the result of an enchanter who is discovered and overcome. With his kingdom freed, Ludd ruled in peace and prosperity.[77] The tale of the dragons is referred to directly in the Trioedd Ynys Prydein (the Triads of the Island of Britain) as part of Triad 37, the Three Concealments and Three Disclosures of the Island of Britain.[78]

It has been suggested that the name and character of Lludd as it appears in the Mabinogion and other early Welsh sources reflects the pre-Roman deity Nodens and possibly also the Irish Nuadu Argatlam (Nuadu 'of the silver hand'), Lludd/Lud and Nudd being interchangeable.[79] Little is really known about Nodens, although he seems to have been equated with the Roman deity Mars, probably in his healing and protective aspects, and also with Silvanus, the Roman god of woodlands.[80] At Lydney in Gloucestershire, a healing sanctuary and associated pilgrimage centre dating to the third century AD has been archaeologically examined,[81] the key attributes of the deity, chiefly fish, sea monsters and anchors, all associating him with fishing and the ocean.[82] Identification of Androgeus/Mandubracius as the 'son of Lud/Lludd', if Lud were indeed equated with a Celtic god, may have had more to do with establishing a semi-divine ancestry than the reality of paternal lineage.

Taking the Lud/Lludd/Nudd/Nodens association further, John Koch has argued that the origins of Lud as father of Androgeus story may, alternatively, have derived from more negative associations. The tradition of the Irish Nuadu Argatlam/Nodens Argantolamos (Nuadu/ Nodens of the silver hand), he observes, is that of a 'divine king who undergoes maiming, disqualification from kingship, and oppression of his kingdom', something which could further correspond with the three plagues as described in Cyfranc Ludd a Llefelys. To call Androgeus/Mandubracius a son of Lludd could, therefore, potentially 'identify him as the mortal counterpart of the victim god' ruling a plague-ridden wasteland.[83] Certainly there is a degree of negativity surrounding the tradition of Mandubracius in both the Mabinogion and the Trioedd Ynys Prydein where as Manawydan 'son of Llyr Half Speech' he is described as a prostrate chieftain, one of three leaders who 'would not seek a dominion and nobody could deny it to them'.[84] Whatever the reasons for establishing Lud as son of Heli, brother of Cassibellaunus and Nennius, king of Trinovantum and, ultimately, father of Androgeus and Tenvantius in the Historia Regum Britanniae, it would seem that he is more likely to represent another example of a divine progenitor.

Cassibellaunus

With the death of King Lud, so the Historia Regum Britanniae tells us, there were concerns regarding a potential succession crisis, his two sons, Androgeus and Tenvantius, being too young to govern.

> Lud's brother Cassibellaunus was preferred in their stead. As soon as he was crowned king he gained such high esteem for his bounty and his prowess that his fame was spread abroad through far-distant kingdoms. As a result the kingship of the entire realm came into his hands, instead of into those of his nephews. However, Cassibellaunus had such a sense of family solidarity that he did not wish the young men to be cut off from the kingship, and he allowed a large share of his realm to the two of them. He granted the town of Trinovantum and the duchy of

Cantia to Androgeus; and to Tenvantius he gave the duchy of Cornubia. Cassibellaunus himself remained in authority over both of them and over the princes of the entire island, for he was the overlord by virtue of his crown.[85]

Intriguingly, no reference is made by Geoffrey of Monmouth to the killing of Mandubracius' father, whom Caesar, in certain manuscript versions of de Bello Gallico, calls Imanenetius (see above). The account preserved within the Historia implies that the transmission of power from Lud to his brother Cassibellaunus was relatively smooth, the new king acting as regent and protector for the Lud's two young sons. As overking controlling, as Geoffrey puts it, 'the entire realm', Cassibellaunus appears a beneficent monarch, granting his two young nephews the town of Trinovantum/London and the duchy of Cantia/Kent to Androgeus and Cornubia/Cornwall to Tenvantius because he had a 'sense of family solidarity'. This could potentially indicate that Caesar's version, describing the murder of Imanenetius and the forcible takeover of his land by Cassivellaunus, was false; a piece of negative propaganda designed to demonise his British foe.

Alternatively, the account preserved within the Historia Regum Britanniae could simply have derived from an overtly positive spin on the character of Cassivellaunus, established later by his supporters and descendants. After all, Geoffrey of Monmouth had earlier commented that Lud refashioned the city of Trinovantum having 'seized command of the government of the kingdom' – from whom is not explained – before renaming it 'Kaerlud, or Lud's city', leading to a bitter quarrel with his second brother, Nennius.[86] This particular family dispute, which suggests that all was not well in the 'House of Heli', is never mentioned again. It does, however, hint at the possibility that variant sources, each with a different point of view, were gathered together and made to fit the single overarching narrative of the Historia. We have already seen that multiple contradictory perspectives on the character of an individual can sit side by side in Geoffrey's account, not least with regard to the hero/tyrant Cassibellaunus. Perhaps Cassibellaunus/Cassivellaunus did indeed murder the father of Androgeus/Mandubracius, forcing the young prince to obtain

Caesar's help, this particular version of events being suppressed in the more pro-Cassivellaunian account that survived to Geoffrey's day.

In the version that is presented in the Historia Regum Britanniae, the kingdom that Cassibellaunus acquires is, of course, equated with 'Britain', Trinovantum or London, Cornubia or Cornwall and Cantia or Kent being three disparate elements within the greater whole of the State. The prehistoric reality, however, if we take the arguments already provided, was something altogether different. Androgeus (Mandubracius), presumably the elder nephew, gained control of the Trinovantes (Trinovantum) and Cantiaci (Cantia) while his brother Tenvantius (Tasciovanus) received the Catuvellauni (Cornubia). Cassibellaunus, it is clear, possessed 'the entire realm', suggesting that he had overall control of all three tribal groups.

This could all reflect the desire of Cassivellaunus to become the pre-eminent force in southern Britain, dominating his immediate neighbours in the process. Certainly this was the view Caesar gives us, noting in de Bello Gallico that the British king had been 'continually at war' with all the other tribes of the region.[87] A unified resistance to Caesar's campaign of 54 BC was only possible if all the different groups came together and agreed on the direction of the war. On his return to battle, following a ten-day lull in fighting, necessitated by the repair to ships damaged in a storm, the Roman general discovered that 'British forces had now been assembled from all sides by Cassivellaunus, to whom the chief command and direction of the campaign had been entrusted by common consent'.[88]

Whether the 'chief command' awarded to Cassivellaunus was as consensual as Caesar implies is unknown. The British leader may already have established himself as 'overking' of the area or he may simply have bullied the other tribes into accepting him. Alternatively, as Caesar notes later, the presence of Roman soldiers in Britain may simply have 'frightened them into appointing him their supreme commander',[89] his experience in regional conflict making him the obvious choice. Infighting between the disparate tribal groups was temporarily suspended by the arrival of Caesar, who was now, for the time being at least, clearly the greater threat. It may be this particular, and perhaps rather unusual, 'election' of Cassivellaunus as commander in chief to fight Rome that was being remembered in the Historia Regum Britanniae. Certainly it would have constituted a major advance in the power and status of Cassivellaunus, arguably bringing him closer to being 'king of the Britons', rather than simply 'a king in Britain' like all his predecessors had been.

The position of overking as described in the Historia Regum Britanniae, Cassibellaunus acting as regent or 'protector' for his young nephews as they nominally governed the Trinovantes/Cantiaci and Catuvellauni, potentially explains a number of discrepancies in Caesar's de Bello Gallico that have perplexed academics for years. Most frustrating has been the fact that Caesar, never one for adding helpful geographical or political detail, does not ascribe his rival to a specific tribe. All the Roman general tells us is that Cassivellaunus' territories bordered the northern edge of 'a river, which is called the Thames', which separated his lands 'from the maritime states [of Kent] at about eighty miles from the sea'.[90] It seems a fair assumption, therefore, that the 'tribe of Cassivellaunus' and the 'Catuvellauni', later recorded as occupying the area of Hertfordshire, were essentially one and the same and that the king's 'capital', which lay 'not far from' the Trinobantes tribe, was probably the enlarged oppidum later referred to as VERLAMIO on coinage.

There is one last aspect of the Cassivellaunus story that requires consideration for some sources suggest that his war against Julius Caesar was not confined to the British Isles. The tradition is particularly strong in the Trioedd Ynys Prydein where, in Triad 35, of the 'Three Levies that departed from this Island, and not one of them came back' we hear that

> ... the third levy went with Caswallawn son of Beli, and Gwenwynwyn and Gwanar, sons of Lliaws son of Nwyfre, and Arianrhod daughter of Beli their mother. And those men came from Arllechwedd. They went with Caswallawn their uncle across the sea in pursuit of the men of Caesar. The place where those men are is in Gascony. And the number that went in each of those Hosts was twenty-one thousand men.

An army of 21,000 men taken by Caswallawn, another variant form of the name Cassivellaunus in early Welsh tradition, seems like a grossly exaggerated figure, but could be an echo of an expedition taken against the Romans in Gaul. In order to legitimise his actions in Britain during late summer 55 BC, Caesar claimed there was evidence to show that the Britons had acted against him, noting that 'in almost all the wars with the Gauls support had been furnished to our enemy from that country'.[91] This has often been viewed as a crude piece of self-justification intended to explain to the senate and people of Rome why their general was messing about overseas. There may, however, be some truth in Caesar's claim for there was much commonality between tribal groups on either side of the English Channel; certainly Caesar's translator, the Belgic King Commios, was apparently able to move between tribes with little or no problem.

To be fair it would seem strange, if Cassivellaunus had taken troops across the Channel in order to attack Caesar, that Geoffrey of Monmouth or Nennius did not bother to mention it. British kings fighting Rome was a popular theme in the Historia Regum Britanniae, as indeed was the idea of carving out an empire in Gaul/ France. Perhaps Geoffrey did mention a speculative conflict between Cassivellaunus and Caesar in Gaul, but, due to the garbled nature of his source material, ascribed the Continental adventure to another, possibly the earlier Belinus and Brennius or later, more overtly Roman and post-Roman leaders such as Maximianus or Arthur. Possibly Geoffrey did not mention that Cassivellaunus led troops over the Channel to fight Caesar in Gaul because the anti-Cassivellaunian sources he had at his disposal simply did not mention it, the adventure being ignored, overlooked or otherwise redacted.

Back in the Trioedd ynys Prydein, Triad 67, dedicated to the 'Three Noble Shoemakers of the Island of Britain', acknowledges 'Caswallawn son of Beli, when he went to Rome to seek Fflur'. This brief mention may allude to a lost tale taken from the semi-legendary life of Caswallawn/Cassivellaunus,[92] something of which is also alluded to in the Mabinogion. Quite who Fflur was is not explained, although a fleeting reference to the relationship between herself and Caswallawn in Triad 71, where both are cited as being among the Three Greatest Lovers of the Island of Britain[93] suggests it was an epic romance. Ultimately the suggestion that Cassivellaunus himself went to Rome may seem unlikely, given the levels of animosity between himself and Caesar, although as a client king, he may have travelled to the city later to make offerings on the Capitol like so many other kings of Britain are supposed to have done. The Historia Regum Britanniae says, almost in passing, that Androgeus (Mandubracius) accompanied Caesar to Rome, so perhaps the tradition later became confused or garbled, the compilers of the Triads substituting the name of one Briton for another.

Androgeus

Androgeus has appeared many times in our discussion of the Historia Regum Britanniae, being one of the few characters for whom, as Mandubracius, independent historical confirmation exists. As we have seen, Mandubracius occurs in many other forms, and with many variant names, in post-Roman and early Welsh literature, suggesting that not only was he remembered as a significant character for many generations after his death, but also that his story embedded itself in folklore, the tradition being extremely old, and much told, by the time Geoffrey of Monmouth came to compile his great work. The name Mandubracius was distorted in a variety of ways, suggesting either a later chronicle writer's unfamiliarity with the basic name-form or that oral tradition had mangled the primary material prior to it being formally recorded. Hence we hear of Andragius in the account of Orosius, Androgius in Bede, Androgeus in the Historia Regum Britanniae, Afarwy son of Lludd son of Beli in the Trioedd Ynys Prydein[94] while he also appears as Manawydan in the Mabinogion.[95] We have also noted that there are good grounds for believing that Morvidus, the evil king devoured by a sea monster, is also the same individual.

The splintering of Mandubracius' name-form through time partially masks the observation that there are, in fact, two very different characterisations of the king and that these almost certainly stem from differential treatment at the hands of discrete tribes each with a different perspective. In the Trioedd ynys Prydein, Triad 51[96] notes that Afarwy/Mandubracius was the first of the 'Three Men of Shame' in the Island of Britain.

Afarwy son of Lludd son of Beli. He first summoned Julius Caesar and the men of Rome to this Island, and he caused the payment of three thousand pounds in money as tribute from this Island every year, because of a quarrel with Caswallawn his uncle.

Earlier in the Trioedd Ynys Prydein, Triad 8, records the 'Three Prostrate (or Humble) Chieftains of the Island of Britain', noting that the second was 'Manawydan, son of Lyr Half-Speech'. Further negative associations may be reflected in the citation of Afarwy/ Manawydan as being the son of Lludd/Lyr, possibly identifying him, as has been noted 'as the mortal counterpart of the victim god' ruling a plague-ridden wasteland.[97] Mandubracius appears to have two strong traditions within the Historia Regum Britanniae: as Androgeus, the fearsome warrior king who helps Caesar defeat Cassibellaunus and of whom Caesar is afraid, and Morvidus, the savage, cruel and sadistic monarch who defeats the king of the Moriani, skinning all prisoners and burning them alive.

In the Second Branch of the Mabinogi, Manawydan serves as advisor to his brother Bendigeidfran (Bran 'the Blessed'), king of Britain, who sits with him at the wedding feast of their sister Branwen to Matholwch, king of Ireland. When Bran and Manawydan hear that Matholwch has been mistreating Branwen, they launch a rescue bid during which Bendigeidfran is killed. Bringing the king's head back to Britain, Manawydan hears that 'Caswallon son of Beli has overrun the Island of the Mighty and is crowned king in London'. Resting within a royal dwelling at Gwales, the party discover that two doors in the hall are open while the third, 'the one facing Cornwall', is closed. Pausing to feast, the group soon forgot all their worries until Heilyn, son of Gwyn, eventually forces open the door and looks out at Cornwall, 'and when he looked, every loss they had ever suffered, and every kinsman and companion they had lost, and every ill that had befallen them was as clear as if they had encountered it in that very place'.[98]

In the context of an early Welsh folktale, of course, Cornwall is another Celtic homeland untainted by Roman or Anglo-Norman aggression. Using the logic of the Historia Regum Britanniae, however, Cornwall/Cornubia is Catuvellaunia, the shut door perhaps acting as a metaphor for either the wrecked nature of filial relations between the Catuvellauni and the Trinovantes of Mandubracius, or the very physical nature of the shared, and now undeniably closed, border. Eventually the party manages to return to London (Trinovantum) where, safe in the bosom of the tribe, they bury the head of Bendigeidfran facing France.

In the Third Branch of the Mabinogi, with Caswallon still dominating the land, Manawydan travels around England seeking a craft. With Pryderi, son of Pwll and Rhiannon, he becomes a shield-maker but, upon angering the people of an unnamed city, they hear that they are about to be killed. Pryderi advises to strike first and attack their would-be assailants. Manawydan advises caution noting that 'Caswallon would hear of it, and his men and we would be ruined'.[99] As their travels continue, Manawydan's fortune declines until he eventually becomes a mouse-trapper. Throughout all of this, 'Manawydan unflinchingly accepts progressive degradation of his rank'.[100] This is not the end of Manawydan for, as we shall see, he later reappears within the ranks of King Arthur's army.

Tenvantius

With the departure of Caesar from Britain together with, so the Historia Regum Britanniae tells us, Androgeus, the kingdom was left to Cassivellaunus. Six years later he died and was buried in York. Without a direct heir, the kingdom passed to Tenuantius.

> Tenuantius was therefore crowned king and he governed his realm diligently. He was a warlike man and he insisted upon the full rigour of the law. After him his son Kimbelinus was raised to royal eminence.[101]

There is little to really go on with regard to the reign of Tenuantius/Tenvantius, second son of Lud and nephew to Cassibellaunus, the period of his rule being summed up in two short sentences, telling us he was both warrior and lawmaker. He is, however, a character who, like Androgeus/Mandubracius and Caswallon/Cassivellaunus before, can be identified, albeit from archaeological rather than written sources.

It has long been established that the Kimbelinus appearing in the Historia as the son of Tenvantius was the same as the 'Cynobellinus king of the Britons' mentioned in passing by the Roman historian Suetonius in an entry dated to AD 40,[102] while coins stamped with CUN / CUNO / CUNOB / CUNOBEL / CUNOBELIN, translated as 'Cunobelinus', were being minted at CAM (Camulodunum) from around the AD 30s. Some of the coin issues marked with CUNOBELIN also had TASC F and TASCIOVANI F, a shortening of a specific family relationship: Tasciovanus Filius or 'son of Tasciovanus'. If Cunobelinus/Cynobellinus was indeed the son of a ruler called Tasciovanus, and was not just a political heir, then we can identify Tenuantius' original name-form.

The suggestion, based on the coin evidence alone, that both Verulamium and Camulodunum were controlled by a single king named Tasciovanus in the final years of the first century BC, does at least appear archaeologically plausible. The expansion of his coinage across Hertfordshire and Essex from the two Iron Age centres of Verulamium and Camulodunum can, of course, be explained within the context of the Historia Regum Britanniae. Here Tenvantius (Tasciovanus), duke of Cornubia (Catuvellauni) and Androgeus (Mandubracius) the duke of Trinovantum (Trinovantes) and Cantia (Cantiaci) were brothers, their youth and inexperience at the point of accession being managed by caretaker rule of an overking, their uncle Cassibellaunus. Unfortunately the 'truth' of the relationship between the Cassivellaunus and Mandubracius appearing in Julius Caesar's de Bello Gallico and the Tasciovanus on coinage cannot be as easily resolved. Caesar does not elaborate on how, if at all, Cassivellaunus and Mandubracius were related; he may well not have known or indeed cared, noting only that Cassivellaunus killed Mandubracius' father, the king Imaneunetius. If the narrative established in the Historia Regum Britanniae can be believed, then Cassibellaunus and Imanuentius had been brothers, proving that fratricide was not just a Roman problem.

The key thing about Tasciovanus is that he is not known from any classical source, the surviving manuscripts of Caesar, Tacitus, Suetonius, Dio Cassius and others failing to mention him at all. This is an important point for, although he does not get a huge amount of attention in the Historia Regum Britanniae, Geoffrey of Monmouth is unusual for mentioning him at all. He was remembered, if not by Rome, then certainly by the British, his name appearing in a number of early Welsh genealogies, the relationship with his successor being recorded as 'Cinbelin map Teuhant' (Cunobelinus son of Tasciovanus).[103] In the same genealogies the son of Cinbelin/Cunobelinus is cited as Caratacus, the same Caratacus whom, we shall see, was a key player in the resistance against Rome during the invasion of AD 43, suggesting that the family of Tasciovanus held special relevance to those of the post-Roman West. Other apparent distortions of Tasciovanus occur in the name-forms Tecvan, Tecmant and Tenewan as well as Tecwant and Tecvann.[104]

Tasciovanus styled himself as RICON/RICONI, the Celtic for king, on his coins, studiously avoiding the Latin equivalent REX, unlike other British rulers like Eppillus and Verica of the Atrebates (Berkshire and northern Hampshire). This may have been because the coins of Tasciovanus were attempting to affirm a more overtly British heritage, rather than claiming legitimacy to rule through use of a Roman title. It could also be that the term RICON/RICONI had a specific usage, perhaps meaning something greater than a REX. Possibly the term implied 'overlordship' of more than one tribal group, in this instance perhaps the Trinovantes and the Catuvellauni, as has been suggested for Cassivellaunus. Perhaps Tasciovanus was too unpredictable, or even too dangerous, a character for the Roman State to recognise, therefore they denied him recognition or opportunity to use a title such as REX. This is certainly possible: a destabilising element in south-east Britain would certainly not have been welcomed by the emperor Augustus and his successors.

Some of the coinage issued by Tasciovanus, a name which may roughly be translated as 'Killer of Badgers' or 'Badger-slayer',[105] also possess the word-forms AND / ANDO / ANDOCO, DIAS, RVII / RVISS / RVES or SE / SIIC / SEC / SEGO. It has been suggested that these may have been the complete or abbreviated form of particular Celtic names, such as Andocomaros, Dias, Rues and Segovax;[106] perhaps representing minor or petty rulers who were subordinate in some way to Tasciovanus. We have no idea how the Catuvellauni and Trinovantes were organized or whether the hierarchy of power was in any way similar from one social group to the next. It is possible, however, that if one king (Tasciovanus) could rule over two tribes (the Trinovantes and the Catuvellauni) then perhaps it is also possible that any given tribe may have possessed multiple leaders, or was itself subdivided into semi-autonomous clan groups. Such a scenario might explain use of the term RICON/RICONI on the coins of Tasciovanus for he could have been in control of many discrete subsects or smaller territories contained within the area of 'the greater tribe'. Alternatively, ANDOCO, DIAS, RVES, SEGO and all their variant forms could represent more egotistical concerns, a form of boasting or one-upmanship, Ande perhaps meaning 'big', Rues meaning 'great' and Sego perhaps meaning 'power' or 'force'.

Tasciovanus evidently lived long enough, or committed sufficient great acts, to be commemorated upon the British coin series by those who claimed direct descent from him. As we have already seen, in the area around Camulodunum, Cunobelinus minted coins marked with the additional name TASCIIOVAN / TASCIOVANI / TASCIIOVANII / TASCIIOVANTI / TASCIIOVANTIS and also with the specific relationship, abbreviated as TASCIOVANI F or son of Tasciovanus. A second set of coinage, attributed to EPA / EPAT / EPATI / EPATICU (Epaticcus), who seems to have been primarily based, according to the coin distribution, around Verulamium also noted the TASCI F relationship. It could be that both men, if indeed the biological sons of Tasciovanus and not simply his political or adopted heirs, later re-established the divide between the Trinovantes and Catuvellauni following the demise of their father. This theory, though undeniably attractive, fails to explain why Cunobelinus also has coins marked with VER and VERV, unless he later took control of Verulamium following the death or subsequent exile of Epaticcus.

The survival of Tasciovanus' name-form, together with the key father-to-son relationship, as recorded in genealogies and king-lists, of 'Caratacus son of Cunobelinus son of Tasciovanus' suggests a strong oral tradition. The sheer variety of name-forms, furthermore, indicates that this tradition was rich and geographically diverse long before Geoffrey of Monmouth incorporated the character into the Historia Regum Britanniae. All this demonstrates that the character was not only key, as an ancestral figure and progenitor of an important house, but that he undoubtedly figured in numerous fables, myths and pieces of tribal folklore. Given the wealth of stories that must have circulated around the Tasciovanus, it perhaps seems strange that he was only accorded a short and not particularly descriptive section in the Historia Regum Britanniae. First appearances, however, can be deceptive.

Bearing in mind the diverse nature of name-forms, we should not be surprised to find Tasciovanus occurring on more than one occasion within the narrative of Geoffrey of Monmouth. Geoffrey, as we have already seen, was not adverse to taking stories and folklore surrounding individuals, if not fixed to an 'anchoring event', such as a specific date or place on a genealogical table, in order to help fill apparent gaps in his narrative. The need to demonstrate a complete and unbroken line of kings is clear enough, for any obvious absences in the timeline could cast doubt on the veracity of the account. Characters were often taken from their correct time and space, only to appear in a different form elsewhere. The extreme variety of spellings that Geoffrey undoubtedly encountered, sometimes with what is clearly the same character appearing with divergent and almost unrecognizable name-forms, furthermore did not help in establishing chronological context. Multiple points of view, from different primary source writers recording the same event in different ways and with opposite perspectives on the outcome, didn't help either.

Perhaps, then, we should not be overly surprised to discover that, in the aftermath of Roman Britain, there exists in the Historia Regum Britanniae an individual with the name Trahern. Trahern is not a name-form we have encountered within the Tenvantius / Teuantius / Teuhant / Tecvan / Tecmant / Tenewan / Tecwant / Tecvann variable as yet, and there would quite rightly be significant doubt as to the veracity of the comparison were it not for significant aspects appearing in his life and story as recorded by Geoffrey of Monmouth. Geoffrey first introduces the character of Trahern in the middle of Book 5 of the Historia within the complex milieu of later Roman Britain. Here we are told that after Constantine, king of the Britons, had overthrown the Roman tyrant Maxentius, thus becoming 'overlord of the whole world', the kingdom was seized by Octavius, duke of the Gewissei, who overthrew 'a certain proconsul' in whose hands the island hand been left.

Fearful of losing Britain entirely, Constantine sent Trahern, his mother's uncle, the brother of a previous king, Cole, 'with three legions to restore the island to Roman sovereignty'.[107] Trahern landed at 'Kaerperis', previously identified by Geoffrey of Monmouth as Portchester,[108] taking the town after a two-day siege. Octavius immediately conscripted an army and marched south, meeting Trahern 'not far from Winchester in a field called Maisuria in the Welsh language'.[109] A battle ensued and Trahern, defeated, fled back to his ships, sailing to Albany, 'the various regions of which he began to ravage'. Octavius followed and the two armies met again 'in the province called Westmorland'. This time Octavius was defeated.

> When Trahern realized that victory was his, he pursued Octavius, and gave him no respite until he had wrested from him the cities and his crown. Octavius was greatly saddened by the loss of his kingdom.[110]

Seeking shelter with King Gunbert of Norway, Octavius sends word to his friends back in Britain 'to do their utmost to assassinate Trahern'. An unnamed but 'leading figure of a certain municipality' immediately set his plans to kill the new king.

> One day when Trahern was on his travels some way from the city of London, this man lay in ambush with a hundred of his own soldiers in a certain valley in the forest through which the king would have to pass. He attacked Trahern unexpectedly as he passed by, and killed him in the midst of his soldiers. When Octavius heard this news he returned to Britain, scattered the Roman forces and drove them in flight, thus regaining the royal throne.[111]

Trahern's ancestry and connections, as provided by the Historia, are rather confused: Constantine, his great-nephew-in-law in reality being Constantine I ('the Great'), proclaimed emperor in York (Eboracum) in AD 306, while Helen, his supposed niece (and the mother of Constantine), was not a British princess but the Greek-born wife of emperor Constantius, later becoming St Helena after her work locating fragments of the True Cross in Jerusalem. The identity of King Cole is something we shall investigate later, but suffice to say here that he would not appear to have been a British king ruling Britain in the late third or early fourth century AD. Maxentius was indeed emperor in Rome, and an unpopular one at that – at least according to later Roman sources, his forces being defeated by Constantine at the Battle of the Milvian Bridge in AD 312. King Gunbert of Norway is not known from any contemporary sources.

Overall, then, the context in which Trahern finds himself is a dynastic and chronological mess, something that is further complicated by the inclusion of Octavius. Octavius can perhaps only really be the first emperor of Rome, Augustus (27 BC–AD 14) who was born Gaius Octavius in 63 BC. Octavius, or Octavian as he is commonly called today, went through a number of name changes through his career, before being granted the title Augustus ('illustrious' or 'revered one') by the Senate in 27 BC. Throughout his period of rule, Augustus maintained strong diplomatic contacts with the 'barbarian' aristocracy of north-western Europe, at least two British rulers, Tincomarus and Dubnovellaunus, seeking refuge with him in Rome, probably around 30 BC. There is no evidence of a king/leader or powerful aristocrat with the name Octavius in Britain during the later Roman period, let alone the early fourth century when Constantine marched to Rome to become emperor. He would appear to be a wholly artificial construct, taken out of time and space from the later years of the first century BC.

Within the political context of the end of the Roman Republic and early years of Empire, the story of Trahern and Octavius appears to make more sense. Stripping away the complicating factors of ancestry and marriage, the basic story as it exists concerns a struggle for power between two individuals. Geoffrey of Monmouth makes Octavius a British king, but if in the original narrative he was the first man of Rome then Geoffrey's comment that Trahern 'had wrested from him the cities and his crown' leaving Octavius 'greatly saddened by the loss of his kingdom' makes more sense. Octavius/Augustus had invested much in the continued stability of Britain, at the northern fringes of his empire, and was no doubt keen to honour all agreements made between the British kings and his adopted father, Julius Caesar.

We know that on three separate occasions during the early part of his rule, troubles in Britain caused him to consider direct military intervention, in 34, 27 and 26 BC. The precise reasons for Roman concern are not recorded, but the presence in Rome of a number of British exiles and the fact that the Roman historian Dio Cassius repeatedly tells us that the Britons 'would not come to terms'[118] suggests a period of significant turmoil.

In this respect it is perhaps also worth recalling that Tasciovanus repeatedly styled himself RICON/RICONI on his coinage, avoiding REX, the Latin term for king. This could, as suggested, reflect a degree of political 'overlordship' of more than one tribe or perhaps because Tasciovanus had not been formally recognized by Rome, choosing instead to use a British equivalent. It may, therefore, be a battle for legitimacy, Augustus trying to instigate a form of regime change in Britain, which is being reflected in the tale of Trahern and Octavius. There was probably no direct military intervention, the garbled account of Trahern landing at Kaerperis 'with three legions to restore the island to Roman sovereignty' being little more than a repeat of the AD 43 invasion, right down to the siege of Portchester and the withdrawal of Roman troops to their ships (see below). The story element of Trahern's death in an ambush, however, could conceivably fit within a remembered account of Roman treachery: a targeted assassination, conducted by either Roman soldiers operating beyond the frontier or British elements loyal to Rome, intended to bring down a troublesome king and replace him with someone more acceptable to Augustus. That, at least, would explain the detail provided of a king cut down 'in the midst of his soldiers' as he passed through a wooded valley.

Such an emotive tale would, from Geoffrey of Monmouth's perspective, be difficult to adequately integrate within the narrative of the Historia Regum Britanniae, especially if the finer details of who was really doing what to whom had become blurred. Rather than attempting to cram the story into the already crowded events of pre-Roman Britain, Geoffrey probably found it easier to slot it into the later Roman era, where there was a distinct lack of royal names with which to link the time of early rulers like Arvirargus, Coilus and Marius et al with Aurelius Ambrosius and Arthur. The emperor, in such a rewrite, becomes the absent King Constantine, the forces of Octavius become simplified to those of a British upstart and Tasciovanus becomes Trahern, a man trying to bring order to a kingdom disrupted by revolt. In such a scenario, the remembered tale of political turmoil against the distant powers of Rome in reality becomes a more localized squabble between two petty kings.

Kimbelinus

Following the death of Tenuantius/Tenvantius, ignoring for a moment the story of Trahern (see above), the succession passed directly, so the Historia Regum Britanniae tells us, to his son.

> Kimbelinus was raised to royal eminence, a powerful warrior whom Augustus Caesar had reared in his household and equipped with weapons. This king was so friendly with the Romans that he might well have kept back their tribute-money, but he paid it of his own free will.[113]

Kimbelinus is, as we have already established, to be equated with Cunobelinus, a name meaning either the cuno ('hound') of Belinos (a Celtic god) or the bel-cuno ('powerful' hound). He is an important character in the story of Iron Age Britain for, as we have seen, shortened versions of his name-form as CVN / CVNO / CVNOB / CVNOBEL / CVNOBELIN / CVNOBELINI appear prominently upon coinage produced in central southern Britain in the early years of the first century AD. Cunobelinus may have been king of either the Catuvellauni, and therefore (perhaps) a descendant, in either politics or blood, of Caesar's great opponent Cassivellaunus, or the Trinovantes, thereby being a descendant of Caesar's ally Mandubracius. At some stage in the AD 30s coins stamped with CUN/CUNO were being minted at CAM – Camulodunum (Colchester), the tribal centre of the 'Trinobantes' for whom Caesar had provided protection in 54 BC and also at VER, Verulamium. It is quite possible, therefore, that Cunobelinus was continuing the expansionist wars of Cassivellaunus, gradually spreading his influence through southern Britain. It is also possible that, as the son of Tasciovanus Ricon (the great king), Cunobelinus simply took control of both the Catuvellauni and the Trinovantes and had, as far as the coin distribution goes, a degree of control of the Cantiaci of Kent.

It may be that the succession of Kimbelinus/Cunobelinus as king was particularly favoured by Rome. The Historia Regum Britanniae notes that this particular son of Tenvantius (Tasciovanus) was someone whom Augustus Caesar 'had reared in his household'. This is a detail that Geoffrey of Monmouth, had he been writing a particularly pro-British patriotic epic, is unlikely to have thought necessary to include or, indeed, invent. It suggests that the 'powerful warrior' was not a proudly independent king but more a Roman puppet; a Romanised king who well appreciated the finer aspects and benefits of Mediterranean culture. Up until fairly recently, the dynasts of Britain were assumed to have been 'unsullied' by Rome, leading an individualistic, self-governing, self-determining existence at the fringes of the Roman world, trading for products that facilitated certain aspects of their lifestyle, but remaining stubbornly autonomous and free from outside influence. This was certainly not the case.

A key element of Roman society was the institution known as clientela (clientage). This ran on the principle that a cliens (client) was obligated through a debt of loyalty to repay favours such as gifts, financial aid, employment, protection or the granting of their own personal freedom, received from a benefactor or patronus (patron). The patron acted, in most instances, as a father figure to his clients, taking a personal interest in all their future business and financial activities as well as their welfare and legal status. In return the client could offer financial, political, legal and, in the old days of the Republic, even military support to his patron. The more clients a patron possessed, the greater his support base and therefore his standing in society. The system worked tolerably well at a personal level, but at an institutional level, when entire families, clans, cities or tribes became clients, the social dynamics could become precarious.

The rulers of states, tribes or kingdoms allied to Rome could perhaps have operated as clients to their patron, the emperor Augustus. In such a framework, particular 'barbarian' monarchs could be influenced or manoeuvred in many different ways and by many varied means. They could, for instance, be obligated to supply slaves, meat, grain or metal ore, pay tribute or tax or provide fighting men for the armies of Rome. They may also have been required to surrender their children to the emperor, a practice which helped ensure their continued loyalty to the Roman state, the royal offspring acting as hostages. The young people handed to Rome would, theoretically, benefit from a good education in the ways of empire, mixing with the great, good and politically influential. Once 'educated', and at a point when the succession of power within a particular kingdom was in doubt, the former hostage could be returned to his or her people, fully conversant with the ways and systems of Rome. The emperor would thus minimise any potentially destabilising event, such as invasion, coup or the unexpectedly sudden death of an allied monarch in a 'client-kingdom' on the fringes of the empire by returning their own preferred, and thoroughly Romanised, candidate to a position of power.

This system ensured that the friendly kingdoms at the boundaries of the Roman world became every more 'closely tied to Augustus' ideological project in the creation of a new network of power'.[114] The hostages (or obsides to give them their Latin term) were fostered out to the Roman State and brought up as Roman. Judging by his coins, Cunobelinus was a fervent supporter of Rome and there seems little doubt that, like other client kings of the period, he spent time in the city being educated under the protection of the emperor, just as Geoffrey of Monmouth claimed.

Cunobelinus is a rare example of a character who is mentioned, albeit briefly, by two Roman historians, Suetonius and Dio Cassius. Suetonius, in his Lives of the Caesars, observed that, in AD 40, the emperor Gaius (Caligula) while engaged in manoeuvres on the north-eastern coast of Gaul received the surrender 'of Adminius, son of Cynobellinus king of the Britons'[115] while Dio Cassius noted that during the invasion of AD 43, the Roman general Aulus Plautius 'had many problems in searching out the sons of Cunobelin' who, by that time, was dead.[116] Both references suggest that Cunobelinus was one of the premier British dynasts; in fact Suetonius seems to imply that he is the only one worth speaking of.

By the early years of the first century AD, Britain and the Britons were well known to the Senate and people of Rome. The empire had been trading with certain British leaders on a semi-regular basis for a considerable time. They had also been interfering with British internal affairs, restoring order where necessary, for a situation of calm stability was good for trade and also for the security of Rome's North West frontier. In peacetime, the Romans benefited from cheap metals, foodstuffs and slave labour, while British monarchs grew fat on the proceeds of Roman trade and began to dominate not only their own lands but also those of their immediate neighbours. Cunobelinus appears to have been one such British magnate.

As with the majority of other Britons appearing in the histories of ancient Rome, we possess no written description of Cunobelinus and there are no known works of that accurately record his image. There are, however, a large number of coins which carry his name, and a series of realistic-looking portraits. Do any of these represent the Great King? Possibly. Some of Cunobelinus' portrait issues may indeed have shown the monarch dressed and styled as a Roman ruler: clean-shaven in a tunic and with a laurel wreath. As these are clearly modelled upon the emperors Augustus and Tiberius, however, the likelihood is that these represented the first citizen of Rome and not the British dynast. One wonders whether, by copying the emperor's face and then superimposing his own name around the edge of the portrait, Cunobelinus was merely creating a facsimile, an imitation designed to flatter his Roman counterpart, or whether he was indicating the debt of loyalty (or obligation of service) that he, as a client, owed his patron.

Guiderius

Kimbelinus, the eighty-third monarch to appear in the Historia Regum Britanniae, ruled the kingdom, so Geoffrey of Monmouth tells us, with due respect and deference to Rome, paying tribute money 'of his own free will'.[117] After ten years Kimbelinus had two sons, 'the older of whom was called Guiderius and the second one Arvirargus'.

> As his life drew towards its end, Kimbelinus handed over the government of his kingdom to Guiderius. Guiderius refused to pay the Romans the tribute which they demanded and as a result Claudius, who had been raised to the position of emperor, crossed over to the island.[118]

The relationship between Britain and Rome had become strained, and once again it was the arrogance of a British king that threatened the integrity of the kingdom, at least according to the Historia Regum Britanniae.

It is fair to say that we know considerably less about the Roman invasion of Britain in AD 43 than we do about Caesar's expeditions of 55 and 54 BC. This is due, in the main, to a lack of reliable primary source material. Although Caesar was a blatant self-promoter and propagandist, at least he was an eyewitness to the key events of the campaign. Our only reliable source for the Claudian invasion of AD 43 is Dio Cassius, a Greek historian writing in the late second and early third century AD, over 100 years after the events he is describing. The relevant sections by the more objective and slightly more contemporary Tacitus, the Annals, written in the early second century, are unfortunately lost. Dio Cassius' work is usually treated as a standard discussion of a major military invasion akin to Caesar's expeditions or to the later Norman conquest of England in 1066. Unfortunately his text is often lacking in specific detail, presenting a narrative that is sometimes vague or incoherent. It is clear that he used a variety of sources in order to compile his History and that, in doing so, may have had access to material, such as Tacitus' earlier account, which contained information that he misunderstood or otherwise garbled. Although he is the closest to a primary source that we have for the Claudian invasion and its immediate aftermath, we must be wary of how closely we use him.

We must also be wary of assuming that the account related in the pages of the Historia Regum Britanniae will in any way be relatable to what we know (or think we know) about the events of AD 43. As we have already seen, the history stitched together by Geoffrey of Monmouth was derived from multiple sources, sometimes reflecting different or competing points of view. If, like the events of 55 and 54 BC, these sources focused upon the Catuvellauni/Trinovantes territorial zone of modern Hertfordshire and Essex, they may not have been all that concerned with events occurring to the immediate south of the Thames. Any landing of Roman troops on the Kent/ Sussex coast, or any engagement with the enemy prior to crossing the Thames, may not, if it did not directly impinge upon the Catuvellauni or Trinovantes, appear in the original narrative and hence it will be absent from Geoffrey of Monmouth's Historia.

The bare detail of the AD 43 invasion, as gleaned from Dio Cassius, may be summarized in the following way. To begin with, Roman troops assembled on the north coast of Gaul under the command of senator Aulus Plautius. After a short crossing, the Romans landed in three discrete divisions somewhere on the south coast of England. A series of inconclusive engagements followed against the two main tribal leaders in Britain, Togodumnus and Caratacus, sons of the recently deceased King Cunobelinus (Kimbelinus). Advancing, the Romans encountered stiff resistance at two major rivers, one of which is named as the Thames. Arriving with reinforcements, the emperor Claudius took full command and marched to Camulodunum (Colchester) where he received the surrender of at least eleven British kings.

Geoffrey of Monmouth recounts two separate invasions in AD 43, although the detail that he supplies suggests that he may have been describing the same invasion twice. Another aspect of the military offensive, as it appears in the Historia Regum Britanniae, which differs from established events is that we are told that Claudius himself came in person during the initial stage, accompanied by 'his chief of staff, who in his own language was called Lelius Hamo'. Hamo, it would appear, was the architect of the campaign for it was he 'who planned all the battles which had to be waged'.[119] Under the instruction of Lelius Hamo, Roman troops disembarked 'in the city of Portcestria and began to block up its gate with a wall, in order to stop the citizens coming out'. Hamo, it appeared, wanted to starve the citizens into submission 'or else he planned to kill them off mercilessly'.[120]

Portcestria, or Portchester, was an important deep-water anchorage at the northern edge of Portsmouth Harbour in Hampshire. Guarded by a late third-century Roman fort, one of the most impressive and well-preserved in Western Europe, the origins of settlement here remain largely unknown. It is difficult to know whether Geoffrey, in mentioning Portchester, was drawing upon an earlier source, linking the invasion with Portsmouth Harbour, or whether he was merely placing the expedition at what was in his day an important coastal base with an impressive royal castle set within a Roman fortress. The idea of a siege following on from a large-scale amphibious landing could relate to a real action in AD 43 or, perhaps, drew directly upon the earlier campaigns of Caesar, when at least one hill fort was attacked. No native centres were recorded as being assaulted during the initial stages of this latter Roman invasion but then, as we have noted, Dio Cassius' account is vague and lacking in specific detail.

Once word of Claudius and Hamo's arrival got round, Geoffrey tells us that Guiderius mobilized an army and marched swiftly to intercept the Romans. Forcing Claudius back to his ships, Guiderius was on the brink of victory when fate intervened.

> The crafty Hamo threw off the armour which he was wearing, put on British arms, and began to fight against his own men as though he were a Briton. Then he encouraged the Britons to charge in pursuit, promising them a speedy victory. He had learned their language and their habits, for in Rome he had been brought up among British hostages. In this way Hamo got nearer and nearer to Guiderius; and when he finally managed to reach the King's side he killed the unsuspecting man with the blade of his sword. He then edged away through the enemy's assault-troops and re-joined his own men, having won an execrable victory.[121]

It is clear that the account related by Geoffrey of Monmouth bears little resemblance to what we understand really happened in AD 43. The biggest anomaly is the inclusion, on the Roman side, of Claudius' Chief of Staff, Lelius Hamo. Thanks to the surviving Roman sources, such as they are, we know that the initial phases of the invasion were directed on the ground by Aulus Plautius, possibly with the support of Gnaeus Sentius Saturninus, whom the late fourth-century Roman historian Eutropius says was also involved in some capacity.[122] Neither 'Aulus Plautius' nor 'Gnaeus Sentius Saturninus' appear to represent plausible original variant forms for the name 'Lelius Hamo' while it is evident that both survived the invasion, stubbornly failing to be killed at Southampton or any other location in Britain. Where, then, did Geoffrey of Monmouth get the information for this particular tale?

A plausible explanation as to the identity of the mysterious Hamo is that he was not a Roman officer at all, but an ethnic Briton operating on the side of the Roman State. We know that, prior to

AD 43 a number of British aristocrats had fled to Rome. We have already encountered Tincomarus and Dubnovellaunus, but there were certainly others, indeed Dio Cassius tells us that one of the primary reasons for the invasion in the first place was that 'a certain Berikos, who had been driven out of the island as a result of an uprising, had persuaded Claudius to send a force there'.[123] 'Berikos' is usually equated with 'Verica', a king whose coins are found around Silchester in northern Hampshire and also along the coastal plain of West Sussex, 'b' sometimes being used instead of 'v' in British and Gallic names appearing in ancient Greek or Latin. If the general distribution of these coins indicate the extent of political power that Verica wielded, then whatever the uprising entailed, it presumably occurred in this part of central southern Britain. If the arrival of Verica/Berikos in Rome really did help persuade the emperor Claudius to intervene militarily in Britain, could it be that the King, or one of his relatives, joined the Roman expeditionary force, acting as an intermediary, supplying tactical information as and when required?

Such an individual, if seen to be actively working with Rome against the tribes from north of the Thames, could have formed the basis of the devious Hamo in the Historia. If Lelius Hamo were a Briton, one who, from the perspective of the original story-teller, was on the wrong side, this would explain why he is portrayed as duplicitous and execrable. It may also help to explain the curious description of Hamo putting on 'British arms' at the height of the conflict, being able to pass himself off as a native. Geoffrey says this was because he 'had learned their language and their habits' having 'been brought up among British hostages' in Rome. It is possible that either Geoffrey or the originator of the tale misunderstood that Hamo had himself been in the imperial court as a hostage, possibly as a descendant of the British aristocratic elite.

Hostages, as we've seen, were traditionally taken by the Roman State as a way of ensuring the loyalty of conquered peoples, the children being indoctrinated into a Mediterranean mindset. Once returned to their people, former hostages could bring a range of new gods, ideas and customs back with them. Having been thus exposed to the inner workings of the Empire, they could also help fast track Roman culture within their own people. Hamo, as an ethnic Briton returning to his homeland, would have been keen to find allies and support to aid his cause, and this could explain Geoffrey's comment that he 'encouraged the Britons to charge in pursuit, promising them a speedy victory'. Is this the garbled reflection of a period of inter-tribal warfare, Briton fighting Briton, tribe competing for power against tribe? It is perhaps interesting to reflect that, just prior to the invasion, the historian Suetonius observed that Britain was in uproar as Rome had refused 'to return certain fugitives'.[124] Was Lelius Hamo one such British fugitive?

Of all the possible candidates for 'Lelius Hamo', perhaps the closest match appears just prior to the Claudian invasion. In AD 40, the emperor Gaius, known to history as 'Caligula', was making plans to cross the English Channel in order, so we are told, to conquer Britain. Our sources for the proposed campaign, however, are overtly hostile, all desperate to establish that Caligula was delusional. 'He had but one experience with military affairs or war', Suetonius tells us, 'and then on a sudden impulse',[125] suggesting that the whole idea for the expedition was based on a whim. His plans ended, we are told, in chaos, his only real achievement being 'to receive the surrender of Adminius, son of Cynobellinus king of the Britons, who had been banished by his father and had deserted to the Romans with a small force'.[126]

'Adminius' is probably a later manuscript garbling of 'Amminus', a name appearing on British coins originally circulating in eastern Kent, the territory of the Cantiaci, during the late 30s and early 40s AD. If Amminus had indeed been the son of Cynobellinus/Cunobelinus/Kimbelinus, rather than, say, merely his political subordinate, it could be that the distribution of his coins indicates a degree of administrative responsibility over Cantium and the Cantiaci. It could be this was gained through a marriage alliance or war or simply that Cunobelinus, the pre-eminent ruler of the time, gave the territory to him to rule over. Caesar, in the final stages of his campaign in 54 BC, mentions four separate kings of Cantium,[127] all of whom seem to have been subservient, in some way, to Cassivellaunus the overking. The possibility that a Catuvellaunian or Trinovantian aristocrat could take control of Kent should not, therefore, be discounted. One of Amminus' coins displays a Pegasus above an abbreviated name DVN/DVNO. Given that many British rulers had a liking for establishing family credentials on coins, DVN/DVNO may have represented the lineage of Amminus, perhaps being the shortened form of a parent or ancestor. Assuming, however, that Suetonius did not get his facts wrong, then the father of Adminius/Amminus was Cunobelinus, not Dunobelinus. More plausibly, perhaps, given that many of Cunobelinus' own coins possess the mint marks CAM and VER, then DVN/DVNO could indicate where the coins were made. The identification of such a site in Kent is still hotly debated, although there is an obvious association with Canterbury; Durovernum in later Roman sources, seems reasonable enough, especially if its Latin form is a garbling of an earlier British name, perhaps Durovernon or Dunovernum.

Suetonius is damning when he describes the defection of Adminius to Rome, claiming that Caligula used the surrender of a petty British princeling to boast that 'the entire island had submitted to him'. What ultimately happened to the aristocrat after his flight from Britain is not recorded, although presumably the emperor would have made much of his catch, the prince becoming the centrepiece of his return to Rome. Whether Adminius/Amminus was able to provide tactical information on Britain, such as possible landing sites, safe havens, friendly tribes, major towns and river crossings necessary for a projected invasion, we cannot say. Neither can we be sure whether the British king was himself actively engaged in any covert action, plotting a coup or counter-insurgency, on behalf of the third emperor.

In hindsight, the court of Caligula was not the safest place in which to seek refuge, at least if we believe the writings of Suetonius. We hear nothing of Amminus' fate in the Roman sources. It is possible that he ended up like Ptolemy, son of the north African King Juba II, and grandson of Mark Antony, whom Caligula executed 'for no other reason than that when giving a gladiatorial show, he noticed that Ptolemy on entering the theatre attracted general attention by the splendour of his purple cloak'.[128] We never hear of Amminus/Adminius again, so we don't know whether he survived Caligula's increasingly paranoid final months or the bloodbath that ushered in the reign of his immediate successor, Claudius.

If Adminius/Amminus represents a good fit, both historically and etymologically for the name-form 'Hamo', what can we make of his praenomen, as recorded in the Historia Regum Britanniae, of Lelius? If we are indeed discussing an ethnic Briton who had fled to the relative security of Rome, then, even as the son of the Iron Age King Cunobelinus, Amminus would have required an official sponsor in order to gain citizenship and protection. Caligula could have provided this, as could his immediate successor Claudius. As a citizen of Rome, the British aristocrat would have received the forenames of his Roman sponsor. If Amminus had survived in Rome long enough to be officially recognized by Claudius, he could he have been enfranchised as Tiberius Claudius Amminus. 'Claudius Amminus' could plausibly degenerate over time to the name-form 'Lelius Hamo', especially in the tales and tradition that undoubtedly surrounded the events of AD 43, well before the time of Geoffrey of Monmouth.

If the identity of Lelius Hamo is difficult to resolve, that of Guiderius should be relatively easy given that Roman sources tell us that Cunobelinus (Kimbelinus) had at least three sons: Adminius (Amminus), Caratacus and Togodumnus. If Adminius had fled to the court of Caligula in AD 40, that left only Caratacus and Togodumnus to defend the kingdom from attack. Surely Guiderius must be one of these two royal sons, but which? We cannot resolve this question without examining the detail provided by the Historia Regum Britanniae for Arvirargus, the third son; so closely is his identity intertwined with that of Guiderius.

Arvirargus

Arvirargus, younger son of Kimbelinus, avenged the death his brother, King Guiderius, so Geoffrey of Monmouth tells us, by killing the deceitful Lelius Hamo during the early stages of the first Roman invasion of AD 43. While this was going on, the Roman emperor Claudius captured the city of Kaerperis, forcing Arvirargus and his army to seek shelter in Winchester. Here, just as the two forces were about to do battle, Claudius asked for a truce, offering Arvirargus his daughter Gewissa in marriage. Now on friendly terms, Claudius and Arvirargus subjugated the Orkneys 'and the other islands in that neighbourhood'.[129] Gewissa, whose 'beauty was such that everyone who saw her was filled with admiration', duly arrived from Rome and was married to the British king. Arvirargus, inflamed 'with such burning passion that he preferred her company to anything else in the world', suggested to Claudius that they should found a city that would 'perpetuate in times to come the memory of so happy a marriage'. The city, duly established, was 'called Kaerglou or Gloucester'.[130] Content that Britain was secure, Claudius left for Rome 'leaving the governorship of the islands of this province in the hands of Arvirargus'.

Arvirargus rebuilt his cities, ruling with such firmness that, Geoffrey tells us 'he was feared by far-distant kings and peoples'.[131] Becoming arrogant, he eventually refused to pay homage to Rome, leaving the emperor Claudius no choice but to send Vespasian to Britain 'either to bring about a reconciliation with Arvirargus or to force him back into subjection to Rome'. The British king raised an army, forcing Vespasian to abandon an attempt to land at Rutupi Portus (Richborough) and land further along the coast near Kaerpenhuelgoit, which Geoffrey identifies as Exeter. While Vespasian was laying siege to the town, Arvirargus arrived and attacked the Romans with great slaughter. The two forces were about to do battle again when Gewissa interceded and mediated a truce. Now acting together, the Romans and Britons subjugated Ireland. Vespasian eventually left, allowing Arvirargus to govern again for Rome.

The two Roman invasions described by Geoffrey of Monmouth in the Historia Regum Britanniae appear broadly similar. The first is triggered by Guiderius' refusal to pay tribute to Rome. When the Romans, led by Claudius and Lelius Hamo, arrived at Portcestria, Guiderius causes 'great havoc amongst the enemy, killing more of them with his own sword than the greater part of his army', forcing them back onto their ships.[132] It also stresses Guiderius' downfall, thanks to the deceit of Lelius Hamo, followed swiftly by bloody vengeance, Arvirargus 'rushing here and there' on the battlefield 'as if he were Guiderius himself'. About to fight Claudius at the gates of Kaerperis, a truce is called and Gewissa is offered up in marriage. The Romans join forces with the Britons and attack Orkney. The second invasion is triggered by Arvirargus' refusal to pay tribute to Rome. When the Romans, led by Vespasian, appear at Rutupi

Portus, Arvirargus arrives in such numbers that the attackers are forced back onto their ships. About to fight Vespasian at the gates of Kaerpenhuelgoit, a truce is called and Gewissa mediates. The Romans join forces with the Britons and attack Ireland.

In the second account of the invasion there is no mention of Guiderius, something that would make sense to Geoffrey of Monmouth if the operation were indeed a sequel, the king having already died during the first assault. Alternatively, the absence of Guiderius in the second account, which replicates significant elements of the first, may have been due to the fact that he was considered irrelevant to the story, the secondary version having been written by the supporters of Arvirargus, who naturally emphasised his bravery in particular. We have already seen the duplication of key events in the Historia when examining the second expedition of Julius Caesar to Britain in 54 BC, something which appears in Geoffrey's narrative no less than three times. Different points of view evidently remembered the same incident in contrasting ways. To the casual reader or researcher, like Geoffrey, divergence in the basic story could be taken to suggest two discrete events.

The differential treatment of the Roman leaders during both invasions could also explain why, in the first, it is Claudius and Lelius Hamo who are cited as leaders while in the second only Vespasian is credited with seeing action. Of course we know that there were indeed two elements to the invasion of AD 43, the earliest stages being led by Aulus Plautius, and in which Vespasian, as a general commanding a legion, played a significant part, Claudius only arriving later in order to oversee the capture of Camulodunum and receive the surrender of the British kings. Mention of Vespasian participating in the second expedition, when in reality he was in Britain long before Claudius arrived with reinforcements, could mean that, if the confusion derived from the fact that discrete aspects of the same invasion were being incorrectly recalled as two separate events, Vespasian's war, which occurred first, was being misremembered and cited as occurring later. Certainly Vespasian did lead an army west across Britain, as testified by the archaeological evidence, his legion eventually establishing a fortress at Exeter.

All this brings us to the issue of character identification. The names Claudius and Vespasian are self-evident, and we have dealt with Lelius Hamo, but what about Guiderius and Arvirargus? The Roman historian Dio Cassius names the two key British protagonists in the war of AD 43 as Caratacus and Togodumnus, whom he says were the 'sons of Cunobelin'.[133] Cunobelinus/Kymbeline we have already met, but what independent archaeological evidence, if any, is there for his two sons? Unlike Togodumnus, Caratacus seems to have minted his own coins, a small series marked with the legend CARA being found across northern Hampshire and southern Oxfordshire. These feature a well-executed portrait bust and a Roman-looking eagle on the reverse, and are almost identical to issues previously minted with the name EPATI (Epaticcus), all being derived from the same general geographic area. Assuming that Dio Cassius was right, and Caratacus was the son of Cunobelinus, then Epaticcus should have been his uncle, both Epaticcus and Cunobelinus being identified on their coins as TASCI F, 'son of Tasciovanus'. That the CARA coins so closely emulate those of EPATI may however indicate that Caratacus was actually the son of Epaticcus, and therefore the nephew of Cunobelinus, Dio Cassius having misunderstood the precise nature of the relationship. Alternatively, Caratacus may have been deliberately copying the style of his uncle's coins, having acquired Epaticcus' kingdom following the latter's demise.

After the events of AD 43, Caratacus disappears, finally remerging in AD 47, stirring the Silures tribe of south-western Wales and coordinating their fight against the advancing Roman army. What happened to him in the intervening years, and how he obtained a position of leadership in such a distant tribe, we do not know, Tacitus noting only that his 'successes, partial or complete, had raised him to a pinnacle above the other British leaders'.[134] Perhaps, like Cassivellaunus before, he was simply the best man for the job: a seasoned warrior with extensive combat experience fighting Rome. Certainly his presence in the west seems to have enlivened things for the second governor of Britain, Publius Ostorius Scapula, whose job it was to capture him dead or alive. Caratacus shifted the theatre of war to the Ordovices in north Wales, further complicating matters for the Romans, but, after a disastrous battle in which his unnamed wife and brothers were captured, he fled to the Brigantes in what is now northern England. Here, the Brigantian queen Cartimandua, realising that where Caratacus went the Roman army would soon follow, had the fugitive arrested and handed over to Scapula. After nine years of living life on the run, Caratacus had finally been captured.

Tacitus relates the arrival of the British king before the emperor in Rome and Claudius' attempts to milk the situation for all it was worth:

> The populace were invited as if to some spectacle of note; the praetorian cohorts stood under arms upon the level ground in front of their camp. Then, while the king's humble vassals filed past, ornaments and neck-rings and prizes won in his foreign wars were borne in parade; next his brothers, wife, and daughter were placed on view; finally, he himself. The rest stooped to unworthy entreaties dictated by fear; but on the part of Caratacus not a downcast look nor a word requested pity. Arriving at the tribunal, he spoke as follows: 'Had my lineage and my rank been matched by my moderation in success, I should have entered this city rather as a friend than as a captive; nor would you have scorned to admit to a peaceful alliance one spring from famous ancestors and holding sway over many peoples. My present lot, if to me a degradation, is to you a glory. I had horses and men, arms and riches: what wonder then if I regret their loss? If you wish to rule the world, does it follow that everyone welcomes servitude? If I were dragged before you after surrendering without a blow, there would have been little heard either of my fall or of your triumph: punishment of me will be followed by oblivion. If on the other hand you spare my life, I shall be an everlasting memorial of your clemency.' In response to this Caesar [Claudius] pardoned Caratacus and his wife and brothers.[135]

Claudius' stage-managed pardon of Caratacus is in direct contrast to the earlier actions of Julius Caesar, who, following the celebration of his victory against the Gauls in 46 BC, had Vercingetorix, the leader of the Gallic resistance, paraded through the streets before being strangled. Claudius had not only surpassed Caesar in achieving a conquest of Britain, he surpassed him in humanity, forgiving his enemies rather than condemning them to death. Caratacus' speech, as recorded, may have been written for him, although given that he was, in his early reign, essentially a pro-Roman client who may in his youth have even lived in Rome as a hostage, he was clearly no 'tourist' lost in an alien environment – he could no doubt understand Latin and knew exactly how to speak to an emperor. Much of his address, however, chimes with what we know about Tacitus' own mindset and attitude, so it could easily be the Roman author's own words coming through the mouth of the captive king.

Is Caratacus the model for Arvirargus in the Historia Regum Britanniae? Certainly he fits the profile of a king who feels confident enough to deny Rome tribute, before bravely fighting the Roman army and making his peace with the emperor. Perhaps the wedding between Arvirargus and the lady Gewissa, who wasn't the daughter of Claudius as he had only the one child (a boy called Britannicus), is in reality the echo of a marriage alliance between Caratacus and a Roman aristocrat, sealing the ties between the bloodline of Cunobelin and the Julio-Claudian house? Perhaps the idea that Arvirargus remained in power, governing Britain for Rome while Claudius went back to Italy, was just an ultra-nationalist piece of propaganda, showing once again how the natives sent the Romans packing. Although we don't know what happened to Caratacus after he was paraded through the streets of Rome, it was unlikely that he would ever have been permitted to return to his kingdom. If Geoffrey of Monmouth needed the royal line of kings to continue in order for his narrative to make sense, perhaps he changed key aspects of the story, allowing Caratacus/Arvirargus to remain in the island until old age claimed him and the throne passed to his son.

There is an alternative interpretation and it lies in the character and identification of Guiderius. In Geoffrey's Historia, Guiderius dies early on in the Claudian war, bravely fighting against the Roman army. Guiderius must, it has always been assumed, be a garbling of the name-form Togodumnus, a son of Cunobelinus whom, it is thought, was also killed resisting Rome during the hard-fought crossing of the River Thames. This is all well and good, but the trouble with this equation of characters is that Togodumnus didn't die fighting Rome; in fact the historical evidence seems to say just the opposite.

In his rather confused account of the war in Britain, Dio Cassius says that the enemy, or 'barbarians' as he calls them, had encamped on one side of a river, blocking access. Before the Roman army could cross, a group of Celts, 'Keltoi', pressed forward in order to attack the barbarians.

> The Celts straight away swam across while others got across by a bridge a little way upstream, engaged with them from many sides and cut many of them down. But in the headlong pursuit of the remainder, chased them into swamps with no way out and many of themselves perished. However, because of this action and also, at the same time, the destruction of Togodumnus, those Britons not greatly involved, but of a gentle and mild disposition, deemed it worthy to stand together at his side, against them.[136]

Here Dio Cassius is describing, in his own convoluted way, the crossing of the Thames by Keltoi/Celts. It is this Celtic army that chases the 'barbarian' enemy from the riverbank, subsequently being destroyed in the swamps. It is not Togodumnus the man being 'killed', then, but his army of Keltoi/Celts, who appear to be on the Roman side.[137] It is only after the ambush in the swamps, and the destruction of the Keltoi, that those 'Britons not greatly involved' in the war were compelled to 'stand together at his [Togodumnus'] side against them [Caratacus' army of barbarians]'. The crucial thing about this rereading is not just that Togodumnus appears as an ally of Claudius, but more importantly that he survived the battle, allowing other British tribes to stand 'together at his side'. This is not the account of British tribes united against Rome, but of two British tribes fighting each other, one with Rome's backing. In every way this seems to echo the conflict between Caesar and Cassivellaunus in which the British prince Mandubracius, of the Trinovantes, sided with the Romans.

Support for this alternative reading of Dio Cassius is provided by what we later know about the Roman province of Britain. Immediately after the invasion, Togodumnus disappears from history. Soon afterwards, however, we hear of an important Briton called

Togidubnus who is credited as a loyal servant of Rome. Togodumnus and Togidubnus are variants of the same name-form and, given the general level of uncertainty over the correct way of spelling British/Celtic names, especially when transcribing them into Latin, there can be little doubt that this was the same individual.[138]

Our first source for Togidubnus in post-invasion Britain comes from the pen of the Roman historian Publius Cornelius Tacitus, who, writing at the very end of the first century AD, comments rather sneeringly that 'certain states were handed over to King Togidubnus – he in fact remained totally loyal down to our times – in accordance with the Roman people's old and long-standing policy of making even kings their agents in enslaving people'.[139] This name-form appears in one other historical document, a monumental inscription found in Chichester in West Sussex. Although damaged, enough of the text survives to name 'Tiberius Claudius Togidubnus, Great King in Britain'.[140] The inscription originally formed the centrepiece of a temple dedicated to Neptune and Minerva and, given the style of text and lettering, it has been suggested that it was made during the either the reign of Claudius (AD 41–54) or Nero (AD 54–68).

We may infer that Togodumnus/Togidubnus, leader of the Keltoi or 'Celts', was the man whom the emperor Claudius supported as 'Great King' in Britain, probably because he was considered to be the obvious heir to succeed the recently deceased Cunobelinus. In this situation his brother (or possibly cousin), Caratacus, leader of the 'Barbarians', was the loser in every sense, for, having failed to support Togidubnus/Togodumnus, he made himself Rome's enemy. Identification of Togodumnus, son of Cunobelinus, with Tiberius Claudius Togidubnus further helps to explain the title of 'Great King in Britain' on the Chichester inscription, for this is very similar to the level of recognition that the Roman historian Suetonius says was accorded by Rome to his father.

As a prominent king, Togidubnus' power would almost certainly not have originally centred on Chichester, where the inscription commemorating his temple was found. As heir to Cunobelinus' estate, Togidubnus should theoretically have been based either at the Trinovantian capital of Camulodunum (in Essex) or the Catuvellaunian centre at Verulamium (in Hertfordshire), the two oppida which

Cunobelinus had claimed lordship over. As Camulodunum became the chief target of Claudius' army, later having a legionary fortress implanted directly across it, while Verulamium became prosperous and successful town whose population, if we believe Tacitus, were all granted Roman citizenship[141] we can only assume that it was with the Catuvellauni in Hertfordshire that Togidubnus reigned supreme.

If Togodumnus/Togidubnus can be equated with the character of Arvirargus, how can we explain the corruption of the name? Arvirargus is a name-form encountered in only one other Roman source, a satirical poem by Juvenal written in the early second century AD. In this, the emperor Domitian, when presented with a giant turbot, is greeted with the cryptic omen 'Some king you will capture or Arvirargus will be hurled from his British chariot pole'.[142] Quite what this means is anyone's guess, though presumably it was an oblique reference to the potential deposition or overthrow of a British leader. For it to have had any meaning, Juvenal's audience would have to know who precisely 'Arvirargus' was. Frustratingly no further reference is made to this chariot-racing monarch, so we remain none the wiser. Geoffrey of Monmouth, however, found Juvenal's aside and quoted it, in Book 4 of the Historia, as an example of how the British king was esteemed and feared more than any other. Unfortunately he gets his emperors wrong, ascribing the statement made to Nero (AD 54–68) rather than Domitian (AD 81–96) as Juvenal intended.

What we don't know, of course, is whether Juvenal's passing reference was projected back to AD 43 by Geoffrey and used as a substitute for Togodumnus/Togidubnus, whose name-form by then may have been hopelessly garbled. It is certainly possible. As Arvirargus itself is a perfectly acceptable British/Celtic name, meaning something like 'manly' or 'true in battle', it could just as plausibly be a title, perhaps awarded to a successful war leader by his own people. If so, then it may be Geoffrey of Monmouth had, in his possession, a source that described Togodumnus/Togidubnus as an 'Arvirargus' or something similar, and he naturally made the link with Juvenal, pushing the quote back in time by three decades to fit.

It should be noted, in this respect, that there is an otherwise unexplained AGR name-form abbreviation appearing on a small number of pre-Roman coins in Britain. If this was an indigenous name, it may have been something like Agricu, possibly meaning 'war dog', or Agriccos/Agrecios, equating with a variant of 'battle'.[143] Just as has been suggested for Arvirargus, the AGR form may represent a title rather than a specific name, for, as well as occurring in its own right, it has also been recorded on the reverse of coins with CAM and CVN set at either side of a stylised ear of corn. Such a combination, citing Camulodunum (Colchester) and Cunobelinus may indicate that Cunobelin was claiming authority over Camulodunum through 'battle'. Alternatively it may be that a putative Agricu/Agriccos/ Agrecios was either displaying his blood-heritage to Cunobelin, an automatic right to govern Camulodunum or that his authority to rule came from, or had been granted by, that particular king. In the latter scenario AGR need not be a blood relative of Cunobelin, merely a close ally or subordinate.

There is another possibility for a parallel for AGR may be found in the more securely Roman name-form, 'Agrippa'.[144] Marcus Vipsanius Agrippa was, as we have seen, a close friend to the emperor Augustus, and would have been well known to the exiled British dynasts and hostages in Rome. Adoption of the name Agrippa is well documented, a fine example of which being Marcus Julius Agrippa, or Herod Agrippa as he is more popularly known, grandson of Herod the Great, who lived in Rome before returning to the east as governor of Judea in the early 40s AD. It is certainly conceivable that a child of Cunobelinus, brought up in Rome, would have been renamed 'in a manner to emphasise loyalty and deference'.[145] The reference to Arvirargus by Juvenal may therefore have been seized on by Geoffrey of Monmouth, struggling to understand the AGR form of Agrippa, Agrippinus, Agrippina or something similar, which by the early twelfth century had become unrecognizable.

If Arvirargus was Togodumnus/Togidubnus then Guiderius was surely Caratacus. A problem immediately arises with such an identification for, although the Historia Regum Britanniae asserts that Guiderius died, killed at the hands of Lelius Hamo fighting near Portsmouth, Caratacus lived on as an exile in Rome. We have already noted that in compiling the Historia Geoffrey seems to have overlooked or ignored detail contained in a number of important primary Roman sources, Julius Caesar's own account concerning the expeditions of 55 and 54 BC, for example, playing little or no part in the story of the conflict as he presents it. If, as seems likely, Geoffrey did not mine the Roman histories for information but utilized a variety of sources skewed by a Romano-British perspective, some of which were roundly dismissive of the anti-Roman children of the southern tribes, then the absence of Caratacus from his narrative and his 'death' is more explicable. He was an enemy of Togodumnus/ Togidubnus who fought his guerrilla campaign in the mountainous uplands of Wales, a significant distance from the area that Geoffrey's sources appear to have been interested in. Whether he died, was killed or was captured, it made no difference; he was gone and that was all that mattered to those who first established the tradition of Togidubnus 'the Great'.

Marius and Sodric

If the Historia Regum Britannia was intended as a blatant piece of historical revisionism, a hopelessly patriotic fantasy concerning the British heroes of the past promoting the political cause of a once proud but now subjugated race, then why, one may ask, are the more obvious heroic figures, attested by Roman sources, left unmentioned? Caratacus, coordinator of the resistance to Claudius, barely features in the book and Boudicca of the Iceni, the most famous of all British insurgents, is completely absent. In his epic Mythology of the British Isles, Geoffrey Ashe suggested that such gaps undermine the Historia, making it appear even more improbable that Geoffrey of Monmouth was using information recovered from a genuine 'lost' source.

> Where Geoffrey tried to deal with the Roman conquest, his fiction grew less persuasive. Here, at last, it was too blatantly at odds with fact. The only Britons of that period who have shown durability are these two, and he ignores them both.[146]

The absence of Caratacus and Boudicca seems even more curious when one considers the prominence of both war leaders in the writings of Tacitus and Dio Cassius. If Geoffrey of Monmouth had been liberally plagiarizing ancient texts in order to create a wholly fictional account of British resistance against a foreign enemy, why did he omit to mention such obvious and well-attested heroes and heroines? Caratacus we have already dealt with, his campaigns perhaps occurring at a sufficient distance from central south-east England for Geoffrey's sources to safely ignore him. Boudicca's war of liberation, however, was fought squarely within the geographical epicentre of Geoffrey's narrative. Why was she ignored?

Geoffrey Ashe has suggested that because Nennius treated the Romans as 'interlopers', whose authority over Britain was rejected by the indigenous population, there was no scope for characters like Boudicca.[147] If Geoffrey of Monmouth took this concept of Britain having never been Roman further, believing that the island was 'a tribute-paying protectorate' rather than a province, then for him to trace the monarchy through a history of defeat would, Ashe notes, 'have been to admit the conquest'. Mentioning Boudicca's war of liberation would suggest there was something to be liberated from, contradicting the belief that Britain remained defiantly free. Caratacus and Boudicca are, by this argument, missing from both the Historia Brittonum and the Historia Regum Britanniae because the fictional world created by Nennius and Geoffrey simply could not support their existence.

There is, however, another explanation. Boudicca and Caratacus were ignored, downplayed or, perhaps, indirectly referred to as a malign influence, because they did not fit the perspective of those directing the tradition. If the original narrative treated the anti-Roman leaders as something that directly threatened the survival of their own people or way of life, why would they endeavour to commemorate them? If anything, the absence of characters like Caratacus and Boudicca from the Historia Regum Britanniae would appear to support the belief that Geoffrey of Monmouth was employing a diverse range of primary source material rather than generating a piece of overtly pro-British propaganda.

The story of Boudicca, as told in the Roman histories, can be briefly summarized. Prasutagus, pro-Roman king of the Iceni (Norfolk), died, citing the emperor Nero as his heir, together with his two (unnamed) daughters in 'an act of deference which he thought would place his kingdom and household beyond the risk of injury'.[148] Unfortunately the will was ignored by Rome, Tacitus noting that the kingdom was 'pillaged by centurions', land being seized, possessions looted and the royal family 'treated as slaves'.[149] Rising up, the Iceni were joined by other disenfranchised groups, most notably the Trinovantes. A pro-Roman client state since the time of Mandubracius in 54 BC, the Trinovantes were the biggest losers in the invasion of AD 43. Their aristocracy broken and their liberty restricted, the tribe had also lost their capital Camulodunum, which was overlain by a legionary fortress before being rebuilt as a Roman town. Premium space in the town was given to ex-soldiers, Camulodunum being rebranded as Colonia Claudia Victricensis, 'the city of Claudius' victory'.

Undefended and ill-prepared, Colonia Claudia Victricensis quickly fell to Boudicca. Those who could fled to the relative protection of the temple, where they held out for two days. No prisoners were taken. The legion closest to the city, the IX Hispana, was ambushed as it raced south, the Britons 'slaughtering the infantry to a man'.[150] Sensing victory, Boudicca's army descended upon Londinium (London) and then Verulamium (St Albans), destroying them both. Finally, the remnants of the Roman garrison met the rebels in an open battle, butchering them so completely that the revolt collapsed overnight. Boudicca, we are told, 'ended her days by poison'.[151]

It could be that Boudicca, as a strong and warlike female protagonist, caused the sermonizing Gildas a problem or two, for women do not feature much within the blood-and-thunder Old Testament world of De Excidio et Conquestu Britanniae. He mentions Boudicca once, and then only in passing and certainly not by name. 'A treacherous lioness,' he spits, 'butchered the governors who had been left to give fuller voice and strength to the endeavours of Roman rule.' Bede neglects to mention her at all. A close examination of the Historia Regum Britanniae, however, shows that, despite our misgivings, all is not what it seems. Boudicca is there, albeit in a rather surprising form.

Sometime after the Roman invasion, Marius, the son of Arvirargus, 'succeeded him in the kingship', Geoffrey notes.

A little later on in his reign a certain king of the Picts called Sodric came from Scythia with a large fleet and landed in the northern part of Britain which is called Albany. He began to ravage Marius' lands. Marius thereupon collected his men together and marched to meet Sodric. He fought a number of battles against him and finally killed him and won a great victory. In token of his triumph Marius set up a stone in the district, which was afterwards called Westmorland after him. The inscription on it records his memory down to this very day. Once Sodric was killed and the people who had come with him were beaten, Marius gave them the part of Albany called Caithness to live in. The land had been desert and untilled for many a long day, for no one lived there. Since they had no wives, the Picts asked the Britons for their daughters and kinswomen; but the Britons refused to marry off their womenfolk to such manner of men. Having suffered this rebuff, the Picts crossed over to Ireland and married women from that country. Children were born to those women and in this way the Picts increased their numbers.[152]

Leaving aside for the moment the tricky issues surrounding the identity of 'Marius', it is clear that 'Sodric' in this particular account can only be Boudicca and the 'Picts'/'Scythians' the Iceni. Here Geoffrey is making what sense he can of a garbling of the British queen's name, although whether it was he who originally changed it to Sodric/Soderic, or whether this had already occurred in the unnamed sources, is unclear. Presumably the primary source did not clarify Sodric/Boudicca's gender and so the Icenian queen seamlessly becomes a king of the Picts/Scythians.

Geoffrey makes no explanation of why a 'king of the Picts' would come 'from Scythia' for this, on the face of it, creates a major geographical problem. Traditionally, in the literature of the later Roman world, the term 'Pict' or 'Picti' may be translated as meaning 'tattooed' or 'painted people'. It was applied in a derogatory way by to the people north of Hadrian's Wall. 'Scythian' on the other hand was a generic term that throughout Antiquity was used by historians of the Mediterranean to cover the nomadic tribes of the Eurasian Steppe. By the mid-fifth century the name seems to have become synonymous with the Huns, the highly mobile 'barbarian' tribe who, under the leadership of Attila, successfully extorted large sums of gold from the Roman Empire. Of unusual appearance, with unfamiliar customs and language, the Huns were, from a Roman perspective, a deeply worrying prospect – unpredictable, violent and unrepentantly pagan.

An explanation for the confusion between Picts and Scythians may lie in the fact that Sodric has been conflated with a much earlier migration account. Bede, in describing the earliest inhabitants of Britain, notes that 'when they had spread northwards and possessed the greater part of the island, it is said that some Picts from Scythia put to sea in a few long ships, and were driven by storms around the coasts of Britain'.[153] The Pict/Scythia connection, therefore, seems to derive from Bede, although he was undoubtedly employing even earlier accounts. Given that the Scythians or Huns were, at the time Bede was writing, considered to have been the most savage and barbaric of all barbarian races, it may be that he was simply linking the two peoples on the basis of their attitude towards civilization and Christianity. Bede goes on to tell us that, having been buffeted by storms onto the shores of Ireland, the Picts 'asked for a grant of land so that they too could make a settlement'.[154] The Irish refused, advising the Picts to cross to Britain, saying 'there is another island not far to the east, which we often see in the distance on clear days. If you choose to go there, you can make it fit to live in; should you meet resistance, we will come to your help.'

Bede's alliance of Pictish and Irish tribes may be an echo or remembrance of a real migratory or raiding coalition, the most significant of which was recorded by the late fourth-century writer Ammianus Marcellinus, which today is referred to as the 'Great Barbarian Conspiracy'. In AD 367, the Picts of northern Britain joined forces with the tribes of Ireland, most notably the Scots and Attacotti, and the Saxons from across the North Sea, plunging Britain 'into the depths of distress'.[155] Whatever the case, it is clear from Bede's next comment that this account is, at least in part, the one used by Geoffrey of Monmouth:

> The Picts crossed into Britain and began to settle in the north of the island, since the Britons were in possession of the south. Having no women with them, these Picts asked wives of the Irish, who

consented on condition that, when any dispute arose, they should choose a king from the female royal line rather than the male.[156]

The version in the Historia Regum Britanniae inverts key aspects of the geography, with the Picts asking the Britons for wives, then moving to Ireland when the request is denied. The origin tale is, it should be noted, presented as an explanation for both the early arrival of the Picts into the British Isles and their curious (from Bede's perspective) custom of following royal descent from the female line. It is not something which appears to relate to an event occurring in the mid-first century AD, shortly after the Claudian invasion, where Geoffrey of Monmouth placed it. Neither is Sodric mentioned, suggesting that he may not originally have been part of the origin myth. 'Scythia' and 'Caithness' could have been used by Geoffrey as a substitute for a place of origin he could not easily translate or identify from his primary source. Both could represent a plausible interpretation of the tribal name 'Iceni', whose form, no doubt, had become irrevocably garbled and meaningless by the time the Historia was being written. This seems to further confirm that Geoffrey was not using, or was unaware of, the writings Roman authors such as Tacitus, Dio Cassius or Ammianus Marcellinus, whose descriptions of both the Boudican revolt and the history of the Picts would have clarified matters of etymology and geographical placement.

If the kingdom of Marius conforms, broadly, with the client kingdom of the Catuvellauni, then the invading Picts/Scythians of Geoffrey's narrative follow the general route of the Icenian insurgency of AD 60–1, invading from the north, after which they 'began to ravage Marius' lands'. The main target was the tribal town of Verulamium which had been accorded the status of a municipium, a self-governing community of Roman citizens. The disparity between the treatment of the Catuvellauni in Verulamium and the Trinovantes, whose centre at Camulodunum had been subjugated by the Roman military, was dramatic. The Catuvellauni were accorded high status while their neighbours, the Trinovantes, were a conquered people, possessing no official place in the new political system. When the Boudiccan revolt began, Verulamium was an obvious target. Tacitus is largely quiet about the fate that befell the citizens of the town, noting only that their numbers contributed to the 'seventy thousand Roman citizens and allies' who died during the war.[157]

We are left with Geoffrey of Monmouth's assertion that the war of AD 60–1 was put down solely through the decisive actions of a British king, there being no Roman aid or military assistance. From the perspective of tribes in central southern Britain, of course, the revolt left them isolated and vulnerable. At the time of the uprising, the Roman governor, Suetonius Paulinus, was engaged in operations in North Wales with two legions while a third was in action somewhere to the west. The only other legion that could conceivably have come to their assistance, the IX Hispana, had been ambushed and destroyed. With no news as to the location and combat status of the Roman military, those in the British tribal aristocracy faced up to the fact that there was no help coming. Their options were limited. They could flee out of harm's way, to the west or across the Channel, abandoning homes, possessions and loved ones. They could join the insurgency, although this would mean rejecting everything they stood for by helping their old enemies as well as facing up to any subsequent Roman reprisals, or they could stand and fight.

The revolt, or war of liberation from the perspective of the Iceni and Trinovantes, would have been an ideal time for the pro-Roman leaders of the south to prove their fidelity to the emperor. That one such British monarch, Togidubnus, was revered into the last decade of the first century AD, as is evident from the writings of Tacitus, would perhaps indicate that at the very least he and his followers had remained loyal to the Roman cause. With this in mind, the absence of pro-Roman British leaders in the histories of the war may seem strange but there is clearly no room in Tacitus' dramatic account for a character like Togidubnus. The Roman writer would perhaps not have been keen to acknowledge British involvement on the side of Rome, for this would have confused the storyline, blurring the Roman distinction between good (Roman) and evil (British), as well as seriously diluting the role played by Paulinus. In the official version, the governor is very much a classic Roman hero: courageous, steadfast and utterly unyielding. Togidubnus' role in supporting the emperor during the uprising must, however, have been crucial to Rome's success.

As a king whose territory included the Roman town of Verulamium, modern-day St Albans, Togidubnus' people were targeted by Boudicca's army, possibly as a result of deep-seated intertribal hatred. The Romano-British aristocracy had everything to lose and nothing to gain by the revolt of the Iceni and Trinovantes and it was in their interests to ensure that the rebels were swiftly crushed. By holding land to the south of the River Thames, containing the rebellion largely to the north, Togidubnus would have ensured Roman investment in the province was saved. Given the armed forces that may have been available to the king in AD 43, it would seem we are not dealing with an effete Roman puppet but a battle-hardened veteran who enjoyed the popular support of his people. Whether he was able to deploy an army in active support of Paulinus' campaign to restore order to the province we will never know, but Geoffrey of Monmouth is adamant that it was a British monarch, in this instance 'Marius', who 'collected his men together and marched to meet Sodric', fighting 'a number of battles against him' before finally killing him and winning a great victory. Just as there is no room for British participation in the Roman account, there is similarly no place for Roman military assistance in the version preserved by Geoffrey of Monmouth.

The revolt proved catastrophic for the Iceni and Trinovantes, the Roman governor Paulinus being in no mood to be merciful afterwards. 'Cohorts and cavalry squadrons were stationed in winter quarters,' Tacitus tells us, 'and any tribe that had wavered in its loyalty or had been hostile was ravaged with fire and sword.'[158] Worse was to come. 'Nothing afflicted the enemy as much as famine,' Tacitus says, 'since they had taken no thought for sowing crops and had actually diverted people of all ages to the war effort, while marking out Roman provisions for their own use.'[159] This picture of post-revolt desolation is mirrored in Geoffrey of Monmouth's observation that when Sodric's followers were settled in Caithness, 'the land had been desert and untilled for many a long day, for no one lived there'.

So who was Marius? We have observed that Togidubnus/ Togodumnus survived the revolt and it could be that he was the basis for Marius as depicted in the Historia Regum Britanniae. There were, undoubtedly, other key members of the British elite of whom we know nothing, for in the late first century AD indigenous aristocrats would have been seeking citizenship and integration rather than minting coins. Their offspring would, furthermore, have been given new Roman identities and, as the generations moved on, ethnic name-forms would have disappeared. There may have been a Marius in the Iron Age British royal family but, given that Roman emperors, usurpers and generals were adopted by Nennius and Geoffrey of Monmouth to serve as British kings, it is also possible that Marius was not originally a Briton.

Coilus

The next king of the Britons after Marius, like a number of characters cited in Geoffrey's Historia Regum Britanniae, seems to appear more than once, albeit in a slightly different guise and with a divergent name-form.

> When Marius finally died, his son Coilus took over the government of the kingdom. From his early childhood this Coilus had been brought up in Rome. He had learnt the ways of the Romans and had conceived the greatest possible liking for them. He paid their tribute without even attempting to argue about it, for he realized that the whole world was subject to them and that their power was greater than that of individual countries or any one province. He therefore paid what was demanded and was left to rule in peace over his possessions. None of the British kings ever held the nobles of their realm in greater honour, for Coilus either left them alone in peace or else rewarded them with frequent gifts.[160]

Coilus is someone praised for his obedience to Rome; not the sort of character one would expect to be celebrated in the Historia Regum Britanniae if it were, as is sometimes suggested, a misguided patriotic tome. In fact, like Cunobelinus before, Coilus is credited as growing up in Rome; presumably he was, therefore, a former hostage who had returned to his homeland determined to imprint it with a new and distinctively Roman identity.

There can be little doubt that of all the areas of early Roman Britain, the wealthiest, at least in the latter half of the first century AD, was the coastal strip of central southern England. Here, in an area unaffected by the Boudiccan uprising, the remains of at least eight palaces have been found, of which Fishbourne is today the most famous.[161] To someone brought up in Rome, these new builds would have appeared normal, but to the indigenous Briton, whose contact with the Roman world had been through trade and exchange, such a display of exotic architectural forms would have been mind-blowing. The private civilian building projects were immense, but who were they for? Were they the official residences of administrators, wanting all the comforts of Rome, or did they belong to Romanised Britons expecting to live apart from their more barbarian neighbours? It is possible that the Emperor Nero's delight over the defeat of Queen Boudicca's rabble may have spilled over into rewarding those members of the native British elite who had not sided with the enemy. The extravagant levels of expenditure displayed within the civilian buildings at Fishbourne and the other palace sites could therefore have derived from imperial patronage.

Less than 2 km away from Fishbourne, in the centre of the Roman town of Chichester, two inscriptions have been found, one set up by 'Gaius Sallustius Lucullus, Legate of the emperor with praetorian powers of the province of Britain', the other by 'Lucullus, son of Amminus'.[162] Either Lucullus could plausibly represent the origin of the name-form 'Coilus', especially if, as prominent and wealthy citizens, they were involved in the planning or construction of a palace. Intriguingly, Amminus, the father of Lucullus on the second inscription, is the same name-form as the British prince (Adminius) who Suetonius tells us fled from his father (Cynobellinus) to the relative safety of the emperor Caligula in AD 40, so there certainly is a connection with the Catuvellauni/Trinovantes/Cantiaci here.

Coilus reappears as Cole, duke of Kaelcolim, 'that is to say Colchester' Geoffrey of Monmouth tells us,[163] a Briton who illegally takes the crown from the rightful king, Asclepiodotus, before surrendering to the Roman legate Constantius later in our story. The form also recurs as Cole Hen, or Cole 'the Old', in a number of early Welsh and northern British genealogies.[164] The epithet 'Old' may mean that Cole/Coilus lived to a grand age or, if he was cited as an ancestor or progenitor, simply that he was from deep time:

a much-celebrated and successful leader with a link to the distant Roman past. Whatever the case, it is clear that Coilus/Cole Hen was remembered as a wealthy and extravagant king, a man who certainly is worthy of the description 'merry old soul'.

Severus

The emperor Hadrian visited Britain in AD 122, establishing a permanent solution to Britain's northern frontier by designing a monumental new wall. He also 'corrected many faults', as the anonymously penned Scriptores Historiae Augustae put it,[165] among which was the final dissolution of any remaining client states.[166] The status of native aristocrats within society was probably now much like any other wealthy individual in the Empire, power being relative to continued financial success rather than bloodline or achievements on the battlefield. At this point 'heroic' nature of the kings and queens of Britain in oral tradition seems to fizzle out, there being no new leaders to commemorate in bardic praise poems, eulogies or panegyrics.

The story of Britain, in the absence of any new native rulers, commanders or trendsetters, skips briskly in both the Historia Brittonum and the Historia Regum Britanniae from the second century to the beginning of the fifth with minimal detail. Neither Gildas nor Bede supply any useful information for the period and the framework constructed by Nennius, further built upon by Geoffrey of Monmouth, is sketchy. Only a few key events in the history of Britannia appear to have been remembered or commemorated in oral tradition, and these towards the latter half of the province's life. No mention is made of the battle for Britain and the conquest of Wales, northern England and Scotland in either Historiae, whilst other major incidents, such as the visit by Hadrian, the 'great northern war' of AD 180–4, or the revolt by the governor Clodius Albinus in AD 196–7, are also ignored. As Nennius puts it:

> The Romans ruled over the Britons for four hundred and nine years. The Britons however scorned the rule of the Romans, neither paying them tribute, nor receiving their kings to rule over them, nor did the Romans come to rule Britain any longer, because the Britons had killed their leaders.[167]

The leaders of Rome who came to Britain are numbered as nine in the Historia Brittonum. First was Julius Caesar, followed shortly after by Claudius. Then, on the death of the British King Lucius – the first, according to Nennius, to receive baptism – came Severus. Severus decided that in order to 'protect the re-taken provinces from barbarian attack' he needed to build 'a wall and a rampart from sea to sea across the breadth of Britain'.[168] This defensive line, which is described as running for 'a hundred and thirty-two miles from Penguaul, which town is called Cenail in Scottish, Peneltun in English, up to the mouth of the river Cluth and Cairpentaloch', was constructed to divide the Britons from the Picts and Scots. Not long after building it Severus died, murdered by Karitius who then seized the throne of Britain.[169]

Nennius' account telescopes a series of important events, including the building of Hadrian's Wall (from AD 122), the building of the Antonine Wall, from the Clyde to the Forth (from AD 138), the arrival in Britain of the emperor Septimius Severus (in AD 207–8) and the usurpation of Carausius (in AD 286). Mention of a wall 132 miles in length was probably taken from the fifth-century writer Orosius,[170] who not only wrongly attributes the frontier construction to Severus, who may have merely overseen repairs to Hadrian's Wall, but also gets the distance wrong, Hadrian's Wall being 80 Roman miles long. Geoffrey of Monmouth expands on the brief detail supplied by Nennius. In the Historia Regum Britanniae, Severus arrives immediately after the death of Lucius, the narrative jumping on a century or so from the start to the second century. Battle is joined between the Roman army and the forces of Fulgenius, who is credited as the leader of the rebellion.[171] Fulgenius is not mentioned in any other source from the period. It is just possible that he represents the corruption of a genuine British name-form, although the only named Briton in the Severan campaign is the Caledonian chief Argentocoxus.[172]

The emperor Septimius Severus did indeed bring a large army to Britain, hoping to win a major victory in the north of the island. He also brought with him his wife, Julia Domna, and two sons, Marcus Aurelius Antoninus, born Lucius Septimius Bassianus (and known to history as 'Caracalla'), and Publius Septimius Geta, establishing the imperial court at York. Although tribal envoys arrived from the Maeatae and the Caledones, the two large native tribal confederacies that existed beyond Hadrian's Wall, with offers of peace, Severus wanted a military resolution and sent them back empty-handed. Initially successful, the Roman campaign soon slowed, the guerrilla hit-and-run tactics employed by native groups denying Severus the victory he so craved. 'Unable to go on,' Dio Cassius tells us, 'as many as 50,000 died in all.'[173] Such a body count may be excessive, for Dio Cassius was known to exaggerate, but it is clear that the decision to invade had been a catastrophic miscalculation. Denied set-piece battles, and with no enemy fortresses or towns to attack, the Roman army succumbed to the inevitable. Crippled by illness and worn out by the war, Severus died in York in AD 211. After his funeral, the campaign was swiftly terminated by Antoninus (Caracalla) and the troops were taken home.

Geoffrey of Monmouth has Severus dying in York but credits this not to illness, but to fighting in a battle outside York in which his enemy Fulgenius is also mortally wounded.[174] With Severus dead, Geoffrey tell us, his two sons, Bassianus and Geta, were left to fight over the throne. This much is certainly true, the two sons being bitter rivals and Antoninus eventually going on to kill his brother in Rome. Geta is commemorated in the Historia Regum Britanniae with his correct name-form, but Antoninus by his birth name Bassianus, instead of by his imperial name or later agnomen, 'Caracalla', which may be how he was remembered in Britain. The Romans supported Geta, Geoffrey continues, but the British supported Bassianus because 'he was related to them through his mother's line'.[175] This aspect of Geoffrey's narrative is certainly not true, for Julia Domna, the mother of Antoninus and Geta, was born in Syria and was of Arabic descent while Septimius Severus was North African. Presumably the tradition surrounding the events of AD 211 had Antoninus/Bassianus returning to Rome then becoming sole emperor after murdering Geta the following year. Geoffrey has Bassianus, a part-British claimant, and Geta fighting over the throne of Britain, Bassianus eventually winning and becoming king.

Carausius and Allectus

Karitius (Carausius) was, according to the Historia Brittonum, the fourth Roman to rule Britain who 'came to Britain tyrannically and who was a tyrant because of the murder of Severus'.[176] Nennius therefore makes Septimius Severus the immediate predecessor to Carausius, even though the former died in AD 211 and the latter did not come to power until AD 286. Once again a significant time gap between two remembered traditions is effortlessly bridged, establishing an apparently seamless, uninterrupted chronology. Geoffrey of Monmouth tells us that Carausius was born in Britain of 'humble parentage', and had proved himself on the field of battle. Going to Rome, he asked the Senate if they would grant him permission to deploy a fleet in order to 'defend the coast of Britain against invasion by the barbarians'.[175] The commission sealed, Carausius returned to Britain.

> Carausius soon collected some ships together, gathered round himself a great force of the young men of the country and put out to sea. He sailed along all the coasts of the kingdom, making the greatest possible upset among the inhabitants. Then he landed in the neighbouring islands, laid waste to the open fields, sacked the cities and the towns, and plundered those who lived there of all that they had. While he was behaving in this way, all those who lusted after someone else's possessions flocked to join him. In a short time he had so great a force under command that no local leader could resist him. His head became so swollen by what he had done that he instructed the Britons to make him their king, promising that he would massacre the Romans and wipe them out of existence and so free the whole island from that foreign race. He was given what he asked for.[178]

Carausius then fought with and killed Bassianus, thanks to the last-minute betrayal of the Roman by his Pictish allies who 'deserted the king and attacked his allies'. Having won the crown, Carausius rewarded the Picts with land in Albany.[179] The treacherous seizure of the British crown being reported in Rome, the senate dispatched Allectus with three legions in order to 'restore the kingdom of Britain to the domination of Rome.[180] Allectus wasted no time after landing in Britain, killing Carausius and taking over the reins of government.

In reality, Marcus Aurelius Carausius was an official who, in the 280s AD, had been given the task of clearing the sea lanes between

Britannia and Gaul of pirates and, just as noted in the Historia Regum Britanniae, of defending the coast 'against invasion by the barbarians'. We know next to nothing about him, the fourth-century writer Eutropius noting that he was indeed 'a man of very low birth',[181] but from the Menapii, a tribe from Flanders in Belgium rather than Britain. From the mid-third century, communication between Britain and Gaul had become difficult due to the presence of increasingly hostile maritime bandits, the Saxons, who operated from bases beyond the control of Rome. We don't know just how disruptive Saxon pirate activity was, but the Roman State clearly viewed them as more than just an irritant. That inland targets were hit during the course of the earliest Saxon raids seems evident enough from the written accounts that survive, the historian Aurelius Victor writing in the fourth century AD that much provincial loot was carried off by the bandits.[182]

Carausius seems to have had some success against the Saxons, but he soon found himself on the wrong side of the law. Word got back to Maximian, the emperor of the West (at this time the Roman Empire was divided between two rulers), that the commander of the British Fleet had been letting the barbarians through, only catching them as they headed home with their booty. Whether or not there was any truth in this, it must have been clear to Carausius that the game was up and he decided the best chance of survival lay in rebellion. Late in AD 286 he formally severed ties with Rome and set up his own government. If Carausius had been corrupt, as the sources suggest, allowing pirates to attack soft Roman targets, it is perhaps unlikely that he would have received much support from the British or Gallic elite. As it was, he appears to have been able to muster widespread support from military and civilian officials on both sides of the English Channel. This in turn suggests that there was a groundswell of alienation with the imperial system in the north-western provinces of the Rome Empire. What Carausius offered the soldiers and people of Britain and Gaul we will never know; perhaps it was the opportunity of having a leader who understood local issues and grievances, not one who was based hundreds of miles away in Italy. Perhaps he simply offered greater security from external threats, tax cuts to landowners or better financial incentives for the military.

It's unlikely that everyone would have welcomed Carausius with open arms or viewed the break with Rome as a good thing. It may well be that, in order to take full control of the machinery of government, Carausius had to imprison or remove those officials who remained loyal to the emperor Maximian, and there may have been summary arrests and executions. Whoever had been previously charged to govern Britannia (the province was, by the third century, divided into two commands – one based in London, the other at York) would certainly not have remained in power for long. Unfortunately we do not know the names of any of the state officials on the island at the time Carausius seized power, but there is no evidence that any were called 'Bassianus'. As noted above, Bassianus, whom Nennius does not mention, seems likely to have been Marcus Aurelius Antoninus, born Lucius Septimius Bassianus (Caracalla), the son of Emperor Septimius Severus who came to power in AD 211 and who died in 217, some seven decades before Karitius/Carausius took control of Britain.

It further seems unlikely that, in a bid to take power, Carausius would have 'laid waste to the open fields' nor sacked the cities and 'plundered those who lived there' for such actions would certainly not have won the hearts and minds of the civil population. This sounds more like the sort of negative propaganda spun by the State in order to demonise their enemy. The evidence from coinage produced by the Carausian regime shows that the new leader was keen to exploit the concept that he was a saviour figure, turning the fortune of Britain around. Some coins carried the words Expectate Veni, meaning 'Come the Awaited One', alluding to a line in Virgil's Aeneid, while others echo further Virgilian themes.[183] Two bronze medallions of Carausius have also been recovered with the initials RSR and INPCDA referring directly to lines from Virgil's Eclogues, one of his earlier epic works, which prophesy the return of a Golden Age: 'Redeunt Saturnia Regna' and 'Iam Nova Progenies Caelo Demittitur Alto', or 'the Saturnian reign returns' and 'now a new generation is let down from Heaven above'.[184] Further coins issues, with images of cows being milked, reflect prosperity and times of plenty.[185]

Virgil, in the late first century BC, had of course been making direct references to the Augustan regime in his work, providing literary support for the new order following the collapse of the Roman Republic. That Carausius was further alluding to Virgil shows his own understanding of Rome's artistic legacy, for 'no other emperor ever made so explicit a reference to Rome's literary heritage'.[186] It also implies that the key players in late third-century Britain, especially those who owned land, ran businesses and served as officials in the government and military, knew their Virgil or, at the very least, would be impressed by the widespread use of quotations.[187] This suggests an astute grasp of the importance of propaganda and spin, using cultural heritage as a weapon, which contrasts with the official view that Carausius was nothing but a corrupt and low-born barbarian. It also seems to contradict the story put forward in the Historia Regum Britanniae, no doubt influenced by later imperial perspectives on the regime, that it was held together purely through threats, intimidation and violence.

The loss of Britain was a substantial blow not just to the prestige of the emperor Maximian, but, more importantly, to the whole Roman economy. Plans were soon drawn up to bring Carausius to heel but initial efforts to defeat the usurper were unsuccessful. A series of at least eleven coastal fortresses, comprising Brancaster, Caister, Burgh Castle, Walton, Bradwell, Reculver, Richborough, Dover, Lympne, Pevensey and Portchester, collectively referred to as the 'Saxon Shore', were built across eastern and south-eastern Britain at this time, probably beginning in AD 286. These forts were created, not as part of a defensive chain designed to guard the eastern seaboard from mass invasion by Germanic pirates, but to protect deep-water harbours from the forces of the Roman emperor. As strongly built masonry installations, with a range of state-of-the-art defensive elements including thickened walls, projecting towers and recessed entrances, the forts sat in prominent locations along the coast, acting as both a warning and a deterrent to those hoping to disembark troops.

An unhappy truce between Carausius and Maximian lasted until AD 293 when, following the loss of his overseas territory in northern Gaul, Carausius was assassinated by Allectus. If we know little of Carausius, we know even less about his successor. The Historia Regum Britanniae records that Allectus was a man sent by the Roman senate 'with three legions to kill the tyrant and restore the kingdom of Britain to the domination of Rome'[188] but history suggests he was in fact a subordinate of Carausius, possibly the praetorian prefect in charge of the British emperor's bodyguard, who staged a palace coup.[189] Geoffrey of Monmouth portrays Allectus as a member of Rome's elite who, on taking control back from Carausius, immediately 'massacred as many of the Britons as he could', claiming that, in joining with the usurper they had 'broken their alliance with the State'.[190] Once again there is no alternative evidence, historical or otherwise, for this, although our sources for the period are admittedly rather sparse, but the story may reflect the sort of purges one might expect in the aftermath of a revolution.

Asclepiodotus

Britain, as a breakaway state, was finally brought down in AD 296 when imperial forces under the command of Flavius Valerius Constantius, or Constantius 'Chlorus' ('the Pale'), and Julius Asclepiodotus invaded and suppressed the regime of Allectus. Constantius was at that time holding the rank of Caesar, or junior emperor, being the nominated successor to Maximian, while Asclepiodotus was evidently his right-hand man. Curiously, although Constantius was later to become emperor, it is his subordinate Asclepiodotus who is remembered in British tradition.

The Historia Regum Britanniae has Asclepiodotus as a native leader, the Duke of Cornwall, whom the Britons supported as king in defiance of the Roman-sponsored Allectus. Allectus' popularity had, according to Geoffrey of Monmouth, never been high, partly due to his official endorsement by the senate and partly because of his brutal treatment of those who had previously supported Carausius. Gathering an army, Asclepiodotus marched on London. On hearing the news, Allectus, whom Geoffrey tells us had been 'celebrating a feast day for the gods of his country', took to the field to meet the challenger in battle.

It was Asclepiodotus who was victorious. He scattered the troops of Allectus, forced him to flee and in the pursuit killed many thousands of his men and the leader himself.[191]

As regards the identification of Asclepiodotus, sadly we know nothing of his ethnicity and background, although he was almost certainly not Cornish. The brief detail supplied by Geoffrey of Monmouth does, however, fit what little we know of the invasion in AD 296. According to the panegyrists, the imperial court poets, the Roman army landed on the south coast of Britain, having avoided detection from 'the hostile fleet on station at the Isle of Vecta', thanks to a thick sea fog.[192] It is not known where precisely this was, though reference to 'Vecta', the Isle of Wight, would perhaps place disembarkation somewhere in the Solent Estuary or Portsmouth Harbour, neatly avoiding the fortress of Portchester. Moving swiftly inland, the forces of the emperor Maximian fought with Allectus' troops and destroyed them. 'In this victory,' the panegyrist cooed, 'scarcely did a single Roman fall', adding that,

> All the plains and hills were littered only with the prostrate corpses of our loathsome enemies. Those bodies of barbarians or those that once feigned barbarous ways in style and dress and long blond hair, now lay besmirched with dust and gore, frozen into various attitudes of death imposed by agony of wounds, and among them the ringleader of that band of brigands himself.[193]

The keenness of the poet to emphasise that only barbarians fell probably reflects the concerns of the State to avoid providing legitimacy to Allectus' government through the acknowledgement that Roman citizens had been fighting on both sides of the conflict. It may also reflect the fact that Allectus had, as Geoffrey of Monmouth infers, been less popular than his predecessor Karitius/Carausius, and had been unable to draw upon units of the regular army, relying instead upon mercenaries (the blond-haired 'barbarians'). Perhaps Allectus had simply been ill-prepared, not believing that Rome would invade in force at that particular time.

With the battle won and Allectus dead, Geoffrey tells us that Livius Gallus, 'one of Allectus' fellow officers', withdrew behind the walls of London with what remained of his forces. Asclepiodotus immediately began to lay siege to the city. Once again no mention is made of Constantius, possibly because he was not referenced in the sources

Geoffrey used to compile the Historia Regum Britanniae. It may be that the bulk of the fighting had indeed fallen to Asclepiodotus, especially if the invasion had been a two-pronged affair, Constantius landing elsewhere. Whatever the case, inclusion of Caesar Constantius at this point would have significantly diluted the impact of Geoffrey's narrative, for he depicts the conflict as a rebellion led by a British aristocrat (Asclepiodotus) against the forces of a tyrannical Roman king (Allectus).

[Asclepiodotus] sent word to all the leaders of Britain that he had killed Allectus and many of his soldiers and was now besieging Gallus and the remnants of the Romans inside London. He begged each and every one of them, as a matter of great urgency, to come and help him as quickly as possible, for now that they were besieged the whole race of the Romans might easily be exterminated from Britain, if only, as he said, the British leaders would attack them with their united strength.[194]

Hearing the call to war, Geoffrey tells us, the Demeti, Venedoti, Deiri, Albani 'and all the Britons without exception' marched on London, an action reminiscent of the assault by Boudicca's army on the city in AD 60. Tearing down the city walls with siege engines, the Britons set about killing everyone they could find. The Romans begged Livius Gallus to surrender 'so that they might be allowed to depart with their lives'.[195] Gallus duly threw himself at the mercy of Asclepiodotus, but the Venedoti managed to get to the Romans first, 'and in one day decapitated the lot of them'. Geoffrey tells us that his atrocity was conducted 'beside a brook in the city which from the name of their leader was afterwards called Nantgallum in Welsh or in Saxon Galobroc'.[196]

The identification of Nantgallum/Galobroc with the Walbrook, an important tributary of the Thames, which effectively divided the Roman settlement of London in two, seems clear enough. The origin of the name however, back-projected by Geoffrey of Monmouth from Livius Gallus,, the unlucky leader of the Romans following the death of Allectus, seems unlikely. It probably derived from either the 'brook by the wall' or the brook or stream of the walas/wealh (the 'Welsh' in Old English). Significant amounts of Romano-British ritual and religious material has been recovered from the river, although it is now, rather sadly, built over and largely forgotten. Human skulls have been found from both the Walbrook and the length of the Thames during multiple phases of dredging and development, particularly in the nineteenth century.[197] Although the majority appear to represent young males, suggesting a degree of selection, they span a range of time periods, and there is no evidence to date that they relate to a single catastrophic event, such as the Boudiccan Revolt when, we are told by Tacitus, the Britons 'rushed to slaughter, hang, burn and crucify'.[198] The tale of Livius Gallus, as told in the Historia Regum Britanniae, could indeed echo a real event, a mass execution of prisoners undertaken during the Roman or any subsequent period, commemorated in oral tradition, or it could, more prosaically, derive from an attempt by Geoffrey of Monmouth to explain the large number of human skulls recovered from the Walbrook at the time he was writing.

Unsurprisingly perhaps, the official account preserved in the Roman panegyrics paints a more joyful 'liberation' of London than that described in the Historia Regum Britanniae. In the sanctioned version, the Britons, we are told, greeted Constantius as 'the longed-for avenger' and were 'borne along by such great joy after so many years of most wretched captivity'.[199] A medallion struck to commemorate the occasion, found at Arras in France, depicts the moment that the haughty Constantius, on horseback and with spear in hand, advanced on a city. A woman, presumably representing the personification of London (as the initials LON appear beneath her), kneels with arms outstretched in adulation while below, in the Thames, an imperial galley rows serenely past. The inscription around the triumphant Caesar Constantius reads 'Redditor Lucis Aeternae' ('the restorer of Eternal Light'). After ten years, Britain was formally back inside the Roman Empire.

6

TWILIGHT OF THE KINGDOM

The basic chronological sequence of events appearing in both the Historia Brittonum and the Historia Regum Britanniae, from the first invasion of Julius Caesar (in 55 BC) to the crushing of the Carausian revolt by Asclepiodotus (in AD 296), follows that established in contemporary historical sources, albeit with substantial gaps in the overall narrative. Nennius, as we have seen, credits only nine Romans as having power over Britain: Caesar, Claudius, Severus, Karitius (Carausius), Constantius, Maximus, Maximianus, Severus the Second and another Constantius. The line of emperors becomes a little confused after Karitius, with significant amounts of event repetition, back-projection and duplication of characters. This may be partially due, as Nennius notes, to the fact that 'the traditions of our elders tell that in those times seven emperors came from Rome to Britain, however the Romans say there were nine'. This not only further indicates a strong oral tradition, that of the 'elders', was being drawn on for the Historia Brittonum, but also there was a written one deriving from the world of Rome. Thankfully Nennius does not gloss over any contradictions evident in the two sources of information but actually drawn attention to them.

Constantine

According to Nennius, the tyrant Karitius 'put to the sword all the rulers of Britain'.[1] After him came Constantius, 'son of the great Constantine' who died in Britain, being buried in Cair Segeint. Constantius can only be Flavius Valerius Constantius (Constantius 'Chlorus'), who, as heir to the imperial throne, led the campaign against Allectus in AD 296 in which Asclepiodotus participated. In AD 305, Constantius was elevated to Augustus (emperor) when his boss, Maximian, retired, returning to Britain in order to campaign on the northern frontier. Constantius died in York, early in 306, the soldiers there proclaiming his son Constantine as successor. It was this Constantine who later earned the title 'the Great', Nennius (or his sources) evidently confusing the identity and sequence of father and son.

Geoffrey of Monmouth has the reign of Asclepiodotus ending ten years after the death of Allectus with a revolt led by Coel, 'duke of Kaelcolim, that is to say Colchester'.² Coel we have already met as a possible repetition of Coilus (Lucullus), credited in the Historia Regum Britanniae as being a leader in Britain in the aftermath of the Claudian invasion. Coel paid tribute to senator Constantius, dispatched from Rome to restore Britain to the empire, as Constantius Chlorus did when sent in AD 296 to depose Allectus. On the death of Cole, from 'a most serious illness', Constantius seized the crown of Britain, marrying Coel's daughter Helen, described as being more beautiful than any other woman in the kingdom.³ In reality, Constantius had earlier married a Helen/Helena, who later became St Helen, but she was not British but from Bithynia in Asia Minor (Turkey). Together the union of Constantius and Helen produced a son, Constantine. Eleven years later, according to Geoffrey of Monmouth, Constantius died in York, passing the throne to his son.

Constantine took an army out of Britain, together with Helen's three uncles, Ioelinus, Trahern and Marius, to crush the tyrant Maxentius, who was ruling Rome with 'oppressive savagery'.⁴ They left the kingdom in the hands 'of a certain proconsul'.⁵ Capturing Rome, Constantine became 'overlord of the entire world'. This, again, broadly follows the established sequence of events, Constantine becoming emperor of Rome after defeating Maxentius at the battle of the Milvian Bridge in AD 312, eventually taking control of the whole empire, after defeating the eastern incumbent Licinius in AD 324. In the Historia Regum Britanniae, Constantine hears that the kingdom of Britain has been seized in his absence by Octavius, Duke of the Gewissei. Sending three legions back to Britain with Trahern, Constantine hopes to reclaim the territory. Octavius and Trahern we have already met, as the alter egos of Augustus and Tasciovanus, both characters taken from the late first century BC. Trahern recovers Britain but, following his death in an ambush, Octavius returns to the island.

As Octavius became weakened by age, and with no son to succeed him, a dispute arose as to the succession, Constantine never having returned to reclaim the throne. Octavius' counsellors advised that his nephew, Conanus Meridiadocus, should be married to the king's (unnamed) daughter, allowing him to take the crown. Others, like Caradocus Duke of Cornwall, suggested that a better match would be found with senator Maximianus, son of Ioelinus and nephew of Cole. Conanus, unhappy with this suggestion, sent his son Mauricius to Rome to talk with Maximianus. Maximianus and Mauricius return to Britain, landing at Southampton. Hearing of their arrival, the elderly Octavius sent Conanus to attack the newcomers, war being averted only by the appearance of Caradocus, Duke of Cornwall. Octavius agreed to give the kingdom of Britain and his daughter to Maximianus. Conanus, aggrieved, returned with an army, determined to wrest Britain from Maximianus. After a protracted battle, the two finally make peace.

This rather convoluted tale of revolt, usurpation, invasion and treachery repeats many of the themes already developed in the Historia Regum Britanniae, such as a Roman invasion establishing itself at Southampton aided by a Briton (here being Mauricius rather than Lelius Hamo/Adminius), as well as reintroducing major characters such as Caradocus of Cornwall (Caratacus and the Catuvellauni) and Marius, the eighty-sixth king.

Maximianus

Magnus Maximus, a Spaniard who, after being illegally made emperor in Britain in the year AD 383, took soldiers from the island to fight a war against Rome which ended in his capture and execution seems, on the face of it, a peculiar choice for a British hero. Yet, aside from Arthur, he seems to have been the most important figure in post-Roman tradition, appearing as Maximus as an ancestor to the dynasty of Powys, Maxim as an ancestor to the kingdoms of Dyfed, Gwynllwg, Dal Riata and the Isle of Man and Maxen in the genealogies of a number of saints.[6] An inscription on the Valle Crucis pillar (or pillar of Eliseg), a stone set up by Concenn, ruler of Powys, in the early ninth century to honour his great-grandfather, Eliseg, traces his lineage back to Sevira, who, so the stone claims, was the wife of Guarthigirn (Gwrtheyrn/Vortigern) and daughter of 'Maximus the king, who killed the king of the Romans'.[7] Magnus Maximus also figures prominently in Welsh folklore as Maxen Wledig in the Trioedd Ynys Prydein and Macsen Wledig in the Mabinogion.[8]

In truth, Magnus Maximus, whose name can be translated as meaning, rather modestly, 'the Great the Greatest', was a career soldier. Promoted to a command in Britain, possibly as dux Britanniarum (military leader of the northern army), Maximus' proclamation as emperor was explained by the early sixth-century historian Zosimus as being due to jealousy that Theodosius, a colleague from his youth, had been 'considered worthy of the throne' in the eastern half of the empire, while Maximus had not received similar recognition.[9] Whatever the real reason for the uprising, Maximus soon crossed to Gaul where the western emperor, Gratian, was swiftly killed. Striking a deal with Justina, Gratian's mother, Maximus allowed her and her second son, Valentinian II, who was then still only twelve, to rule Italy, leaving Maximus in charge of the remaining areas of the west. Eventually tiring of the relationship, and perhaps feeling confident having been, as the fifth-century historian Sozomenus tells us, reinforced with 'a very large army of Britons, neighbouring Gauls, Celts and the tribes thereabouts', Maximus entered Italy determined to take Rome. Valentinian and Justina fled and, faced with no real alternative, Theodosius, the eastern emperor (son of Maximus' erstwhile colleague), brought an army into Italy, catching Maximus at Aquileia in AD 388, where the usurper was executed. Flavius Victor, the son whom Maximus had left in charge of Gaul, was also killed later the same year.

Gildas, the first British source to mention Maximus, is hardly complimentary.

[Britain] cast forth a sprig of its own bitter planting, and sent Maximus to Gaul with a great retinue of hangers-on and even the imperial insignia, which he was never fit to bear; he had no legal claim to the title, but was raised to it like a tyrant by rebellious soldiery. Applying cunning rather than virtue, Maximus turned the neighbouring lands and provinces against Rome, and attached them to his kingdoms of wickedness with the nets of his perjury and lying. One of his wings he stretched to Spain, one to Italy, the throne of his wicked empire he placed at Trier, where he raged so madly against his masters that of the two legitimate emperors, he drove one from Rome, the other from his life, which was a very holy one.[10]

The end result of this futile and 'wicked war' in Gildas' view was catastrophic:

Britain was despoiled of her whole army, her military resources, her governors, brutal as they were, and her study youth, who followed in the tyrant's footsteps, never to return home. Quite ignorant of the ways of war, she groaned aghast for many years, trodden underfoot first by two exceedingly savage overseas nations, the Scots from the north west and the Picts from the north.[11]

In the Historia Brittonum, Maximus is the sixth Roman emperor to rule Britain,[12] the seventh being Maximianus.[13] Nennius ultimately has very little to say about Maximus, other than he 'conversed with Saint Martin'. If this is, as seems likely, Saint Martin of Tours, then 'Maximus' can only have been Magnus Maximus, who is credited as meeting the saint in Gaul in AD 385. This creates an obvious problem in the narrative for the seventh emperor of the Historia Brittonum, Maximianus, is then established as leaving Britain 'with all the soldiers' and gaining imperium over Europe after killing 'Gratian, king of the Romans'.[14] This, as is evident, is also a description of Magnus Maximus who, after departing Britain with the soldiery, fought with and killed the emperor Gratian at Lyons in AD 383. Presumably Nennius was working with two separate traditions, one describing a meeting between Maximus and St Martin, the other, with the corrupted name-form Maximianus, commemorating his victory against Gratian and his seizure of the western half of the empire.

Nennius explains that having gained imperium, Maximianus was unwilling to allow his troops to return home 'to their wives and their sons and their possessions', instead granting them land 'from the lake at the top of Mont Jovis to the city called Cantguic and as far as the western summit that is Cruc Occident', explaining that they now became 'the Amoric Britons'.[15] The geographical placement provided in the Historia Brittonum is vague, but evidently equates with Armorica, later to become Brittany ('little Britain'). This statement builds on Gildas' earlier view that the soldiers leaving with Maximus never returned, a point also picked up in Triad 35 of the Trioedd Ynys Prydein, being the second of the 'Three Levies that departed from this Island and not one of them came back'.[16] It is also a key element in the story of Maximianus as told in the Historia Regum Britanniae, the settlement of Brittany being of major concern to Geoffrey of Monmouth.

Typically, having dispensed with Maximus/Maximianus and moved on with the story, Nennius returns 'to the tyrant' in section 29 of the Historia Brittonum. Presumably this narrative flashback reflects an additional primary source or oral tradition that required inclusion. Unfortunately it only serves to muddy the sequence presented in the chronicle yet further, the readers being informed that at the same time as the soldiers serving the usurper took control of Gaul, 'Martin, bishop of Tours, was renowned for his great virtues'. To add further confusion, Nennius suddenly switches between name-forms, the tyrant being Maximianus when he is in Britain, but Maximus when he arrives in Gaul.[17]

The story of Maximianus/Maximus as it unfolds in the Historia Brittonum broadly follows the established sequence of historical events, right up to the capture and execution of Magnus Maximus and his son Flavius Victor. Geoffrey of Monmouth, however, picks up the name-form Maximianus but changes a critical aspect of the story. In the Historia Regum Britanniae, Maximianus, as we have already seen, was a Roman senator, his parents being Ioelinus, the British uncle of Helen, wife of Constantine, and an unnamed Roman woman 'by birth of royal blood'.[18] Annoyed at having been overlooked for the imperial throne, it going instead to Gracianus and Valentinianus, Maximinanus is pleased to be invited to Britain where he takes the kingdom and marries the daughter of King Octavius.

Five years into his reign, Maximianus, having 'developed an obsession with power', decides to invade Gaul. Conscripting 'every armed soldier in Britain', he leads a fleet across the Channel to attack the 'kingdom of the Armorici'. Defeating duke Himbaldus and slaughtering 15,000 of his men, Maximianus observes that 'we have seized one of the fairest kingdoms of Gaul', promptly granting it to Conanus Meridiadocus, nephew of King Octavius.[19] Marching on through Gaul, the Britons 'massacred the men, sparing only the women', eventually wiping out 'every single male in the whole land'. Determined to restock his new territory with people from Britain, Maximianus summoned 100,000 'ordinary men and women' from the island whom, with 30,000 soldiers to protect them, he redistributed through Armorica. 'In this way,' Geoffrey tells us, 'he created a second Britain.'[20] Moving on to conquer Germany, Maximianus 'vented his fury on the two emperors', killing Gracianus and driving Valentianus from Rome.

Meanwhile Conanus, 'returning bloodshed for bloodshed' in 'defending with great manliness' his new kingdom of Armorica (much like the Trojan Corineus defended Cornwall for his overking Brutus), decides that he needs wives for his soldiers. In order to 'prevent any mixture of blood with the Gauls', the ethnically sensitive Conanus sends word to Britain to Dionotus, Duke of Cornwall, whom Geoffrey tells us 'had succeeded his brother Caradocus in the kingship of Britain', to assemble 11,000 daughters of noblemen, together with 60,000 'others born to the lower orders'.[21] Unfortunately the ships transporting the women across the sea were hit by a storm, those who did not drown being slaughtered or sold into slavery by 'the execrable army of Wanius and Melga', kings of the Huns and Picts respectively.[22] Learning that Britain was now denuded of its military, leaving only the 'unarmed and witless peasantry', Wanius and Melga invaded from Albany, slaughtering the population 'as though they had been so many sheepfolds'.[23]

In essence this story appears to represent the conflation of many diverse elements. King Dionotus of Cornwall, replacing his brother Caradocus in power, appears to be an echo of Togidubnus replacing Caratacus of the Catuvellauni in the years immediately following the Claudian invasion of AD 43, while the combined attack on

Britain by Wanius and Melga may reflect the events of the 'Great Barbarian Conspiracy' of AD 367. The 71,000 female migrants, of whom 11,000 were 'daughters of noblemen', is also found in the tradition of St Ursula, who is supposed to have travelled with 11,000 handmaidens from Britain to meet her future husband. Captured by the Rhine, the entire party, it is said, were executed by the Huns, relics from the martyrs being held today in Cologne. The origins of the St Ursula story are not known, but it is evident that Geoffrey of Monmouth was conflating the tale with a tradition of mass migration to Armorica,[24] which he has already alluded to when describing the 100,000 'ordinary men and women' gathered by Maximianus earlier in the Historia.

Overall, the story of Conanus and Brittany sounds very much like a foundation myth or origin story similar to those we have already encountered in both the Historia Brittonum and the Historia Regum Britanniae, with the Promised Land, large numbers of migrants and a heroic leader. Cynan/Conan Meriodoc appears as 'one of the two promised deliverers who will one day return and lead the Britons to victory' in tenth- and eleventh-century Welsh prophetic verse.[25] He is generally considered a founding figure or progenitor of the Bretons, the name Conan being popular among the dukes of Brittany right up to the mid-twelfth century; indeed, just prior to invading England in 1066, Duke William of Normandy had been at war with Conan II. Armorica/Brittany seems to have been important to Geoffrey of Monmouth and it has been suggested that he was himself part Breton.[26]

The colonization of Brittany also features in Breudwyt Macsen Wledig (the Dream of Prince Macsen/Maxen), an early Welsh tale first written down in the early twelfth century and often incorporated together with the four branches of the Mabinogion. In this, Macsen Wledig, already the emperor of Rome, repeatedly dreams of a beautiful woman in a distant land. Determined to find her, Macsen dispatches men all over his empire until she is found, eventually, in Britain at Caer Seint (Caernarfon), the Roman fort of Segontium in Gwynedd. Refusing to go to Rome, the maiden, Elen Lluydawc, insists that the emperor come to her in person. This he does, conquering Britain by defeating Beli Mawr, son of Manogan, along the way. Marrying Elen,

Macsen grants the whole island to her father, Eudaf Hen, but stays in Britain for so long that his position in Rome is usurped. With the help of Elen's brother Cynan, Macsen recaptures Rome and, in reward, grants him Armorica/Brittany.

Geoffrey of Monmouth does not mention the name of Maximianus' wife, the daughter of Octavius, but the Breudwt Macsen Wledig calls her Elen, daughter of Eudaf Hen. The epithet Lluydawc 'of the Hosts', which the writer of Breudawt Macsen applies to Elen, is not explained but it has been suggested that the name originally belonged to 'an independent figure in native tradition', possibly a deity.[27] If so, it could be that Elen was viewed as a primary ancestor or progenitor, the union between her and Macsen Wledig helping to bring two royal pedigrees together.[28] Further confusion arose in British tradition with regard to the mother of Constantine the Great, whom history records as Helena and who later became St Helena/St Helen. The Historia Regum Britanniae tries to make Constantine's mother British, the daughter of King Coel, perhaps because tradition already had a Helen/Elen as the wife of Magnus Maximus/Maximianus.

Although the name-form Maxim in early Welsh tradition has clearly derived from 'Maximus' and 'Maximianus', Macsen (or Maxen as he is in most English accounts) seems to have evolved from something else entirely – perhaps a variant form of Maxentius. We have already seen the confusion, evident in the Historia Brittonum, surrounding the names Maximus and Maximianus, but Maxentius is different. It is possible that this name-form derived from the emperor Maxentius, who famously fought against Constantine 'the Great' in AD 312. Alternatively, however, it could have originated from another usurper who, like Magnus Maximus, also challenged the power of Rome in the latter half of the fourth century.

Flavius Magnus Magnentius, was a Roman officer who was proclaimed emperor in AD 350 at Autun in eastern Gaul. Large numbers of soldiers in the western army defected to his cause and the legitimate emperor, Constans, was killed. Invading the eastern half of the empire, after Constantius II, the emperor there had refused to acknowledge him. Magnentius' army was defeated at the battle of Mursa, a conflict that would prove catastrophic for the Roman world. Estimates of the dead at Mursa suggested that 24,000 fell on Magnentius' side and 30,000 on Constantius', a casualty figure that permanently compromised the Roman military.[29] Despite failing to defeat Constantius II, Magnentius managed to retain control of the west until AD 353. Sources at the time claimed he had a British father and Frankish mother, although more recent writers have suggested this story may have ultimately derived from negative imperial propaganda.[30] Whatever the case, Magnentius, whose coinage was the first to prominently display Christian imagery, clearly enjoyed significant support in Britain. When Constantius took control of the island in 353, after defeating Magnentius, the reprisals were particularly harsh. Ammianus Marcellinus noted that the man sent to Britain, a Spaniard called Paulus, exceeded his instructions to seek out and punish conspirators.

> Like a flood he suddenly overwhelmed the fortunes of many, sweeping forward amidst widespread slaughter and ruin, casting freeborn men into prison and degrading some with fetters, all this by fabricating charges which were far removed from the truth. Thus was perpetrated an impious crime which branded Constantius' time with an everlasting mark of shame.

The rebellion of Flavius Magnus Magnentius had a debilitating effect on Britain, leaving its military significantly weakened and its political and aristocratic elite compromised. Given that the revolt occurred just thirty years before the revolt of Flavius Magnus Maximus, and had been led by someone with an extremely similar name, it is possible that later chronicle writers confused the name-forms Magnentius and Maximus, creating Maxentius/Maxen/Macsen in the process.

The importance of Magnus Maximus in British tradition does not appear to have been due to his bloody struggle against Rome, nor his establishment of Brittany as an independent kingdom of Britons/Bretons, although these were both major areas of interest for Geoffrey of Monmouth. The value of Maximus/Maximianus/Macsen was that he embodied the link between the ancient Britons and Rome by 'not only making Britain Roman, but also by making the Roman Empire British'.[32] He may, furthermore, have been remembered as the man who reorganized the political structure of the British tribes, permitting a greater degree of autonomy in those areas where the official Roman garrison had been denuded. That too would perhaps have made him seem like the prime mover or progenitor in certain post-Roman households.

Vortigern

The Historia Regum Britanniae says that after Maximianus 'was killed in Rome by friends of Gracianus', the former emperor, those Britons in his army 'were either slain or scattered', the few who did escape fleeing to Armorica/Brittany.[32] In Britain the throne was seized by another Gracianus who, after acting tyrannically, was deposed. Acting on the requests of the Britons, Geoffrey tells us, in a lengthy section culled almost word for word from Gildas' De Excidio Britanniae, Rome sent a legion to Britain but then, tired of such 'wearisome expeditions' the Romans finally left the Britons to their own devices.[34] Constantine, the brother of Alrdroneus, King of Brittany, then came to Britain, at the request of Archbishop Guithelinus, to be king, landing at Totnes. Married to an (unnamed) woman 'born of a noble family', Constantine's rule is cut short by a murderous Pict with a knife.[35]

Gratian (Gratianus) is briefly noted as a 'a citizen of the island' of Britain who rose in revolt against Rome early in the fifth century by Orosius in his Adversum Paganos,[36] a text which Bede and Nennius had access to. Unfortunately nothing is known about him other than he was swiftly killed and replaced by Constantine, an usurper who survived just long enough to go down in history as Constantine III. Unlike the Constantine appearing in the Historia Regum Britanniae, this one left Britain for Gaul, in the year AD 407, taking a large part of the Roman field army with him where he immediately started to expand his empire. Two years later, whatever officials were left in Britain rebelled against both Constantine III and the government of the legitimate emperor Honorius, taking the island out of the Roman Empire for good. From this point we can no longer rely on Roman histories to supply information with which we can compare accounts appearing in either the Historia Regum Britanniae or the Historia Brittonum. This is a shame because it's at this point that things really start to get interesting.

With the assassination of Constantine, so Geoffrey tells us, a disagreement arose among the leaders of Britain concerning the succession. Constantine had three sons, two of which, Aurelius Ambrosius and Utherpendragon, were still infants while the third, Constans, was in a monastery. Vortigern, 'leader of the Gewissei', and chief among the royal advisors, persuaded Constans to take the throne but, in a secret deal, convinced him to pass governmental control of the kingdom over. Eventually tiring of Constans, Vortigern had him killed. Fearing for the safety of the two remaining younger brothers, those looking after them 'fled with their charges to Little Britain' (Brittany) where King Budicius received them 'with due honour'.[37] Vortigern was now left in charge as king.

Vortigern is perhaps one of the more infamous of characters to appear in the Historia Regum Britanniae and the Historia Brittonum. Geoffrey of Monmouth and Nennius both make it clear that it was he who first invited the Saxons into Britain, giving them land on which to settle; it was Vortigern, therefore, who ultimately brought about the ruin of the kingdom. This critical point in British history, with English migrants first gaining a foothold in the island, unsurprisingly features strongly in Gildas' narrative. To Gildas, this was the source of all the woes to affect the wretched Britons. 'The method of destruction they devised for our land was that the ferocious Saxons, name not to be spoken, hated by man and God, should be let into the island like wolves to the fold,' Gildas fumes, adding that 'nothing more bitter has ever befallen the land.'[38]

The name of the man responsible for the catastrophe is not given by Gildas, either because it was too hurtful – he could after all hardly bring himself to say the word 'Saxon' – or because his congregation knew only too well to whom he was referring. All he is able to say is that the decision to invite the Saxons was made by 'all the members of the council, together with the Superbus Tyrannus'.[39] There have been many guesses as to the precise identity of this unnamed 'tyrant'. Most writers have plumped for 'Vortigern', partly because this is the name later given by Bede, who notes that 'the Angles or Saxons came to Britain at the invitation of King Vurtigerno in three longships'.[40] Partly also the association is made because the title that Gildas gives to the fateful British leader, Superbus Tyrannus, can be translated literally as the 'arrogant tyrant' while Vurtigerno/Vertigernus/Vortigern is an equivalent British form, meaning something like 'overlord'. Ultimately, as these are all titles rather than birthnames, we are left in the dark as to the true identity of the man behind the name-form Vortigern.

Gildas makes the claim that the council, led by the arrogant tyrant, invited the Saxons to Britain to 'beat back the peoples of the north',[41] suggesting, perhaps, either military operations at the limits of Britannia, along Hadrian's Wall, or, perhaps more realistically given that the Germanic groups seem to have been settled in Kent, as hired muscle to defend Cantia/Kent from its immediate neighbours. The hiring of mercenaries or federates from Germanic and other tribes was standard practice in the Later Roman Empire and if, in the early years of the fifth century, Britain was indeed fragmenting into separate tribal kingdoms, multiple warlords attempting to seize and maintain control of their new territories, perhaps it seemed the sensible thing to do.

The deliberate early settlement of Saxon groups in Kent may further explain why Canterbury is unique among Romano-British towns in preserving the tribal suffix 'Cantiaci', becoming 'Cantiaci-burgh'. All other urban centres appear to have lost the tribal element of their name in the immediate post-Roman period, focusing instead on the element 'Castrum', from the Latin term for 'fortress'.[42] Hence towns like Venta Belgarum, the Roman market town created for the Belgae, became Venta Castrum or Winchester while Isca Dumnoniorum, the market town for the Dumnonii, became Isca Castrum or Exeter. This did not happen in Gaul, where the tribal suffix remained intact, to be transmitted to subsequent Germanic groups suggesting that here, unlike in Britain 'the idea of the urban centre encapsulating the people and its land remained important'.[43] Perhaps the comparatively early switch from British to Germanic-speaking groups in south-eastern England occurred at a time when Romano-British tribal identities still meant something. The transfer of power to 'barbarian' control in Cantium/Kent could therefore have been different to that occurring elsewhere in Britannia, the territory inheriting something of its political structure directly from its British past.[44]

Gildas tells us, in his own distinctive way, that 'a pack of cubs' who 'burst forth from the lair of the barbarian lioness' came across the North Sea and 'fixed their dreadful claws on the east side of the island', the ill-fated Superbus Tyrannus hoping that they would fight to protect 'our country'.[45] Unfortunately for both tyrant and council, 'the mother lioness learnt that her first contingent had prospered, and she sent a second and larger troop of satellite dogs', suggesting a second wave of wholly unexpected, or unwanted, English migrants. The increase in numbers sparked a request for more supplies, which were at first granted and which, for the time being at least, 'shut the dog's mouth'.[46] Demands for further food and payment were accompanied, so Gildas tells us, with threats 'to plunder the whole island'. Non-payment by the British council led to a tearing up of the agreement, the newcomers putting 'their threats into immediate effect'.

Bede, as we have already noted, adds small, but significant, amounts of detail to Gildas' Old Testament, blood-and-thunder account, providing names not only for the Superbus Tyrannus but also the leaders of the Saxon warband, noting that 'their first chieftains are said to have been the brothers Hengist and Horsa'.[47] The element of doubt expressed by Bede, claiming that Saxon leaders are 'said to have been called' Hengist and Horsa, may relate back to the strength of oral tradition at the time he was writing, rather than something more definite; something derived from a creation myth perhaps, rather than any form of dynastic or documented certainty.[48] We have already noted that most early royal houses claimed decent from a divine, or semi-divine, progenitor and it is possible that Hengist and Horsa were, in reality, just that. It has long been established that the names are both variants of an equine form in Old English, meaning 'stallion' and 'horse' respectively.[49] It is just possible, therefore, that the story handed down to Bede was one corrupted or modified from a more literal origin myth whereby the first settlers in Kent claimed descent from a divine stallion and mare. If 'Horsa' was originally the feminine name-form in the pairing, gender and relationship to Hengist being altered when the animal deities were anthropomorphized, it could be that patriarchal later Christian society changed the two into founding twin brothers, akin to Romulus and Remus.

The Anglo-Saxon Chronicle provides further detail following the revolt against Vortigern mentioned in Gildas and Bede, citing, as one would perhaps expect, a successful series of battles in which additional territory was added to the kingdom of Kent. In 455, according to the Chronicle, Hengist and Horsa fought Vortigern 'in the place called Aegelesthrep' where Horsa is recorded as dying. In 456 Hengest and his son Aesc 'fought the Britons in the place called Crecganford' where four companies of the enemy were killed, the Britons giving up Kent 'and in great fear fled to London'. In 465 Hengest and Aesc 'fought the Welsh near Wippedesfleot' where twelve 'Welsh' (British) ealdormen were killed. In 473 Hengest and Aesc again 'fought the Welsh', this time seizing 'countless spoils of war'. The rather mangled name-forms supplied by the Chronicle for Ypwinesfleot, the original landing site of the Saxon warband, as well as the battles of Aegelesthrep and Crecganford, for Ebbsfleet, Aylesford and Crayford respectively, have suggested that the compilers were not copying information directly from a written account of the Kentish kingdom, 'but rather drawing on oral tradition'. Hence the West Saxon (Wessex) Chronicle writers were consequently corrupting the place names 'in a way that would not have been acceptable to a Kentish audience'.[50]

The character of Vortigern, or 'Guorthigirnus' as Nennius calls him, expands significantly within the Historia Brittonum, his story developing over sections 31–49, filling almost a quarter of the overall word count for the work. The tale begins, as with Gildas, Bede and the Anglo-Saxon Chronicle, with the Saxons under Hengest and Horsa being provided with land on the proviso that they fight in support of the British king. At the point where the Britons are considering releasing the Saxons from the deal, Hengest, we are told, prepares a feast where, after plying Guorthigirnus with copious amounts of alcohol, the king is introduced to Hengest's daughter. Fuelled by lust, Guorthigirnus asks for her hand in marriage, to which the Saxon leader demands in return 'the region that in their language was called Cantguaraland, but in our language Cantia'.[51] This could of course be entirely fictional, a lurid detail added to entertain, but it is just possible, as Nicolas Brooks has observed, that it echoes the transfer of territory 'from British to English control by legal means' through a marriage alliance, not by warfare and conquest.[52]

The Houses of Guorthigirnus and Hengest being thus joined, Hengest, as the father-in-law of the British king, began to act as chief counsellor to Guorthigirnus, simultaneously increasing his grip on Kent. 'Adding to his wickedness,' the Historia Brittonum tells us, 'Guorthigirnus took his own daughter in marriage and she bore him a son.'[53] Evidently now lost in sin, Guorthigirnus is hounded by Germanus, a Christian envoy from Rome, and after taking advice from his magicians he elects to flee to the furthest part of his kingdom where he starts building a fortress. At this point in the narrative there may be a degree of textual confusion: Nennius just described two marriages in relatively short time, one between Guorthigirnus and the (unnamed) daughter of Hengist (Geoffrey of Monmouth later calls her Ronwein[54]) and another, incestuous one with his own (again unnamed) daughter. Quite how Gildas missed this particularly reprehensible aspect of the Superbus Tyrannus' character is unclear given how much he revels in the base depravity of the 'five tyrants' featured in de Excidio Britanniae. It is possible, however, that he didn't overlook this detail of regal incest; it's just he allotted it to a different person entirely.

Gildas records the immoral nature of 'Vortipor, tyrant of the Demetae' whom, among his many sins, is singled out for 'the despoilment of a shameless daughter' following 'the removal and honourable death' of Vortipor's own wife.[55] Vortipor, whose name also may have been a title, meaning something like 'overking', was leader of the Demetae, the pre-Roman name for the tribe of Dyfed in Wales. Little is known about him, other than information contained in Gildas' colourful rant. Given the mangling of name-forms that we have already seen, however, it is possible that the Vortipor/Vortiporius appearing in de Excidio Britanniae was also the Voteporigis commemorated on a tombstone found at Castell Dwyran and now in Carmarthenshire Museum. The inscription reads MEMORIA VOTEPORIGIS PROTICTORIS, which translates as 'in memory of Voteporigis / Voteporix / Voteporius / Vortepor the protector'. Whoever the stone remembers, and whether or not it is the same person as Gildas' 'tyrant of the Demetae', it is evident that this particular individual was favoured by those whom he had 'protected'.

It may be that the similarity in Vort/Vorti- name-forms led Nennius, or those who had a hand in establishing the tradition before him, to confuse the daughter-marrying king of the Demetae with the Saxon-marrying king of the Gewissiae; hence 'Vortipor' was conflated with 'Vortigern'/Guorthigirnus, the unpleasant story of a family affair being used to further discredit the king who first invited Hengest and Horsa to Britain. Such a scenario would certainly resolve the apparent double marriage confusion in the Historia Brittonum, Vortigern/Guorthigirnus committing bigamy as well as incest in a relatively short space of time. This would also explain why Geoffrey of Monmouth, although concentrating on the duplicitous and treacherous nature of Vortigern, fails to dwell on the more unpleasant aspects of his private life for it simply did not feature in the sources that he examined.

Textual/name-form confusion may also explain why Geoffrey further confuses aspects of the lives and respective reigns of Vortigern and Vortiporius in the Historia Regum Britanniae. The latter part of Vortigern's life, in particular the flight from Aurelius Ambrosius, is, for example, inexplicably transferred from central south-east England (especially Kent) to Wales, where Vortiporius ruled, while the reign of Vortiporius (of Wales) seems, in its basic details, to mirror that of Vortigern, Geoffrey telling us that

> Vortiporius came after Conanus. The Saxons rose against him and brought over their fellow countrymen from Germany in a huge fleet. Voriporius fought a battle against them, beat them and so gained control of the entire kingdom. After this he governed the people frugally and peacefully.[56]

We are left with one further element of Vortigern left unexplained: who, precisely, were the 'Gewissei', the people of whom Vortigern led prior to becoming king? The Gewissei are singled out for mention by Geoffrey of Monmouth on a few notable occasions. Aside from Vortigern, we hear that Octavius, Duke of the Gewissei, led a revolt against Constantine's government[57] and later arranged for his daughter to marry the senator Maximianus[58] while later the magician Merlin was found 'in the territory of the Gewissei' at the Galabes Springs, a place he often frequented.[59] More intriguingly, Cadwallader, whom Geoffrey credits as being the last of the British kings, had a grandmother who is credited as being 'a woman born from a noble family of the

Gewissei'[60] while Arvirargus, the king who forged an alliance with Rome, married Gewissa, said to have been daughter to the emperor Claudius.[61] Whoever the Gewissei were, and sadly Geoffrey does not elaborate, they were clearly important and figured in much of the tradition that filtered into the Historia Regum Britanniae.

It is perhaps natural to assume that by using the term Gewissei, Geoffrey meant 'the people of Gwent'.[62] Confusingly, however, the West Saxons were also known as 'Gewisse', something apparently meaning 'allies' or 'confederates'.[63] The term first seems to have appeared in the Historia Ecclesiastica Gentis Anglorum where Bede tells us that Cynigils, king of the West Saxons 'anciently known as the Geuissae' accepted Christianity,[64] then Cadwalla, 'a daring young man of the royal house of the Geuissae', killed King Ethelwalh,[65] while finally Wilfred, friend of King Alchfrid and subsequently Bishop of Northumbria, was first ordained a priest by Agilbert 'Bishop of the Geuissae'.[66] At this stage, therefore, the term Gewisse/Geuissae seems to have been broadly interchangeable with 'Wessex'. Later, as with all curious name-forms, an attempt was made to establish a distant ancestor for the kingdom of Wessex with the name Gewis – hence in the preface to the Anglo-Saxon Chronicle we hear that Cerdic, the primary dynast, 'was the son of Elesa, son of Elsa, son of Gewis, son of Wig, son of Freawine, son of Freothogar, son of Brand, son of Baeldaeg, son of Woden'.

To make matters even worse, etymologically speaking, Gewisse could also equate with Hwicce, a people occupying the south-west midlands (roughly Worcestershire, Gloucestershire and south-west Warwickshire) in the late sixth and seventh centuries. Probably having a similar meaning to the modern Welsh 'gwych', meaning 'excellent', the name Hwicce seems to be of Celtic British origin, whose ultimate meaning was something like 'the most excellent ones'.[67] Whatever the nature of the people calling themselves, or being called by others, Hwicce and Gewisse, it would appear that the name-forms derived from a Celtic/British rather than Saxon/English source. This has potentially significant ramifications with regard to the progenitor of the House of Wessex, Cerdic, a king claimed by the Anglo-Saxon Chronicle but whom, as we shall see, has a British name.

Aurelius Ambrosius

Vortigern's rule was seriously compromised, so Geoffrey of Monmouth tells us, by his marriage to Ronwein, Hengist's daughter, and the increasingly subservient role played by the king of the Britons to his erstwhile Saxon employee. The task of dealing with the growing threat posed by additional quantities of Saxon migrants fell to Vortimer, Vortigern's son. Winning a number of significant victories against the Saxons, Vortimer was eventually poisoned by Ronwein while remaining elements of British council were treacherously slaughtered by Hengist's men 'at the Cloister of Ambrius' whilst attending a peace conference.[68]

The disastrous nature of Vortigern's reign was finally terminated, with extreme prejudice, by the next man to claim the throne: Aurelius Ambrosius. Ambrosius, in the pages of the Historia Regum Britanniae, is an old-fashioned hero, returning in order to bring 'fiery vengeance' down on the man who betrayed his father and invited the accursed Saxons into the kingdom. He and his brother Uther had been too young to take the throne on the death of their father, Constantine, power passing instead to their uncle, Constans, who was assassinated on the orders of Vortigern. Taken in secrecy to the court of King Budicius in Brittany, Aurelius Ambrosius and Uther grew up, determined to reclaim their kingdom in Britain. Aurelius Ambrosius plays a major role in Geoffrey of Monmouth's narrative, especially as he effectively sets the scene for the glorious later reign of his nephew, Arthur. Ambrosius also has the distinction of being mentioned in glowing terms by Nennius, Bede and Gildas; indeed he is just about the only person named in de Excidio Britanniae for whom Gildas has a positive word to say.

After describing in detail the horrors that befell Britain at the hands of the Saxons, with fires burning 'almost the whole surface of the island' destroying town and country and 'licking the western ocean with its fierce red tongue', Gildas comments that 'the wretched survivors were caught in the mountains and butchered wholesale'.[69] Just at the point where they feared total extermination, however, a saviour appeared in the form of Ambrosius Aurelianus. Aurelianus was 'a gentleman', Gildas assures us, and one of the last of the Romans to have survived 'the storm' of war, invasion and plague, adding that his parents, 'who had worn the purple', had evidently died in it.[70] 'Wearing the purple' was a euphemism for being emperor, given that the purple clothing dye used in Roman times was so prohibitively expensive that it was reserved for the imperial incumbent. The fact that Gildas uses the term with regard to the parents of Aurelianus, albeit in a rather loose and vague way, suggests that he was not only in awe of the man, but also that he was crediting him with a significant degree of dynastic authority. Given that Britannia had been in a state of near continual rebellion against the official government in Rome for the final decades of the fourth century AD, it is likely that, had Aurelianus' parents indeed 'worn the purple', then it would have been as usurpers.

Bede follows Gildas' overtly praiseworthy tone when mentioning Ambrosius Aurelianus[71] but it is left to Nennius to supply further information as to the nature of his life and deeds. The Historia Brittonum, after outlining at some length the wickedness of Guorthigirnus/Vortigern and the duplicity of the Saxons Hengist and Horsa, becomes extremely descriptive when introducing the character of Ambrosius (he is not given his full name by Nennius); in fact the greatly expanded section here, with its magical and fantastical elements of folklore, suggests the inclusion of a separate story or tradition into the body of the Historia. Guorthigirnus, we are told, fleeing from the envy of the Saxons and the religious fury of St Germanus, is advised by his magicians to 'go to the furthest borders of your kingdom and build a fortress that you may defend yourself'.[72] Arriving in Gwynedd, in north Wales, Guorthigirnus identifies an ideal spot perched high on a mountain. Gathering together workmen and materials, Guorthigirnus was surprised, and no doubt rather annoyed, to discover that, one morning, all the stone and timber necessary for the building enterprise had vanished. Three further times material was gathered, only for it to disappear again. Guorthigirnus' magicians told him that the stronghold would never be completed 'unless you find a boy without a father, and he is killed, and the fortress is sprinkled with his blood'.[73]

Eventually, after searching 'the whole of Britain', messengers located a boy whose mother confirmed that she had 'not ever known a man'. The boy was duly brought before the king and, in a long discussion with both Guorthigirnus and his magicians, he proceeded to explain to them the cause of the problem. Persuading the royal entourage to dig beneath the floor, the boy revealed a pool in which were set two vases separated by a folded tent. Within the tent were two snakes: one red one white and both asleep. The youth then urged the assembled crowd to watch carefully.

> The snakes began, one to drive out the other, one set its shoulders to drive out the other from its half of the tent, and this happened three times. After some time the red snake seemed the weaker, nevertheless it then became stronger than the white and drove it beyond the edge of the pool, and the tent vanished.[74]

Guorthigirnus questioned the boy, demanding to know the meaning of this. Aurelius replied:

> The tent represents your kingdom; the two snakes are two dragons; the red snake is your dragon, and the pool represents this world. But the white dragon is of the peoples who have overrun many provinces and peoples in Britain, and will hold it almost from sea to sea; and afterwards our people will rise up, and will violently throw out the tribe of the Angles from across the sea.[75]

Explaining that he could not build his fortress here, whether or not sacrificial blood was spilt, the boy told Guorthigirnus that he should depart, adding, 'I will remain here.' Amazed by all he had seen and heard, the king asked the boy his name, to which he replied, 'I am called Ambrosius', Nennius adding 'that is Embries Guleitic that he was seen to be', presumably inferring a degree of aristocratic or princely status. As if that weren't enough, Ambrosius went on to explain, 'My father is one of the consuls of the Roman people.' This particular revelation, of course, immediately contradicts the earlier part of the story in which it was stated that Ambrosius' selection for sacrifice had been due to the fact that he had no father. Presumably this discrepancy in the narrative arose because two separate myths, or folklore elements, were welded together: the first emphasising Ambrosius' miraculous conception, possibly due to the intervention of a deity, such as is encountered in Egyptian, Greek, Roman and Christian mythology; the other stressing his aristocratic pedigree and royal blood-heritage.

Geoffrey of Monmouth follows the same descriptive path as the Historia Brittonum, changing, or adding, a few details along the way; hence we hear that the fortress, or tower, that Vortigern decides to build was planned for Erir montis ('Mount Erith') and that, rather than just the building material disappearing overnight, the foundations established for the tower were 'swallowed up'. Once again it is the magicians in his court who advise Vortigern to search for 'a lad without a father', eventually locating him in the town 'which was afterwards called Kaermerdin', presumably Carmarthen in west Wales. His mother was identified as a 'daughter of a king of Demetia' living with nuns in the nearby church of St Peter.[76] The boy, Geoffrey tells us, was called Merlin, but unfortunately he fails to name either the princess or her father, the former king. The story of immaculate conception is provided with more detail in the Historia Regum Britanniae, the mother of the boy confirming that the father had been invisible at the moment of procreation, again reflecting the supernatural nature of the deed. Astounded by all he had heard, Vortigern asked 'a certain Maugantius' for his advice, Maugantius confirming that he knew of many men born this way, probably through the direct intervention of 'incubus demons'.[77]

Merlin demands to know why he and his mother have been brought before the king and Vortigern explains the need for the blood of a fatherless youth to be sprinkled on the mortar and stones of his great building project. Telling the king that his magicians have lied, Merlin, whom at this point in the narrative Geoffrey informs us 'was also called Ambrosius', suggests that the foundations be ripped up in order to expose a pool beneath. Ambrosius Merlin (as Geoffrey now calls him) explains that, if the pool is drained, the magicians will find two hollow stones at the bottom in which 'you will see two dragons sleeping'.

At this point in the Historia Regum Britanniae, Geoffrey of Monmouth inserts another, slightly earlier work, the Prophesies of Merlin, in its entirety, as Book 7. Geoffrey suggests that these were quoted directly by Ambrosius Merlin to Vortigern and his counsellors and, only when finished does Book 8 and the narrative continue. Curious to know what lay in his own immediate future, Vortigern asked the boy if he could elaborate. The response was probably not what he wanted to hear:

> Run from the fiery vengeance of the sons of Constantine, that is if you have the power to escape it. At this very moment they are fitting out their ships. Even as I speak they are leaving the coasts of Armorica and spreading their sails to cross the sea. They will make for the island of Britain, attack the Saxon people and conquer the race which they detest. The first thing they will do will be to burn you alive, shut up inside your tower. You made a fatal mistake when you betrayed their father and invited the Saxons to your island.[78]

Geoffrey calls the sons of Constantine 'Aurelius and Uther', thus avoiding potential confusion with Ambrosius Merlin, whom he has only just named. Quite why he felt the need to change the identity of Ambrosius, who prophesised Vortigern's downfall in the Historia Brittonum, to Merlin in the Historia Regum Britanniae is unclear. Nennius implies that Ambrosius of the snake/dragon prophesy and Ambrosius the successful general were one and the same. Geoffrey, of course, cannot afford that luxury for, as his narrative was constructed, Ambrosius the boy could hardly explain that Prince Ambrosius, an older version of himself, was currently on his way from Gaul to reclaim the kingdom. Given that Geoffrey had already written about the prophesies of Merlin, it must have made sense to insert them into the Historia at this point, as part of a wider 'prophetic trance',[79] and make the boy at Erir montis a youthful version of the famous soothsayer. Given the strength of the tradition that it was in fact Ambrosius who delivered the dragon prophesy to Vortigern, Geoffrey evidently was compelled to clarify that Merlin 'was also called Ambrosius'.

Textual confusion aside, folklore places the meeting of Vortigern and Ambrosius/Merlin at Dinas Emrys, the 'fortress of Emrys' (Emrys Wledig being another early Welsh name-form for Ambrosius), an impressive rocky outcrop near Beddgelert in Gwynedd, at the southern fringes of Snowdonia. Archaeological fieldwork has demonstrated the presence of an Iron Age hill fort here, covering just over a hectare, with some evidence of reoccupation, or at least reuse, in the immediate sub- and post-Roman periods. Excavations conducted in the mid-1950s[80] revealed part of a pool or cistern/water tank. Modification of the site in the thirteenth century, possibly during the reign of Llywelyn the Great (Llwelyn ap Iorwerth), Prince of Gwynedd, may reflect the deliberate appropriation of a site with strong mythic associations. Something similar would also occur at Tintagel in the early thirteenth century, on the orders of Richard, 1st Earl of Cornwall, and also at Caernarfon in Gwynedd during the late thirteenth century under Edward I.

With the prophesises of Ambrosius Merlin no doubt still ringing in his ears, Geoffrey tells us that Vortigern fled to 'the castle of Genoriu', which was in 'Hergign country, beside the River Guaiae on a hill called Doartius' in Kambria.[81] Here Aurelius Ambrosius, the son of Constantine, having recently landed in Britain, lay siege to the castle, attacking it with fire, which 'once it took hold, went on blazing until it burned up the tower and Vortigern with it'.[82] Having defeated the tyrant Vortigern and destroyed his fortress, Ambrosius set about establishing himself as master of Britain. Geoffrey describes him as an archetypal good king in the making, 'brave and hardy' in single combat and 'most skilled in commanding an army'. He was also 'liberal in his gifts, regular in his attendance at divine services, modest in all his behaviour and unwilling ever to tell a lie'.[83] In fear of the new order, the Saxon leader Hengist decided to retreat north but was duly overtaken by Aurelius Ambrosius. The battle that followed took place 'in a field called Maibeli'. Eldol, Duke of Gloucester, who had escaped the massacre of British leaders organized by Hengist in the reign of Vortigern, desperately sought out the Saxon so he could have his revenge. Hengist fled to Kaerconan, which Geoffrey tells us 'is now called Cunungeburg'. There, in a second battle, Eldol and Hengist came face to face and the Historia provides us with another example of single combat taken, presumably, from a lost source, oral tradition or bardic praise poem.

What men they were, and how much more war-like than the others! As each in turn slashed at the other with his sword, the sparks flew from his blows, as if he were at once a source of thunder-claps and of lightening-flashes. For a long time it was not clear on which side lay the greater strength. At one moment Eldol pressed forward and Hengist yielded; and then Eldol drew back and Hengist advanced.[84]

Eldol prevailed, and with the Saxon warband defeated. Hengist's son Octa retreated to York where his kinsman Eosa had a garrison. Resting in 'the town of Conan', Aurelius allowed Eldol to execute Hengist, decreeing that the Saxon could be buried in 'the pagan custom' in a barrow.[85] Next, laying siege to York, Aurelius received the unconditional surrender of Octa and Eosa, whom he pardoned, granting them 'the region near Scotland' in which to settle.[86] With his enemies now beaten, Aurelius Ambrosius set about restoring the kingdom.

Gildas, although praising the leader whom he calls Ambrosius Aurelianus, is vague when it comes to citing specific battles or victories over the Saxons, providing no dates, names, or any secure form of geographical placement. What De Excidio Britanniae does supply, however, is the earliest reference to the 'proud tyrant' (Vortigern) and the arrival of the Saxons, introducing Ambrosius as the leader of what may be termed 'the British resistance movement'. Gildas is also the first writer whose works survive to mention the battle of Badonici Montis (Badon Hill), a struggle which later writers such as Geoffrey of Monmouth place at the heart of King Arthur's campaigns. Badon is, in Gildas's mind, 'pretty well the last defeat of the villains, and certainly not the least',[86] but it is not clear from his account who is besieging whom – nor, indeed, where the action occurred.

Gildas' brief mention of the siege of Badon Hill (or 'Battle of Mount Badon') is cited in all Arthurian literature. For most, it provides the only near-contemporary source for what proved to be the most decisive victory in King Arthur's long career. Unfortunately, Gildas never mentions Arthur by name and neither does he credit the battle of Badonici Montis to him. This could, it has been argued, be because although Gildas appreciated the significance of the battle, it occurring in 'the year of my birth', some forty or so years prior to the compilation of De Excidio Britanniae,[88] he was in some way unhappy with Arthur as a leader and could not, therefore, bring himself to specifically name him.

We are, as with all 'primary' texts from the period, reliant upon modern translations of later manuscript copies, no original version surviving exactly as it was written. For De Excidio Britanniae, the earliest manuscript copy to exist is a badly burnt, and therefore only partial, tenth-century manuscript held in the British Library.[89] Few academics today have gone back to the source material, preferring instead to work with later transcriptions, mostly generated in the sixteenth and seventeenth century. One historian who has returned to the thirty-seven surviving pages, 'most illegible, shrunk, shrivelled and split; some blackened and water-stained', is Michael Wood, whose forensic examination of Cotton MS Vitellius A vi has produced interesting results.[90]

The first revelation is that the tenth-century manuscript, upon which all later translations rely, 'has no chapter headings and divisions'.[91] This is an important observation for, as Wood notes, the modern division of De Excidio Britanniae into discrete, ordered chapters 'would appear to have no authority'. Quite why anyone felt that Gildas's work required ordered subdivision is unclear, although it may have aided reading and referencing in the Tudor period. Removal of the chapter headings, together with a new, literal translation of the surviving Latin text, free of modern rules surrounding punctuation and grammar, provides a startlingly different account of the war against the Saxon horde to the one normally given.

... not be altogether destroyed, led by Ambrosius Aurelianus, a gentleman who alone perhaps of a Roman noble family the shock of such a storm, though certainly killed in it his parents were who the purple had worn, had survived; whose descendants in our own day from the excellence of their ancestor a long way have degenerated; our people regained their strength; the victors challenged to battle, to whom the victory god willing was given; from that time now our citizens now the enemy won, so that in this people could make trial the Lord, as he does, of this latter-day Israel to see if it loves him or not; up to the year of the siege of Badon Hill this lasted.[91]

Stripped from the straitjacket of modern translation, which has imposed a rigid grammatical order upon De Excidio Britanniae, creating a 'meaning' that may not originally have been intended, this is, as Wood himself notes, 'probably as near as we can hope to get to what Gildas actually wrote'. Without the artificial modern break between chapters that separate Ambrosius Aurelianus from the battle of Badon Hill, it clear that Badon itself is being treated as if it were the climax of Ambrosius' career: it is central to his campaign against the Saxons and part, we must assume, of the reason why Gildas viewed him with such admiration. Removal of uncertainty concerning the authorship of Badon resolves a major concern regarding the interpretation of an historical Arthur, for, if we take Gildas at face value, Arthur was never there.

With the Saxons defeated, Aurelius Ambrosius, so the Historia Regum Britanniae tells us, began the process of reconstruction. York was rebuilt first, 'the churches which the Saxon people had destroyed' being restored to their former glory.[92] Then he set his mind to London, 'which the fury of the enemy had not spared', establishing himself there in order to reconfigure the legal system of the kingdom. Next he travelled to Winchester, completing another programme of works, before going on to visit a monastery near Kaercaradduc, which Geoffrey tells us 'is now called Salisbury'. There, in the monastery 'of three hundred brethren' located on a place called Mount Ambrius, were buried 'the leaders whom the infamous Hengist had betrayed'. Given the placement of Kaercaradduc/Salisbury, Mount Ambrius is usually equated with Amesbury in Wiltshire. Certainly the name 'Amesbury', which evolved from Ambresbyrig, could have derived from something like Ambre's burh or 'the burh of Ambrosius', although whether this was the same Ambrosius as commemorated in the Historia Regum Britanniae, or was simply a back-projection of the name-form in order to explain the place name, is unknown. As Lewis Thorpe noted in his 1966 translation of the Historia, by describing Mount Ambrius, and later 'the Cloister of Ambrius', Geoffrey of Monmouth 'may be thinking of Avebury and muddling it with Amesbury'.[93]

There then follows one of the most famous, and certainly most curious, events recorded in the Historia Regum Britanniae. Convinced he needed to commemorate both the place of the massacre, and the poor victims who represented 'so many noble men who had died for their fatherland', Aurelius decided a memorial was required. No one, however, could decide on a suitable monument until Tremorinus, archbishop of the City of the Legions, suggested that they should ask Merlin 'the prophet of Vortigern'.[94] Locating him 'in the territory of the Gewissei', Merlin, who interestingly is no longer called Ambrosius, was brought before Aurelius. 'If you want to grace the burial place of these men with some lasting monument,' Merlin said to the king, then 'send for the Giant's Ring' situated on Mount Killaraus in Ireland.

> In that place there is a stone construction which no man of this period could ever erect, unless he combined great skill and artistry. The stones are enormous and there is no one alive strong enough to move them. If they are placed in position round this site, in the way in which they are erected over there, they will stand forever.[95]

Aurelius questioned why they needed to travel so far to gather large stones when Britain was full of such things, but Merlin explained that the Giant's Ring possessed healing properties being 'connected with certain religious rites': the sick being cured if they bathed in water that had been poured over them.[96] Charged with recovering the stones, the king's brother, Utherpendragon set sail with 15,000 men, destroying an army sent by the Irish King Gillomanius to protect the Ring. Merlin then 'dismantled the stones more easily than you could ever believe' using hawsers, ropes and ladders. Landing back in Britain, the stones were taken to the king.

> Aurelius dispatched messengers to all the different regions of Britain, ordering the clergy and the people to assemble and, as they gathered, to converge on Mount Ambrius, where with due ceremony and rejoicing to re-dedicate the burial place ... At the summons from Aurelius the bishops and abbots duly assembled with men from every rank and file under the king's command. All came together on the appointed day. Aurelius placed the

crown on his head and celebrated the feast of Whitsun in right
royal fashion, devoting the next three days to one long festival.
As part of this, he bestowed lands on those who had no holdings
of their own, thus rewarding them for the efforts they had made
to serve him.[97]

The tale of the Giant's Ring is, perhaps understandably, often presented
as a slice of pure fiction; a fantastical episode in the far-fetched and
utterly bizarre world that Geoffrey of Monmouth inhabited. We know
now, of course, that the earliest major event at Stonehenge was the
construction of a circular bank and ditch around 3000 BC, the site
being used, among other things, as a cremation cemetery.[98] In around
2500 BC, the first sarsen stones were set up within the enclosure in
two great concentric settings, an inner horseshoe and an outer circle,
with smaller bluestones erected between them in a double arc.[99] Two
centuries later the bluestones appear to have been rearranged to form
a circle and inner oval, later modified again to form a horseshoe
setting. Whether the monument was ever finished, or remained
a continuously developing building project throughout the later
Neolithic and Early Bronze Age, is a matter for debate.

It has long been recognized that although the immense sarsen blocks
forming the Trilithon settlings at Stonehenge were locally sourced, the
bluestones at the centre of the monument were derived from a more
distant place, almost certainly a quarry site in Pembrokeshire some
225 km (140 miles) to the west of Salisbury Plain. The bluestones
themselves may, furthermore, have been part of an earlier structure,
dismantled prior to re-erection in Wiltshire, although, given the amount
of resetting and modification evident within the structure today, there
is no guarantee that this speculative earlier phase of monument was
actually in Wales. The sourcing of stones from a distant site west
of Salisbury Plain, coupled with the suggestion that they may have
originally been part of a Welsh circle, led archaeologist Stuart Piggott,
when considering the tale preserved in the Historia Regum Britanniae,
to note that such 'correspondence between legend and fact is so
remarkable that it can hardly be dismissed as mere coincidence'.[100]
While the suggestion that oral tradition could have extended over
three millennia, from the quarrying of the stones in Pembrokeshire

(rather than Ireland as the Historia tells us) to the time that Geoffrey of Monmouth was writing, seems unlikely – as Piggott himself acknowledged, we must remember that geographical precision is not something that the Historia is particularly renowned for. The fact that a westerly source was correctly identified by Geoffrey of Monmouth for the bluestones doesn't mean that independent verification for the story of Merlin and the Giant's Ring has been established. Recent archaeological work conducted within the Stonehenge monument itself, however, suggests that Geoffrey's story may actually contain a deeper truth.

In 2008, excavations were conducted at Stonehenge, within the south-eastern sector of the monument, in an area between the Trilithons and the outer sarsen circle, in the hope that by locating and examining the sockets for the bluestone circle a date for this phase of the structure could be established. Intriguingly, a large number of the features discovered were of late or sub-Roman date. One such cut, described as a small shaft, lay in the centre of the trench, while a smaller, square-ended cut, possibly a grave, was found nearby.[101] Both features contained pieces of bluestone, Roman pottery and at least one extremely worn coin of the late fourth century AD. The fill of the shaft also incorporated 'a substantial amount of animal bone' including sheep/goat, pig, horse, dog, red deer, hare and rabbit. The amount of bluestone recovered suggested to the excavators that in the late or sub-Roman period, 'pieces of the bluestones around Stonehenge and within it were being broken off and used in the construction of these features'.[102]

The rediscovery, in 1999, of a human skeleton excavated from Stonehenge in 1923, thought to have been destroyed during the Second World War when the stores of the Royal College of Surgeons in London was bombed, has added further information concerning reuse of the monument in the post-Roman era. Reanalysis of the bone has shown that the individual concerned, an adult male in his late twenties or early thirties, had been decapitated with a sharp-blade weapon, probably a sword, in the seventh century.[103] So-called 'deviant burials', execution victims set down at territorial boundaries or at liminal places some distance from contemporary settlements or more established cemeteries, are relatively well established from the post-Roman and early Saxon period, although such burials are not commonly found within earlier prehistoric stone circles. Whether skeleton 4.10.4 (as numbered by the Royal College of Surgeons) was the only such victim to be interred at Stonehenge, or whether there were others, will only be resolved by further excavation.

All this, perhaps, really shouldn't surprise us, for Stonehenge was, and remains, a powerful and awe-inspiring monument, within and around which people have, until fairly recently, been carving and chipping away at the stone as well as burying objects for posterity. It would seem strange if the stones had not been the focus for religious or ritual deposition during the later prehistoric and Roman period, or indeed as a liminal place ideal for 'deviant burial', including those of execution victims, in the sixth and seventh centuries. In fact, the sheer quantity of Roman metalwork and pottery finds recovered from excavations conducted at Stonehenge during the early half of the twentieth century seems to indicate a significant amount of later ritualized activity here. This is intriguing for, aside from the burial, the archaeological evidence suggests a major phase of modification to the bluestone circle in the fifth century AD, the same period in which the Historia Regum Britanniae describes the activities of Merlin and Ambrosius Aurelianus.

What if the operations that Geoffrey of Monmouth described in the Historia actually had nothing to do with the transportation of the stones, either sarsen or bluestone, to Salisbury Plain, but the deliberate alteration and modification of those stones set at the very heart of the prehistoric monument? The latter part of Geoffrey's narrative concerning the 'Giant's Ring', with the clergy rededicating part of the site and Aurelius himself placing 'the crown on his head' before an assembled throng, then bestowing land and property to his followers, sounds suspiciously like the festivities surrounding a formal coronation rather than just a commemoration of those assassinated by the Saxon leader Hengist. Where better than Stonehenge, the single largest prehistoric stone structure in Europe, built by the 'giants of old', to hold such an open-air celebration of the restoration of the monarchy and of the 'House of Constantine'?

As we have noted, Ambrosius Aurelianus was, according to Gildas, a major figure in the British resistance movement against the Anglo Saxons, inflicting many major defeats on them including the much-celebrated Battle of Badon Hill. We should, therefore, perhaps not be too surprised if his political and military prowess, which Gildas (uncharacteristically) praises, do not feature much in the equivalent early Saxon histories. Bede, as we have established, does mention him in passing, but his reference is lifted, almost word for word, from Gildas. As someone who may significantly have curtailed the activities of the first Saxon kings, however, it is not inconceivable that an echo of his martial achievements would resonate, perhaps indirectly, in other English sources.

There are, in the Anglo-Saxon Chronicle, a number of foundation myths concerning the establishment of the kingdoms of Kent, Sussex and Wessex. We have already noted the activities of Hengist and Horsa in Kent, and Wessex will concern us later. Only the creation of Sussex seems to fit the, admittedly vague, chronology that we have for Ambrosius Aurelianus in the later half of the fifth century. There are, unfortunately, only three short references to the establishment of the kingdom of Sussex in the Chronicle, although these are undoubtedly important, providing a date and setting for the first English settlers in the region. As with all entries in this sometimes frustrating document, no attempt is made to provide a detailed or historically accurate account of Germanic first contact, only those events considered essential to a ninth-century compiler being recorded for posterity.

In 477 Aelle and his three sons, Cymen, Wlencing and Cissa, came to Britain in three ships, at the place called Cymensora, and there slew many Welsh, driving some of them to flight to the wood called Andredsleag;

In 485 Aelle fought the Welsh on the bank near Merecredesburna;

In 491 Aelle and Cissa besieged Andredescester and killed all who were inside, so there was not one Briton left.

The details are vague, just three sentences covering the political turmoil of fourteen years. Perhaps we are fortunate that anything is mentioned at all, for many other areas of Britain are simply ignored in the pages of the Chronicle. The reason that Sussex was mentioned in any detail was purely because it was one of the three early Saxon territories which, by the late ninth century, comprised the kingdom of Wessex. It was also the seat of power of Aelle, apparently one of the foremost early Saxon leaders in Britain.

We shall come on to the political significance and possible geographical context of Aelle in a moment, but it is worth pausing briefly in order to note one aspect of the language used within the Anglo-Saxon Chronicle to categorise and define the enemy. As we have already noted, the Germanic aristocracy generally referred to the Britons as 'Welsh' (wylisc, walas or wealh in Old English). This was originally a pejorative term, loosely translated as 'foreigners', 'serfs' or 'slaves'. In Sussex and Surrey, place names such as Walton and Wallington may have derived from identifiable British communities at the margins of important early Saxon settlements.[104] Hence, when the Anglo-Saxon Chronicle records the landing of Aelle at Cymensora in Sussex in 477, it is the 'Welsh' that he drives into 'wood called Andredsleag' and it is the 'Welsh' that he again fights again in 485 'on the bank near Merecredesburna'. Such terminology, perhaps understandably, may well have caused confusion within the minds of subsequent authors, such as Nennius and Geoffrey of Monmouth, to whom 'Welsh' had more specific geographical associations. The casual way in which the terms 'Welsh' and 'British' were employed and interchanged throughout the disparate English sources could, as we have already noted, explain why so many of the stories in the Historia Brittonum and the Historia Regum Britanniae which appear to have an origin in the pre-Saxon lowlands of what is now central southern and south-eastern England, were, from the ninth century AD, shifted to the upland landscapes of Wales.

Alternate use of the term Welsh and British in the brief account of Aelle's fledgling kingdom preserved within the Anglo-Saxon Chronicle may, furthermore, hint at the use by the compilers of different primary source materials. Hence, although it is the Welsh that Aelle drives into the woods shortly after disembarkation and following the battle at Merecredesburna, at Andredescester, in 491, he besieges only the British, slaughtering them all in the aftermath 'so there was not one Briton left'. It is a curious anomaly, but one which may well aid our interpretation of the events in fifth-century Sussex, helping us to better understand precisely who Aelle was.

Overall, the story of Aelle as presented in the Anglo-Saxon Chronicle is rather cursory: he came, he saw, he conquered. There is no reference given to his status before first footfall in Britain, nor is there any indication of his importance in society given beyond a purely regional level. As a Saxon, Aelle, we may assume, hailed from the ethnic homeland of the Saxon people, situated somewhere between the rivers Ems, Weser and Elbe on what is now the north-western coast of Germany. We know nothing of his background, his reasons for crossing the North Sea, the number of people in his entourage nor of his relations with the self-proclaimed leaders of Britain. Bede, however, writing in Jarrow in the early eighth century, mentions Aelle, indicating that the king had an importance that extended beyond a local level.

> In the year of our lord 66 King Ethelbert of the Kentish folk died after a glorious reign of 56 years, and entered the eternal joys of the kingdom of heaven. He was the third English king to hold sway of all the provinces south of the River Humber, but he was the first to enter the kingdom of heaven. The first king to hold such overlordship was Aelle, king of the South Saxons; the second was Caelin, king of the West Saxons, known in the speech of his people as Caeulin; the third, as I have mentioned, was Ethelbert.[105]

This, admittedly rather brief, mention by Bede of Aelle records that the Sussex king was the first Saxon to hold the office of Bretwalda, or Lord of Britain. Bretwalda is a title that by Bede's time seems to have conferred ultimate power over all the English peoples to the south of the Humber. Though the Anglo-Saxon Chronicle is cursory in its treatment of Aelle, there can be little doubt that he was remembered as the pre-eminent King of the Germanic people during the mid to latter half of the fifth century. Sadly, Aelle's curriculum vitae does not survive and there is nothing in either the Anglo-Saxon Chronicle or the writings of Bede which obviously explain his claim to primacy. Perhaps he was simply perceived by later writers to have been the elder statesman of Saxon society; perhaps he was the most respected politician or, following his exploits in Sussex, the most fearsome warrior. Whatever the case, on the face of it, Aelle as Bretwalda was evidently the champion of the whole English movement against the Britons in the south.[106]

The Chronicle's account of Aelle's entry into Britain, although supplying more detail than Bede, is presented as a relatively straightforward origin myth, the primary dynast arriving with a small group of followers – in this case three sons and three ships – overcoming significant local opposition and establishing a kingdom. It is presented in terms akin to the classic myth of Aeneas, who led a band of refugees to Italy in three ships following the events of the Trojan War. Similar accounts also appear in the Anglo Saxon Chronicle, the founders of Kent, Hengist and Horsa arriving in three ships (in 449) as do later Wessex leaders Port, Bieda and Maegla (in 501) and Stuf and Wihtgar (in 514) while the primary dynasts of Wessex, Cerdic and Cynric land in Hampshire with five boatloads in (495). The exploits of Aelle as he forged the kingdom of Sussex may have come down to the compilers of the Chronicle via a now lost saga, or through oral tradition, but either way the primary source for the early history of the South Saxons dynasty is unlikely to have been either wholly unbiased or objective.

The basic sequence provided in the Anglo-Saxon Chronicle for Aelle's landing, battles and violent liquidation of the enemy seems logical, but the dates provided should not necessarily be believed. It has, for example, been argued that the time sequence has been distorted by at least two decades,[107] which would mean that Aelle's landings occurred in the mid- to late 450s rather than 477, and the storming of Andredescester around AD 471. Identification of Merecredesburna, where the Anglo-Saxon Chronicle says that Aelle fought a battle against 'the Welsh' is problematic. The name has been interpreted as meaning the as the 'River of the frontier agreed by treaty'.[108] This could fit a suggestion that, having forced his way into Britain, Aelle signed a non-aggression pact with British leaders, allowing him land on which his people could settle. The battle of Merecredesburna could, in such a scenario, have been fought as Aelle attempted to expand his territory beyond a small enclave, or it could have been a defensive struggle against a revitalised local resistance. Either way the target of his next campaign is clear enough for Andredescester, as mentioned in the Chronicle entry for AD 491, can only be Anderitum: the Roman fortress of Pevensey, in East Sussex.

In the early years of the fifth century AD, Anderitum remained a more than serviceable stronghold, the harbour that it protected being a vital point of access to the iron and timber resources of the Weald. Whoever possessed the fortress controlled a significant block of south-eastern England and the English Channel. Whether it was the remnants of the original garrison, mutating into a local militia, or a roaming warband that saw the opportunities of being based in a prominent and easily defensible position, it would appear that Anderitum remained a key player in the regional politics of post-Roman Britain. This would be the obvious place for Aelle to concentrate his forces for Anderitum could block good access to the resources of the Weald while simultaneously disrupting Saxon communications along the English Channel. Worse, the proximity of the fortress must have represented an ever-present threat to Aelle's fledgling kingdom.

This is the conventional story of Aelle, founder of the Kingdom of Sussex and first Bretwalda: a landing, consolidation, small-scale skirmish and an epic siege ending with an atrocity at a Roman fortress. Aelle does not make an appearance in the Historia Regum Britanniae, the Historia Brittonum or the sermons of Gildas, which is perhaps unsurprising as an enemy of the Britons would not expect recognition within the pages of a resolutely British history; Hengist and Horsa are mentioned, but in extremely unflattering terms. The epic siege of Andredescester also fails to be mentioned by Geoffrey of Monmouth, unless of course it appears in a different form. As we have already noted, the Anglo-Saxon Chronicle was created in the ninth century by a Saxon monarchy keen to legitimize its position but also to more solidly define the ethnicity of its people through the judicious rewriting of history. Could it be that the 'Saxon' King Aelle's ultimate origin as primary dynast of the South Saxons lay somewhere other than the Germanic world? Could his career in the Anglo-Saxon Chronicle, such that it is, be mirrored in the exploits of another leader, buried deep within the Historia Regum Britanniae or Historia Brittonum? Could the unusual title of Bretwalda actually have come about because Aelle was not a Saxon overlord of Britain but, in fact, simply a British king?

Geoffrey of Monmouth provides significant detail concerning the character and life of Aurelius Ambrosius, the Ambrosius Aurelianus so briefly, but enthusiastically, mentioned by Gildas. According to Geoffrey, Ambrosius fled Britain following the murder of his father by the usurper Vortigern. Later, returning from Brittany with his brother Uther and a force of supporters, Ambrosius landed unopposed, gathering those Britons 'who had been scattered with such great slaughter' in order to march against the tyrant. Having cornered the villain in 'the castle of Genoreu', Ambrosius, now thirsting for revenge, began the attack.

> They lost no time, but moved into position with their siege-engines and did their utmost to break down the walls. When everything else had failed, they tried fire; and this, once it took hold, went on blazing until it burned up the tower and Vortigern with it.[109]

The Historia Brittonum provides a more Biblical, Old Testament-style end to Vortigern: 'The earth opened up and engulfed him on the night that his fortress burned around him, because no remains of those who were burnt in the fortress with him were found.'[110] Which is perhaps another way of saying that no one got out alive.

At a basic level, this all sounds horribly familiar; both the 'Saxon' warlord Aelle and the 'Roman' general Aurelius Ambrosius lead invasion armies across the Channel, albeit one was reclaiming a lost kingdom, the other trying to establish a new one. Both went on to besiege their enemy, who had taken shelter behind the walls of a mighty fortress. Finally, having gained access to the fortress, both Aelle and Aurelius Ambrosius slaughter all those they find within. The key here, of course, is that in both stories, the enemy being attacked and annihilated is British; in fact, as noted, the Anglo-Saxon Chronicle, for once, fails to call them 'Welsh'. Could it be that both the English warlord in the Anglo-Saxon Chronicle and the British king of the Historia Brittonum/Historia Regum Britanniae were, in fact, the same person – Aelle being in essence a corruption of Aur-ELI-us/Aur-ELI-anus? Such an explanation would, of course, explain why Aelle was remembered as an important leader, commemorated in later histories. He was not an obscure king or princeling in a small and rather insignificant coastal territory, but a prominent British warlord whose identity was later hijacked by the English. It would also help explain the term Bretwalda as a distorted version of British leader or British king.

In such a reconstruction of events, the fortress of Genoreu was not a strongly defended hilltop enclosure in Wales, but Anderitum (Andredescester), a Roman shore fort on the south coast of Sussex. Was it here, in the later fifth century AD, that two British warlords fought out the final stages of their own personal vendetta with such ruthlessness that it was remembered and commemorated by subsequent generations, an epic saga surviving in oral tradition until the time of the Saxon and Norman kings? If so it is clear that by then 'Aurelius Ambrosius/Ambrosius Aurelianus' had become 'Aelle'. Now he could be claimed by an English hierarchy desperate to establish their legitimacy and unified identity in the struggle against the Danes.

Arthur

The curious irony about King Arthur is that while everyone agrees that his rise to fame came thanks to Geoffrey of Monmouth, the search for a real 'historical' Arthur means that few people look in detail, or indeed at all, at the Historia Regum Britanniae for clues to his context and possible identity. If one is trying to establish the existence of the true Arthur as a warlord in fifth-/sixth-century Britain, then it is usually reasoned that the Historia is too implausible, too fictional and, to be frank, just too weird to be taken seriously. The anachronistic detail, coupled with the unreal and obviously fantastical elements, all conspire to make Geoffrey's book unreliable. Hence when we look at the hundreds of articles and books generated year on year which either re-examine the evidence, or which claim to have unearthed new and exciting clues as to his secret identity, the Historia Regum Britanniae is not consulted. More often it is rejected out of hand in favour of 'more reliable' sources. If we wish to resolve who King Arthur was, however, we cannot afford to be so picky.

Key elements of the Arthur story, such as his parentage, conception, association with Merlin, marriage to Guinevere, establishment of a great kingdom, betrayal and final disappearance, all take form in the Historia Regum Britanniae. Major plot details, however, are notably absent: there is no Lancelot, no Camelot, no Holy Grail, no sword in the stone and no chivalric order of the round table. These represent later 'add-ons', which significantly expand the original narrative, reordering key events and making it relevant for each subsequent age. This process continues to the present day. Throughout the twentieth and early twenty-first century there has been an ever-increasing slew of Arthurian literature, factual, semi-factual, fictional and, at times it is fair to say, completely delusional as well as made-for-television drama, plays, musicals and films. At the time of writing, adverts for *King Arthur: Legend of the Sword*, a new cinematic production, are being screened, which, it is said, will reimagine the story for a new generation. Again. Whatever happens to the film, it will no doubt add new elements to the already well-trodden tale.

So what does Geoffrey of Monmouth actually tell us about the life and deeds of Arthur? It is important to understand exactly what he says, and indeed the order in which he says it, cutting away all later elaboration and exaggeration.

At the start, Arthur is conceived at Tintagel in Cornwall, the result of an identity deception triggered through drug use. Merlin, the wise man, teller of prophesies and part-time advisor to Uther Pendragon, king of Britain, following the death of his brother Aurelius, concocts a potion transforming the lusty monarch into the exact image of Gorlois, the Duke of Cornwall, so that Uther can spend the night with Ygerna, Gorlois' wife. Following the death of Gorlois, Uther marries Ygerna and they live 'together as equals'.[111] In time Arthur is born, as is his sister, Anna. When Uther dies, from poison administered in a Saxon-sponsored plot, the leaders of Britain convene at Silchester where they agree that Arthur should be crowned king. At this time, Geoffrey of Monmouth tells us, the Saxons invited more of their countrymen over from Germany. With Colgrin appointed as their leader, the Saxons 'began to do their utmost to exterminate the Britons', overrunning 'all that section of the island which stretches from the River Humber to the sea named Caithness'.[112]

Arthur, although still only fifteen, had been recognized as a young man of 'outstanding generosity and courage', his evident goodness giving him 'such grace that he was loved by almost all of the people'. Invested with royal insignia at the coronation, the king 'observed the normal custom of giving gifts freely to everyone'. Deciding to attack the Saxons 'so that with their wealth he might reward the retainers who served his own household', Arthur marched to York. In a battle on the River Douglas, he defeated Colgrin's army of Saxons, Scots and Picts, Colgrin seeking refuge in the city. Badulf, Colgrin's brother, then brought 6,000 men north to attack the Britons besieging York, but was ambushed by Cador, Duke of Cornwall. Badulf escaped, getting into York disguised as a minstrel. At this point Cheldric, another Saxon leader, arrived in Albany with 600 ships. Arthur, realizing he couldn't fight such an army, swiftly returned to London where he sent word to Hoel, king of Brittany, requesting assistance. Hoel, Geoffrey tells us, 'was the son of Arthur's sister', his father being 'Budicius, the king of the Armorican Britons'.[113]

The statement that Hoel was the son of Arthur's sister and King Budicius appears to contradict an earlier statement Arthur's father, King Uther Pendragon, had given his daughter Anna to Loth of Lodonesia, putting him in charge of the kingdom when ill.[114] To be fair, Geoffrey doesn't explicitly state that Loth and Anna were married or, if they were, that the marriage lasted, Arthur's sister perhaps marrying Budicius later. Alternatively Arthur could have had a second sister, although if so she is not mentioned again. More likely, perhaps, Geoffrey simply got his facts wrong, being confused by multiple discrepant traditions relating to the family of Uther. Later on in the *Historia*, for example, we hear that Loth of Lodonesia had married the unnamed sister of Aurelius Ambrosius (who, rather confusingly, had himself been brought up by King Budicius of Armorica), the partnership producing two sons, Gualguainus (Gawain) and Mordred. This particular marriage made Loth the brother-in-law of Aurelius Ambrosius and therefore the uncle-in-law of Arthur rather than Arthur's brother-in-law (had Loth married Anna). This would make Gualguainus and Mordred first cousins of Arthur, although both are later repeatedly referred to in the *Historia* as being Arthur's nephews.[115]

With 15,000 warriors assembled, Hoel landed at Southampton and Arthur 'received him with all the honour due to him'. Together, the two went on to liberate Kaerluideoit, which Geoffrey equates with Lincoln, from a Saxon siege. There 'they inflicted unheard-of slaughter upon them; for on one day six thousand of the Saxons were killed, some being drowned in the rivers and the others being hit by weapons'.[116] Retreating to Caledon Wood, the Saxons regrouped, attacking the Britons, killing 'a number' of them. Arthur ordered the trees around the wood to be cut down and placed in a circle, trapping the enemy inside. After a three-day stalemate the Saxons surrendered and, leaving their gold and silver, Arthur granted them safe passage to their ships, demanding that on their arrival in Germany they should send hostages and tribute.

Once at sea, however, the Saxons rejected the agreement, turning to make landfall at Totnes. Taking possession of the land, they 'depopulated the countryside as far as the Severn Sea killing off a great number of the peasantry'.[117] Astonished 'at their extraordinary duplicity', Arthur immediately hanged his Saxon hostages and marched west, leaving Hoel, at this point seriously ill, behind 'in the city of Alclud'. Arriving in Somerset, Arthur discovered the Saxon army besieging the city of Bath. After an epic battle in which 'fell Colgrin, with his brother Badulf and many thousands of others', Cheldric fled with what small numbers of troops he had left. Arthur returned to Alclud, where Hoel was being besieged by an army of Scots and Picts, while Cador, Duke of Cornwall, pursued the Saxons and 'cut them to pieces without pity'.[118]

The Saxons, who only a short time before used to attack like lightning in the most ferocious way imaginable, now ran away with fear in their hearts. Some of them fled to secret hiding places in the woods, others sought the mountains, and caves in the hills, in an attempt to add some little breathing space to their lives. In the end they discovered safety nowhere; and so they came to the Isle of Thanet, with their line of battle cut to pieces. The duke of Cornwall pursued them thither and renewed the slaughter.

Here King Cheldric was killed.

Arthur relieved Alclud and, with Cador joining him, the Britons followed the Picts and Scots to Morray, the enemy taking control of the islands in Loch Lomond. Surrounding them for fifteen days, Arthur 'reduced them to such a state of famine that they died in their thousands'. Too late, Gilmaurius, the king of Ireland, arrived with an army, hoping to save his compatriots. Turning his forces to meet the invaders, Arthur 'cut them to pieces mercilessly', forcing the survivors to return home.

> Once he had conquered the Irish, he was at liberty once more to wipe out the Scots and Picts. He treated them with unparalleled severity, sparing no one who fell into his hands. As a result all the bishops of this pitiful country, with all the clergy under their command, their feet bare and in their hands the relics of their saints and the treasures of their churches, assembled to beg pity of the king for the relief of their people.[119]

Moved to tears by 'their patriotism', Arthur agreed to show clemency. With Hoel restored to health, the two men spend time at Loch Lomond sightseeing and catching up on the legends of Britain. Then, riding south to York, the king was 'grieved to see the desolate state of the holy churches' following their treatment at the hands of the pagans. He rebuilt the churches and restored the noble families whom the Saxons had driven out. To three brothers in York, who were 'sprung from the royal line', Arthur granted back all hereditary rights. To Auguselus he 'returned the kingship of the Scots'; to Urian he gave back rule 'over the men of Moray; and to Loth, who had married the sister of Aurelius Ambrosius and had two sons, Gualguainus and Morded, he 'restored to the dukedom of Lothian and other near-by territories which formed part of it'.[120] With the island restored, Arthur married Ganhumara, a woman 'descended from a noble Roman family' who had been brought up in the household of Cador, Duke of Cornwall.

The next summer, Arthur sailed to Ireland with a large fleet. There, King Gilmaurius' poorly equipped army was cut to pieces. Gilmaurius submitted to Arthur and all the princes of Ireland followed his example. Arthur then sailed on to Iceland which also surrendered to him. Hearing of this, Doldavius, king of Gotland, and Gunhpar, king of the Orkneys, came to Arthur 'of their own free will' to do homage and to promise tribute. Returning to Britain, Arthur ruled in peace for the next twelve years.

> Arthur then began to increase his personal entourage by inviting very distinguished men from far-distant kingdoms to join it. In this way he developed such a code of courtliness in his household that he inspired peoples living far away to imitate him. The result was that even the man of noblest birth, once he was roused to rivalry, thought nothing at all of himself unless he wore his arms and dressed in the same way as Arthur's knights.[121]

Stories of his prowess now spread far and wide:

> The kings of countries far across the sea trembled at the thought that they might be attacked and invaded by him, and so lose control of the lands under their dominion. They were so harassed by these tormenting anxieties that they re-built their towns and the towers in their towns, and then went so far as to construct castles on carefully chosen sites, so that, if invasion should bring Arthur against them, they might have a refuge in their time of need.[122]

Realizing how much he was feared, Arthur conceived the idea of becoming master of Europe. Fitting out his fleets, he sailed to Norway. Here, Sichelm the king had just died, bequeathing the kingdom to Loth, his nephew and someone whom Geoffrey calls the brother-in-law of Arthur (in reality, and if we read the relationship correctly, Loth was actually Arthur's uncle-in-law). The Norwegians refused to acknowledge Loth as their king, making Riculf their monarch instead. Gualguainus (Gawain), the eldest son of Loth (so the Historia Regum Britanniae tells us), was at this time only twelve but had served 'in the household of Pope Sulpicius' who had dubbed him a knight. The forces of Arthur and Riculf met in battle, 'much blood' being shed on both sides. Victorious, Arthur's army 'invested the cities of

Norway and set fire to them everywhere'[123] forcing all of Norway and Denmark to accept his rule.

Leaving Loth in charge of Norway, Arthur sailed to Gaul. Here he began to 'lay waste the countryside in all directions'.[124] Tribune Frollo, who governed Gaul for the emperor Leo, marched to face Arthur but could not make any headway, the British king having 'so powerful a force that it could hardly have been conquered by anyone'.[125] Retreating to Paris, Frollo tried to assemble a force but instead found himself trapped within the city by Arthur. The siege lasted a month before Frollo sent word to ask if the war could be settled by single combat. Arthur gladly agreed and, in a lengthy battle, described in enthusiastic detail,[126] Frollo is defeated and Paris falls to the Britons. Dividing his forces, Arthur sent Hoel to attack Guitardus, leader of the Poitevins while he subdued Aquitania and ravaged Gascony 'with fire and sword'. Nine years passed and, with all of Gaul conquered, Arthur held court in Paris where he 'settled the government of the realm peacefully and legally' dividing the territory up between his noblemen, giving 'Neustria, now called Normandy, to his cup-bearer Beduerus and the province of Anjou to his seneschal Kaius'.[127]

As Whitsun approached, Arthur decided to establish a plenary court where he could 'place the crown of the kingdom on his head'[128] and where all the leaders 'who owed him homage' could be summoned. Duly, the City of the Legions, which Geoffrey equates with Caerleon in south-east Wales, is prepared. A lengthy description of the city then appears in the Historia, accompanied by a list of visitors, which includes crowned heads, religious leaders and 'other famous men of equal importance'. A protracted description of the procession, feast, fashions and subsequent party games played by the assembled guests follows. The celebrations, however, are interrupted after four days by envoys who arrive from Rome with a message.

Lucius Hiberius, the Procurator of Rome, outraged by Arthur's 'tyrannical behaviour' demands that the king should immediately submit himself to the Roman authorities.

You have had the presumption to disobey this mighty empire by holding back the tribute of Britain, which tribute the senate has ordered you to pay, seeing that Gaius Julius Caesar and other men of high place in the Roman State had received it for many years. You have torn Gaul away from the empire, you have seized the province of the Allobroges and you have laid hands on all the islands of the ocean, the kings of which paid tribute to my ancestors from the first moment when the might of Rome prevailed in those regions. As a result the senate has decreed that punishment should be exacted for this long series of wrongs which you have done.[129]

Lucius then instructed Arthur to appear in person before him by August. Failing to do this, he noted, would risk the anger of Rome, forcing him to invade Arthur's territory 'and do my best to restore to the Roman State all that you have taken from it'.

Incensed, Arthur withdrew from the party with his advisors, Cador Duke of Cornwall, Hoel King of the Armorican Britons and Auguselus King of Albany being chief among them. Cador tried to lighten the mood by joking that a war is just what the Britons needed, the long period of peace having dampened 'their reputation for bravery on the battlefield'. Arthur, however, was greatly angered by the demands of Lucius, and delivered a long speech on liberty and justice to the assembled group. There was no reason to fear Rome, he reminded them, for they could absorb any attack once they had worked out how to join forces in order to resist it. The key demand of Lucius, that the payment to Rome of tribute money should be restarted, was something that particularly upset him, however.

He says that he ought to be given it because it used to be paid to Julius Caesar and those who succeeded him. When these men landed with their armed band and conquered our fatherland by force and violence at a time when it was weakened by civil dissensions, they had been encouraged to come here by the disunity of our ancestors. Seeing that they seized the country in this way, it was wrong of them to exact tribute from it. Nothing that is acquired by force and violence can ever be held legally by anyone.[130]

Reminding the council that his ancestors had conquered Rome no less than three times, under Belinus 'that most glorious of the kings of the Britons, with the help of his brother Brennius' and later Constantine and Maximianus, 'both close relations of mine', Arthur suggested that Rome should pay tribute to *him*. As for the 'illegal' conquest of Gaul and neighbouring territories, Arthur told his band of brothers that they need not respond to the Roman communication given that 'when we snatched those lands from their empire they made no effort to defend them'.[131]

Hoel replied that he was in agreement with Arthur, reminding everyone that the Sybilline Prophecies had testified that 'someone born of British blood shall seize the empire of Rome' on three occasions. Conveniently forgetting Maximianus, Hoel said that as far as the first two were concerned, 'princes Belinus and Constantine once wore the imperial crown of Rome'. Now it was Arthur's turn. Auguselus of Albany concurred, saying, 'I thirst for their blood, as I would thirst for a spring if I had been prevented from drinking for three whole days.' One after another, Arthur's followers pledged their support, troops being subsequently raised from Britain, Armorica, Ireland, Iceland, Gotland, Orkney, Norway, Denmark and Gaul so that 'the total number of the army, not including the foot soldiers, who were not at all easy to count, was one hundred and eighty three thousand, three hundred'.[132]

Word was sent 'to the emperors' that Arthur was not intending to pay tribute. Instead, the British king made preparations for war. Lucius Hiberius immediately dispatched orders 'to the Orient' to gather an army to conquer Britain. Troops being raised, Lucius was joined by the kings of Greece, Africa, Spain, Parthia, Media, Libya, Israel, Egypt, Babylon, Bithynia, Phrygia, Syria, Boetha and Crete. Together with the soldiery of Rome, the army at Lucius' disposal numbered 'up to four hundred thousand, one hundred and sixty when all counted'.[133] Hearing about this Roman coalition, Arthur 'handed over the task of defending Britain to his nephew Mordred and to his queen Ganhumara', marched to Southampton and crossed over to Gaul. As they sailed, Arthur dreams of a dragon fighting a bear, something which his followers take as a good omen.

Landing at Barfleur, news is brought to Arthur that a giant 'of monstrous size had emerged from certain regions in Spain' to terrorise the locals. Discovering that Helena, the niece of duke Hoel, had been taken captive by the giant, Arthur takes Kaius (Kay) and Beduerus (Bedevere) and climbs Mont-Saint-Michel where the creature is hiding, Geoffrey of Monmouth noting that 'being a man of such outstanding courage, he had no need to lead a whole army against monsters of this sort'.[134] Discovering he is too late, the giant having already killed Helena, Arthur, in another lengthy digression, fights an epic battle with the giant and destroys it. Ordering Beduerus to saw off its head, they return to camp, Arthur reminiscing about the time that he killed the giant Retho 'on Mount Arvaius' following a dispute about which of them should take the other's beard for a trophy.

His army now assembled, Arthur marched to Autun. Pausing by the River Aube 'he was informed that the emperor had pitched his camp not far away and was advancing with such an enormous army that no one could possibly resist him'.[135] Undismayed, Arthur sent two of his leaders, Boso of Oxford and Gerin of Chartres, together with his nephew Gualguainus, to Lucius Hiberius, telling him to either withdraw from Gaul or else to fight 'to see which of them had more right' to the territory. In the meeting, Gaius Quintillianus, Lucius' nephew, muttered an insult to the British delegation, whereupon Gualguainus beheaded him on the spot. Escaping from the Roman camp, all three of the British envoys turn and kill their pursuers. Chasing them to the fringes of a wood, the Romans are ambushed by 6,000 Britons who 'had concealed themselves there in order to bring help'[136] and are driven back. Roman reinforcements arrive and the conflict escalates, Geoffrey of Monmouth supplying significant epic detail as to the nature of combat. Finally both sides withdraw, the Britons in triumph with large numbers of prisoners, including the senator Peteius Cocta.

Arthur, elated at the result of the battle (although he took no part in it), instructed a detachment of his army, under the protection of Duke Cador of Cornwall, Beduerus, Borellus and Richerius, to take the prisoners to Paris where they could be locked up. The emperor, hearing this, selected 15,000 men to attack the British escort and free their countrymen. Surprised, the Britons nevertheless put up a stiff resistance until Guitardus, Duke of Poitevins, arrived with a relief army of 3,000 men, beating the Romans back. Many of the Britons died in fighting; however, Geoffrey of Monmouth singled out Borellus, 'the famous leader of the Cenomanni', Hirelgas of Periron, Maurice of Cardorcan, Ailduc of Tintagel and Her, the son of Hider for special mention, adding 'it would not have been easy to find braver men than these'.[137] On the Roman side Vulteius Catellus and Evander, king of Syria, fell.

Lucius Hiberius now faced a difficult decision: should he engage Arthur directly or withdraw to Autun, where he could safely 'await reinforcements from the emperor Leo'?[138] Fearing the British, Lucius took the latter option and began the march to Autun. Arthur saw his chance and outmarched the Roman, drawing up his troops in 'a valley called Siesia'. Ordering one of his legions 'the command of which he entrusted to earl Morvid' to stay in reserve, Arthur drew up the rest of his troops in seven divisions, each comprising one part cavalry to one part infantry.

> They were given the following standing orders: whenever the infantry showed signs of advancing to the attack, the cavalry of that division, moving forward obliquely with closed ranks, should do its utmost to break the force of the enemy.[139]

Auguselus, king of Albany, was placed in command of the British right flank; Duke Cador of Cornwall the left. A second division was headed up by Gerin of Chartres and Boso of Oxford; Aschil, king of the Danes, and Loth, king of Norway, were put in charge of a third whilst others were led by Hoel, king of the Bretons, Gualguainus, Arthur's nephew, Kaius the seneschal, Beduerus the cup-bearer, Holdin leader of the Ruteni, Guitardus duke of the Poitevins, Jugein of Leicester, Jonathel of Dorchester, Cursalem of Caistor and Urbgennius of Bath.[140] Behind these Arthur set his position next to the 'Golden Dragon which he had as his personal standard'.

After the obligatory speeches to the troops, Arthur urging his men to capture and occupy Rome, Lucius Hiberius commending his followers to recall the great deeds of the Republic, battle was joined. Once again, specific details surrounding the fighting are provided by

Geoffrey of Monmouth, individuals being singled out for their heroic action. In the furnace of combat, Beduerus of the Neustrians and Kaius of the Angevins were among the first to fall on the British side, followed by Holdin, Leodegarius, Cursalem, Guallauc, Urbgennius Chinmarchocus, Riddomarcus, Bloctonius and Iaginvius, Geoffrey lamenting that had they been kings, 'succeeding ages would have celebrated their fame for their courage was immense'.[141]

Gualguainus and Hoel pressed a fierce attack upon the emperor's bodyguard, Gualguainus and Lucius fighting in single combat. Each dealt 'mighty blows, holding out their shields to the opponent's onslaught and each planning how he could kill the other'.[142] Eventually the Romans recovered, repulsing the forces of Hoel and Gualguainus. At this point in the battle, Arthur raised his sword Caliburn and dashed headlong at the enemy. Seeing Arthur in action, the Britons were greatly encouraged. Morvid, the Earl of Gloucester, moving from the hills with his troops, attacked the Roman army in the rear, scattering them 'with tremendous slaughter'.[143] Many thousands of Romans were killed, Geoffrey of Monmouth tells us, Lucius himself being struck down in the midst of battle 'pierced through by an unknown hand'. Arthur's forces chased their enemy from the field, Geoffrey reiterating that the Britons made every effort to protect their freedom, 'which the Romans were trying to take away from them, by refusing the tribute which was wrongly demanded of them'.[144] With the battle over, Arthur oversaw the burial of the dead, the body of Lucius Hiberius being conveyed to Rome with the message that 'no further tribute could be expected from Britain'.[145]

Arthur spent the winter in Gaul, subduing the cities of the Allobroges. As summer approached he made his army ready for the final march on Rome. As the first wave of his troops were making their way through the mountain passes into Italy, however, the king received dire news from Britain: his nephew Mordred, together with queen Ganhumara, had stolen the crown. Abandoning his attack on Rome, Arthur returned to Britain 'accompanied only by the island kings and their troops',[146] the remainder of his army he left in Gaul with Hoel in order 'to restore peace in those parts'. Hearing that Arthur had learned of his treachery, Mordred sent word to Chelric, leader of the Saxons in Germany, inviting him to Britain and offering him all of Britain from the River Humber to Scotland and 'all that Hengist and Horsa had held in Kent in Vortigern's day'. Chelric landed with 800 ships 'filled with armed pagans' and pledged allegiance to Mordred. Mordred further 'brought the Scots, Picts and Irish into his alliance', forming a coalition of all those whom he knew 'to be filled with hatred for his uncle'.

Attempting to land at Richborough, Arthur's army was attacked by Mordred. In the battle that followed, Auguselus of Albany and Gualguainus fell. Finally, after much desperate fighting, Arthur managed to establish a beachhead, driving Mordred from the shore. Using tactics developed from their long experience in war, Geoffrey tells us (again) that Arthur's officers 'drew up their troops most skilfully. They mixed their infantry with their cavalry and fought in such a way that when the line of foot soldiers moved up to the attack, or was merely holding its position, the horse charged at an angle and did all that they could do to break through the enemy lines and to force them to run away.'[147]

Mordred retreated to Winchester, deserting Ganhumara who, fleeing from York to the City of Legions, took holy vows with nuns in the church of Julius the martyr, promising to lead a chaste life thereafter. Burying the slain, Arthur advanced on Mordred and lay siege to him. In a battle outside the walls of Winchester there is once again 'immense slaughter on both sides'. Mordred flees 'in shame from the battlefield' by ship to Cornwall with Arthur in close pursuit. At the River Camblam both sides square up for the final reckoning.

Mordred, who Geoffrey acknowledges to be 'the boldest of men', mustered the remaining 60,000 soldiers in his army, promising them the possessions of his enemies should they win. Arthur too exhorted his men 'to kill these perjured villains and robbers' who had committed treason, telling them that Mordred's army was no more than 'a miscellaneous collection of barbarians', unlike his veterans. So eager were both sides for the fight, they came together before both commanders had finished their pre-battle speeches. 'Combat was joined,' says Geoffrey 'and they all strove with might and main to deal each other as many blows as possible',[148] neither side wishing to give quarter.

Everywhere men were receiving wounds themselves or inflicting them, dying or dealing out death. In the end, when they had passed much of the day in this way, Arthur, with a single division in which he had posted six thousand, six hundred and sixty six men, charged at the squadron where he knew Mordred was. They hacked a way through with their swords and Arthur continued to advance, inflicting terrible slaughter as he went. It was at this point that the accursed traitor was killed and many thousands of his men with him.[149]

Unfortunately the fighting didn't cease with the fall of Mordred. Almost all the leaders on both sides were present in the final stages of the conflict and no one was prepared to give way. On Mordred's side, Geoffrey tells us, fell Chelric, Elaf, Egbrict and Bruning 'all of the Saxons' as well as the Irish chiefs Gillapatric, Gillasel and Gillarvus and all the Scottish and Pictish leaders. On Arthur's side fell Odbrict, the new king of Norway, Aschil king of Denmark, Cador Limenich and Cassivellaunus. Then, in what is probably the most famous sentence in the Historia Regum Britanniae, Geoffrey of Monmouth tells us that 'Arthur himself, our renowned king, was mortally wounded and was carried off to the Isle of Avalon, so that his wounds might be attended to'.[150]

With both Arthur and Mordred gone, together with Gualguainus and most of the crowned heads of western Europe, the kingdom was handed to Arthur's cousin, Constantine, the son of Cador of Cornwall. So significant was the Battle of Camblam that Geoffrey, for once, supplies us with a year: AD 542.

The tale of King Arthur in the Historia Regum Britanniae seems, at first, rather strange, given the focus on Arthur's overseas empire and the lack of interest shown in more familiar elements, such as the roles of Merlin and Lancelot, the significance of Camelot and the romance between Arthur and Guinevere, none of which feature. Arthur has a schizophrenic persona which makes him hard to like. Capable of tenderness one moment and utter savagery the next, he defends his homeland against the Saxons, but also wages a cruel and unprovoked war against the people of Norway and Gaul, burning towns and laying waste to the land. He rails against those who subjugate the innocent, stating 'nothing that is acquired by force and violence can ever be held legally', without realizing the irony of this, given his brutal and unjustified seizure of land in Gaul. He may have established a code of courtliness in the City of the Legions, surely a template for the later creation of Camelot, but he also kills without mercy, slaughtering all those who will not submit and accept him as king. He is hardly the model of chivalric nobility.

Of all the elements in Arthur's life as it appears in the Historia Regum Britanniae, arguably it is the story of Arthur's conception at Tintagel that has probably caused most interest among archaeologists, historians, writers, journalists and the general public. Many sites in Britain have 'Arthurian connections' thanks to folklore or local tradition, yet perhaps none are today as obviously linked to the legend of Arthur as Tintagel Castle. The site is certainly dramatic, a windswept craggy headland projecting out into the churning sea; a battered series of walls clinging desperately to the cliff edge above. Geoffrey's decision to select Tintagel would undoubtedly have been informed by many things. Cornwall, of course, already featured heavily in his narrative, albeit for the wrong reasons – the leaders of Cornubia, up to this point, deriving from the Catuvellauni tribe of central south-eastern Britain. Tintagel was, however, an important site that had flourished at exactly the right time in the post-Roman period.

There was almost certainly an Iron Age hill fort or promontory enclosure at Tintagel, which, by the sixth century AD, whether inhabited or not, overlooked an important port with trade connections through the Atlantic Seaway to Ireland, France, Portugal, Spain and the Mediterranean. Tin and copper were exported from here in return for wine, olive oil and other exotic consumables from the Late Roman world. Tintagel was a dominant part of the regional landscape and it is probable, as the Romano-British administration collapsed in the later fourth century, that the local economy was controlled by a business entrepreneur or warlord, much as it had been in prehistory. Relatively large amounts of fifth- to seventh-century pottery have been found all over the island together with faint traces of what may have been a large hall or residential building. Following its heyday in the later fifth century, Tintagel slipped into relative obscurity as the markets shrank and trade connections became less certain and secure. Something remained, however, to influence local legend and folklore – a memory, perhaps, or an association embedded deep within oral tradition. In the 1230s, nine decades after the Historia Regum Britanniae, Earl Richard of Cornwall, the brother of King Henry III, initiated a great building project at Tintagel. Comprising a curtain wall, two courtyards and a gate tower, the new-build dominated both village and coastline, and remains an extremely popular tourist attraction today.

Like many Norman aristocrats, Earl Richard was entranced by folklore, and especially the legends associated with King Arthur. What better way, he thought, of establishing a bond with the ancient British king, whose bloodline stretched back to Troy, than to choose the very place of Arthur's conception to build a home? Establishing a castle here made no sense militarily speaking, but as a political move it proved extremely canny. Richard's desire to establish himself as a latter-day Arthur was reflected in the castle design, for the walls, which are too thin to resist a concerted siege, were created with rough slate in antiquated style. Richard was not attempting to construct a state-of-the-art stronghold but a romanticised building that harked back to the ancient world of King Arthur.

Tintagel Castle is in one sense an early medieval theme park, albeit one created for one very individual taste. The key buildings established by Earl Richard on the plateau beyond the castle, a rock-cut tunnel, a chapel and a curious 'walled garden', all link to a particular Cornish legend, but it is not one relating to Arthur but of Tristan and Yseult. As with all legends, there are multiple versions of the tale of Tristan and Yseult but, as Mark Bowden has noted, 'large parts of this story are set at the site, which is one of the named courts of King Mark of Cornwall'.[151] The landscape setting depicted in all versions of the legend resolves around three key architectural elements: 'a garden or orchard; a chapel on a cliff; and an "underground" grotto, cave or cellar'. There is a distinct possibility, therefore, that in an attempt to make the site of Tintagel fit the mythology Richard appropriated the island, building structures that helped create 'a theatrical landscape designed to embody the legend'.[152]

Given the length of the 'Arthurian' section in the Historia Regum Britanniae, the presence of individual story elements, where there is a clear disparity in content and narrative style, is more apparent than in any other part of Geoffrey's book. From what we have already seen in studying the content of the Historia, and from what has already been discussed from the time of Brutus the Trojan through to the arrival of the Saxons, there is much here that sounds familiar – worryingly so.

An obvious parallel can immediately be drawn with the story of a heroic and fearless king slaying a giant immediately after making landfall in a new land. Arthur kills the giant 'of monstrous size' on Mont-Saint-Michel[153] while Corineus kills Gogmagog, 'a particularly repulsive' example, at Totnes.[154] A further piece of giant-folklore also occurs in the Arthur story, as a tale within a tale, probably because Geoffrey of Monmouth wasn't sure quite where to place it in the narrative without things sounding overly repetitive. Hence, after descending from Mont-Saint-Michel Arthur reminisces about Retho, the beard-stealing giant 'on Mount Arvaius' who, before the encounter in Gaul, had been the strongest person the king had encountered.[155]

Earlier in Arthur's story, after returning from Lothian with Hoel, the king decides it is time for a wedding.

> Finally, when he had restored the whole country to its earlier dignity, he himself married a woman called Ganhumara. She was descended from a noble Roman family and had been brought up in the household of duke Cador. She was the most beautiful woman in the entire island.[156]

If this seems familiar, it should, for the sequence of events broadly echo those that followed the Roman invasion of AD 43 when, returning from the Orkneys with Claudius, Arvirargus consents to a marriage partnership.

> At the end of that winter the messengers returned with Claudius' daughter and handed her over to her father. The girl's name was Gewissa. Her beauty was such that everyone who saw her was filled with admiration. Once she had been united to him in lawful marriage, she inflamed the king with such burning passion that he preferred her company to anything else in the world.[158]

Unless there was a very great coincidence, with both Arvirargus and Arthur returning home from conquests in the north accompanied by a powerful ally from overseas in order to arrange a marriage, this seems like blatant repetition. Similarity in name-forms for the bride of Arvirargus/Arthur, as Gewissa (or some instances Genvissa) and Ganhumara (Guinevere), is heightened as both women are described as being exceptionally alluring, Ganhumara in particular as the most beautiful in the entire island. This sounds like the sort accolade taken directly from a panegyric or court poem written in high praise of the royal partnership. In the case of Arvirargus, the wedding may be the remembrance of a marriage alliance, binding two tribal groups together following the completion of a war fought with enemies 'to the north'. The closeness of both male and female name-forms, combined with the correlation of events and parallel descriptive elements, all strongly suggest that the marriage of Arthur and Ganhumara is a duplication of that between Arvirargus and Gewissa.

The disjointed nature of the overall narrative, sometimes overly descriptive and sometimes just a bald sequence of events, can be explained by the inclusion of material which included folklore, epic poems, panegyrics and dynastic lists. The presence of genealogical tables, cut and pasted into the Historia Regum Britanniae without any form of editing, can certainly be detected; for example in the description of the guests at Arthur's plenary court where Geoffrey of Monmouth simply, and without any form of explanation, states:

> In addition to these great leaders there came other famous men of equal importance: Donaut map Papo, Cheneus map Coil, Peredur map Peridur, Grifud map Nogord, Regin map Claut, Eddeliui map Oledauc, Kynar map Bangan, Kynmaroc, Gorbonian map Goit, Worloit, Run map Neton, Kymbelin, Edelnauth map Trunant, Cathleus map Kathel, Kynlit map Tieton and many others whose names it is too tedious to tell.[158]

No doubt this was taken directly from an early Welsh king-list. The mention of Kymbelin, or Cunobelinus, is particularly suggestive given how often he appears as a celebrated ancestor figure. Kynlit map Tierton, who also appears as an attendee at Arthur's royal party, may also have derived from a distortion of the 'Cunobelinus son of Tasciovanus' relationship that is recorded on both Iron Age coins and in early Welsh dynastic tables.

Echoes of the Caesarean wars resonate through the story of Arthur as related in the Historia Regum Britanniae. For example, when Arthur races to intercept the retreating army of the proconsul Lucius Hiberius at Siesia, Geoffrey tells us that the Britons have a method of fighting in which mounted and foot soldiers operate in unison so that 'whenever the infantry showed signs of advancing to the attack, the cavalry of that division, moving forward obliquely with closed ranks, should do its utmost to break the force of the enemy'.[159] This particular strategy seems somewhat confusing, until one recalls Julius Caesar's description of the Britons at war.

> Our cavalry found it very dangerous work fighting the charioteers, for the Britons would generally give ground on purpose and after drawing them some distance from the legions, would jump down from their chariots and fight on foot, with the odds in their favour. In engaging their cavalry our men were not much better off; their tactics were such that the danger was exactly the same for both pursuers and pursued. A further difficulty was that they never fought in very close order, but in open formations and had reserves posted here and there, in this way the various groups covered one another's retreat and fresh troops replaced those who were tired.[160]

Of course Geoffrey does not mention chariots, but his rather curious description of infantry and cavalry interchanging and moving 'forward obliquely' could be a garbled reference to the style of fighting that Caesar and his troops found strange and almost impossible to combat. The likelihood that the tactics of Arthur's men was in fact a corrupted version of the chariot tactics deployed by Cassivellaunus is made more explicit by Geoffrey's second reference to the mixed cavalry/ infantry fighting units deployed when Arthur lands at Richborough to fight Mordred. Here the British 'fought in such a way that when the line of foot soldiers moved up to the attack, or was merely holding its position, the horse charged at an angle and did all that they could do to break through the enemy lines and to force them to run away'.[161]

Additional reflections of Caesar's war can be seen in the way that certain name-forms cited in the course of his expeditions reappear during Arthur's campaigns in Gaul. The Cenimagni, for example, mentioned only once by Caesar, as a tribe that surrendered to him in 54 BC, are referenced as the 'Cenomanni', a people who support Arthur against the Romans,[162] their leader Borellus[163] being pierced through the throat by Evander, king of Syria.[164] Morvidus, whom we have already met as a substitute, Mandubracius/Androgeus,[165] fighting 'a certain king of the Moriani' (i.e. Caesar) appears with name-form Morvid with Arthur, his warriors attacking the Roman army in the rear, scattering them 'with tremendous slaughter'[166] during the battle of Siesia, effectively winning the war for Arthur. A remarkably similar tactic is deployed to great effect by Androgeus at the battle of Durobernia[167] where the prince 'made a rear attack upon Cassibellaunus' battle-line', scattering the British enemy and winning the war for Caesar. Even Cassibellaunus/Cassivellaunus himself is resurrected as a general fighting in Arthur's army and dying at the battle of Camblam.[168]

The appropriation of characters and events from earlier in the Historia Regum Britanniae is further discernible in the continual reference made by both Arthur and Geoffrey of Monmouth to the tribute payment made to Rome, a key sticking point in the relationship between Cassibellaunus and Caesar and Arvirargus and Claudius. A sense of dé jà vu is even more apparent with regard to Arthur's overseas conquests, the nature and sequence of which directly builds upon those of Brennius and Belinus, Maximianus and Constantine, something that Arthur himself observes when he reminds his royal council that his ancestors had conquered Rome no less than three times, Constantine and Maximianus both being cited as close relations of his.[169] The ferocity of Arthur towards his continental enemies, which directly contrasts with his more reasonable actions at home, looks, in this respect, like an attempt to portray him as a warrior far greater in stature than any of his Celtic and Roman predecessors.

The replication of past events and repetition of characters from earlier sections in the Historia Regum Britanniae establishes Arthur as little more than a composite character, formed from the deeds of others. In retrospect, many of his activities, both in Britain and across Europe, can perhaps be more sensibly brought back to their place of origin: the tribal zones of the Trinovantes and Catuvellauni. In this, the placement for the final battle between Arthur and Mordred at Camblam can be perhaps be suggested. Many have tried to find a context for this in Cornwall, just as Geoffrey of Monmouth did, establishing a link with the River Camel in the north of the county. If the description of the battle is actually an echo of a conflict fought in central southern Britain, conflating details and people from stories generated in the mid-first century BC, there can only really be one origin for the name: Camulodunum.

Camulodunum (Colchester) was, as we have seen, the premier Late Iron Age oppidum in Britain, a prestigious centre of economic, political and religious power that was celebrated on coins, repeatedly fought over and, in AD 43, became the main target of the Roman army. More critically, in the story of Mandubracius and Cassivellaunus, Camulodunum (Trinovantum) was the centre of Trinovantian power, protected from attack by Julius Caesar who concentrated his forces on Cassivellaunus' capital at Verulamium. In the Historia Regum Britanniae, the third invasion by Caesar against the Britons is preceded by an account of Cassivellaunus attacking Trinovantum in an attempt to capture it. Wherever Camblam is placed in our chronology and whatever the reality of a battle fought there, it would seem that Camulodunum was the ultimate inspiration.

The relationship between Cassibellaunus and Androgeus can further help us resolve the identity of Mordred in the Historia Regum Britanniae, for there is only one other treacherous nephew with a similar name: once again it is Mandubracius. We have already encountered the many divergent name-forms for Mandubracius, heir to the Trinovantian throne, encountered by Julius Caesar during the British campaign of 54 BC. The multiplicity of names, as Mandubracius, Manawydan 'son of Llyr Half Speech', Morvidus, Andragius, Androgius, Androgeus and Afarwy son of Lludd son of Beli, suggest the presence of a long and extremely varied oral tradition. The nature of his character, being depicted either as heroic or evil, furthermore implies the existence of two discrete narratives, the nature of which depended upon the perspective of the original story-writers. Mordred, or Medraut as it appears in the Historia Brittonum, is a more than plausible variant of the name-forms recorded, something which could be taken as coincidence were it not for the fact that the usurper king is cited by Geoffrey as a 'treacherous tyrant' and 'infamous traitor' who had committed a 'flagrant crime' by illegally placing 'the crown on his head'. Mordred's betrayal of his uncle Arthur was, of course, far worse than Mandubracius' betrayal of his uncle Cassibellaunus, 'living adulterously and out of wedlock' with Queen Ganhumara. Mordred deprives Arthur of his kingdom at the very point the king is about to destroy the armies of Rome, further echoing the actions of Mandubracius, who in the negative tradition of Androgeus the traitor, treacherously joins the Romans, granting victory to Caesar at the point Cassibellaunus looks likely to win.

Mordred, furthermore, just prior to Arthur's return,

> had sent Chelric, the leader of the Saxons, to Germany, to conscript as many troops as possible there, and to come back as quickly as he could with those whom he was to persuade to join him. Mordred had made an agreement with Cheldric that he would give him that part of the island which stretched from the River Humber to Scotland and all that Hengist and Horsa had held in Kent in Vortigern's day. In obedience to Mordred's command, Cheldric landed with 800 ships filled with armed pagans. A treaty was agreed and Cheldric pledged his obedience to the traitor Mordred as if to the king.[170]

This much-overlooked incident unlocks a further element in the resolution of the identity of Mordred and the association with Mandubracius for, just as the Trinovantian king undermined Cassibellaunus by secretly sending envoys to Caesar, then in Gaul, so Mordred sends deputations to Chelric. Chelric 'the Saxon' does not feature in any other account (such as they are) and it seems clear that Mordred's plea and the subsequent agreement to hand over land, especially that of Cantium/Kent, followed by the arrival of the German king, is all an echo of the Mandubracius/Caesar relationship as it unfolded in 54 BC. The specific mention of Chelric landing 'with 800 ships filled with armed pagans' is particularly insightful here as

Caesar had made a great point of stressing the nature of shock and awe during his second expedition:

> Caesar discovered afterwards from prisoners that, although large numbers had assembled at the spot, they were frightened by the sight of so many ships and had quitted the shore to conceal themselves on higher ground. Including those retained from the previous year and the privately owned vessels built for their own use, over eight hundred ships were visible simultaneously.[171]

The arrival of so large an invasion fleet undoubtedly left an impact on the native population and may have been remembered for some time thereafter. Even if the story had not been commemorated in oral verse or epic tradition, the number of ships in the Roman expedition, cited as 'over eight hundred', was certainly a matter of record.

That the oral tradition surrounding the character of Arthur was particularly strong in Geoffrey of Monmouth's day is noted at several points in the narrative of the Historia. With regard to the final battle between Arthur and Mordred, Geoffrey observes that he would prefer to say nothing, implying that the conflict was too upsetting, but (describing himself in the third person) adds,

> He will, however, in his own poor style and without wasting words, describe the battle which our most famous king fought against his nephew, once he had returned to Britain after his victory; for that he found in the British treatise already referred to. He heard it, too, from Walter of Oxford, a man most learned in all branches of history.[172]

This form of story-transmission is noted by Geoffrey in the very first paragraph of the Historia where says:

> The deeds of these men were such that they deserve to be praised for all time. What is more, these deeds were handed joyfully down in oral tradition, just as if they had been committed to writing, by many peoples who only had their memory to rely on.[173]

Of course Geoffrey is not saying that he was able to speak to people who had been there with Arthur, but that memory of the king had been passed down through many countless generations. That there were many stories on the 'deeds of Arthur' in circulation in the early twelfth century is confirmed by William of Malmesbury, who observes that 'it is of this Arthur that the Britons fondly tell so many fables, even to the present day; a man worthy to be celebrated, not by idle fictions, but by authentic history'.[174] Interestingly, William appears to have been irritated by these many 'fables'. Presumably the unauthenticated and highly variable nature of oral transmission was not something that he was particularly happy about, for it did not equate with the sort of serious historical account he was trying to establish. Having said that, it is also true that William incorporated a lot of unverifiable information in the Gestum Regum Anglorum, the source to the 'lost' life of Athelstan being one case in particular. The important point here, which many have overlooked, is that William of Malmesbury supplies earlier independent proof for the existence of a rich oral tradition surrounding the character of Arthur; a tradition within which, no doubt, Arthur's life, deeds and history was becoming evermore convoluted, confused and garbled, incorporating information from other tales, poems, panegyrics and pieces of folklore.

It is worth pausing a little longer with the brief account supplied by William of Malmesbury, for, as an antecedent to Geoffrey of Monmouth, it provides a tantalizing clue on the nature of Arthurian information available to this most English of historians. The Arthur in the Gesta Regum Anglorum is certainly a great warrior, but does not appear as a king or ruler in his own right, William noting that:

> British strength decayed, and all hope fled from them; and they would soon have perished altogether, had not Ambrosius, the sole survivor of the Romans, who became monarch after Vortigern, quelled the presumptuous barbarians by the powerful aid of warlike Arthur.[175]

William's account, with Ambrosius being the 'sole survivor of the Romans', has evidently been appropriated from both Gildas and

Bede. Gildas describes the British leader as 'a gentleman who, perhaps alone of the Romans, had survived the shock of this notable storm',[176] something which Bede paraphrases as 'a man of good character and the sole survivor of the Roman race from the catastrophe'.[177] Obviously this doesn't leave much space for Arthur, unless he is the second-to-last of the Romans? Neither Gildas nor Bede mention Arthur and yet there he is in the Historia Brittonum, with Nennius summarizing the nature of his twelve great battles. Interestingly, Nennius is unspecific with regard to the status of Arthur at this time, observing simply that when the Saxons arrived in great numbers 'Arthur, with the kings of Britain, fought against them, though he was the commander in battle'.[178] This sounds uncomfortably as if Arthur, although war leader, was not himself king, fighting 'with the kings of Britain' rather than being the king of the Britons. Possibly he was simply the premier field commander or generalissimo of all British forces, the 'dux Bellorum' or commander in chief, rather than the supreme political leader. Perhaps, alternatively, his position was actually greater than that of the petty kings, acting as an overking or single unifying leader, echoing the role of Cassivellaunus, leader of British resistance against Julius Caesar in the campaign of 54 BC.

This clear absence of Arthur from Gildas and Bede, combined with the ambiguity of his role in Nennius, presumably created a problem for William of Malmesbury, for what precisely was Arthur's position and status within post-Roman Britain? Add to this the large number of (no doubt mutually contradictory and semi-legendary) accounts of Arthur that seem to have been in circulation at the time William was conducting research and we can perhaps begin to understand why he was both frustrated, at the absence of tangible fact and concerned as to how Arthur could be satisfactorily integrated into the narrative. Describing him as providing 'powerful aid' in war is suitably vague, providing Arthur with due credit for wining battles, but without according him a title. It is Geoffrey, then, who seems to be the first writer to credit Arthur as king, although this could have been something stated more clearly, or at least could have been implicit, within the oral tradition that both William and Geoffrey allude to.

The battles that Geoffrey of Monmouth says were fought and won by King Arthur equate tolerably well with those credited to him by Nennius in the Historia Brittonum. It is Nennius who first introduces the concept of the twelve great battles of Arthur, namely the River Glein; the four battles at the River Dubglas in the region of Linnuis; the River Bassus; the wood of Celidon or Cat Coit Celidon; the fortress of Guinnion; the City of the Legions; the River Tribruit; the mountain called Agned; and Mount Badon. Gildas, in citing the campaign of Ambrosius Aurelianus, and the inconclusive nature of early skirmishes, only names the final conflict, at Badon Hill. Where Nennius obtained the other eleven battles, and whether these were all part of the same campaign or if some were duplicated (such as the 'four' battles at the River Dubglas), is unclear. At least two of the battles, however, were considered to be of such significance that, at some later date, additional heroic detail was added – hence at the battle at the fortress of Guinnion we hear that

> Arthur carried an image of the Holy Virgin Mary on his shoulders, and the pagans were put to flight on that day, and there was great slaughter of them, through the power of our Lord Jesus Christ, and the Holy Virgin Mary his mother.[179]

At Mount Badon 'in one day there fell nine hundred and sixty men to the assault of Arthur; and none fell except by his hand alone'.[180]

Geoffrey of Monmouth, although not citing a specific battle list comprising twelve individual points of conflict, does supply additional information for the fighting. In Geoffrey's narrative, combat moves straight from Caledon Wood, where Arthur allows the defeated Saxons 'to return to Germany with nothing but their boats' to 'the neighbourhood of Bath'.[181] Geoffrey therefore, although missing Guinnion, supplies a geographical placement for Kaerbadum/Badonici Montis, the Roman city of Bath. The prelude to battle, as recounted by Geoffrey of Monmouth, follows the standard Celtic-warrior trope, the detail sitting awkwardly in the text, suggesting it has probably been culled wholesale from a separate saga or praise poem:

> Arthur himself put on a leather jerkin worthy of so great a king. On his head he placed a golden helmet, with crest carved in the

shape of a dragon; and across his shoulders a circular shield called Pridwen, on which there was painted a likeness of the Blessed Mary, Mother of God, which forced him to be thinking perpetually of her. He girded on his peerless sword, called Caliburn, which was forged in the Isle of Avalon. A spear called Ron graced his right hand; long, broad in the blade and thirsty for slaughter.[182]

Similar staged preparation of armour and weaponry is recounted in the in epic Táin Bó Cúailnge (Cattle Raid on Cooley), first transcribed in the late eleventh or early twelfth century, which sets out the activities of Ulster hero Cú Chulainn prior to battle.

Over him he put on the outside his battle-girdle of a champion … he took his eight little swords together with the bright-faced, tusk-hilted straight-sword; he took his eight little spears besides his five-pronged spear, he took his eight little darts together with his javelin with its walrus tooth ornaments; he took his eight little shafts along with his play-staff; he took his eight shields for feats together with his dark-red bent-shield, whereon a show-boar could lie in its hollow boss, with its very sharp razor-like, keen cutting, hard iron rim … next he put round his head his crested war-helm of battle and fight and combat.[183]

Mention of Arthur's shield, upon which was painted a 'likeness of the Blessed Mary', in the Historia Regum Britanniae may indicate that the source employed by Geoffrey either confused or collated the battles of Guinnion and Badon, for the 'image of the Holy Virgin Mary', which annotated versions of Guinnion in Nennius tells us that Arthur carried on his shoulder, is surely the same thing. Either that or the poetic battle preparation presented by Geoffrey, with Arthur gathering together his named shield, sword and spear, actually came from a panegyric composed for a separate battle (possibly Guinnion), which has become conflated with the prelude to Badon Hill in the pages of the Historia.

Dressed for war, Arthur leads his men to attack the Saxon host, drawn up in battle array outside the city of Bath. The battle of 'Badon' then commences.

Arthur drew up his men in companies and then bravely attacked the Saxons, who as usual were arrayed in wedges. All that day they resisted the Britons bravely, although the latter launched attack upon attack. Finally towards sunset, the Saxons occupied a neighbouring hill, on which they proposed to camp. Relying on their vast numbers, they considered that the hill in itself offered sufficient protection. However, when the next day dawned, Arthur climbed to the top of the peak with his army, losing many of his men on the way. Naturally enough, the Saxons, rushing down from their high position, could inflict wounds more easily, for the impetus of their descent gave them more speed than the others, who were toiling up. For all that, the Britons reached the summit by a superlative effort and immediately engaged the enemy in hand-to-hand conflict. The Saxons stood shoulder to shoulder and strove their utmost to resist. When the greater part of the day had passed in this way, Arthur went berserk, for he realized that things were still going well for the enemy and that victory for his own side was not yet in sight. He drew his sword Caliburn, called upon the name of the Blessed Virgin, and rushed forward at full speed into the thickest ranks of the enemy. Every man whom he struck, calling upon God as he did so, he killed at a single blow. He did not slacken his onslaught until he had dispatched four hundred and seventy men with his sword Caliburn. When the Britons saw this, they poured after him in close formation, dealing death on every side. In this battle fell Colgrin, with his brother Badulf and many thousands of others with them. Cheldric, on the contrary, when he saw the danger threatening his men, immediately turned away in flight with what troops were left to him.[184]

This epic battle has uncanny echoes of the battle fought between the armies of Cassibellaunus/Cassivellaunus and Julius Caesar recounted earlier in the *Historia Regum Britanniae*.[185] There, of course, it had been Nennius, brother of Lud, who, with the sword 'called Yellow Death', had gone berserk, so vigorously assaulting the enemy, raging up and down the line, so that 'everyone he struck with this sword either had his head cut off or else was so seriously wounded as Nennius passed that he had no hope of recovery'. There too Geoffrey notes 'so passed the greater part of the day', the Britons ultimately pressing forward 'with their ranks undivided'. Finally, as at Kaerbadum/Bath, 'God favoured them and victory was theirs.'[186] At this battle, however, it is Arthur who leads his men to victory against the foe Cheldric who, like Caesar before, flees the battlefield with what few troops he could muster.

The berserker, or warrior undergoing 'warp-spasm' in battle, whose rage transforms them into a crazed fighting machine capable of slaughtering huge numbers of the enemy, is also a popular theme in Celtic literature. The transformation clearly affects Arthur in the Historia Regum Britanniae during the battle of Bath/Badon where, in the thickest part of the enemy, he 'dispatched four hundred and seventy men with his sword'. A more extreme example of the 'warp-spasm' affects Cú Chulainn following his dressing for battle: 'his flesh trembled about him like a pole against the torrent or like a bulrush against the stream, every member and every joint and every point and every knuckle of him from crown to ground. He made a mad whirling-feat of his body within his hide.'[187] Careful battle preparation and berserker combat also echoes through the epic poem Y Gododdin, first transcribed in the ninth or tenth century:

> On Tuesday they put on their dark-brown garments / On Wednesday they purified their enamelled armour / On Thursday their destruction was certain / On Friday was brought carnage all around / On Saturday their joint labour was useless / On Sunday their blades assumed a ruddy hue / On Monday was seen a pool knee deep of blood.[188]

Badon/Kaerbadum/Bath seems, therefore, to have acquired mythical status by the time Geoffrey of Monmouth transcribed the details into the Historia Regum Britanniae. This may, as has been suggested before, simply prove to be a case of him simply making it all up; however, the change in writing style prior to the battle, with Arthur gathering his favoured (named) weaponry, swiftly followed by the hero (Arthur) morphing into a berserker, striking down large numbers of the enemy, suggests that Geoffrey has indeed acquired access to a series of independently written sagas. The battle of Badon, as recounted by Nennius, does not possess the slow build of armament, but does record the 960 victims claimed only by Arthur (as opposed to the 470 he dispatches in the Historia), also hinting at a lost, epic source.

A similar account, describing careful preparation for war and subsequent berserker-like frenzy, appears later in the Historia Regum Britanniae for the battles fought by Arthur in Gaul. At Saussy, for example, the Romans come face to face with Arthur as the British front line starts to collapse in upon itself.

Arthur dashed straight at the enemy. He flung them to the ground and cut them to pieces. Whoever came his way was either killed himself or had his horse killed under him at a single blow. They ran away from him as sheep run from a fierce lion who raging hunger compels to devour all that chance throws in his way. Their armour offered them no protection capable of preventing Caliburn, when wielded in the right way of this mighty king, from forcing them to vomit forth their souls with their life-blood. Ill luck brought two kings, Sertorius of Libya and Polietes of Bithynia, in Arthur's way. He hacked off their heads and bundled them off to hell.[189]

Apart from fulfilling the Celtic hero trope of an unstoppable warrior in warp-spasm slicing his way single-handedly through the ranks of the enemy, it is interesting that the way Arthur is described also echoes that of Nennius, the brother of Cassivellaunus, as he brings death to the army of Caesar using Caesar's own sword.[190]

Another curious interruption where an overly descriptive aspect of combat disrupts the narrative flow occurs when Boso of Oxford, Gerin of Chartres and Gualguainus flee the camp of Lucius Hiberius following the decapitation of Gaius Quintillianus. The heavily stylized nature of the text at this point, suggests that the story has been appropriated from a bardic praise poem or other, more formulaic text, such as encountered in the Trioedd Ynys Prydein.

Gerin of Chartres suddenly turned around, just as one of the Romans was straining to hit him, couched his lance, pierced the enemy through his protective armour and the middle of his body, and hurled him to the ground with all his might. Boso of Oxford, envious of the mighty deed done by the man from Chartres, wheeled his own horse round and stuck his spear into the throat of the first man he met, mortally wounding him and dashing him from the nag on which he was careering along. In the meantime Marcellus Mutius was making every effort to avenge Quintillianus. He was already threatening Gualguainus from the rear, and was on the point of laying hold of him, when Gualguainus swung round and with the sword which he brandished clove him through helm and head to his chest.[191]

As noted in the previous chapter, it would seem, from a careful rereading of Gildas' de Excidio et Conquestu Britannia, that the battle of Badon Hill was actually the climax of Ambrosius Aurelianus' military career and did not form part of Arthur's. The theory that it was Ambrosius, not Arthur, who triumphed at Badon is not, of course, a new one, for a number of writers have suggested that this might be the case.[192] What is worth noting, however, is that it is Nennius and Geoffrey of Monmouth who make the connection between the siege of Badon and Arthur, writing Ambrosius out of the picture entirely. Both men have already been shown to duplicate stories, confusing the exploits of particular individuals, possibly because they were trying to make sense of multiple versions of the same event, or at least the same event recorded from different perspectives, each discrete tale having corrupted the major name-forms in a variety of surprising new ways. Is it possible that the same thing happened here – that Ambrosius Aurelianus and Arthur were in fact the same person? In conclusion it is clear that there was no Arthur after all, the character as he appears in the Historia Regum Britanniae being no more than a composite, a great compilation of all that has gone before.

Keredic

After Arthur, the narrative of the Historia Regum Britanniae seems to lose focus. Characters such as Vortiporius, 'who governed the people frugally and peacefully',[193] and Maglo, who 'strove hard to do away with those who ruled the people harshly'[194] and who can be matched with Vortipor and Maglocunus, both listed by Gildas as two of the 'five tyrants',[195] are swiftly dealt with by Geoffrey of Monmouth. Unlike the outraged Gildas, who happily lists all their faults, Geoffrey does not dwell upon any perceived 'negative character traits', being more concerned about the political ramifications of their individual rule. An element of moral sermonizing can, however, be seen in Geoffrey's comment that Maglo was given 'to the vice of sodomy',[196] echoing Gildas, who complained that Maglocunus wallowed 'like a man drunk on wine pressed from the vine of the Sodomites'.[197]

After Maglo came Keredic, whom Geoffrey notes was 'a fomenter of civil discords, hateful to God and to the Britons also'.[198] Quite why Keredic was so hated, and what precisely was the civil discord he fomented, is not explained, although it is clear that the king was not well liked, at least by those responsible for preserving his tradition.

> When the Saxons came to understand his fickleness, they sent to Hibernia for Gormundus the king of the Affricani, who had gone there with an enormous fleet and conquered the people of that country. As a result of this treachery by the Saxons, Gormundus, accompanied by a hundred and sixty thousand Affricani, came over to Britain, which, between them, the Saxons and the local inhabitants were completely devastating: the former by breaking their oath of fealty, the latter by continually waging civil wars among themselves.[199]

Treachery by the Saxons is not a new theme for Geoffrey of Monmouth, who, like Gildas before, made a point of chronicling every aspect of their duplicity and faithlessness. By specifically noting that they broke 'their oath of fealty', it would appear that the Saxons described here were mercenaries, brought in as a force with which Keredic no doubt hoped to crush rebellion and protect his borders.

Presumably, as a 'fomenter of discords', Keredic was attempting to establish himself as a strong leader as the political map of Britain started to fracture, multiple independent states, each with a defendable stronghold, town or recommissioned hill fort, at its heart, competing for resources and land. The discord attached to Keredic, rather than being a relatively clear-cut struggle of Briton against Saxon, in the traditional 'Arthurian' sense, may have been more like a grubby and distinctly localized war of attrition in which ethnic origin, cultural background, religious belief or tribal affiliation no longer had any meaning. Certainly this is the image that Geoffrey of Monmouth provides, noting that the kingdom of Keredic was being devastated by both the deceitful Saxon horde and the 'local inhabitants' alike.

Mention of Gormundus, 'king of the Affricani', arriving with an army of 160,000 soldiers provides a significant degree of geographical uncertainty at this point in the narrative. Why would a large body of Africans descend upon Britain in the post-Roman period? The clue, evidently is in the name given to Gormandus' people, not as Africans but 'Affricani' which, given that they emerged from Ireland, was probably more like 'Attacotti'. The Attacotti (or Atecotti), whose name may have derived from a term meaning 'the old ones' or 'oldest/first inhabitants',[200] were an Irish tribe who first appeared in the pages of history as a marauding band of raiders, harassing the western coastal fringes of Roman Britain in the later fourth century AD. The Roman historian Ammianus Marcellinus observed that, together with the Scotti, also from Ireland, and the Picts and Saxons, the Attacotti 'harassed the Britons with continual calamities'.[202] In AD 367 the tribe formed part of what became known as 'the Great Barbarian Conspiracy' when raiders joined forces, acting in concert to attack the province of Britannia.

At the time in question the Picts were divided into two tribes, the Dicalydones and the Verturiones. These, together with the warlike Attacotti and the Scots, were ranging over a wide area causing much devastation, while the Franks and their neighbours the Saxons ravaged the coast of Gaul with vicious acts of pillage, arson and the murder of all prisoners, wherever they could burst in by land or sea.[203]

With no parallel or comparison for Attacotti/Atecotti, or whatever corrupted variant the name had taken by the twelfth century, we can see why Geoffrey of Monmouth equated it with the name-form 'Affricani'. Given that Geoffrey records Gormundus as emerging 'from Hibernia' and that Irish raiding and settling parties had long made their influence felt along the western seaboard of Britain, it seems far more likely that it was the Attacotti who were being invited over in large numbers by the Saxons to attack Keredic, especially when one considers the history of co-operation, in military affairs, between the Germanic and Irish tribes in the final years of Roman Britain.

Gormundus swiftly made a treaty with the Saxons 'and then attacked King Keredic'. After many battles, Gormundus 'drove the king from city to city and then forced him to take refuge in Cirecestriam, where he besieged him'.[203] Cirecestriam, or Cirencester in Gloucestershire, was then captured and burnt.

> Gormandus then fought Keredic and chased him over the Severn into Wales. Next he ravaged the fields, set fire to all the neighbouring cities, and gave free vent to his fury until he had burnt almost all the land in the island, from one sea to another. All the settlements were smashed to the ground with a great force of battering rams. All the inhabitants were destroyed by flashing swords and crackling flames, and the priests of their church along with them. Those left alive fled, shattered by these dreadful disasters, but wherever they went, no havens of safety remained open to them in their flight.[204]

Clearly now on a roll, Geoffrey of Monmouth spills into a diatribe against the ineptitude and weakness of the British people in a sermon-like rant which appears to have been taken directly from the pages of Gildas, criticising them for being foolish, 'weighed down by the sheer burden of ... monstrous crimes' and never being happy 'but when you are fighting one another'.[205]

The reign of Keredic, however much it was coloured in the *Historia Regum Britanniae* by the earlier apocalyptic writings of Gildas, appears to mark a turning point in the fortunes of the British kings. The arrival of Gormandus and his Affricani/Attacotti 'destroyed almost all the island', Geoffrey of Monmouth despairs, later having Brian, the nephew of Cadwallo (father of Cadwallader whom Geoffrey cites as the last of the British kings), lament that 'by this invasion, our fatherland was snatched away from our fellow countrymen'.[206] Keredic was driven 'into shameful exile' and Britain was handed to the Saxons.

> For many years after this the Britons were deprived of the right to govern their own kingdom and were without sovereign power over their own land. They made no attempt to recover their former greatness. On the contrary, they continued to ravage with civil war the part of their fatherland which still remained theirs, this part being ruled over by three tyrants instead of by a single king. In the same way the Saxons too, did not establish a single kingship in the island. They also owed allegiance to three kings and divided their energy between attacking their own side and assaulting the Britons.[207]

If this was such a critical moment in British history, surely the 'shameful' and destructive reign of Keredic, if not visible in the archaeological record, should at least be mentioned in alternative sources for the period? Resolution can perhaps be found in the Anglo-Saxon Chronicle, where the arrival and subsequent activities of Cerdic, and his son Cynric, later acknowledged as the founders of the Saxon kingdom of Wessex, feature strongly.

> In 495 came two ealdormen, Cerdic and Cynric his son, to Britain with five ships at a place called Cerdices ora, and on the same day fought against the Welsh;
> In 501 Port and his two sons, Bieda and Maegla came with two ships to Britain at the place called Portesmupa. They soon landed killed a certain young British man of very high rank;
> In 508 Cerdic and Cynric slew a certain British king, whose name was Natanleod, and five thousand men with him, after whom the land as far as Cerdices ford was named Natanleag;
> In 514 came the West Saxons to Britain, with three ships at the place called Cerdices ora and Stuff and Wihtgar fought against the Britons and put them to flight;
> In 519 Cerdic and Cynric succeeded to the kingdom of the West Saxons; and the same year they fought against the Britons

at a place they now call Cerdices ford; and the royal family of the West Saxons ruled from that day on;

In 527 Cerdic and Cynric fought against the Britons at the place which is called Cerdices leag;

In 530 Cerdic and Cynric took the Isle of Wight, and slew many men at Wihtgaraesbyrg;

In 534 Cerdic died, the first king of the West-Saxons. Cynric his son reigned afterwards for twenty-six winters; and they gave all Wight to their nephews Stuff and Wihtgar.

This is the only account of the origins of the kingdom of Wessex to survive but, as a solid piece of ninth-century propaganda authorized by the ruling family themselves, we should not of course accept it entirely at face value. There is, in fact, much within the narrative that follows the general pattern of other Germanic or Scandinavian royal foundation myths, such as the landing of primary dynasts in a small number of ships and the bitter struggle for survival against an indigenous foe. It has already been observed that serious concerns arise with regard to the basic account provided for Wessex when it is compared to the Anglo-Saxon Chronicle's own version of the foundation of Kent, which is worryingly similar.[208] The story of Cerdic and Cynric seems to broadly parallel that of Hengist and Horsa and may similarly comprise much that is either legendary or derived from folklore.

It is equally difficult to place the campaigns of Cerdic and Cynric geographically. That both were enthusiastically claimed as founders of the royal line in Wessex would naturally place their activities broadly within modern-day Hampshire and Wiltshire, although the place names provided by the Anglo-Saxon Chronicle, Cerdices ora, Portesmupa, Cerdices ford, Natanleag, Cerdices leag and Wihtgaraesbyrg, are not particularly helpful for the purposes of identification. That Portesmupa was Portchester/Portsmouth seems likely, although this raises doubts as to the likelihood that 'Port' was a real person rather than being a way of explaining a curious place name. The same could, of course, be said of Natanleag and the British king 'Natanleod' and Wihtgaraesbyrg and Wihtgar as well as Cerdic himself and Cerdices ora, Cerdices ford and Cerdices leag.

Uncertainty over both the man and the places he is supposed to have fought over stopped people from trying to identify the locations and make sense of the king's campaign strategy.[209]

It is nigh-on impossible to reconstruct specific details of Cerdic and Cynric's kingdom-building activities in central southern England. It is, however, worth reiterating that the main task facing the compilers of the Anglo-Saxon Chronicle was to place the founders of the house of Wessex squarely within their own understanding of the kingdom as it was in the ninth century. The judicious retailoring of fith- and sixth-century events, even to the point of copying key elements of the foundation myth established for Kent, was all part of the strategy, helping to legitimize the later rulers' claim to the land.

There is a more significant issue to address at this point, rather than the suspicious chronology, dubious geography and mythological self-justification contained in the Anglo-Saxon Chronicle, and it relates to the names of the primary dynasts themselves. 'Cerdic' and 'Cynric' are not Germanic names; they are British, Cerdic deriving from Caraticos/Caratacus and Cynric plausibly from Cunorix. Not only that but subsequent members of the royal Wessex house, such as Ceawlin, Cedda and Caedwalla, are also arguably of Brittonic/British as opposed to Germanic derivation.[210] This is, on the face of it, difficult to resolve. Were Cerdic and Cynric Germanic leaders whose names had, in some way, been 'Celticised', or did they possess a degree of Anglo-Celtic ancestry? Both are possible.

Far more likely perhaps, given the context in which the Anglo-Saxon Chronicle was written, Cerdic and Cynric were British dynasts, albeit ones who were subsequently 'hijacked' by a fledgling English kingdom desperately searching for a founder or progenitor. If no Germanic hero could be found, why not take a pre-existing British one? Support for this, of course, may be found within the pages of the Historia Regum Britanniae for here we find King Keredic, whom Geoffrey of Monmouth describedas 'a fomenter of civil discords'; a British king disfavoured in British tradition. Whether Keredic's kingdom covered the whole of Britain, as Geoffrey implies, or, more likely a small territory within it, his reign appears to have been momentous. Based on what we can gather from the vague description contained within the Historia, Keredic fought against his fellow Britons, killing a large number of his enemies, some of whom no doubt compiled his overtly negative tradition. He also hired Saxon mercenaries, possibly to use against his neighbours or perhaps as a deterrent against the Attecotti or other roaming Irish warbands.

The Cerdic of the Anglo-Saxon Chronicle is therefore less likely to have been an early English adventurer establishing a kingdom deep in enemy territory than a British dynast of the Geswissi locked in a war of mutually assured destruction with his fellow Britons. Despite his evident disfavour in British tradition, as Keredic 'hateful to God and to the Britons also', Cerdic/Keredic was a strong warleader, an employer of Germanic mercenaries and the first if we note the reference to him taking shelter from Gormandus in Cirecestriam (Cirencester) before fleeing across the River Severn to bring the Saxons into the West Country. He was, from that perspective, just the right man to act as progenitor of the house of Wessex, his name-form remaining intact, with no attempt being made to Germanise/Anglicise it. Is it possible, then, that the Saxon dynasties of southern England were established upon very British foundations?

7

CONCLUSIONS

There are three broad conclusions to be drawn from this study of the Historia Brittonum and the Historia Regum Britanniae. The first is that both texts, despite being compiled many centuries after the period that they claim to be describing, contain significant demonstrable fact. Both Nennius and Geoffrey of Monmouth were writing for a purpose, bringing together a disparate mass of source material including folklore, chronicles, king-lists, dynastic tables, oral tales and bardic praise poems, some of which was irrevocably garbled or corrupted, original meaning and context having been lost over time. Nennius was happy to identify contradictions where they occurred, drawing attention to the alternative points of view. Geoffrey of Monmouth, however, exercised more editorial control, massaging the information and smoothing out inconsistencies in order to create a single grand narrative. In doing so he hijacked certain characters and stories from different time periods, rearranging them in such a way that they created a continuous chronology; a line of monarchs stretching from 'prehistory' to the seventh century AD.

Much of the information that both Geoffrey and Nennius used was, in fact, gathered from two discrete sources. The first was the orally transmitted heroic tales of the Catuvellauni and Trinovantes, two pro-Roman tribes inhabiting central south-eastern Britain at the very end of the Iron Age. The second were the king-lists of important post-Roman dynasties ruling territories in western Britain. Stretching this source material out, chopping, changing and re-editing it in the process, Geoffrey evidently added additional information culled from later Roman histories and also those of 'Dark Age' and early medieval writers such as Gildas and Bede. At its core, then, the Historia Regum Britanniae is the tale of two tribes at a critical moment in history: the period of first contact with Rome. What Nennius, Geoffrey of Monmouth and the many anonymous bards, storytellers and compilers of the triads and other epic works like the Mabinogion did was expand the geography away from the Catuvellauni and Trinovantes in central south-eastern England in order to provide a greater sweep of the British Isles.

What Geoffrey of Monmouth also did was to 'back-project' events from closer to his own time period into the past, presumably in order to generate a comforting sense of familiarity; a divine plan endlessly repeating itself through history. This helped to establish the feeling that, whatever the Saxons and Normans did, the Britons had got there first. Overall, then, although both the Historia Brittonum and the Historia Regum Britanniae do not comprise single stories, setting down a series of unfortunate events in largely chronological order, they do represent a mass of information, some of it unrelated, some of it duplicated, that has been made to fit by medieval writers. Yes, both historiae contain much deviation, hesitation and repetition, but the stories, information and data sets presented can be shown, in some cases, to derive from events that occurred as early as the first century BC.

Second, perhaps more explosively, given that Nennius and Geoffrey of Monmouth are cited as the primary sources for the legend of King Arthur – the Historia Brittonum supplying the evidence for his twelve great battles, the Historia Regum Britanniae laying the foundations of his life story – a detailed examination of both texts clearly shows that King Arthur cannot have existed, at least in the form in which he is presented. In Geoffrey's Historia, Arthur is the ultimate composite character, inhabiting a world where everything that happens to him has already happened to other people, there being nothing in his story that is truly original. Even the battle of Badon Hill, which Geoffrey places at Bath/Kaerbadum, and which is usually treated as the ultimate victory of Arthur's career and is credited as a great slaughter of the Saxons by no less a primary source than Gildas, can be shown to be a battle won by Ambrosius Aurelianus and not Arthur at all. Aurelianus clearly existed, as did Constantine, Magnus Maximus

(Maximianus), Togidubnus (Arvirargus), Mandubracius (Androgeus) and Cassivellaunus (Cassibellaunus), all of whom, directly or indirectly, seem to have provided the inspiration for Arthur the king. Once you take their stories away there is nothing left for Arthur.

The character of King Arthur, great and fearsome warleader, probably evolved in oral tradition thanks to the commemoration, celebration, preservation and modification of the very real Ambrosius Aurelianus. In the process of this storytelling, the identity, character and name-form of Ambrosius Aurelianus changed. Much as Magnus Maximus became Macsen Wledig, Tasciovanus became Tenvatius/ Teuhant, Cassivellaunus became Casswallon and Mandubracius became Androgeus/Mordred in early Welsh legend, so Ambrosius Aurelianus became Arthur to the British, desperate for a heroic figure from deep time, and Aelle to the English, who needed a royal progenitor for the kingdom of Sussex.

The idea that King Arthur did not exist is, of course, not new, Caitlin Green and Guy Halsall for example having both recently produced excellent summaries of the evidence for 'Arthur', suggesting that he may indeed be fictional.[1] It is only by studying the text of Nennius' Historia Brittonum and Geoffrey of Monmouth's Historia Regum Britanniae, however, that we can start to understand the precise nature and significance of the character, seeing how the legend developed up to the beginning of the twelfth century. In establishing Arthur as a figure independent of Ambrosius Aurelianus, Arvirargus and all the other hazily remembered kings of Britain, Geoffrey of Monmouth established a new chapter in British mythology. But it should not be forgotten that in doing so he was artfully editing information derived from genuine prehistoric and post-Roman sources.

Last but by no means least is the fact that although the account presented in the Historia Regum Britanniae has been altered and dramatized, creating a version of the past that fitted Geoffrey's own distinctive viewpoint, it does nonetheless contain much that is archaeologically and historically verifiable. Hence, when we hear, following Cassibellaunus' second victory over the Roman general Julius Caesar had been secured, that the British king celebrated a major feast, this was almost certainly a real event enacted by Britons in the first century BC and commemorated thereafter in oral tradition:

He issued an edict that all the British leaders should assemble with their wives in the town of Trinovantum to do honour to their country's gods who had given them victory over so mighty an emperor. They all gathered together without delay. Sacrifices of various kinds were made and many cattle were killed. They offered forty thousand cows, a hundred thousand sheep and so many fowl of every kind that it was impossible to count them. They also sacrificed three hundred thousand wild animals of various species which they had caught in the woods. When they had done honour to the gods, they feasted on the viands left over, as the custom was on sacrificial occasions. What remained of that day and night they spent in various sporting events.[2]

This feast, occurring within the native centre of Camulodunum, was something unrecorded by our more 'reliable' Roman and Greek sources. It is something that was originally remembered and celebrated by Iron Age tribes living in a period that we still, mistakenly, call prehistory.

NOTES

1 *Introduction to Source Material*

1. Gildas, de Excidio et Conquestu Britanniae 19.
2. Halsall 2013, 53.
3. Alcock 1971, 21.
4. Nennius, Historia Brittonum 3.
5. Dumville 1974; Green 2007, 16.
6. Thorpe 1966, 13-4.
7. Geoffrey of Monmouth, Historia Regum Britanniae i.1.
8. William of Newburgh, Historia Rerum Anglicarum I.ii.
9. Ashe 1982, 12.
10. Burrow 2007, 238.
11. Creighton 2000, 143.
12. Ammianus Marcellinus, Rerum Gestarum IX.5.
13. Braund 1980, 422.
14. Lucan Pharsalia I, 420-30.
15. Caesar de Bello Gallico i, 33.
16. Roymans 2009, 220-1.
17. Geoffrey of Monmouth i.1.
18. William of Malmesbury, Gesta Regum Anglorum xi.

19. Scott 2009, 31-2.
20. Wood 1999, 153.
21. William of Malmesbury vi.
22. William of Malmesbury vi.
23. Thompson 1999, 116-7.
24. Thompson 1999, 117.
25. Wood 1999, 154.
26. Lapidge 1980.
27. Wood 1999, 155.
28. Wood 1999, 147-68.
29. Wright 2007, lii.
30. Wright 2007, lii.
31. Geoffrey of Monmouth ix.9.
32. Geoffrey of Monmouth x.13.
33 Geoffrey of Monmouth xi.1.
34. Geoffrey of Monmouth x.2.
35. Thorpe 1966, 34-5.
36. Wright 2007, lxxv.
37. Wright 2007, lxxv.

2 *Unlocking the Historiae*
1. Caesar, de Bello Gallico V.9.
2. Caesar V. 11.
3. Caesar V.11.
4. Caesar V. 15.

5. Caesar V. 17.

6. Caesar V. 19.

7. Caesar V, 19.

8. Caesar V 20.

9. Caesar V.21.

10. Caesar V.22.

11. Caesar V.21.

12. Caesar V.22.

13. Caesar V.22.

14. Gildas, de Excidio et Conquestu Britanniae 5.2.

15. Gildas 5.2.

16. Gildas 6.1.

17. Bede, Historia Ecclesiastica Gentis Anglorum 2.

18. Orosius, Historiarum Adversum Paganos 6.9.

19. Orosius 6.9.

20. Caesar IV.38.

21. Caesar V.8.

22. Caesar V.15.

23. Bede I.2.

24. Nennius, Historia Brittonum 20.

25. Rivet and Smith 1979, 340.

26. Rivet and Smith 1979, 353-4.

27. Caesar V.9.

28. Caesar V.21.

29. Nennius 20.

30. Nennius 20.

31. Geoffrey of Monmouth Historia Regum Britanniae iv.3.

32. Geoffrey of Monmouth iv.3.

33. Geoffrey of Monmouth iii.20.

34. Orosius 6.9.

35. Bede 1.2.

36. Geoffrey of Monmouth iii.20.

37. Geoffrey of Monmouth iv.3.

38. Geoffrey of Monmouth iv.3.

39. Geoffrey of Monmouth iv.3.

40. Geoffrey of Monmouth iv.3.

41. Geoffrey of Monmouth iv.3.

42. Geoffrey of Monmouth iv.3.

43. Geoffrey of Monmouth iv.3.

44. Geoffrey of Monmouth iv.4.

45. Geoffrey of Monmouth iv.6.

46. Geoffrey of Monmouth iv.7.

47. Geoffrey of Monmouth iv.7.

48. Caesar iv.24.

49. Caesar iv.26.

50. Nennius 20.

51. Geoffrey of Monmouth iv.8.

52. Geoffrey of Monmouth iv.8

53. Geoffrey of Monmouth iv.8.

54. Geoffrey of Monmouth iv.9.

55. Caesar V.20.

56. Rivet and Smith 1979, 353-4.

57. Rivet and Smith 1979, 354.

58. Geoffrey of Monmouth vi.10.

59. Rivet and Smith 1979, 346-7.

60. Geoffrey of Monmouth iv.9.

61. Geoffrey of Monmouth iv.9.

62. Geoffrey of Monmouth iv.9.

63. Geoffrey of Monmouth iv.9.

64. Geoffrey of Monmouth iv.9.

65. Geoffrey of Monmouth iv.9.

66. Geoffrey of Monmouth iv.10.

67. Caesar V.9.

68. Caesar V.11.

69. Caesar V.15.

71. Caesar V.17.

72. Geoffrey of Monmouth iv.3.

73. Geoffrey of Monmouth iv.9.

74. Geoffrey of Monmouth iv.3.

75. Geoffrey of Monmouth iv.9.

3 In the Beginning

1. Geoffrey of Monmouth, Historia Regum Britanniae iv.1.

2. Geoffrey of Monmouth iv.2.

3. Geoffrey of Monmouth i.16.

4. Bede, Historia Ecclesiastica Gentis Anglorum 1.15.

5. Creighton 2000, 137-8.

6. Creighton 2000, 139.

7. Caesar, de Bello Gallico V.12.

8. Creighton 2000, 124.

9. Nennius, Historia Brittonum 10.

10. Jankulak 2010, 23, 39.

11. Nennius 10.

12. Nennius 7.

13. Nennius 47.

14. Nennius 48.

15. Nennius 11.

16. Nennius 17.

17. Nennius 18.

18. e.g. Jankulak 2010, 39-40.

19. Geoffrey of Monmouth i.3.

20. Geoffrey of Monmouth i.16.

21. Geoffrey of Monmouth i.12.

22. Geoffrey of Monmouth i.12.

23. Geoffrey of Monmouth i.13.

24. Geoffrey of Monmouth i.14.

25. Geoffrey of Monmouth i.15.

26. Geoffrey of Monmouth iv.16.

27. Geoffrey of Monmouth i.16.

28. Geoffrey of Monmouth i.16.

29. Geoffrey of Monmouth i.16.

30. Geoffrey of Monmouth i.16.

31. Geoffrey of Monmouth i.17.

32. Clark 1981, 148.

33. Geoffrey of Monmouth i.12.

34. Geoffrey of Monmouth i.12.

35. Geoffrey of Monmouth i.18.

36. Geoffrey of Monmouth i.18.

37. Geoffrey of Monmouth iii.20.

38. Geoffrey of Monmouth ii.1.

39. Crummy 1997, 22-8.

40. Geoffrey of Monmouth ii.16.

41. Gildas de Excidio et Conquestu Britanniae 33.1.

42. Geoffrey of Monmouth xi.7.

43. Cottam et al 2010, 104-5.

44. Dio Cassius, Historia Romana LX.20.

45. Cottam 2010, 104.

46. Geoffrey of Monmouth iii.19.

47. Jankulak 2010, 73.

48. Geoffrey of Monmouth ii.1.

49. Geoffrey of Monmouth ii.2.

50. Geoffrey of Monmouth ii.3.

51. Geoffrey of Monmouth ii.4.

52. Geoffrey of Monmouth ii.5.

53. Geoffrey of Monmouth ii.5.

54. Geoffrey of Monmouth ii.6.

55. Jankulak 2010, 49.

56. Morris 1973, 41-3.

57. Geoffrey of Monmouth ii.17.

58. Caesar V.22.

59. Hamp 1982, 83-5.

60. Koch 2003, 46-8.

4 A Trojan Dynasty

1. Cottam et al 2010, 39-40.

2. Cottam et al 2010, 121-2.

3. e.g. Nash 1987; Van Arsdell 1989.

4. Creighton 2000, 75.

5. Dio Cassius Historia Romana LIII.25.

6. Creighton 2000, 78-9.

7. Cottam et al 2010, 39.

8. Creighton 2000, 204-5.

9. Creighton 2000, 204.

10. Geoffrey of Monmouth Historia Regum Britanniae ii.16.

11. Geoffrey of Monmouth ii.17.

12. Caesar, de Bello Gallico V.11.

13. Cottam et al 2010, 39, 45.

14. Geoffrey of Monmouth ii.17.

15. Creighton 2000, 204-5.

16. Geoffrey of Monmouth ii.9.

17. Creighton 2000, 209-10.
18. Braund 1984, 108; Creighton 2000, 208.
19. Creighton 2000, 211.
20. Creighton 2000, 211.
21. Geoffrey of Monmouth i.16.
22. Dio Cassius LX.20.
23. Cottam et al 2010, 126.
24. Koch 1987a, 259; Cottam 2010, 126.
25. Cottam et al 2010, 126.
26. Enweu Ynys Prydein translated by Bromwich 2014, 247.
27. Bromwich 2014, ciii.
28. Geoffrey of Monmouth ii.10.
29. Geoffrey of Monmouth ii.10.
30. Wheeler and Wheeler 1932.
31. Collingwood and Wright 1965, 62.
32. Collingwood and Wright 1965, 316.
33. Crummy 1997, 59-60.
34. Cunliffe and Davenport 1985.
35. Solinus, Collectanea Rerum Memorabilium 22, 1-12.
36. Ireland 2008, 186.
37. Geoffrey of Monmouth ii.10.
38. Clark 1994, 41.
39. Cunliffe 1984, 14-18.
40. Haverfield 1906, 221; Cunliffe 1984, 15.
41. Russell 2006, 35-8.
42. de la Bedoyere 2002, 56.
43. Henig 2002, 48.
44. Tacitus, Agricola 14.
45. Henig 1999; Russell 2006, 213-4.
46. Geoffrey of Monmouth ii.10.
47. William of Malmesbury, Gesta Regum Anglorum 11.
48. quoted in Thomson 1999, 211.
49. Sayce 1889, 216.
50. Fear 1992, 222.
51. Fear 1992, 223.
52. Clark 1994, 40.
53 Clark 1994, 44.
54. Hedeager 2011, 177-84.
55. Clark 1994, 41.
56. Cunliffe 1984, 16-19.
57. Cunliffe 1984, 208-19; Gerrard 2007, 149-50.
58. quoted in Kershaw 1922, 55.
59. Cunliffe and Davenport 1985, 72-3, 185.
60. Gerrard 2007, 159.
61. Gerrard 2007, 159.
62. Gerrard 2007, 161.
63. Cunliffe 1984, 212.
64. Gerrard 2007, 151.
65. Cunliffe and Davenport 1985, pls xxix and xxxvi.
66. Geoffrey of Monmouth ii.11.
67. Geoffrey of Monmouth ii.11.
68. Geoffrey of Monmouth ii.12.
69. Geoffrey of Monmouth ii.12.
70. Geoffrey of Monmouth ii.13.
71. Geoffrey of Monmouth ii.14.
72. Bromwich 2014, 420.
73. Bromwich 2014, 419.
74. Green 1983, 51.
75. Geoffrey of Monmouth ii.11.
76. Geoffrey of Monmouth ii.11.
77. Geoffrey of Monmouth ii.9.
78. Cottam et al 2010, 39-40.
79. Geoffrey of Monmouth ii.17.
80. Bate and Thornton 2012, 217.
81. Geoffrey of Monmouth ii.14.

5 *Life with the Empire*

1. Geoffrey of Monmouth, Historia Regum Britanniae ii.15.
2. Geoffrey of Monmouth ii.16.

3. Geoffrey of Monmouth iii.1.
4. Geoffrey of Monmouth iii.1.
5. Geoffrey of Monmouth iii.2.
6. Geoffrey of Monmouth iii.3.
7. Geoffrey of Monmouth iii.5.
8. Geoffrey of Monmouth iii.5.
9. Geoffrey of Monmouth iii.6.
10. Geoffrey of Monmouth iii.6.
11. Geoffrey of Monmouth iii.7.
12. William of Malmesbury, Gesta Regum Anglorum 13.
13. Wood 1981, 219.
14. Geoffrey of Monmouth iii.7.
15. Geoffrey of Monmouth i.15.
16. Geoffrey of Monmouth iii.8.
17. Geoffrey of Monmouth iii.9.
18. Geoffrey of Monmouth iii.9.
19. Plutarch, Camillus 22.1.
20. Livy, Ab Urbe Condita Libri 5.48.
21. Geoffrey of Monmouth iii.9.
22. Geoffrey of Monmouth iii.9.
23. Geoffrey of Monmouth iii.10.
24. Geoffrey of Monmouth iii.9.
25. Geoffrey of Monmouth iii.5.
26. Geoffrey of Monmouth iii.11.
27. Geoffrey of Monmouth iii.11.
28. Geoffrey of Monmouth iii.5.
29. Geoffrey of Monmouth iii.6.
30. Nennius, Historia Brittonum 19.
31. Suetonius, Caligula 44.
32. Bromwich 2014, 288-9.
33. Koch 1987a, 265.
34. Koch 1987a, 264.
35. Bromwich 2014, 288-9.
36. Geoffrey of Monmouth iv.6.
37. Geoffrey of Monmouth xii.6.
38. Geoffrey of Monmouth iii.20.
39. Koch 1987a, 265.
40. MacKillop 2005, 35.

41. Green 1992, 30-1; James 2005, 144; Mackillop 2005, 21, 34-5.
42. Green 1992, 30; James 2005, 89.
43. Green 1992, 31.
44. Geoffrey of Monmouth iii.11.
45. Geoffrey of Monmouth iii.1.
46. Hawkes and Crummy 1995; Crummy 1997, 9-28.
47. Geoffrey of Monmouth iii.11.
48. Geoffrey of Monmouth iii.11.
49. Geoffrey of Monmouth iii.12.
50. Nennius 13.
51. Nennius 13.
52. Nennius 14.
53. Nennius 15.
54. Geoffrey of Monmouth iii.13.
55. Geoffrey of Monmouth iii.14.
56. Livy, Ab Urbe Condita Libri 5.36.
57. Geoffrey of Monmouth iii.15.
58. Caesar, de Bello Gallico IV.21.
59. Caesar IV.37.
60. Caesar IV.38.
61. Bede, Historia Ecclesiastica Gentis Anglorum 2.
62. Geoffrey of Monmouth iv.3.
63. Geoffrey of Monmouth iii.15.
64. Geoffrey of Monmouth iii.15.
65. Geoffrey of Monmouth iv.11.
66. Geoffrey of Monmouth iii.16.
67. Geoffrey of Monmouth iii.17.
68. Geoffrey of Monmouth iii.20.
69. Caesar V.50.
70. Ellis Evans 1967, 452-4.
71. Crummy 1997, 22-8.
72. Cottam et al 2010; Crummy 1997, 14-15.
73. Crummy 1997, 13-14.
74. Geoffrey of Monmouth iii.20.
75. Bebbington 1972, 207.
76. Davies 2007, 233.

77. Davies 2007, 115.
78. Bromwich 2014, 94.
79. Bromwich 2014, 419; Koch 1987, 41; Green 1992, 162.
80. Green 1992, 162.
81. Wheeler and Wheeler 1932.
82. Woodward 1992, 76-7; Bromwich 2014, 419-20.
83. Koch 1987, 41-2.
84. Bromwich 2014, 15.
85. Geoffrey of Monmouth iii.20.
86. Geoffrey of Monmouth i.18.
87. Caesar V.11.
88. Caesar V.11.
89. Caesar V.11.
90. Caesar V.11.
91. Caesar IV.20.
92. Bromwich 2014, 185.
93. Bromwich 2014, 199-201.
94. Bromwich 2014, 276-7.
95. Koch 1987.
96. Bromwich 2014.
97. Koch 1987, 41-2.
98. quoted in Davies 2008, 34.
99. Davies 2008, 38.
100. Koch 1987, 37.
101. Geoffrey of Monmouth iv.11.
102. Suetonius, Caligula 44.
103. Koch 1987a, 266.
104. Koch 1987a, 266-8.
105. Koch 1987a, 268-9; Cottam et al 2010, 127.
106. Cottam 2010, 173-6.
107. Geoffrey of Monmouth v.8.
108. Geoffrey of Monmouth iv.13-14.
109. Geoffrey of Monmouth v.8.
110. Geoffrey of Monmouth v.8.
111. Geoffrey of Monmouth v.8.
112. Dio Cassius, Historia Romana, LIII.25.
113. Geoffrey of Monmouth iv.11.
114. Creighton 2006, 3.
115. Suetonius, Caligula 44.
116. Dio Cassius LX.20.
117. Geoffrey of Monmouth iv.11.
118. Geoffrey of Monmouth iv.11.
119. Geoffrey of Monmouth iv.12.
120. Geoffrey of Monmouth iv.12.
121. Geoffrey of Monmouth iv.13.
122. Eutropius Breviarium Historiae Romanae 7.13.2.
123. Dio Cassius LX 19.1.
124. Suetonius, Claudius 17.
125. Suetonius, Caligula 43.
126. Suetonius, Caligula 44.
127. Caesar V.22.
128. Suetonius Caligula 35.
129. Geoffrey of Monmouth iv.14.
130. Geoffrey of Monmouth iv.15.
131. Geoffrey of Monmouth iv.16.
132. Geoffrey of Monmouth iv.13.
133. Dio Cassius LX.20.
134. Tacitus, Annales XII.33.
135. Tacitus, XII.36-7.
136. Dio Cassius, LX.20.
137. Russell 2009, 104-8.
138. Russell 2006, 39-43; Hind 2007; Russell 2009, 108-12.
139. Tacitus, Agricola 14.
140. Russell 2006, 35-7.
141. Tacitus, Annales XIV.33.
142. Juvenal, Satires iv.126.
143. Cottam et al 2010, 142.
144. de la Bedoyere 2003, 32.
145. de la Bedoyere 2003, 32-3.
146. Ashe 1990, 142.
147. Ashe 1990, 144.
148. Tacitus, Annales XIV, 31.
149. Tacitus XIV, 31.
150. Tacitus XIV, 32.

151. Tacitus XIV, 37.
152. Geoffrey of Monmouth iv.17.
153. Bede, Historia Ecclesiastica Gentis Anglorum 2.
154. Bede 1.1.
155. Ammianus Marcellinus, Rerum Gestarum XXVII.8.
156. Bede 1.1.
157. Tacitus XIV, 33.
158. Tacitus XIV, 38.
159. Tacitus XIV, 38.
160. Geoffrey of Monmouth iv.19.
161. Rudling 1998; Russell 2006, 132-45.
162. Russell 2006, 45-51.
163. Geoffrey of Monmouth v.6.
164. Morris 1973, 213.
165. Scriptores Historiae Augustae, Hadrian 5.11.
166. Russell 2006, 145-8.
167. Nennius 28.
168. Nennius 23.
169. Nennius 24.
170. Orosius, Historiarum Adversum Paganos VIII.17.8.
171. Geoffrey of Monmouth v.6.
172. Dio Cassius LXXVII.16.
173. Dio Cassius LXXVI.13.
174. Geoffrey of Monmouth v.2.
175. Geoffrey of Monmouth v.2.
176. Nennius 24.
177. Geoffrey of Monmouth v.3.
178. Geoffrey of Monmouth v.3.
179. Geoffrey of Monmouth v.3.
180. Geoffrey of Monmouth v.4.
181. Eutropius, Breviarium Historiae Romanae IX.21.
182. Aurelius Victor, Liber de Caesaribus 39.20.
183. de la Bedoyere 2003, 146.
184. de la Bedoyere 2003, 146-7.
185. Casey 1994, 80-1.
186. Bedoyere 2003, 147.
187. Birley 2005, 376-7.
188. Geoffrey of Monmouth v.4.
189. Birley 2005, 385-6.
190. Geoffrey of Monmouth v.4.
191. Geoffrey of Monmouth v.4.
192. Panegyric on Constantius Caesar, 15
193. Panegyric on Constantius Caesar, 16
194. Geoffrey of Monmouth v.4
195. Geoffrey of Monmouth v.4
196. Geoffrey of Monmouth v.4
197. e.g. Bradley and Gordon 1988
198. Tacitus Annales XIV.33
199. Panegyric on Constantius Caesar, 18.

6 *Twilight of the Kingdom*

1. Nennius, Historia Brittonum 24.
2. Geoffrey of Monmouth, Historia Regum Britanniae v.6.
3. Geoffrey of Monmouth v.6.
4. Geoffrey of Monmouth v.7.
5. Geoffrey of Monmouth v.8.
6. Jankulak 2010, 56-7.
7. Edwards 2009, 165-6.
8. Bromwich 2014, 441-4.
9. Zosimus, Historia Nova iv.35.
10. Gildas de Excidio et Conquestu Britannia 13.2.
11. Gildas 14.
12. Nennius 26.
13. Nennius 27.
14. Nennius 27.
15. Nennius 27.
16. Bromwich 2014, 81-4.
17. Nennius 29.

18. Geoffrey of Monmouth v.9.
19. Geoffrey of Monmouth v.12.
20. Geoffrey of Monmouth v.14.
21. Geoffrey of Monmouth v.15.
22. Geoffrey of Monmouth v.16.
23. Geoffrey of Monmouth v.16.
24. Jankulak 2010, 58-9.
25. Bromwich 2010, 320-1.
26. Thorpe 1966, 13.
27. Bromwich 2014, 443.
28. Williams 1927; Bromwich 2014, 443.
29. de la Bedoyere 2003, 165.
30. Birley 2005, 418.
31. Ammianus Marcellinus, Rerum Gestarum xiv.6-7.
32. Jankulak 2010, 54.
33. Geoffrey of Monmouth v.16.
34. Geoffrey of Monmouth vi.1-3.
35. Geoffrey of Monmouth v.5.
36. Orosius, Historiarum Adversum Paganos vii.40.4.
37. Geoffrey of Monmouth vi.9.
38. Gildas 23.1-2.
39. Gildas 23.1.
40. Bede, Historia Ecclesiastica Gentis Anglorum 1.15.
41. Gildas 23.2.
42. Millett 1990, 222.
43. Millett 1990, 223.
44. Brooks 1989, 57; Millett 1990, 222-3.
45. Gildas 23.3-4.
46. Gildas 23.5.
47. Bede 1.15.
48. Brooks 1989, 58.
49. Brooks 1989, 59; Mallory 1991, 135.
50. Brooks 1989, 61.
51. Nennius 37.
52. Brooks 1989, 57.
53. Nennius 39.
54. Geoffrey of Monmouth vi.12.
55. Gildas 31.1.
56. Geoffrey of Monmouth xi.6.
57. Geoffrey of Monmouth v.8.
58. Geoffrey of Monmouth v.11.
59. Geoffrey of Monmouth viii.10.
60. Geoffrey of Monmouth xii.14.
61. Geoffrey of Monmouth iv.15.
62. Ashe 2000, 69, 94.
63. Ashe 2000, 147; Venning 2011, 18.
64. Bede 3.7.
65. Bede 4.15.
66. Bede 5.19.
67. Coates 2013, 61.
68. Geoffrey of Monmouth vi.15.
69. Gildas 24-5.
70. Gildas 25.3.
71. Bede 1.16.
72. Nennius 40.
73. Nennius 40.
74. Nennius 42.
75. Nennius 42.
76. Geoffrey of Monmouth vi.17.
77. Geoffrey of Monmouth vi.19.
78. Geoffrey of Monmouth viii.1.
79. Geoffrey of Monmouth vii.3.
80. Savory 1960.
81. Geoffrey of Monmouth viii.2.
82. Geoffrey of Monmouth viii.3.
83. Geoffrey of Monmouth viii.3.
84. Geoffrey of Monmouth viii.6.
85. Geoffrey of Monmouth viii.7.
86. Geoffrey of Monmouth viii.8.
87. Gildas 26.1.
88. Gildas 26.1.
89. British Library Cotton MS Vitellius A vi.
90. Wood 1999, 33-8.

91. Wood 1999, 36.
92. Geoffrey of Monmouth viii.9.
93. Thorpe 1966, 195.
94. Geoffrey of Monmouth viii.10.
95. Geoffrey of Monmouth viii.10.
96. Geoffrey of Monmouth viii.11.
97. Geoffrey of Monmouth viii.12.
98. Parker Pearson et al 2009.
99. Darvill et al 2012.
100. Piggott 1941, 306.
101. Darvill and Wainwright 2009, 14.
102. Darvill and Wainwright 2009, 15.
103. Pitts et al 2002.
104. Drewett et al 1988, 265.
105. Bede 2.5.
106. Stenton 1971, 19.
107. e.g. Down 1988, 104.
108. Morris 1973, 94; Welch 1989, 81.
109. Geoffrey of Monmouth viii.2.
110. Nennius 47.
111. Geoffrey of Monmouth viii.20.
112. Geoffrey of Monmouth ix.1.
113. Geoffrey of Monmouth ix.2.
114. Geoffrey of Monmouth viii.21.
115. Geoffrey of Monmouth x.2; x.4; xi.1.
116. Geoffrey of Monmouth ix.3.
117. Geoffrey of Monmouth ix.3.
118. Geoffrey of Monmouth ix.5.
119. Geoffrey of Monmouth ix.6.
120. Geoffrey of Monmouth ix.9.
121. Geoffrey of Monmouth ix.11.
122. Geoffrey of Monmouth ix.11.
123. Geoffrey of Monmouth ix.11.
124. Geoffrey of Monmouth ix.11.
125. Geoffrey of Monmouth ix.11.
126. Geoffrey of Monmouth ix.11.
127. Geoffrey of Monmouth ix.11.
128. Geoffrey of Monmouth ix.12.
129. Geoffrey of Monmouth ix.15.
130. Geoffrey of Monmouth ix.16.
131. Geoffrey of Monmouth ix.16.
132. Geoffrey of Monmouth ix.19.
133. Geoffrey of Monmouth x.1.
134. Geoffrey of Monmouth x.3.
135. Geoffrey of Monmouth x.4.
136. Geoffrey of Monmouth x.4.
137. Geoffrey of Monmouth x.5.
138. Geoffrey of Monmouth x.6.
139. Geoffrey of Monmouth x.6.
140. Geoffrey of Monmouth x.6.
141. Geoffrey of Monmouth x.10.
142. Geoffrey of Monmouth x.11.
143. Geoffrey of Monmouth x.11.
144. Geoffrey of Monmouth x.12.
145. Geoffrey of Monmouth x.13.
146. Geoffrey of Monmouth xi.1.
147. Geoffrey of Monmouth xi.1.
148. Geoffrey of Monmouth xi.2.
149. Geoffrey of Monmouth xi.2.
150. Geoffrey of Monmouth xi.2.
151. Bowden 2015, 13.
152. Bowden 2015, 13.
153. Geoffrey of Monmouth x.3.
154. Geoffrey of Monmouth i.16.
155. Geoffrey of Monmouth x.3.
156. Geoffrey of Monmouth ix.9.
157. Geoffrey of Monmouth iv.15.
158. Geoffrey of Monmouth ix.12.
159. Geoffrey of Monmouth x.6.
160. Caesar, de Bello Gallico v.16.
161. Geoffrey of Monmouth xi.1.
162. Geoffrey of Monmouth ix.19.
163. Geoffrey of Monmouth ix.12.
164. Geoffrey of Monmouth x.5.
165. Geoffrey of Monmouth iii.15.
166. Geoffrey of Monmouth x.11.

167. Geoffrey of Monmouth iv.9.
168. Geoffrey of Monmouth xi.2.
169. Geoffrey of Monmouth ix.16.
170. Geoffrey of Monmouth xi.1.
171. Caesar v.9.8.
172. Geoffrey of Monmouth xi.1.
173. Geoffrey of Monmouth i.1.
174. William of Malmesbury, Gesta Regum Anglorum 1.9.
175. William of Malmesbury, 1.9.
176. Gildas 55.3.
177. Bede 16.
178. Nennius 56.
179. Nennius 56.
180. Nennius 56.
181. Geoffrey of Monmouth ix.3.
182. Geoffrey of Monmouth ix.4.
183. Táin Bó Cúailnge 17.
184. Geoffrey of Monmouth ix.4.
185. Geoffrey of Monmouth iv.3.
186. Geoffrey of Monmouth iv.3.
187. Táin Bó Cúailnge 17.
188. Y Gododdin lxviii.
189. Geoffrey of Monmouth x.11.
190. Geoffrey of Monmouth iv.3-4.
191. Geoffrey of Monmouth x.4.

192. e.g. Wood 1999, 36-8; Green 2007, 203-6.
193. Geoffrey of Monmouth xi.6.
194. Geoffrey of Monmouth xi.7.
195. Gildas 31, 33-36.
196. Geoffrey of Monmouth xi.7.
197. Gildas 33.1.
198. Geoffrey of Monmouth xi.8.
199. Geoffrey of Monmouth xi.8.
200. Rivet and Smith 1979, 259.
201. Ammianus Marcellinus, Rerum Gestarum xxvi.4.
202. Ammianus Marcellinus, xxvii.8.
203. Geoffrey of Monmouth xi.8.
204. Geoffrey of Monmouth xi.8.
205. Geoffrey of Monmouth xi.9.
206. Geoffrey of Monmouth xii.2.
207. Geoffrey of Monmouth xi.11.
208. Yorke 1989, 84.
209. Ashley 2005, 162-4.
210. Yorke 1995, 190-1.

7 Conclusions

1. Green 2007; Halsall 2013.
2. Geoffrey of Monmouth iv.8.

BIBLIOGRAPHY

Alcock, L. 1971 *Arthur's Britain: history and archaeology AD 367-634*. Aylesbury: Penguin.

Aldhouse-Green, M. 2015 *The Celtic myths: a guide to the ancient gods and legends*. London: Thames and Hudson.

Ashe, G. 1982 *Kings and Queens of Early Britain*. London: Methuen.

Ashe, G. 1990 *Mythology of the British Isles*. London: Methuen.

Ashe, G. 2000 *Kings and Queens of Early Britain* (Revised Edition). London: Methuen.

Bassett, S. 1989 *The origins of the Anglo-Saxon kingdoms*. Leicester: Leicester University Press.

Bate, J. and Thornton, D. 2012 *Shakespeare: staging the world*. London: British Museum Press.

Bebbington, G. 1972 *London street names*. London: Batsford.

Birley, A. 2005 *The Roman government of Britain*. Oxford: Oxford University Press.

Bowden, M. 2015 *Tintagel and the legend of Tristan and Yseult*. Historic England Research 2, 12-15.

Bradley, R. and Gordon, K. 1988 'Human skulls from the River Thames, their dating and significance.' *Antiquity* 62, 503-9.

Braund, D. 1980 'The Aedui, Troy, and the Apocolocyntosis.' *The Classical Quarterly* 30, 420-425.

Bromwich, R. 2014 *Trioedd ynys Prydein: the triads of the Islands of Britain*. Cardiff: University of Wales Press.

Brooks, N. 1989 'The creation and early structure of the kingdom of Kent.' in S.Bassett (ed.) *The origins of the Anglo-Saxon kingdoms. Leicester*: Leicester University Press; 55-74.

Burrow, J. 2007 *A history of histories*. London: Allen Lane.

Clark, J. 1981 'Trinovantum: the evolution of a legend.' *Journal of Medieval History* 7, 135-51.

Clark, J. 1994 'Bladud of Bath: the archaeology of a legend.' *Folklore* 105, 39-50.

Clark, J. 2010 'London Stone: Stone of Brutus or fetish stone – Making the Myth.' *Folklore* 121, 38-60.

Coates, R. 2013 'The name of the Hwicce: A discussion.' *Anglo-Saxon England* 42, 51-61.

Collingwood and Wright 1965 *The Roman inscriptions of Britain: inscriptions on stone*. Oxford: Clarendon.

Constable, G. 1983 'Forgery and plagiarism in the Middle Ages.' *Archiv für Diplomatik* 29, 1-41.

Cottam, E., de Jersey, P., Rudd, C. and Sills, J. 2010 *Ancient British coins*. Aylsham: Chris Rudd.

Creighton, J. 2000 *Coins and power in Late Iron Age Britain*. Cambridge: Cambridge University Press.

Creighton, J. 2006 *Britannia: the creation of a Roman province*. London: Routledge.

Crummy, P. 1997 *City of victory: the story of Colchester – Britain's first Roman town*. Colchester: Colchester Archaeological Trust.

Cunliffe, B. 1984 *Roman Bath rediscovered*. London: Routledge and Kegan Paul.

Cunliffe, B. and Davenport, P. (eds) 1985 'The temple of Sulis Minerva at Bath. Volume 1: the site.' Oxford: *Oxford University Archaeology* Monograph 7.

Davies, S. 2007 *The Mabinogion: a new translation*. Oxford: Oxford University Press.

Darvill, T., Marshall, P., Parker Pearson, M. and Wainwright, G. 2012 'Stonehenge remodelled.' *Antiquity* 86, 1021–40.

Darvill, T. and Wainwright, G. 2009 'Stonehenge excavations 2008.' *The Antiquaries Journal* 89, 1–19.

de la Bedoyere, G. 2002 *Gods with thunderbolts: religion in Roman Britain*. Stroud: Tempus.

de la Bedoyere, G. 2003 *Defying Rome: the rebels of Roman Britain*. Stroud: Tempus.

Down, A. 1988 *Roman Chichester*. Chichester: Phillimore.

Drewett, P., Rudling, D. and Gardiner, M. 1988 *The south east to AD 1000*. London: Longman.

Dumville, D. 1974 'Some aspects of the chronology of the Historia Brittonum.' *Studia Celtica* 10, 78-95.

Edwards, N. 2009 'Rethinking the Pillar of Eliseg.' *Antiquaries Journal* 89, 2009, 143–77.

Ellis Evans. D. 1967 *Gaulish personal names: a study of some continental Celtic formations*. Oxford: Clarendon Press.

Fear, A. 1992 'Bladud: the flying king of Bath.' *Folklore* Vol. 103, 222-224.

Gerrard, J. 2007 'The temple of Sulis Minerva at Bath and the end of Roman Britain.' *The Antiquaries Journal* 87, 148-64.

Green, M. 1983 *The gods of Roman Britain*. Gloucester: Alan Sutton.

Green, M. 1992 *Dictionary of Celtic myth and Legend*. London: Thames and Hudson.

Green, T. 2007 *Concepts of Arthur*. Stroud: Tempus.

Halsall, G. 2013 *Worlds of Arthur: facts and fictions of the Dark Ages*. Oxford: Oxford University Press.

Hamp, E. 1982 'Lloegr: the Welsh name for England.' *Cambridge Medieval Celtic Studies* 4, 83–85.

Handford, S. 1951 *Caesar: the conquest of Gaul*. London: Penguin.

Haverfield, F. 1906 'The Romanization of Roman Britain.' *Proceedings of the British Academy* 1905-1906, 185-217.

Hawkes, C. and Crummy, P. 1995 Camulodunum 2. Colchester: Colchester Archaeological Trust Report 11.

Hedeager, L. 2011 *Iron Age myth and materiality: an archaeology of Scandinavia AD 400-1000*. London: Routledge.

Henig, M. 1999 'A new star shining over Bath.' *Oxford Journal of Archaeology* 18, 419-25.

Henig, M. 2002 *The heirs of King Verica: culture and politics in Roman Britain*. Stroud: Tempus.

Higham, N. and Ryan, M. 2013 *The Anglo-Saxon world*. London: Yale University Press.

Hind, J. 2007 'Plautius' Campaign in Britain: an alternative reading of the narrative in Cassius Dio.' *Britannia* 38, 93-106.

Ireland, S. 2008 *Roman Britain: a sourcebook*. London: Routledge.

James, S. 2005 *Exploring the world of the Celts*. London: Thames and Hudson.

Jankulak, K. 2010 *Geoffrey of Monmouth*. Cardiff: University of Wales Press.

Kershaw, N. 1922 *Anglo-Saxon and Norse poems*. Cambridge: Cambridge University Press.

Koch, J. 1987 'a Llawr en assed (CA 932) "the laureate hero in the war-chariot": some recollections of the Iron Age in the Gododdin.' Études celtiques 24, 253–78.

Koch, J. 1987b 'A Welsh window on the Iron Age: Manawydan, Mandubracios.' *Cambridge Medieval Celtic Studies* 14, 17–52.

Koch, J. 1990 'Brân, Brennos: an instance of Early Gallo-Brittonic history and mythology.' *Cambridge Medieval Celtic Studies* 20, 1–20.

Koch, J. 1992. 'Gallo-Brittonic Tasc(i)ouanos "Badger-slayer" and the reflex of Indo-European "gwh."' *Journal of Celtic Linguistics* 1, 101–18.

Koch, J. 2003 'Celts, Britons, and Gaels – names, peoples, and identities.' *Transactions of the Honourable Society of Cymmrodorion* 9, 41–56.

Koch, J. 2005 'Why was Welsh literature first written down?' In *Medieval Celtic Literature and Society*, (ed.) H.Fulton. Dublin: Four Courts Press; 15–31.

Koch, J. and Carey, J. 2003 *The Celtic Heroic Age: literary sources for ancient Celtic Europe and Early Ireland and Wales* (4th edition). Aberystwyth: Celtic Studies Publications.

Lapidge, M. 1980 'Some Latin poems as evidence for the reign of Athelstan.' *Anglo-Saxon England* 9, 61-98.

MacKillop, J. 2005 *Myths and legends of the Celts*. London: Penguin.

Mallory, J. 1991 *In Search of the Indo-Europeans: Language, Archaeology and Myth*. London: Thames and Hudson.

Millett, M. 1990 *The Romanization of Britain*. Cambridge: Cambridge University Press.

Morris, J. 1973 *The age of Arthur: a history of the British Isles from AD 350–650*. London: Weidenfeld and Nicolson.

Nash, D. 1987 *Coinage in the Celtic world*. London: Seaby.

Padell, O. 2000 *Arthur in medieval Welsh literature*. Cardiff: University of Wales Press.

Parker Pearson, M., Chamberlain, A., Jay, M., Marshall, P., Pollard, J., Richards, C., Thomas, J., Tilley, C. and Welham, K. 2009 'Who was buried at Stonehenge?' *Antiquity* 83, 23–39.

Piggott, S. 1941 'The Sources of Geoffrey of Monmouth ii: The Stonehenge Story.' *Antiquity* 60, 305-19.

Pitts, M., Bayliss, A., McKinley, J., Boylston, A., Budd, P., Evans, J., Chenery, C., Reynolds, A. and Semple, S. 2002 'An Anglo-Saxon Decapitation and Burial at Stonehenge.' *Wiltshire Archaeological and Natural History Magazine* 95, 131-46.

Rivet, A. and Smith, C. 1979 *The place-names of Roman Britain*. London: Batsford.

Roymans, N. 2009 'Hercules and the construction of a Batavian identity in the context of the Roman Empire.' In T.Derks and N.Roymans (eds) *Ethnic Constructs in Antiquity: the role of power and tradition*. Amsterdam: Amsterdam University Press; 19-38.

Rudling, D. 1998 'The development of Roman villas in Sussex.' *Sussex Archaeological Collections* 136, 41-65.

Russell, M. 2006 *Roman Sussex*. Stroud: Tempus.

Russell, M. 2009 *Bloodline: the Celtic kings of Roman Britain*. Stroud: Amberley.

Savory, H. 1960 'Excavations at Dinas Emrys, Beddgelert (Caern), 1954-56.' *Archaeologia Cambrensis* 109, 13-77.

Sayce, A. 1889 'The legend of King Bladud.' *Y Cymmrodor* 10, 207-222.

Scott, R. 2009 'Byzantine Chronicles.' *The Medieval Chronicle* 6, 31-59.

Stenton, F. 1971 *Anglo-Saxon England*. Oxford: Oxford University Press.

Thompson, R. 1999 *De gestis regum Anglorum*. Oxford: Oxford University Press.

Thorpe, L. 1966 *The history of the kings of Britain*. London: Penguin.

Van Arsdell, R. 1989 *Celtic coinage of Britain*. London: Spink and Son.

Venning, T. 2011 *The Anglo-Saxon Kings*. Stroud: Amberley.

Welch, M. 1989 'The kingdom of the South Saxons: the origins.' In S.Bassett (ed.) *The origins of the Anglo-Saxon kingdoms*. Leicester: Leicester University Press; 75-83.

Wheeler, R. and Wheeler, T. 1932 'Report on the excavation of the prehistoric, Roman and post-Roman site in Lydney Park, Gloucestershire.' *Society of Antiquaries of London* Research Report 9.

Williams, I. (ed.) 1927 *Breudwyt Maxen*. Bangor: Jarvis A Foster.

Wood, M. 1981 *In search of the Dark Ages*. London: BBC Books.

Wood, M. 1999 *In search of England: journeys into the English past*. London: Penguin.

Wood, M. 2005 *In search of myths and heroes*. London: BBC Books.

Woodward, A. 1992 *Shrines and sacrifice*. London: Batsford.

Wright, M. 2007 *The history of the kings of Britain*. Woodbridge: Boydell.

Yorke, B. 1989 'The Jutes of Hampshire and Wight and the origins of Wessex.' In S. Bassett (ed.) *The origins of the Anglo-Saxon kingdoms*. Leicester: Leicester University Press; 84-96.

Yorke, B. 1995 *Wessex in the Early Middle Ages*. Leicester: Leicester University Press.

INDEX

Index